AIA

S T U D Y

PAPER 8
COMPANY LAW

T E X T

In this 2020 edition

- A **user-friendly format** for easy navigation
- **Exam-centred topic coverage,** directly linked to AIA's syllabus and study guide
- **Exam focus points** showing you what the examiner will want you to do
- Regular **fast forward** summaries emphasising the key points in each chapter
- **Questions** and **quick quizzes** to test your understanding
- **Exam question bank** containing exam standard questions with answers
- **2 Mock exams** containing the November 2017 and May 2018 papers
- **A full index**

FOR EXAMS IN 2020

First edition 2007
Eleventh edition January 2020

ISBN 9781 5097 8723 4
(previous ISBN 9781 5097 2506 9)

eISBN 9781 5097 2895 4
(previous eISBN 9781 5097 2573 1)

British Library Cataloguing-in-Publication Data
A catalogue record for this book
is available from the British Library

Published by

BPP Learning Media Ltd
BPP House, Aldine Place
142-144 Uxbridge Road
London W12 8AA

www.bpp.com/learningmedia

Printed in the United Kingdom

Your learning materials, published by BPP Learning Media Ltd, are printed on paper obtained from traceable, sustainable sources.

All rights reserved. No part of this publication may be reproduced, stored in a retrieval system or transmitted in any form or by any means, electronic, mechanical, photocopying, recording or otherwise, without the prior written permission of BPP Learning Media.

Contains public sector information licensed under the Open Government Licence v3.0.

The contents of this book are intended as a guide and not professional advice. Although every effort has been made to ensure that the contents of this book are correct at the time of going to press, BPP Learning Media makes no warranty that the information in this book is accurate or complete and accepts no liability for any loss or damage suffered by any person acting or refraining from acting as a result of the material in this book.

We are grateful to the Association of International Accountants for permission to reproduce past examination questions. The suggested solutions in the exam answer bank have been prepared by BPP Learning Media Ltd.

©
BPP Learning Media Ltd
2020

A note about copyright

Dear Customer

What does the little © mean and why does it matter?

Your market-leading BPP books, course materials and e-learning materials do not write and update themselves. People write them: on their own behalf or as employees of an organisation that invests in this activity. Copyright law protects their livelihoods. It does so by creating rights over the use of the content.

Breach of copyright is a form of theft – as well as being a criminal offence in some jurisdictions, it is potentially a serious breach of professional ethics.

With current technology, things might seem a bit hazy but, basically, without the express permission of BPP Learning Media:

- Photocopying our materials is a breach of copyright

- Scanning, ripcasting or conversion of our digital materials into different file formats, uploading them to Facebook or emailing them to your friends is a breach of copyright

You can, of course, sell your books, in the form in which you have bought them – once you have finished with them. (Is this fair to your fellow students? We update for a reason.) But the e-products are sold on a single user license basis: we do not supply 'unlock' codes to people who have bought them second hand.

And what about outside the UK? BPP Learning Media strives to make our materials available at prices students can afford by local printing arrangements, pricing policies and partnerships which are clearly listed on our website. A tiny minority ignore this and indulge in criminal activity by illegally photocopying our material or supporting organisations that do. If they act illegally and unethically in one area, can you really trust them?

Contents

Page

Introduction

The introduction pages contain lots of valuable advice and information. They include tips on studying for and passing the exam, also the content of the syllabus and what has been examined.

How the BPP Learning Media Study Text can help you pass – Help yourself study for your AIA exams – Syllabus – Command words and descriptors – The exam paper

Part A Incorporation
1. Companies 3
2. Company formation 23
3. Constitution of a company 37

Part B Capitalisation
4. Share capital 55
5. Borrowing and loan capital 73
6. Capital maintenance and dividends 89

Part C Administration and control
7. Corporate governance 111
8. Meetings and resolutions 129
9. Company directors and other company officers 147
10. Majority control and minority protection 177
11. Accounts and audit 189

Part D Insolvency
12. Insolvency 205

Part E Criminal law
13. Criminal law 231

Answers to end of chapter questions 251
Exam question bank 265
Exam answer bank 275
Mock exam 1 297
Mock exam 2 313
Case index 331
Index 337

How the BPP Learning Media Study Text can help you pass

> It provides you with the knowledge and understanding, skills and application techniques that you need to be successful in your exams

This Study Text has been targeted at the **Company Law** syllabus.

- It is **comprehensive**. It covers the syllabus content. No more, no less.
- It is written at the **right level**. Each chapter is written with AIA's syllabus in mind.
- It is aimed at the **exam**. We have taken account of recent exams, guidance the examiner has given and the assessment methodology.

> It allows you to study in the way that best suits your learning style and the time you have available, by following your personal Study Plan (see page vi)

You may be studying at home on your own or you may be attending a course. You may like to read every word, or you may prefer to do a fast read through and learn through doing practise questions the rest of the time. However you study, you will find the BPP Learning Media Study Text meets your needs in designing and following your personal Study Plan.

Help yourself study for your AIA exams

Exams for professional bodies such as AIA are very different from those you have taken at college or university. You will be under **greater time pressure before** the exam – as you may be combining your study with work. Here are some hints and tips.

The right approach

1 **Develop the right attitude**

Believe in yourself	Yes, there is a lot to learn. But thousands have succeeded before and you can too.
Remember why you're doing it	You are studying for a good reason: to advance your career.

2 **Focus on the exam**

Read through the Syllabus	This tells you what you are expected to know and is supplemented by **Exam focus points** in the text.
Study the Exam paper section	Past papers are likely to be good guides to what you should expect in the exam.

3 **The right method**

See the whole picture	Keeping in mind how all the detail you need to know fits into the whole picture will help you understand it better. • The **Introduction** of each chapter puts the material in context. • The **Syllabus content** and **Exam focus points** show you what you need to **grasp**.
Use your own words	To absorb the information (and to practise your written communication skills), you need to **put it into your own words**. • Take **notes**. • Answer the **questions** in each chapter. • Draw **mindmaps**. • Try **'teaching' a subject** to a colleague or friend.
Give yourself cues to jog your memory	The Study Text uses **bold** to **highlight key points**. • Try **colour coding** with a highlighter pen. • Write **key points** on cards.

4 **The right recap**

Review, review, review	Regularly reviewing a topic in summary form can **fix it in your memory**. The Study Text helps you review in many ways. • **Chapter roundups** summarise the 'Fast forward' key points in each chapter. Use them to recap each study session. • The **Quick quiz** actively tests your grasp of the essentials. • Go through the **Examples** in each chapter a second or third time.

Developing your personal Study Plan

BPP recommends that you follow a study plan. Planning and sticking to the plan are key elements of learning successfully.

There are five steps you should work through.

Step 1 **How do you learn?**

What types of intelligence do you display when learning? You might be advised to brush up on certain study skills before launching into this Study Text, but refer to the 'tackling your studies' section below which will help.

Step 2 **What do you prefer to do first?**

If you prefer to get to grips with a theory before seeing how it is applied, we suggest you concentrate first on the explanations we give in each chapter before looking at the examples and case studies. If you prefer to see first how things work in practice, read through the detail in each chapter, and concentrate on the examples and case studies, before supplementing your understanding by reading the detail.

Step 3 **How much time do you have?**

Work out the time you have available per week, given the following.

- The standard you have set yourself
- The other exam(s) you are sitting
- Practical matters such as work, travel, exercise, sleep and social life

		Hours
Note your time available in box A.	A	

Step 4 **Allocate your time**

- Take the time you have available per week for this Study Text shown in box A, multiply it by the number of weeks available and insert the result in box B.   B
- Divide the figure in box B by the number of chapters in this text and insert the result in box C.   C

Remember that this is only a rough guide. Some of the chapters in this book are longer and more complicated than others, and you will find some subjects easier to understand than others.

Step 5 **Implement**

Set about studying each chapter in the time shown in box C, following the key study steps in the order suggested by your particular learning style.

This is your personal **Study Plan**. You should try to combine it with the study sequence outlined below. You may want to modify the sequence to adapt it to your **personal style**.

Tackling your studies

The best way to approach this Study Text is to tackle the chapters in order. Taking into account your individual learning style, you could follow this sequence for each chapter.

Key study steps	Activity
Step 1 **Topic list**	This topic list helps you navigate each chapter; each numbered topic is a numbered section in the chapter.
Step 2 **Introduction**	This sets your objectives for study by giving you the big picture in terms of the context of the chapter. The content is referenced to the syllabus, and Exam guidance shows how the topic is likely to be examined. The Introduction tells you **why** the topics covered in the chapter need to be studied.
Step 3 **Fast forward**	Fast forward boxes give you a quick summary of the content of each of the main chapter sections. They are listed together in the roundup at the end of each chapter to help you review each chapter quickly.
Step 4 **Explanations**	Proceed methodically through each chapter, particularly focusing on areas highlighted as significant in the chapter introduction, or areas that are frequently examined.
Step 5 **Key terms and Exam focus points**	• Key terms can often earn you **easy marks** if you state them clearly and correctly in an exam answer. They are highlighted in the index at the back of this text. • Exam focus points state how the topic has been or may be examined, difficulties that can occur in questions about the topic, and examiner feedback on common weaknesses in answers.
Step 6 **Note taking**	Take brief notes, if you wish. Don't copy out too much. Remember that being able to record something yourself is a sign of being able to understand it. Your notes can be in whatever format you find most helpful; lists, diagrams, mindmaps.
Step 7 **Examples**	Work through the examples very carefully as they illustrate key knowledge and techniques.
Step 8 **Case studies**	Study each one, and try to add flesh to them from your own experience. They are designed to show how the topics you are studying come alive in the real world.
Step 9 **Questions**	Attempt each one, as they will illustrate how well you've understood what you've read.
Step 10 **Answers**	Check yours against ours, and make sure you understand any discrepancies.
Step 11 **Chapter roundup**	Review it carefully, to make sure you have grasped the significance of all the important points in the chapter.
Step 12 **Quick quiz**	Use the Quick quiz to check how much you have remembered of the topics covered and to practise questions in a variety of formats.
Step 13 **Question practice**	Attempt the Question suggested at the very end of the chapter. These are all AIA past exam questions, so provide an excellent indication of the type and standard of question that you can expect in your real exam. Some of these questions cover more than one subject area, which is a common feature of exam questions.

AIA Achieve

AIA provides an interactive course of study AIA Achieve, which offers students the tools, resources and learning environment to study for the exams. The study tools include a course of study e-book, marked practice questions, marked mock exam paper and feedback and technical advice via an e-Tutor. Contact the Study Support team at: Achieve@aiaworldwide.com.

Moving on...

When you are ready to start revising, you should still refer back to this Study Text.

- As a source of **reference** (you should find the index particularly helpful for this)
- As a way to **review** (the Fast forwards, Exam focus points, Chapter roundups and Quick quizzes help you here)

Syllabus

For variant papers please refer to appropriate variant syllabus: Hong Kong SAR, Malaysia.

Aims

The aim of the Company Law paper is to examine the candidate's knowledge, understanding and application of the principles of and practice relating to Company Law.

FIG. 8 INTER-RELATIONSHIP OF UNITS

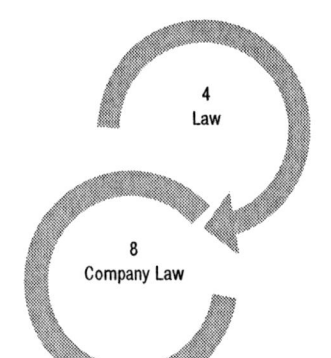

The objective of the paper is to ensure that candidates have:

- Comprehensive knowledge and understanding of the principles of Company Law.
- A thorough understanding of the practical aspects of Company Law.
- An ability to analyse practical scenarios and apply relevant principles and procedures of Company Law.

The syllabus covers key areas of Company Law which are:

- Incorporation
- Capitalisation
- Administration and control
- Accounts and audit
- Reconstructions
- Winding up

For each area of the syllabus, candidates should have knowledge of both relevant statute and case law.

Descriptors

After successfully completing this paper candidates should be able to:

- Discuss principles of law comprehensively and clearly, based on a sound knowledge and understanding of company law and practice.
- Analyse practical scenarios and apply relevant legal principles and procedures.
- Demonstrate reasoned conclusions following the application of legal rules and procedures.

Structure of the Paper

- A three-hour 15 minute paper consisting of eight questions. Questions 1, 2 and 3 are compulsory and candidates must attempt two from the remaining five questions.
- All questions carry equal marks.
- Where appropriate the allocation of marks to individual parts of a question is stated.
- Generally, the paper includes at least two essay type questions, the remaining questions being case studies.

Candidates are expected to support answers with references to statute and case law where appropriate.

Syllabus

Candidates should be familiar with relevant case law, pertinent documentation and the Companies Acts currently in force.

8.1 Incorporation

Topic Weighting   20%

This part of the syllabus covers:

- The procedures relating to the formation and registration of a company and the role and liability of corporate promoters.
- The nature, contents and legal effect of the key documents required for registration.
- The legal effects of company registration including the concept of separate legal personality and the circumstances in which the veil of incorporation may be lifted.

8.2 Capitalisation

Topic Weighting   20%

This part of the syllabus covers:

- The nature of share capital and principles relating to the maintenance of share capital, including procedures for returning capital to members such as buy-back of shares and financial assistance for the acquisition of a companies own shares.
- Alterations to authorised share capital, such as increases to facilitate a further issue of shares or reductions and the appropriate procedures to be followed.
- Types of share and the legal rules relating to alteration of class rights.
- Procedures relating to the allotment of shares, directors' authority to allot shares and the effect of statutory pre-emption rights.
- Share transfers and transmissions, including consideration of restrictions on share transfer and procedures and documents required to effect share transfer.
- Borrowing powers and the nature of debentures, including consideration of the legal and practical effects of fixed and floating charges.

8.3 Administration and Control

Topic Weighting   20%

This part of the syllabus covers:

- The position of company directors, their powers, functions and duties, including duties of care and skill and the fiduciary duties of directors at common law and under ss 171–177 Companies Act 2006.
- Procedures for managing the company and corporate decision making.
- Dealings between the company and its directors and connected persons, such as loans and substantial property transactions covered by section 190 Companies Act 2006.
- The methods of appointing directors, the roles of executive and non-executive directors.

INTRODUCTION

- The procedure for removing a director under section 168 Companies Act 2006, compensation payable for breach of a service contract and the circumstances in which directors can be disqualified from acting.

- The position of the members regarding corporate decision making, the calling and conduct of general meetings and the different types of members' resolutions under Part 13 Companies Act 2006 and the exercise of members' rights under Part 9 Companies Act 2006.

- The principle of majority rule and minority protection including the exceptions to the rule in *Foss v Harbottle*, the new derivative action under ss 260–264 Companies Act 2006, the use of the unfairly prejudicial conduct remedy in section 994 Companies Act 2006 and the just and equitable winding up remedy in section 122(1)(g) Insolvency Act 1986.

8.4 Accounts and Audit

Topic Weighting   20%

This part of the syllabus covers:

- The company's duty to keep accounting records and the nature of those records.
- The effect of the accounting reference date.
- The requirement for the production of directors and auditors reports and the nature of these reports.
- The nature of the duty to lay accounts before the members in general meeting.
- Procedures for the declaration of dividends.
- Financial records which must be sent to members, debenture holders, and the registrar of companies.
- Penalties for non-compliance with filing requirements.
- Details of the audit thresholds and when it is necessary to file statutory accounts and the filing requirements.
- Liability for negligence and professional ethics.
- Professional indemnity insurance.
- Auditor independence.

8.5 Reconstructions

Topic Weighting   10%

This part of the syllabus covers:

- The procedures which must be followed in take-overs, including those relating to the compulsory acquisition of the minority's shares.
- The nature of the offence of insider dealing, the circumstances in which it can be committed and the defences available.
- The concept of market abuse, types of market abuse and sanctions available.

8.6 Winding up

Topic Weighting   10%

This part of the syllabus covers:

- Duties and powers of the Liquidator and the order of payment of creditors.
- Methods of increasing the assets available to the creditors, including undervalue transactions, preferences, the avoidance of floating charges, wrongful and fraudulent trading.
- Corporate rescue procedures, including voluntary arrangements and administration orders.
- The procedure which must be followed in a compulsory and voluntary liquidation and the nature of these processes.

Relationship to Overall Syllabus

The Company Law paper builds on knowledge acquired by candidates who have successfully completed the Law module.

Knowledge of the nature of the English legal system and of Contract and Tort is an essential basis for candidates studying Company Law.

The Legal Relationships section of the Law module introduces candidates to different types of business entity, allowing comparisons to be made between partnerships and companies and introducing the concept of limited liability. This section also covers the concept of agency, which is essential in understanding the nature of the role of company directors.

Ethics

Candidates are advised that the standards outlined in The Code of Ethics for Professional Accountants issued by the International Ethics Standards Board for Accountants (IESBA Code) are implicit in, and examinable throughout, the AIA syllabus. The Code can be accessed via the AIA website at www.aiaworldwide.com

Candidates following the RPQ (statutory auditor qualification) route will be expected to refer, where appropriate, to the Revised Ethical Standard 2016 (ES) published by the FRC. Candidates following other routes will not be penalized if they refer to ESs in preference to the IFAC Code of Ethics. ESs can be accessed via the Financial Reporting Council's website at https://www.frc.org.uk/Our-Work/Codes-Standards/Audit-and-assurance/Standards-and-guidance/Standards-and-guidance-for-auditors/Ethical-standards-for-auditors.aspx

Recommended Reading

AIA Magazine – International Accountant

ISSN: 1465-5144

AIA Text Book

Paper 8 Company Law

Publisher: BPP Learning Media
ISBN: 9781509787234

The e-Book is available at: exams@aiaworldwide.com

Contact our publisher BPP for information on purchasing a hard copy of the text book at:
https://www.bpp.com/learning-media-listing/lmlist/6293

You can purchase any of the books listed below quickly and easily through the publisher's website or link stated below.

Mayson, French and Ryan on Company Law (35th Edition)

Authors: Mayson, S, French, D and Ryan, C
Publisher: Oxford University Press
ISBN: 9780198815105
Website: https://global.oup.com/academic/product/mayson-french-and-ryan-on-company-law-9780198797234?q=mayson%20french&lang=en&cc=gb

Company Law (10th Edition)

Author: Dignam, A, Lowry, L
Publisher: Oxford University Press
ISBN: 9780198811831
Website: https://global.oup.com/academic/product/company-law-9780198753285?q=Company%20law%20dignam&lang=en&cc=gb

Command words and learning outcomes

The following list contains active command words and generic learning outcomes appropriate for use at each stage of the AIA qualification. Reference to the learning outcomes and use of the command words is essential to understanding how the assessment is applied in AIA exams.

Professional Level 1 Command Words

WORD	DEFINITION
ADVISE	To inform as necessary
ANALYSE	Examine in detail in order to interpret its meaning or essential features
APPLY	To use information or a technique
CALCULATE	Work out a value mathematically
CATEGORISE	To put into a group things or people with common qualities
COMPARE & CONTRAST	To explain the similarities and differences between things in order to interpret them
DEMONSTRATE	To show or prove by reasoning or evidence
DERIVE	To formulate or decide based on a particular source of information
DEVELOP	To bring to a more advanced stage
DIFFERENTIATE	To show the difference between
DISCUSS	To examine in detail by argument
IMPLEMENT	To carry out
INTERPRET	To explain the meaning of and to work out the significance of
ILLUSTRATE USING THE CASE	To clarify or explain by use of example or comparison
PRIORITISE	Place in order of importance
PRODUCE	To create or bring into existence
RELATE	To have reference or relation to
SOLVE	Find an answer to
VALUE	To assess the worth of something

Please note:

1. The word 'Calculate' may be used at all levels of the syllabus

    CALCULATE Select the appropriate method and techniques and apply your knowledge and understanding to work out and show how figures were arrived at.

2. The word 'Advise' may be used at all levels of the syllabus

    ADVISE Notify or inform

3. For the Professional Level 1 exams, examiners may include a command word from the Foundation Level providing it is linked to another command word selected from the Professional 1 list. For example:

    '... prepare and discuss a set of accounts...'

4   For the Professional Level 2 exams, examiners may include a command word from the Foundation and Professional Level 1 providing it is linked to another command word from the Professional 2 list. For example:

    '…recommend the appropriate action and prepare a memo…'

The exam paper

Analysis of past papers

The analysis below shows the topics which were examined in the current syllabus.

May 2018

1. Company charges and guarantees
2. Shareholder and debentureholder rights
3. Incorporation procedures and production and filing of accounts
4. Issue of shares and transactions with directors
5. Share buyback
6. Transfer of shares, replacement of director and service contracts
7. Advantages of incorporation and pre-incorporation contracts
8. Bribery

November 2017

1. Articles of association and allotment of shares
2. Resolutions and procedures
3. Compulsory liquidation: statutory test and order of payments on liquidation
4. Takeover and sale and purchase of shares
5. Dealings with directors
6. Company relationships and off-the-shelf companies
7. Floating charges and loan approval
8. Money laundering and offences

May 2017

1. Incorporation, shareholders' agreements and liquidation
2. Private limited company record keeping and reporting
3. Allotment and transfer of shares
4. Company incorporation, power to bind the company, and accounts and auditing
5. Increasing assets available to creditors on liquidation
6. Company meetings, voting and proxies
7. Directors: appointment and removal, and the differences between executives and non-executives
8. Financial assistance for the purchase of shares

November 2016

1. Directors: removal and disqualification
2. Incorporation v partnership
3. Compulsory liquidation: personal liability and offences of directors of insolvent companies
4. Borrowing and rights issues
5. Distribution of dividends
6. Meetings and resolutions
7. Issuing shares, alteration of articles and share premium accounting
8. Market abuse and money laundering

May 2016

1. Incorporation and promoters
2. Administration and the role of administrators
3. Company directors and allotting shares
4. Insider dealing
5. Ordinary and preference shares; class rights
6. Share transfers and minority protection
7. Company charges, personal guarantees and loans from directors
8. Auditors eligibility, appointment duties and rights

November 2015

1. Small companies and loan repayments
2. Separate legal personality
3. Share transfers and statutory pre-emption rights
4. Director appointment and minority protection
5. Company registration documents
6. Transactions with directors and directors' duties
7. Personal guarantees, company charges and loans from directors
8. Takeover

May 2015

1. Legal personality and shares
2. Market abuse
3. Director transactions
4. Financial statements and auditor liability
5. Maintenance of share capital
6. Liquidation
7. Allotting shares and company name
8. Shareholder and debentureholder rights

November 2014

1. Incorporation procedures and obligations
2. Compulsory liquidation
3. Company directors and shares
4. Company charges and personal guarantees
5. Directors and corporate governance
6. Minority shareholder rights
7. Director liability and disqualification
8. Allotting shares and transactions with directors

May 2014

1. Incorporation
2. Company director rules
3. Corporate rescue
4. Dividends and financial information
5. Acquisition of shares and company re-registration
6. Minority protection
7. Removal of directors and property transactions
8. Debentures, auditors and voting

November 2013

1. Liquidation
2. Separate legal personality
3. Company directors
4. Share capital
5. Insider dealing and market abuse
6. Company rules
7. Financial statements
8. Shares and loan capital

May 2013

1. Loans to directors
2. Debt v equity
3. Promoters and personal guarantees
4. Insider dealing
5. Share buy-backs
6. Accounts
7. Removal of directors
8. Allotment and transfer of shares

November 2012

1. Registering a company and legal personality
2. Transfer of shares and pre-emption rights
3. Appointment and removal of directors
4. Market abuse
5. Takeovers
6. Duties of directors
7. Accounts
8. Rights of shares

May 2012

1. Pre-insolvency transactions
2. Allotment and transfer of shares
3. Reduction of share capital and buyback
4. Incorporation; alteration of articles; power to bind the company
5. Insider dealing
6. Members' meetings; removal of a director
7. Accounting requirements in Companies Act 2006
8. Directors fiduciary duties; transactions with directors

November 2011

1. Insolvency
2. Limited liability
3. Removal of directors
4. Shareholder rights against directors
5. Allotment of shares
6. Borrowing, charges and share buy-backs
7. Preparation of accounts
8. Auditing

May 2011

1. Separate legal personality
2. Challenge of transactions by a liquidator
3. Duties of directors
4. Challenging transactions made by directors
5. Insider dealing
6. Removal of directors
7. Borrowing and charges
8. Allotment v purchase of shares

November 2010

1. Accounting records
2. Voluntary and compulsory winding up
3. Rights of shareholders
4. Minority protection
5. Directors and their removal
6. Powers of directors
7. Incorporation and pre-incorporation contracts
8. Allotment and transfer of shares

May 2010

1. Liabilities on liquidation
2. Preparation and approval of accounts
3. Removal of director – minority rights
4. Insider dealing
5. Procedures on incorporation
6. Maintenance of share capital
7. Allotment of shares
8. Appointment of new director – voting issues

November 2009

1. Directors' fiduciary duties
2. Insider dealing
3. Removal of director
4. Limited liability
5. Appointment of new director
6. Rights under articles
7. Rights of chargeholders on liquidation
8. Loans to directors

May 2009

1. Accounting records
2. Insolvency – administration and pre-insolvency transactions
3. Position of minority shareholders
4. Maintenance of share capital – financial assistance
5. Procedures on incorporation
6. Directors' duties and breach of duty
7. Removal of director and minority rights
8. Allotment of shares and corporate borrowing

INTRODUCTION

November 2008

1. Charges and liquidations
2. Fiduciary duties of directors
3. Insider dealing
4. Capital maintenance
5. Removal of directors
6. Transfer of shares and issue of shares
7. Company names and limited liability
8. Directors' transactions with the company

PART A

Incorporation

Companies

Topic list	Syllabus reference
1 A company's legal identity	8.1
2 Limited liability of members	8.1
3 Types of company	8.1
4 Additional classifications	8.1
5 Effect of legal personality	8.1
6 Ignoring separate personality	8.1
7 Comparison of companies and partnerships	8.1

Introduction

The most popular vehicle for business in the world is the **corporate form**, the joint stock company. Company shares are traded round the world on stock exchanges, and many businesses and individuals possess shares, that is they have invested in part-ownership of other companies.

We will introduce companies as business vehicles that are distinct from sole traders and partnerships. The key difference between them is the concept of **separate legal personality**. This chapter outlines this doctrine, and also discusses its implications (primarily **limited liability** for members) and the exceptions to it (lifting the **veil of incorporation**).

In Section 3, we shall look at the different types of company that can be used to carry out business.

The **Companies Act 2006**, (TSO, 2006) and the **Small Business, Enterprise and Employment Act 2015**, (TSO, 2015) apply to this and all chapters unless otherwise stated.

PART A   INCORPORATION

1 A company's legal identity

FAST FORWARD

A company has a **legal personality** separate from its owners (known as members). It is a formal arrangement, surrounded by formality and publicity, but its chief advantage is that members' **liability** for the company's debts is typically **limited**.

A company is the most popular form of business association.

By its nature, a company is more **formal** than a partnership or a sole trader. There is often substantially **more legislation** on the formation and procedures of companies than any other business association, hence the weighting towards company law of most of the rest of this Study Text. In particular, a great deal of information about individual companies is available in the public domain because there is a Registrar of Companies who maintains information on public registers about each one. We shall see more about the Registrar throughout this Study Text.

The key reason why the company is a popular form of business association is that the **liability of its members to contribute to the debts of the entity is significantly limited**. This will be explained more later in this chapter. For many people, this benefit outweighs the disadvantage of the formality and publicity surrounding companies, and encourages them not to trade as sole traders or (unlimited) partnerships.

1.1 Definition of a company

Key terms

> For the purposes of this Study Text, a **company** is an entity registered as such under the Companies Act 2006.
>
> The key feature of a company is that it has a **legal personality** (existence) distinct from its members and directors.

1.2 Legal personality

A person possesses legal rights and is subject to legal obligations. In law, the term 'person' is used to denote two categories of legal person.

- An individual human being is a **natural person**. A sole trader is a natural person, and there is legally no distinction between the individual and the business entity in sole tradership

- The law also recognises **artificial persons** in the form of companies and limited partnerships. Unlimited partnerships are not artificial persons.

Key term

> **Corporate personality** is a common law principle that grants a company a legal identity, separate from the members who comprise it. It follows that the property of a company belongs to that company, debts of the company must be satisfied from the assets of that company, and the company has perpetual succession until wound up.

A corporation is a **legal entity** separate from the natural persons connected with it, for example as members or directors. We shall come back to this later.

2 Limited liability of members

FAST FORWARD

The fact that a company's members – not the company itself – have **limited liability** for its debts **protects** the **members** from the company's creditors and ultimately from the full risk of business failure.

A key consequence of the fact that the company is distinct from its members is that its members have **limited liability**.

Key term

> **Limited liability** is a protection offered to members of certain types of company. In the event of business failure, the members will only be asked to contribute identifiable amounts to the assets of the business.

2.1 Protection for members against creditors

The **company** itself is **liable without limit for its own debts.** If the company buys plastic from another company, for example, it owes the other company money.

Limited liability is a benefit to members. They own the business, so might be the people whom the creditors logically asked to pay the debts of the company if the company is unable to pay them itself.

Limited liability prevents this by stipulating the **creditors** of a limited company **cannot demand payment of the company's debts** from members of the company.

2.2 Protection from business failure

As the company is liable for all its own debts, limited liability only becomes an issue in the event of a business failure when the **company is unable to pay its own debts**.

This will result in the **winding up** of the company which will enable the creditors to be paid from the proceeds of any assets remaining in the company. It is at winding up that limited liability becomes most relevant.

2.3 Members asked to contribute identifiable amounts

Although the creditors of the company cannot ask the members of the company to pay the debts of the company, there are some amounts that **members are required to pay, in the event of a winding up.**

Type of company	Amount owed by member at winding up
Company limited by shares	Any **outstanding amount** from when they originally purchased their shares from the company.
	If the member's shares are fully paid, they **do not have to contribute anything in the event of a winding up**.
Company limited by guarantee	The **amount they guaranteed** to pay in the event of a winding up.

Question — Limitations of liability

Hattie and two friends wish to set up a small business. Hattie is concerned that, following her initial investment, she will have no access to additional funds, and is worried what might happen if anything goes wrong. Advise her on the relative merits of a company and an unlimited partnership.

Answer

The question of liability appears to be important to Hattie. As a member of a limited company, her liability would be limited – as a member at least – to any outstanding amount payable for her shares. If the three friends decide to form an unlimited partnership, they should be advised that they will have **unlimited** liability for the debts of the partnership. (An unlimited partnership does **not** have a legal personality distinct from the partners.)

2.4 Liability of the company for tort and crime

As a company has a separate legal identity, it may also have liabilities in **tort** and **crime**. Criminal liability of companies in particular is a topical area but, is outside the scope of your syllabus.

PART A INCORPORATION

3 Types of company

FAST FORWARD

Most companies are those **incorporated** under the **Companies Act**. However there are other types of company such as **corporations sole, chartered corporations, statutory corporations** and **community interest companies**.

Corporations are classified in one of the following categories.

Categories	Description
Corporations sole	A corporation sole is an **official position** which is filled by one person who is replaced from time to time. The Public Trustee and the Treasury Solicitor are corporations sole.
Chartered corporations	These are usually **charities** or bodies such as the Association of Chartered Certified Accountants, formed by Royal Charter.
Statutory corporations	Statutory corporations are formed by special Acts of Parliament. This method is little used now, as it is slow and expensive. It was used in the nineteenth century to form railway and canal companies.
Registered companies	Registration under the Companies Act is the normal method of incorporating a commercial concern. Any body of this type is properly called a company.
Community Interest Companies (CICs)	A special form of company for use by 'social' enterprises pursuing purposes that are beneficial to the community, rather than the maximisation of profit for the benefit of owners, created by the Companies (Audit, Investigation and Community Enterprise) Act 2004 (TSO, 2004).

3.1 Limited companies

The meaning of limited liability has already been explained. It is the **member**, not the company, whose liability for the company's debts may be limited.

3.1.1 Liability limited by shares

Liability is usually **limited by shares**. This is the position when a company which has share capital states in its constitution that 'the liability of members is limited'.

3.1.2 Liability limited by guarantee

Alternatively a company may be **limited by guarantee**. Its constitution states the amount which each member **undertakes** to **contribute** in a winding up (also known as a liquidation). A creditor has no direct claim against a member under his guarantee, nor can the company require a member to pay up under his guarantee until the company goes into liquidation.

Companies limited by guarantee are appropriate to **non-commercial activities**, such as a charity or a trade association which is non-profit making but wish to have a form of reserve capital if it becomes insolvent. They do not have **share capital**.

3.2 Unlimited liability companies

Key term

An **unlimited liability company** is a company in which members do not have limited liability. In the event of business failure, the liquidator can require members to contribute as much as may be required to pay the company's debts in full.

An unlimited company **can only be a private company** as, by definition, a **public company is always limited**.

An unlimited company need not **file** a copy of its **annual accounts** and reports with the Registrar, unless during the relevant accounting reference period:

(a) It is (to its knowledge) a **subsidiary** of a limited company.

(b) **Two** or more **limited companies** have **exercised rights** over the **company**, which (had they been exercised by only one of them) would have **made** the **company** a **subsidiary** of that one company.

(c) It is the **parent company** of a limited liability company.

Attention! | Some of these requirements and terms will seem unfamiliar to you, but we will look at them in more detail in the following chapters.

The unlimited company certainly has its uses. It provides a **corporate body** (a separate legal entity) which can conveniently hold assets to which liabilities do not attach.

Question — Limited liability

Explain the liability of members of companies limited by guarantee.

Answer

Members of companies limited by guarantee are required to pay the amount they guaranteed if required when the company is wound up.

3.3 Public and private companies

FAST FORWARD | A company may be **private** or **public**. Only the latter may offer its share to the public.

Key terms | A **public company** is a company whose constitution states that it is public and that it has complied with the registration procedures for such a company.

A **private company** is a company which has not been registered as a public company under the Companies Act. The major practical distinction between a private and public company is that the former may not offer its securities to the public.

A **public** company is a company registered as such under the Companies Act 2006 (TSO, 2006) with the Registrar. **Any company not registered as public is a private company**.

A public company may be one which was **originally incorporated** as a public company or one which re-registered as a public company having been previously a private company.

3.4 Conditions for being a public company

FAST FORWARD | To trade, a public company must hold a **Registrar's trading certificate** having met the requirements, including **minimum capital** of £50,000.

3.4.1 Registrar's trading certificate

Before it can trade a company originally incorporated as a public company must have a trading certificate issued by the Registrar. The conditions for this are:

- The **name** of the company identifies it as a public company by ending with the words 'public limited company' or 'plc' or their Welsh equivalents, 'ccc', for a Welsh company.

- The **constitution** of the company states that 'the company is a public company' or words to that effect.
- The **allotted share capital** of the company is not less than the authorised minimum which is currently £50,000.
- It is a **company** limited by shares.

With regard to the minimum share capital of £50,000:

- A company originally incorporated as a public company will not be permitted to trade until its **allotted** share capital is at least £50,000.
- A private company which re-registers as a public company will not be permitted to trade until it has **allotted** share capital of at least £50,000; this needs only be paid up to one quarter of its nominal value (plus the whole of any premium).
- A private company which has share capital of £50,000 or more may of course continue as a private company; it is always **optional** to become a public company.

A company limited by guarantee which has no share capital, and an unlimited company, **cannot** be public companies.

3.4.2 Minimum membership and directors

A public company must have a minimum of **one member**. This is the same as a private company. However, unlike a private company it must have at least **two directors**. A private company may have just one director. All companies must have at least one director who is **a 'natural person'** (that is a person as opposed to a company). Directors do not usually have liability for the company's debts.

3.5 Private companies

A private company is the residual category and so does not need to satisfy any special conditions. Private companies are generally small to medium-sized enterprises in which some if not all shareholders are also directors and *vice versa*. Ownership and management are combined in the same individuals. Therefore, it is unnecessary to impose on the directors complicated restrictions to safeguard the interests of members, and so the number of rules that apply to public companies are reduced for private companies.

3.6 Differences between private and public companies

FAST FORWARD

> The main differences between public and private companies relate to: **capital**, **dealings** in **shares**, **accounts**, **commencement of business**, **general meetings**, **names**, **identification**, and **disclosure requirements**.

Some differences between public and private companies imposed by law relate to the following factors.

3.6.1 Capital

The main differences are:

(a) There is a minimum amount of **£50,000** for a **public** company, but **no minimum** for a **private** company.

(b) A public company may **raise capital** by **offering** its **shares** or debentures to the public; a **private** company is **prohibited** from doing so.

(c) Both **public** and **private companies** must generally **offer** to **existing members first** any ordinary shares to be allotted for cash. However a **private** company **may permanently disapply** this pre-emption rule.

3.6.2 Dealings in shares

Only a **public company** can obtain a listing for its shares on the **Stock Exchange** or other investment exchange. To obtain the advantages of listing the company must agree to elaborate conditions contained in particulars in a **listing agreement** with The London Stock Exchange. However, by no means all public companies are listed.

3.6.3 Accounts

(a) A **public** company has **six** months from the end of its accounting reference period in which to produce its statutory audited accounts. The period for a **private** company is **nine** months.

(b) A **private** company, if qualified by its size, may have **partial exemption** from various **accounting provisions** (discussed later in this text). These exemptions are not available to a public company or to its subsidiaries (even if they are private companies).

(c) A **listed public company** must publish its full accounts and reports on its **website**.

(d) Public companies must lay their **accounts** and reports before a general meeting of shareholders annually. Private companies have no such requirement.

3.6.4 Commencement of business

A **private** company can commence business **as soon** as it is **incorporated**. A **public** company, if incorporated as such, must first **obtain a trading certificate from the Registrar**.

3.6.5 General meetings

Private companies are not required to hold annual general meetings (AGMs). **Public companies** must hold one within six months of their financial year end.

3.6.6 Names and identification

The rules on identification as public or private are as follows.

- The word **'limited'** or **'Ltd'** (or the Welsh equivalent) in the name denotes a private company; **'public limited company'** or **'plc'** (or the Welsh equivalent) must appear at the end of the name of a public company.

- The **constitution** of a **public** company must state that it is a public company. A **private company** should be identified as private.

3.6.7 Disclosure requirements

There are **special disclosure and publicity requirements** for public companies.

The main advantage of carrying on business through a public rather than a private company is that a public company, by the issue of listing particulars, may obtain a **listing** on The London Stock Exchange and so access capital from the investing public generally.

Attention!

> There is an important distinction between public companies and **listed public companies**. Listed (or quoted) companies are those which trade their shares (and other securities) on stock exchanges. Not all public companies sell their shares on stock exchanges (although, in law, they are entitled to sell their shares to the public). **Private** companies are not entitled to sell shares to the public in this way.
>
> In practice, only public companies meeting certain criteria are allowed to obtain a listing on the Main Market of the London Stock Exchange.

Private companies may be broadly classified into two groups: independent (also called **free-standing**) private companies and **subsidiaries** of other companies.

4 Additional classifications

FAST FORWARD — There are a number of other ways in which companies can be **classified**.

4.1 Parent (holding) and subsidiary companies

The Companies Act 2006 (TSO, 2006) draws a distinction between an 'accounting' definition and a 'legal' definition in s 1162.

A company will be the **parent** (or **holding**) **company** of another company, its **subsidiary company**, according to the following rules.

Key term

Parent company

(a) It holds a **majority of the voting rights** in the subsidiary.

(b) **It is a member of the subsidiary and has the right to appoint or remove a majority of its board of directors.**

(c) **It has the right to exercise a dominant influence over the subsidiary**:
   (i) By virtue of provisions contained in the subsidiary's articles.
   (ii) By virtue of a control contract.

(d) **It is a member of the subsidiary and controls alone**, under an agreement with other members, **a majority of the voting rights in the company**.

(e) **A company is also a parent if:**
   (i) It has the power to exercise, or actually exercises, a dominant influence or control over the subsidiary.
   (ii) It and the subsidiary are managed on a unified basis.

(f) **A company is also treated as the parent of the subsidiaries of its subsidiaries.**

A company (A Ltd) is a **wholly owned subsidiary** of another company (B Ltd) if it has no other members except B Ltd and its wholly owned subsidiaries, or persons acting on B Ltd's or its subsidiaries' behalf.

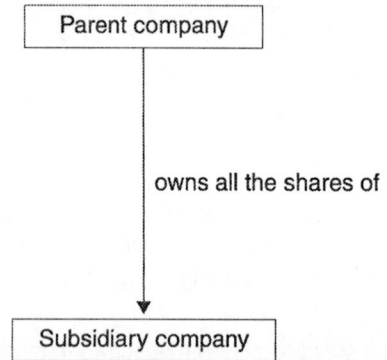

The diagram illustrates a **simple group**. In practice, such groups might be much larger and much more complex.

The importance of the parent and subsidiary company relationship is recognised in company law in a number of rules.

(a) A parent company must generally prepare **group accounts** in which the financial situation of parent and subsidiary companies is consolidated as if they were one person.

(b) A subsidiary may **not ordinarily be a member** of its parent company.

(c) Since directors of a parent company can **control** its **subsidiary**, some rules designed to regulate the dealings of companies with directors also apply to its subsidiaries, particularly loans to directors.

4.2 Quoted companies

As we have seen public companies may seek a listing on a public exchange. This option is not open to private companies, who are not allowed to offer their shares for sale to the public. Listed companies are sometimes referred to as quoted companies (because the price of their shares are quoted publicly).

4.3 Medium companies regime

Medium-sized companies are permitted to take advantage of more **relaxed accounting rules** and **disclosure requirements** as compared to larger companies. For example, the format of the profit and loss account is simpler and there are reduced reporting requirements in respect of their business review or strategic report.

A company is classed as **'medium-sized'** if it meets at least **two** of the following **conditions**:

- Annual turnover must be not more than £36 million
- The balance sheet total must be not more than £18 million
- The average number of employees must be not more than 250.

4.4 Small companies regime

Small companies benefit from the **small companies regime's** reduced legal requirements in terms of accounting rules, abridged accounts filing and exemption from obtaining an audit.

In **accounting terms**, a company is small if it meets **two** of the following applicable **criteria**:

(a) Balance sheet total of not more than £5.1 million.
(b) Turnover of not more than £10.2 million.
(c) 50 employees or fewer on average.

4.5 Micro-entities regime

A **micro-entity** has to option to take advantage of **accounting** exemptions that are not available to small companies.

An **entity** is classed as **'micro'** if it meets at least **two** of the following **conditions**:

(a) Annual turnover must be not more than £632,000.
(b) The balance sheet total must be not more than £316,000.
(c) The average number of employees must be not more than 10.

We shall look at the accounting requirements of small, medium and micro entities further in Chapter 11.

4.6 Multinational companies

Key term

> The vast majority of companies will simply operate in one country. However, some of the larger companies in the world will operate in more than one country. Such companies are **multinational**. A **multinational company** is a company that produces and markets its products in more than one country.

Some examples of multinational companies include:

- Wal-mart Stores Inc
- Royal Dutch Shell plc
- Exxon Mobil Corporation

Such companies sell their shares on stock exchanges around the world.

PART A   INCORPORATION

4.7 European companies

A European company is a **public company** which since **8 October 2004** can be **formed** under **European law**. The main requirement is that the **business must operate** in **two member states** and may be formed as a result of a merger of two companies in separate states.

Such companies are not likely to be a common form of business until rules on areas such as tax, insolvency and employment are harmonised across the European Union.

Question — Small companies

State the criteria that a company must meet to be classified as small.

Answer

A small company must meet two of the following criteria:

- Its balance sheet total must not exceed £5.1 million.
- Turnover must be no more than £10.2 million.
- It must employ fewer than 50 employees.

5 Effect of legal personality

FAST FORWARD

The case of *Salomon v Salomon & Co Ltd 1897* clearly demonstrates the **separate legal personality** of companies and is of great significance to any study of company law.

Salomon v Salomon & Co Ltd 1897

The facts: The claimant, S, had carried on business for 30 years. He decided to form a limited company to purchase the business so he and six members of his family each subscribed for one share.

The company then purchased the business from S for £38,782, the purchase price being payable to the claimant by way of the issue of 20,000 £1 shares, the issue of debentures, £10,000 of debentures and £8,782 in cash thereby making him a secured creditor.

The company did not prosper and was wound up a year later, at which point its liabilities exceeded its assets. The liquidator, representing unsecured trade creditors of the company, claimed that the company's business was in effect still the claimant's (he owned 20,001 of 20,007 shares). Therefore he should bear liability for its debts and that payment of the secured debt to him should be postponed until the company's trade creditors were paid.

Decision: The House of Lords held that the business was owned by, and its debts were liabilities of, the company. The claimant was under no liability to the company or its creditors, his debentures were validly issued and the security created by them over the company's assets was effective. This was because the company was a legal entity separate and distinct from S.

The principle of separate legal personality was confirmed in the following case.

Lee v Lee's Air Farming Ltd 1960

The facts: Mr Lee, who owned the majority of the shares of an aerial crop-spraying business, and was the sole working director of the company, was killed while piloting the aircraft.

Decision: Although he was the majority shareholder and sole working director of the company, he and the company were separate legal persons. Therefore he could also be an employee with rights against it when killed in an accident in the course of his employment.

The following is a more **recent case** on separate legal personality which confirms the previous case law is still valid.

> *MacDonald v Costello 2011*
>
> *The facts:* Mr and Mrs Costello entered into an agreement with MacDonald (a firm of builders) to develop land which they owned. For tax purposes, the Costellos used a special purpose vehicle (Oakwood Residential Limited) to finance the work and the contract was between Oakwood and MacDonald. Oakwood had been used in previous dealings between the parties. Oakwood failed to pay some invoices when there was disagreement about the work which had been done. MacDonald was awarded a payment order against Oakwood and an award in restitution against the Costellos personally for unjust enrichment. The Costellos appealed the award for unjust enrichment.
>
> *Decision:* Although the Costellos had been enriched by the work done by MacDonald, it was decided that the award against them should not be upheld. They were not party to the contract and, as shareholders of Oakwood, they were protected by the 'veil of incorporation'.

5.1 Veil of incorporation

> **FAST FORWARD**
>
> Incorporation '**veils**' members from outsiders' view but this veil may be lifted in **some circumstances**, so creditors and others can seek redress directly from members. The veil may be lifted: by statute to enforce the law; to prevent the evasion of obligations; and in certain situations where companies trade as a group.

Because a company has separate legal personality from the people who own or run it (the members/shareholders/directors), people can look at a company and not know who or what owns or runs it. The fact that members are 'hidden' in this way is sometimes referred to as the '**veil of incorporation**'. Literally, the members are 'veiled' from view.

6 Ignoring separate personality

> **FAST FORWARD**
>
> It is sometimes necessary by law to look at who the owners of a company are. This is referred to as '**lifting the veil**'.

Separate personality can be ignored to:

- **Identify** the **company** with its **members** and/or directors.
- Treat a **group of companies** as a **single commercial entity** (if a company is owned by another company).

The more important of these two reasons is the first one, although the second reason can sometimes be more complex. The main instances for lifting the veil are given below.

6.1 Lifting the veil by statute to enforce the law

Lifting of the veil is permitted under a number of statutes to enforce the law.

6.1.1 Liability for trading without trading certificate

A public company must obtain a trading certificate from the Registrar before it may commence to trade. Failure to do so leads to **personal liability** of the directors for any loss or damage suffered by a third party resulting from a transaction made in contravention of the trading certificate requirement. They are also liable for a fine.

6.1.2 Fraudulent and wrongful trading

When a company ceases to trade because of insolvency or some other reason, and is 'wound up', it may appear that its business has been carried on with **intent** to **defraud creditors** or others. In this case the court may decide that the persons (usually the directors) who were knowingly parties to the **fraudulent trading** shall be **personally responsible** under civil law for debts and other liabilities of the company: s 213 Insolvency Act 1986 (HMSO, 1986).

Fraudulent trading is also a criminal offence; under s 993 of the Companies Act 2006 any person guilty of the offence, even if the company has not been or is not being wound up, is liable for a fine or imprisonment for up to 10 years.

If a company in insolvency proceedings is found to have traded when there is no reasonable prospect of avoiding insolvent winding up, its directors may be liable under civil law for **wrongful trading**. Again a court may order such directors to make a contribution to the company's assets: s 214 Insolvency Act 1986.

6.1.3 Disqualified directors

Directors who participate in the management of a company in contravention of an order under the Company Directors Disqualification Act 1986 (HMSO, 1986) will be **jointly** or **severally liable** along with the company for the company's debts.

6.1.4 Abuse of company names

In the past there were a number of instances where directors of companies which went into **insolvent liquidation** formed another company with an identical or similar name, as a so-called 'phoenix' company. This new company bought the original company's business and assets from its liquidator.

The Insolvency Act 1986 (s 217) makes it a criminal offence and the directors personally liable where they are a director of a company that goes into insolvent liquidation and they become involved with the directing, managing or promoting of a business which has an **identical name** to the original company, or a **name similar** enough to suggest a connection. The directors are also likely to be disqualified from acting as a director.

Exam focus point

> It is very important to know the statutory reasons for lifting the veil.

6.2 Lifting the veil to prevent evasion of obligations

A company may be identified with those who control it, for instance to determine its residence for tax purposes. The courts may also ignore the distinction between a company and its members and managers if the latter use that distinction to **evade** their **existing legal obligations**.

> *Gilford Motor Co Ltd v Home 1933*
>
> *The facts:* The defendant had been employed by the claimant company under a contract which forbade him to solicit its customers after leaving its service. After the termination of his employment he formed a company of which his wife and an employee were the sole directors and shareholders. However he managed the company and through it evaded the covenant that prevented him from soliciting customers of his former employer.
>
> *Decision:* An injunction requiring observance of the covenant would be made both against the defendant and the company which he had formed as a 'a mere cloak or sham'.

6.2.1 Public interest

In time of war a company is not permitted to trade with '**enemy aliens**'. The courts may draw aside the veil if, despite a company being registered in the UK, it is suspected that it is controlled by aliens.

The question of nationality may also arise in peacetime, where it is convenient for a foreign entity to have a British **facade** on its operations.

> *Re F G Films Ltd 1953*
>
> *The facts:* An English company was formed by an American company to 'make' a film which would obtain certain marketing and other advantages from being called a British film. Staff and finance were American and there were neither premises nor employees in England. The film was produced in India.
>
> *Decision:* The British company was the American company's agent and so the film did not qualify as British. Effectively, the corporate entity of the British company was swept away and it was exposed as a 'sham' company.

6.2.2 Evasion of liabilities

The veil of may also be lifted where directors **ignore** the separate legal personality of two companies and transfer assets from one to the other in disregard of their duties in order to avoid an existing liability.

> *Re H and Others 1996*
>
> *The facts:* The court was asked to rule that various companies within a group, together with the minority shareholders, should be treated as one entity in order to restrain assets prior to trial.
>
> *Decision:* The order was granted. The court thought there was evidence that the companies had been used for the fraudulent evasion of excise duty.

6.2.3 Evasion of taxation

The court may lift the veil of incorporation where it is being used to **conceal** the nationality of the company.

> *Unit Construction Co Ltd v Bullock 1960*
>
> *The facts:* Three companies, wholly owned by a UK company, were registered in Kenya. Although the companies' constitutions required board meetings to be held in Kenya, all three were in fact managed entirely by the holding company.
>
> *Decision:* The companies were resident in the UK and liable to UK tax. The Kenyan connection was a sham, the question being not where they ought to have been managed, but where they were actually managed.

6.2.4 Quasi-partnership

An application to wind up a company on the 'just and equitable' ground under the Insolvency Act 1986 may involve the court lifting the veil to reveal the company as a **quasi-partnership.** This may happen where the company only has a few members, all of whom are actively involved in its affairs. Typically the individuals have operated contentedly as a company for years but then fall out, and one or more of them seeks to remove the others.

The courts are willing in such cases to treat the central relationship between the directors as being that of partners, and rule that it would be unfair therefore to allow the company to continue with only some of its original members. This is illustrated by the case of *Ebrahimi v Westbourne Galleries Ltd 1973* (see Chapter 11).

PART A   INCORPORATION

Question
Quasi-partnership

Sandy and Pat have carried on business together for twenty years, most recently through a limited company in which each holds 500 shares. They share the profits equally in the form of directors' remuneration. Pat's son Craig joins the business, buying 100 shares from each of Sandy and Pat. Disputes arise and Pat and Craig use their voting majority to remove Sandy from the board. Advise Sandy.

Answer

Sandy cannot prevent her removal from her directorship. However, a court may find that, on the basis of the past relationship, it is unjust and inequitable to determine the case solely on legal rights. It could, on equitable principles, order liquidation of the company.

The veil of the company may be lifted to reveal a quasi-partnership.

6.3 Lifting the veil in group situations

The principle of the veil of incorporation extends to the holding (parent) company/subsidiary relationship. Although holding companies and subsidiaries are part of a group under company law, they retain their **separate legal personalities**.

In *Adams v Cape Industries plc 1990*, three reasons were put forward for identifying the companies as one, and lifting the veil of incorporation. They are:

- The subsidiary is acting as **agent** for the holding company.
- The group is to be treated as a **single economic entity** because of statutory provision.
- The **corporate structure** is being used as a **facade** (or sham) to conceal the truth.

Adams v Cape Industries plc 1990

The facts: Cape, an English company, headed a group which included many wholly-owned subsidiaries. Some of these mined asbestos in South Africa, and others marketed the asbestos in various countries including the USA.

Several hundred claimants had been awarded damages by a Texas court for personal injuries suffered as a result of exposure to asbestos dust. The defendants in Texas included one of Cape's subsidiaries, NAAC. The courts also considered the position of AMC, another subsidiary, and CPC, a company linked to Cape Industries.

Decision: The judgement would not be enforced against the English holding company, either on the basis that Cape had been 'present' in the US through its local subsidiaries or because it had carried on business in the US through the agency of NAAC. Slade LJ commented in giving the judgement that English law 'for better or worse recognises the creation of subsidiary companies ... which would fall to be treated as separate legal entities, with all the rights and liabilities which would normally be attached to separate legal entities'.

Whether desirable or not, English law allowed a group structure to be used so that legal liability fell on an individual member of a group rather than the group as a whole.

Exam focus point

Lifting the veil in group situations is easily forgotten. Ensure you know the *Cape Industries* case and the three reasons for lifting the veil in groups which it sets out.

6.4 Summary of situations in which the veil can be lifted

The instances in which the veil will be lifted are as follows.

Lifting the veil by statute to enforce the law	• Liability for trading without a trading certificate • Fraudulent and wrongful trading • Disqualified directors • Abuse of company names
Evasion of obligations	• Evasion of legal obligations • Public interest • Evasion of liabilities • Evasion of taxation • Quasi-partnership
Group situations	• Subsidiary acting as agent for the holding company • The group is to be treated as a single economic entity • The corporate structure is being used as a sham

6.5 Lifting the veil and limited liability

The above examples of lifting the veil include examples of where, if they have broken the law, **directors** can be made **personally liable** for a company's debts. This is very rare.

If those directors are also members, then limited liability **does not apply**. This is the only time that limited liability is overridden and that the **member** becomes **personally liable** for the company's debts **due to their actions as a director**.

7 Comparison of companies and partnerships

FAST FORWARD

> Because it is a separate legal entity, a company has a number of features which are different from a partnership. The most important difference between a company and a traditional partnership is that a company has a **separate legal personality** from its members, while a traditional partnership does not.

7.1 The differences

The separate legal personality of a company gives rise to a number of characteristics which mark it out from a traditional partnership. These are outlined below. The other key differences relate to the **formality** of a company as opposed to a partnership and the **regulations** it has to adhere to.

Factor	Company	Traditional partnership
Entity	Is a legal entity separate from its members	Has no existence outside of its members
Liability	Members' liability can be limited	Partners' liability is usually unlimited
Size	May have any number of members (at least one)	Some partnerships are limited to twenty members (professional partnerships excluded)
Succession	Perpetual succession – change in ownership does not affect existence	Partnerships are dissolved when any of the partners leaves it
Owners' interests	Members own transferable shares	Partners cannot assign their interests in a partnership
Assets	Company owns the assets	Partners own assets jointly
Management	Company must have at least one director (two for a public company)	All partners can participate in management

PART A INCORPORATION

Factor	Company	Traditional partnership
Constitution	Company must have a written constitution.	A partnership may have a written partnership agreement, but also may not.
Accounts	A company must usually deliver accounts to the Registrar.	Partners do not have to send their accounts to the Registrar.
Security	A company may offer a floating charge over its assets.	A partnership may not usually give a floating charge on assets.
Withdrawal of capital	Strict rules concerning repayment of subscribed capital.	More straightforward for a partner to withdraw capital.
Taxation	Company pays tax on its profit. Directors are taxed through PAYE system. Shareholders receive dividends which are taxed 10 months after the tax year.	Partners extract 'drawings' weekly or monthly. No tax is deducted. Income tax is payable on their share of the final profit for the year.
Management	Members elect directors to manage the company.	All partners have a right to be involved in management.

Revise this table above when you have studied the rest of the book and know more of the details concerning the distinctive factors of companies.

Chapter roundup

- A company has a **legal personality** separate from its owners (known as members). It is a formal arrangement, surrounded by formality and publicity, but its chief advantage is that members' **liability** for the company's debts is typically **limited**.

- The fact that a company's members – not the company itself – have **limited liability** for its debts **protects** the **members** from the company's creditors and ultimately from the full risk of business failure.

- Most companies are those **incorporated** under the **Companies Act**. However there are other types of company such as **corporations sole**, **chartered corporations**, **statutory corporations** and **community interest companies**.

- A company may be **private** or **public**. Only the latter may offer its shares to the public.

- To trade, a public company must hold a **Registrar's trading certificate** having met the requirements, including **minimum capital** of £50,000.

- The main differences between public and private companies relate to: **capital**; **dealings** in **shares**; **accounts**; **commencement of business**; **general meetings**; **names**; **identification**; and **disclosure requirements**.

- There are a number of other ways in which companies can be **classified**.

- The case of *Salomon v Salomon & Co Ltd 1897* clearly demonstrates the **separate legal personality** of companies and is of great significance to any study of company law.

- Incorporation '**veils**' members from outsiders' view but this veil may be lifted in **some circumstances**, so creditors and others can seek redress directly from members. The veil may be lifted: by statute to enforce the law; to prevent the evasion of obligations; and in certain situations where companies trade as a group.

- It is sometimes necessary by law to look at who the owners of a company are. This is referred to as '**lifting the veil**'.

- Because it is a separate legal entity, a company has a number of features which are different from a partnership. The most important difference between a company and a traditional partnership is that a company has a **separate legal personality** from its members, while a traditional partnership does not.

PART A   INCORPORATION

Quick quiz

1. Which of the following types of company can be incorporated under the Companies Act 2006?

    A   A private limited company
    B   A public limited company
    C   A company limited by guarantee with a share capital
    D   A company limited by guarantee with no share capital
    E   A private unlimited company
    F   A public unlimited company

2. Which TWO of the following statements are true? A private company:

    A   Is defined as any company that is not a public company
    B   Sells its shares on the junior stock market known as the Alternative Investment Market and on the Stock Exchange
    C   Must have at least one director with unlimited liability
    D   Is a significant form of business organisation in areas of the economy that do not require large amounts of capital

3. Under which circumstance would a member of a limited company have to contribute funds on winding up?

    A   Where there is not enough cash to pay the creditors
    B   Where they have an outstanding amount from when they originally purchased their shares
    C   To allow the company to repurchase debentures it issued
    D   Where the company is a community interest company and the funds are required to complete a community project

4. The minimum allotted and paid up share capital of a company incorporated as a public limited company is

    A   £12,500
    B   £50,000
    C   £100,000
    D   £500,000

5. **Fill in the blanks** in the statement below using the figures in the box.

    A micro company must meet two of the following criteria.

    Its balance sheet total must be less than £ … ,000,000 and its turnover must be less than £ … ,000,000. The number of employees must be less than … people.

10	632
316	50

6. Which TWO of the following are correct? A public company or plc:

    A   Is defined as any company which is not a private company
    B   Has a legal personality that is separate from its members or owners
    C   Must have at least one director with unlimited liability
    D   Can own property and make contracts in its own name

7. State the main advantage of forming an unlimited company.

8. What was the name of the case that originally demonstrated the principle of separate legal personality?

9. Businesses in the form of sole traders are legally distinct from their owners.

    True ☐
    False ☐

10 Put the examples given below in the correct category box.

- Wrong use of company name
- Single economic entity
- Corporate structure a sham
- Disqualified directors
- Fraudulent and wrongful trading
- Legal obligations
- Quasi-partnership
- Public interest

WHEN THE VEIL OF INCORPORATION IS LIFTED		
To enforce law	**To enforce obligations**	**To expose groups**

PART A   INCORPORATION

Answers to quick quiz

1. A, B, D and E are correct. It is not possible to incorporate a company limited by guarantee with a share capital, so C is incorrect. A public limited company is by definition limited, so F is wrong.

2. A and D are correct. A private company cannot sell its shares to the public on any stock market, so B is incorrect. Directors need not have unlimited liability, so C is incorrect.

3. B   Members only have a liability for any outstanding amounts of share capital partly paid for.

4. B   £50,000. Where the company was incorporated as a private one but subsequently re-registered as a public one, only a quarter of the minimum must be paid up (£12,500).

5. Balance sheet total £316,000,000
   Turnover £632,000,000
   Employees less than 10

6. B and D are correct. A public company has to be defined as such in its constitution so A is incorrect. No directors **need** have unlimited liability, so C is incorrect.

7. An unlimited company need not usually file annual accounts.

8. *Salomon v Salomon Ltd 1897.*

9. False. Sole trader businesses are not legally distinct from their owners.

10.

WHEN THE VEIL OF INCORPORATION IS LIFTED		
To enforce law	**To enforce obligations**	**To expose groups**
Wrong use of company name Disqualified directors Fraudulent and wrongful trading	Legal obligations Quasi-partnership Public interest	Single economic entity Corporate structure a sham

End of chapter question

Companies

In relation to companies explain the following:

(a) A public limited company   (3 marks)
(b) Parent and subsidiary companies   (4 marks)
(c) A multinational company   (3 marks)

(Total = 10 marks)

Company formation

Topic list	Syllabus reference
1 Promoters and pre-incorporation contracts	8.1
2 Pre-incorporation expenses and contracts	8.1
3 Registration procedures	8.1
4 Statutory books and records	8.4
5 Confirmation statements	8.4

Introduction

In Chapter 1 of this Study Text, you were introduced to the idea of the separate legal personality of a company.

Sections 1 to 3 of this chapter concentrate on the **procedural aspects** of **company formation**. Important topics in these sections include the **formalities** that a company must observe in order to be formed, and the liability of **promoters for pre-incorporation contracts**.

Sections 4 and 5 of this chapter consider the concept of the **public accountability** of **limited companies**. Later on in your coverage of the syllabus you will meet references to a company's obligation to publicise certain decisions, so it is important to understand at this stage how and why this should be done.

The **Companies Act 2006**, (TSO, 2006) and the **Small Business, Enterprise and Employment Act 2015**, (TSO, 2015) apply to this and all chapters unless otherwise stated.

PART A   INCORPORATION

1 Promoters and pre-incorporation contracts

> **FAST FORWARD**
>
> A promoter **forms** a company. They must act with **reasonable skill** and **care**, and if shares are to be allotted they are the agent of the company, with an agent's fiduciary duties.

A company cannot form itself. The person who forms it is called a '**promoter**'. A promoter is an example of an **agent**, that is someone who acts on behalf of another person (the **principal**).

Key term

> A **promoter** is one who undertakes to form a company with reference to a given project and to set it going and who takes the necessary steps to accomplish that purpose: *Twycross v Grant 1877*.

In addition to the person who takes the procedural steps to get a company incorporated, the term 'promoter' includes anyone who makes **business preparations** for the company. **However** a person who acts **merely** in a **professional capacity** in company formation, such as a solicitor or an accountant, **is not** on that account a **promoter**.

1.1 Duties of promoters

Promoters have the general duty to exercise **reasonable skill and care**.

If the promoter is to be the owner of the company there is no conflict of interest and it does not matter if the promoter obtains some advantage from this position, for example, by selling their existing business to the company for 100% of its shares.

If, however, **some or all the shares** of the company when formed **are to be allotted to other people**, the promoter is as **agent** of the company. This means they have the customary **duties** of an agent and the following fiduciary duties towards the principal.

(a) A promoter must account for any **benefits obtained** through acting as a promoter.
(b) Promoters must not put themselves in a position where their own **interests conflict** with those of the company.
(c) A promoter must provide **full information** on their transactions and account for all monies arising from them. The promoter must therefore make **proper disclosure** of any personal advantage to **existing** and **prospective** company **members** or to an **independent board of directors**.

A promoter may make a **profit** as a result of their position.

(a) A **legitimate** profit is made by a promoter who acquires interest in property **before promoting** a company and then makes a profit when they sell the property to the promoted company, provided they disclose it.
(b) A **wrongful** profit is made by a promoter who enters into and makes a profit personally in a contract as a promoter. They are in breach of fiduciary duty.

A promoter of a public company makes their disclosure of legitimate profit through listing particulars or a prospectus. If they make proper disclosure of a legitimate profit, they may retain it.

1.1.1 Remedy for breach of promoter's fiduciary duty

If the promoter does not make a proper disclosure of legitimate profits or if they make wrongful profits the primary remedy of the company is to **rescind** the **contract** and **recover its money**.

However sometimes it is too late to rescind because the property can no longer be returned or the company prefers to keep it. In such a case the company can **only recover** from the promoter their **wrongful profit**, unless some special circumstances dictate otherwise.

Where shares are sold under a **prospectus offer**, promoters have a statutory liability to compensate any person who acquires securities to which the prospectus relates and suffered loss as a result of any untrue or misleading statement, or omission.

Statutory and listing regulations together with rigorous investigation by merchant banks have greatly lessened the problem of the dishonest promoter.

2 Pre-incorporation expenses and contracts

> **FAST FORWARD**
>
> A promoter has **no automatic right** to be reimbursed **pre-incorporation expenses** by the company, though this can be expressly agreed.

2.1 Pre-incorporation expenses

A promoter usually incurs **expenses** in preparations, such as drafting legal documents, made before the company is formed. They have **no automatic right to recover these 'pre-incorporation expenses'** from the company. However they can generally arrange that the first directors, of whom they may be one, **agree** that the company shall pay the bills or refund to them their expenditure. They could also include a special article in the company's constitution containing an indemnity for the promoter.

2.2 Pre-incorporation contracts

> **FAST FORWARD**
>
> Pre-incorporation contracts **cannot** be ratified by the company. A new contract on the same terms must be expressly created.

Key term

A **pre-incorporation contract** is a contract purported to be made by a company or its agent at a time before the company has been formed.

In agency law a principal may ratify a contract made by an agent retrospectively. However, a company can **never ratify** a contract made on its behalf **before it was incorporated**. It did not exist when the pre-incorporation contract was made so one of the conditions for ratification fails.

A company may enter into a **new contract** on **similar terms** after it has been incorporated (**novation**). However there must be **sufficient evidence** that the company has made a new contract. Mere recognition of the pre-incorporation contract by performing it or accepting benefits under it is not the same as making a new contract.

2.3 Liability of promoters for pre-incorporation contracts

The company's **agent** is **liable** on a contract to which they are deemed to be a party. The agent may also be entitled to enforce the contract against the other party and so they could transfer the right to **enforce** the contract to the company. Liability is determined by s 51(1) of the Companies Act 2006.

'A contract that purports to be made by or on behalf of a company at a time when the company has not been formed has effect, subject to any agreement to the contrary, as one made with the person purporting to act for the company or as agent for it, and he is personally liable on the contract accordingly.'

2.4 Other ways of avoiding liability as a promoter for pre-incorporation contracts

There are various other ways for promoters to avoid liability for a pre-incorporation contract.

(a) The contract remains as a **draft** (so not binding) until the company is formed. The promoters are the directors, and the company has the power to enter the contract. Once the company is formed, the directors take office and the company enters into the contract.

(b) If the contract has to be finalised before incorporation it should contain a clause that the personal liability of promoters is to cease if the company, when formed, enters a **new contract** on identical terms. This is known as **novation**.

PART A INCORPORATION

(c) A common way to avoid the problem concerning pre-incorporation contracts is to buy a company **'off the shelf'** (see Section 3 of this chapter). Even if a person contracts on behalf of the new company before it is bought the company should be able to ratify the contract since it existed 'on the shelf' at the time the contract was made.

| Exam focus point | A favourite question in law exams is the status of a pre-incorporation contract. |

Question   Promoter

Fiona is the promoter of Enterprise Ltd. Before the company is incorporated, she enters into a contract purportedly on its behalf. After the certificate of incorporation is issued, the contract is breached. Who is liable?

Answer

Fiona is liable as promoters are liable for pre-incorporation contracts: s 51(1).

3 Registration procedures

FAST FORWARD

A company is **formed** and registered under the Companies Act 2006 when it is issued with a **certificate of incorporation** by the Registrar, after submission to the Registrar of a number of documents and a fee.

Most companies are registered under the Companies Act 2006 (TSO, 2006). The **Small Business, Enterprise and Employment Act 2015** (TSO, 2015) improved registration procedures and improved the transparency and simplified filing requirements for corporations. We shall come to these aspects throughout your study of company law.

A company is formed under the Companies Act 2006 by one or more persons subscribing to a memorandum of association who comply with the requirements regarding registration.

A company may not be formed for an unlawful purpose.

3.1 Documents to be delivered to the Registrar

To obtain registration of a company limited by shares, an application for registration, various documents and a fee must be sent to the Registrar (usually electronically). We shall look at two of them (the articles and the memorandum of association) in detail, later in this Study Text.

3.1.1 Application for registration: Form IN01

S 9 requires an **application for registration** to be made on Form IN01 and submitted to the Registrar with the other documents described in the table below.

The application must contain:

- The company's proposed name (prior to completing form IN01, a check should be made of the register of names at Companies House, to ensure that there is no company already registered with the proposed name).
- The **location** of its **registered office** (England and Wales, Wales, Scotland or Northern Ireland).
- That the **liability of members** is to be **limited** by shares or **guarantee**.
- Whether the company is to be **private** or **public**.
- A statement of the **intended address** of the **registered office**.

2: COMPANY FORMATION

Documents to be delivered	Description
Memorandum of association	This is a **prescribed form** signed by the subscribers. The memorandum states that the subscribers wish to form a company and they agree to become members of it. If the company has share capital each subscriber agrees to subscribe for at least one share.
Articles of association (only required if the company does not adopt model articles)	Articles are signed by the same subscriber(s), dated and witnessed. **Model articles** are provided by statute and are adopted by a new company if: • No other articles are registered, or • If the articles supplied do not exclude or modify the model articles.
Statement of proposed officers	The statement gives the particulars of the proposed **director(s)** and **company secretary** if applicable. The persons named as directors must consent to act in this capacity. When the company is incorporated they are deemed to be appointed.
Statement of compliance	The statement that the **requirements** of the **Companies Act** in respect of registration have been **complied** with.
Statement of capital and initial shareholdings (only required for companies limited by shares)	A statement of capital and initial shareholdings must be delivered by all companies with **share capital**. (See Chapter 4 for the contents of this statement.) Alternatively, a statement of guarantee is required by companies limited by guarantee.
Registration fee	A registration fee (currently £40 if paper documentation is used, £13 if incorporation software is used) is also payable on registration.

Exam focus point

Questions on incorporation could require you to identify the documents which should be sent to the Registrar.

3.2 Certificate of incorporation

The Registrar considers whether the documents are formally in order. If satisfied, the company is given a **'registered number'**. A **certificate of incorporation** is issued and notice of it is publicised.

A company is registered by the inclusion of the company in the register, and the issue of a **certificate of incorporation** by the Registrar. The certificate:

- Identifies the company by its **name** and **registered number**.
- States that it is **limited** (if appropriate) and whether it is a **private** or **public** company.
- States whether the **registered office** is in England and Wales, Wales, Scotland or Northern Ireland.
- States the **date of incorporation**.
- Is **signed** by the **Registrar**, or authenticated by the Registrar's official seal.

Key term

A **certificate of incorporation** is a certificate issued by the Registrar which denotes the date of incorporation, 'the subscribers, together with any persons who from time to time become members, become a body corporate capable of exercising all the functions of an incorporated company'.

The certificate of incorporation is conclusive evidence that:

- All the **requirements** of the **Companies Act** have been **followed.**
- The company is a **company authorised** to be **registered** and has been **duly registered.**

If the certificate states that the company is a **public company**, the certificate is conclusive evidence of this.

If irregularities in formation procedure or an error in the certificate itself are later discovered, the certificate is nonetheless **valid** and **conclusive**: *Jubilee Cotton Mills Ltd v Lewes 1924*.

Upon incorporation persons named as **directors** and **secretary** in the statement of proposed officers automatically become such officers.

3.3 Companies 'off the shelf'

> **FAST FORWARD**
>
> Buying a company 'off the shelf' avoids the administrative burden of registering a company.

Despite the **Small Business, Enterprise and Employment Act 2015** introducing changes to streamline company administration, the registration of a new company can be a lengthy business and it is often easiest for people wishing to operate as a company to purchase an **'off-the-shelf' company**.

This is possible by contacting enterprises specialising in registering a stock of companies, ready for sale when a person comes along who needs the advantages of incorporation.

Normally the persons associated with the company formation enterprise are registered as the company's subscribers, and its first secretary and director. When the company is purchased, the **shares** are **transferred** to the **buyer**, and the Registrar is notified of the director's and the secretary's resignation.

The principal **advantages** for the purchaser of purchasing an off the shelf company are as follows.

(a) The **following documents** will **not need** to be **filed** with the Registrar by the purchaser:

    (i) Memorandum and articles (unless the articles are not model articles)
    (ii) Application for registration
    (iii) Statement of proposed officers
    (iv) Statement of compliance
    (v) Statement of capital and initial shareholdings
    (vi) Fee

This is because the specialist has already registered the company. It will therefore be a quicker, and very possibly cheaper, way of incorporating a business.

(b) There will be **no risk** of **potential liability** arising from pre-incorporation contracts. The company can trade without needing to worry about waiting for the Registrar's certificate of incorporation.

The **disadvantages** relate to the changes that will be required to the off-the-shelf company to make it compatible with the members' needs.

(a) The off-the-shelf company is likely to have **model articles**. The directors may wish to amend these.
(b) The directors may want to **change** the **name** of the company.
(c) The **subscriber shares** will need to be **transferred**, and the transfer recorded in the register of members. Stamp duty will be payable.

Question — Documents required on formation of a company

What are the documents which must be delivered to the Registrar for registration of a company?

Answer

The memorandum of association (and articles if not in model form), application for registration, a statement of proposed officers, a statement of intended registered office address, a statement of compliance, a statement of capital and initial shareholdings, and a fee.

3.4 Re-registration procedures

> **FAST FORWARD**
>
> A **private company** with share capital may be able to re-register as a **public company** if the share capital requirement is met. A public company may re-register as a private one.

Note. For a private company to re-register as a public company it must fulfil the share capital requirement of a public company: Its allotted share capital must be at least £50,000 of which a quarter must be paid up, plus the whole of any premium.

	Re-registering as a public company	Re-registering as a private company
Resolution	The **shareholders must agree** to the company going public. • Convene a general meeting. • Pass a **special resolution** (75% majority) since this decision the company's constitution.	The **shareholders must agree** to the company going private. • Convene a general meeting. • Pass a **special resolution** (75% majority of those present and voting) since this decision the company's constitution.

Application	The **company must** then **apply** to the Registrar to go public.
	• Send application to the Registrar.
	• Send additional information to the Registrar, comprising:
	  – Copy of the special resolution.
	  – Copy of proposed new public company articles.
	  – Statement of the company's proposed name on re-registration.
	  – Statement of proposed company secretary.
	  – Balance sheet and related auditors' statement which states that at the balance sheet date the company's net assets are not less than its called-up share capital and undistributable reserves.
	  – Statement of compliance.
	  – Valuation report regarding allotment of shares for non-cash consideration since the balance sheet date.
		The **company must** then **apply** to the Registrar to go private.
		• Send the application to the Registrar.
		• Send additional information to the Registrar, comprising:
		  – Copy of the special resolution.
		  – Copy of altered new private company articles.
		  – Statement of Compliance.
		  – Statement of the company's proposed name on re-registration.

Approval	The Registrar must accept the statement of compliance as sufficient evidence that the company is entitled to be re-registered as public. A certificate of incorporation on re-registration is issued.	The Registrar issues a certificate of incorporation on re-registration.
Compulsory re-registration	If the **share capital** of a public company **falls below £50,000**, it must re-register as a private company.	There is **no such compulsion** for a private company.

3.5 Commencement of business rules

> **FAST FORWARD**
>
> To **trade** or **borrow**, a public company needs a **trading certificate**. Private companies may commence business on **registration**.

3.5.1 Public companies

A **public company** incorporated as such may not do business or exercise any borrowing powers unless it has obtained a **trading certificate** from the Registrar: s 761. This is obtained by sending an application to the Registrar. A private company which is re-registered as a public company is not subject to this rule.

The application:

- States the nominal value of the allotted share capital is not less than £50,000 (s 763).
- States the particulars of preliminary expenses and payments or benefits to promoters.
- Must be accompanied by a statement of compliance.

If a public company does business or borrows before obtaining a certificate the other party is protected since the **transaction is valid**. However the company and any officer in default have committed an offence **punishable** by a **fine**. They may also have to indemnify the third party.

Under s 122 of the Insolvency Act 1986 a court may **wind up** a public company which does not obtain a trading certificate within **one year** of incorporation.

3.5.2 Private company

A **private company** may do business and exercise its borrowing powers from the date of its incorporation. After registration the following procedures are important.

(a) A **first meeting** of the directors should be held at which the chairman, secretary and sometimes the auditors are appointed, shares are allotted to raise capital, authority is given to open a bank account and other commercial arrangements are made.

(b) A **return of allotments** should be made to the Registrar.

(c) The company may give notice to the Registrar of the **accounting reference date** on which its annual accounts will be made up. If no such notice is given within the prescribed period, companies are deemed to have an accounting reference date of the **last day of the month** in which the **anniversary of incorporation** falls.

4 Statutory books and records

4.1 The requirement for public accountability

> **FAST FORWARD**
>
> The price of limited liability is greater **public accountability** via the Companies Registry, registers, the *London Gazette* and company letterheads.

Under the Companies Act 2006 (TSO, 2006) the privileges of trading through a separate corporate body are matched by the duty to provide information which is available to the public about the company.

Basic sources of information on UK companies
The Registrar keeps a file at **Companies House** which holds all documents delivered by the company for filing. Any member of the public, for example someone who intends to do business with the company, may inspect the file (usually electronically).
The **registers and other documents** which the company is required to hold at its registered office (or in some cases at a different address). These are looked at later in this chapter.
The *London Gazette*, a specialist publication in which the company itself or the Registrar is required to publish certain notices or publicise the receipt of certain documents.
The **company's letterheads** and other forms which must give particulars of the company's place of registration, its identifying number and the address of its office.

4.2 The Registrar of Companies

The Registrar of Companies ('the Registrar') and the Registrar's department within the Government is usually called Companies House (in full it is 'the Companies Registration Office').

For **English** and **Welsh** companies the Registrar is located at the Companies House in **Cardiff**; for **Scottish** companies the Registrar is in **Edinburgh**.

The company is identified by its **name** and **company registration number** which must be stated on every document sent to Companies House for filing.

On first incorporation the company's file includes a copy of its **certificate of incorporation** and the **original documents** presented to secure its incorporation.

Once a company has been in existence for some time the file is likely to include the following.

- Certificate of incorporation
- Public company trading certificate
- Each year's annual accounts and return
- Copies of special and some ordinary resolutions
- A copy of the altered articles of association if relevant
- Notices of various events such as a change of directors or secretary
- If a company issues a prospectus, a signed copy with all annexed documents

4.3 Statutory books

FAST FORWARD

> A company must keep **registers** of certain aspects of its constitution, including the registers of members and directors.

Various people are entitled to have access to **registers** and copies of records that the company must keep. To enable the documents to be found easily the company must keep them at its **registered office** or a **single alternative inspection location** (SAIL) which is registered with Companies House. All documents may be kept at either location or a combination of the two. Companies are not permitted to have more than one single alternative inspection location. Private companies are permitted to file their registers of members, directors and secretaries, PSC and directors' residential addresses at **Companies House** instead of a registered office or SAIL.

Register/copies of records
Register of **members**
Register of **people with significant control (PSC)**
Register of **directors (and secretaries)**
Register of **directors' residential addresses**
Records of **directors' service contracts and indemnities**
Records of **resolutions and meetings** of the company
Register of **debentureholders**
Register of disclosed **interests** in shares (public company **only**)

Attention!

> We will learn more about the **registered office** in Chapter 3. Some of the registers below contain details of shares and classes of shares. We will learn more about types of share in Chapter 4. Similarly, others refer to charges, directors and debentures. We shall learn about all of these later. For now you must just learn the content of each register.

4.4 Register of members

Every company must keep a register of members. It must contain:

(a) The **name** and **address** of **each member**.

(b) **The shareholder class** (if more than one) to which they belong unless this is indicated in the particulars of their shareholding.

(c) If the company has a share capital, the **number of shares** held by each member. In addition:

　(i) If the shares have **distinguishing numbers**, the member's shares must be identified in the register by those numbers.

　(ii) If the company has more than one class of share the member's shares must be **distinguished** by their **class**, such as preference, ordinary, or non-voting shares.

(d) The date on which each member **became** and eventually the date on which they **ceased** to be a member.

The company may choose where it keeps the register of members available for inspection from:

- The registered office
- Another office of the company
- The office of a professional registrar

Any member of the company can inspect the register of members of a company without charge. A member of the public must pay but has the right of inspection.

A company with more than 50 members must keep a separate index of those members, unless the register itself functions as an index.

4.5 Register of people with significant control (PSC)

All private and public companies are required to keep a **register of people with significant control**. This register contains information on individuals who own or control over 25% of a company's shares or voting rights, or who exercise control over the company and its management in other ways (for example through the ability to appoint or remove directors).

The information which is required to be collected includes the individual's **name**, **date of birth**, **nationality** and **service address** and **details of their interest in the company**. This information will be checked and updated each year when the company submits its confirmation statement and is available for public inspection. It an **offence** not to comply with the requirement to file this register.

4.6 Register of directors

The register of directors must contain the following details in respect of a director who is an individual (that is, not a company).

- **Present** and **former** forenames and surnames
- A **service address** (may be the company's registered address rather than the director's home address)
- **Residency** and **nationality**
- **Business occupation** (if any)
- Date of birth

The register does not include shadow directors (discussed in a later chapter). It must be open to inspection by a member (free of charge), or by any other person (for a fee).

Note. The company must keep a separate **register** of **directors' residential addresses** but this is not available to members of the general public.

4.7 Records of directors' service contracts

The company should keep **copies** or written memoranda of all **service contracts** for its directors, including contracts for services which are not performed in the capacity of director. Members are entitled to view these copies for free, or request a copy on payment of a set fee.

> **Key term**
>
> Under s 227 a director's **service contract**, means a contract under which:
>
> (a) A director of the company undertakes personally to perform services (as director or otherwise) for a company, or for a subsidiary of the company, or
>
> (b) Services (as director or otherwise) that a director of the company undertakes personally to perform are made available by a third party to the company, or to a subsidiary of the company.

4.8 Register of debenture holders

Companies with debentures issued nearly always keep a **register of debenture holders**, but there is no statutory compulsion to do so.

5 Confirmation statements

> **FAST FORWARD**
>
> Every twelve months a company must send a **confirmation statement** to the Registrar.

Every company must send a **confirmation statement** to the Registrar. The statement can be sent at any time, but no more than twelve months may elapse between statement submissions.

The purpose of the **confirmation statement** is to keep the Registrar informed about certain changes to the company. Much of this information would have been submitted when the company is formed.

Confirmation statements are used to **confirm** that there have been **no changes** to the information held by the Registrar during the previous twelve months, if none have been made. If changes have been made, it records just the changes have occurred.

Examples of information requiring confirmation are:

- The address of the **registered office** of the company
- The address (if different) at which the **register of members** or **debentureholders** is kept
- The type of company and its principal **business activities**
- The total number of **issued shares,** their **aggregate nominal value** and the amounts paid and unpaid on each share
- For each **class of share**, the **rights** of those shares, the **total number** of shares in that class and their **total nominal value**
- Particulars of **members** of the company
- Changes to the **Register of people with significant control**
- Particulars of those who have **ceased** to be members since the last return
- The number of shares of each **class** held by members at the return date, and transferred by members since incorporation or the last return date
- The particulars of **directors,** and **secretary (if applicable)**

PART A INCORPORATION

Chapter roundup

- A promoter **forms** a company. They must act with **reasonable skill** and **care**, and if shares are allotted they are the agent of the company, with an agent's fiduciary duties.

- A promoter has **no automatic right** to be reimbursed pre-incorporation expenses by the company, though this can be expressly agreed.

- Pre-incorporation contracts **cannot** be ratified by the company. A new contract on the same terms must be expressly created.

- A company is **formed and registered** under the Companies Act 2006 when it is issued with a **certificate of incorporation** by the Registrar, after submission to the Registrar of a number of documents and a fee.

- Buying a company **'off the shelf'** avoids the administrative burden of registering a company.

- A **private company** with share capital may be able to re-register as a **public company** if the share capital requirement is met. A public company may re-register as a private one.

- To **trade** or **borrow**, a public company needs a **trading certificate**. Private companies may commence business on **registration**.

- The price of limited liability is greater **public accountability** is via the Companies Registry, registers, the *London Gazette* and company letterheads.

- A company must keep **registers** of certain aspects of its constitution, including the registers of members and directors.

- Every twelve months a company must send a **confirmation statement** to the Registrar.

Quick quiz

1. A company can confirm a pre-incorporation contract by performing it or obtaining benefits from it.

    True ☐

    False ☐

2. If a public company does business or borrows before obtaining a trading certificate from the Registrar, the transaction is:

    A   Invalid, and the third party cannot recover any loss
    B   Invalid, but the third party may recover any loss from the directors
    C   Valid, and the directors are punishable by a fine
    D   Valid, but the third party can sue the directors for further damages

3. A company must keep a register of directors. What details must be revealed?

    A   Full name
    B   Service address
    C   Nationality
    D   Date of birth
    E   Business occupation

4. An accountant or solicitor acting in their professional capacity during the registration of a company may be deemed a promoter.

    True ☐

    False ☐

5. If a certificate of incorporation is dated 6 March, but is not signed and issued until 8 March, when is the company deemed to have come into existence?

PART A   INCORPORATION

Answers to quick quiz

1. False. The company must make a new contract on similar terms.
2. C. The directors are punished for allowing the company to trade before it is allowed to.
3. All of them.
4. False. A person acting in a professional capacity will not be deemed a promoter.
5. 6 March. The date on the certificate is conclusive.

End of chapter question

Incorporation and promoters

(a) Explain what is meant by the following in company law:
    (i) A promoter (3 marks)
    (ii) A pre-incorporation contract (3 marks)

(b) Describe the liability of a promoter on a pre-incorporation contract. (4 marks)

(Total = 10 marks)

Constitution of a company

Topic list	Syllabus reference
1 Memorandum of association	8.1
2 A company's constitution	8.1
3 Company objects and capacity	8.1
4 The constitution as a contract	8.1
5 Company name and registered office	8.1

Introduction

In the previous chapter, the **articles of association** was mentioned briefly as one of the documents that may be required to be submitted to the Registrar when applying for registration. The articles, together with any resolutions and agreements which may affect them, form the company's **constitution**.

The constitution sets out what the company does; if there are no restrictions specified then the company may do anything provided it is legal. Clearly this includes the capacity to contract, an important aspect of legal personality. Also significant is the concept of *ultra vires*, a term used to describe transactions that are outside the scope of the company's capacity.

The **Companies Act 2006**, (TSO, 2006) and the **Small Business, Enterprise and Employment Act 2015**, (TSO, 2015) apply to this and all chapters unless otherwise stated.

1 Memorandum of association

> **FAST FORWARD**
>
> The memorandum is a **simple document** which states that the subscribers wish to form a company and become members of it.

Before the Companies Act 2006 (TSO, 2006), the **memorandum of association** was an extremely important document containing information concerning the relationship between the company and the outside world – for example its aims and purpose (its objects).

The position changed with the 2006 Act and most of the information contained in the old memorandum is now to be found in the Articles of Association, which we will come to shortly. The **essence** of the memorandum has been retained, although it is now a very simple historical document which states that the **subscribers** (the initial shareholders):

(a) Wish to **form a company** under the Act, and

(b) Agree to **become members** of the company and, to take at least one share each if the company is to have share capital.

The memorandum must be in the **prescribed form** and must be **signed** by each subscriber.

In relation to a company which was incorporated under a **previous** Act and whose memorandum contains provisions now found in the articles, the Companies Act 2006 interprets these provisions as if they are part of the articles.

2 A company's constitution

> **FAST FORWARD**
>
> A **company's constitution** comprises the **articles of association** and any **resolutions and agreements** it makes which affect its constitution.

According to s 17 of the Companies Act 2006 (TSO, 2006), the constitution of a company consists of:

- The **articles of association**.
- **Resolutions and agreements** that it makes that affect the constitution.

We shall consider resolutions and agreements first as an understanding of what they are is required to understand how the articles of association are amended.

2.1 Resolutions and agreements

In addition to the main **constitutional document** (the articles of association), **resolutions** and **agreements** also form part of a company's constitution. Resolutions are covered in Chapter 8 of this Study Text. You may find it beneficial to study Section 3 of that chapter now so that you understand the various types of resolution that a company may pass.

Resolutions directly affect the constitution of a company as they are used to **introduce** new provisions, or to **amend** or **remove** existing ones. **Agreements** made, for example between the company and members of specific classes of share (see Chapter 4), are also deemed as amending the constitution.

Copies of resolutions or agreements that amend the constitution must be sent to the Registrar within **15 days** of being passed or agreed. If a company fails to do this then every officer who is in default commits an offence punishable by fine. Where a **resolution** or **agreement** which affects a company's constitution is **not in writing**, the company is required to send the Registrar a **written memorandum** that sets out the terms of the resolution or agreement in question.

2.2 Articles of association

Key term

The **articles of association** consist of the internal rules that relate to the management and administration of the company.

The articles contain detailed **rules** and **regulations** setting out how the company is to be **managed** and **administered**. The Act states that the registered articles should be contained in a **single document** which is divided into **consecutively numbered paragraphs**. Articles should contain rules on a number of areas, the most important being summarised in the table below.

CONTENTS OF ARTICLES	
Appointment and dismissal of directors	Communication with members
Powers, responsibilities and liabilities of directors	Class meetings
Directors' meetings	Issue of shares
General meetings; calling, conduct and voting	Transfer of shares
Members' rights	Documents and records
Dividends	Company secretary
Decision-making by directors	Decision-making by shareholders

2.2.1 Model articles

Rather than each company having to draft their own articles, and to allow companies to be set up **quickly** and **easily**, the Act allows the provision of **Model** (or standard) **articles** that companies can adopt. Different models under the Companies Act 2006 are available for different types of company; most companies would adopt Model **private** or **public company** articles.

Companies are free to use **any** of the Model articles that they wish to by registering them on incorporation. If **no articles** are registered then the company will be **automatically incorporated** with the **default Model articles** which are relevant to the type of company being formed. Model articles can be **amended** by the members and therefore tailored to the specific needs of the company.

Model articles are effectively a **'safety net'** which allow directors and members to take decisions if the company has failed to include suitable provisions in its registered articles or registered no articles at all.

Many companies still in existence were registered with and therefore retain articles that were available under the previous legislation, that is the Companies Act 1985 as amended. This Act specified a standard set of articles, known as **Table A**, and it is fair to say that most companies operated under Table A without alteration of them.

Where relevant we will make reference to Table A in this Study Text so you are aware of particularly key rules that Table A articles incorporated.

Alteration of the articles

FAST FORWARD

The articles may be altered by a **special resolution**. The basic test is whether the alteration is for the **benefit of the company as a whole**.

Any company has a statutory power to alter its articles by **special resolution**: s 21. A private company may pass a **written resolution** with a **75% majority**. The alteration will be valid and binding on **all** members of the company. **Copies** of the amended articles must be sent to the **Registrar** within 15 days of the amendment taking effect.

2.2.2 Making the company's constitution unalterable

There are devices by which some provisions of the company's constitution can be made **unalterable** unless the member who wishes to prevent any alteration consents.

(a) The articles may give to a member **additional votes** so that he can block a resolution to alter articles on particular points (including the removal of his weighted voting rights from the articles): *Bushell v Faith 1970*. However, to be effective, the articles must also limit the powers of members to alter the articles that give extra votes.

(b) The articles may provide that when a meeting is held to vote on a proposed alteration of the articles the **quorum present must include** the **member concerned**. They can then deny the meeting a quorum by absenting themselves (see Chapter 8).

(c) Section 22 of the Act permits companies to **'entrench' provisions** in its articles. This means specific provisions may only be **amended** or **removed** if certain **conditions** are met which are more restrictive than a special resolution such as agreement of all the members. However, such 'entrenched provisions' **cannot** be drafted so that the articles can never be amended or removed.

2.2.3 Restrictions on alteration

Even when it is possible to hold a meeting and pass a special resolution, alteration of the articles is **restricted** by the following principles.

(a) The alteration is **void** if it **conflicts with the Companies Act** or with general law.

(b) In various circumstances, such as to protect a minority (s 994), the **court may order** that an alteration be made or, alternatively, that an existing article shall not be altered.

(c) An existing **member may not be compelled** by alteration of the articles to **subscribe for additional shares** or to accept increased liability for the shares which they hold unless they have given their consent: s 25.

(d) An alteration of the articles which varies the rights attached to a class of shares may only be made if the correct rights variation procedure has been followed to obtain the consent of the class: s 630. A 15 per cent minority of the holders of shares of the class in question may apply to the court to cancel the variation under s 633.

(e) A person whose **contract** is contained in the articles cannot obtain an injunction to prevent the articles being altered, **but** they may be entitled to **damages** for breach of contract: *Southern Foundries 1926 Ltd v Shirlaw 1940* in Chapter 9. Alteration cannot take away rights already acquired by performing the contract.

(f) An alteration may be **void** if the **majority** who approve it are **not acting *bona fide* in what they deem to be the interests of the company as a whole** (see below).

The case law on the *bona fide* test is an effort to hold the balance between two principles:

(a) The **majority** is **entitled** to **alter articles** even though a minority considers that the alteration is prejudicial to its interests.

(b) A minority is entitled to protection against an alteration which is intended to **benefit** the **majority** rather than the company and which is **unjustified discrimination** against the minority.

Principle (b) tends to be **restricted** to cases where the majority seeks to expel the minority from the company.

The most elaborate analysis of this subject was made by the Court of Appeal in the case of *Greenhalgh v Arderne Cinemas Ltd 1950*. Two main propositions were laid down by Evershed MR.

(a) **'Bona fide for the benefit of the company as a whole'** is a **single test** and also a **subjective test** (what did the majority believe?). The court will not substitute its own view.

(b) 'The company as a whole' means, in this context, **the general body of shareholders.** The test is whether every 'individual hypothetical member' would in the honest opinion of the majority benefit from the alteration.

If the purpose is to benefit the company as a whole the alteration is valid even though it can be shown that the minority does in fact suffer special detriment and that other members escape loss. In *Allen v Gold Reefs of West Africa Ltd 1900* the articles were altered to extend the company's lien from just partly paid shares to all shares. In fact only one member held fully paid shares. The court overruled his objections on the grounds that:

- The alteration was for the benefit of the company as a whole and applied to any member who held fully paid shares.
- The members held their shares subject to the constitution, and hence were subject to any changes to those documents.

2.2.4 Expulsion of minorities

Expulsion cases are concerned with:

- Alteration of the articles for the purpose of **removing** a **director from office**.
- Alteration of the articles to permit a majority of members to **enforce** a **transfer** to themselves of the shareholding of a minority.

The action of the majority in altering the articles to achieve 'expulsion' will generally be treated as **valid** even though it is discriminatory, if the majority were concerned to **benefit the company** or to remove some detriment to its interests.

If on the other hand the majority was **blatantly seeking** to secure an **advantage** to themselves by their discrimination, the alteration made to the articles by their voting control of the company will be invalid. The cases below illustrate how the distinctions are applied in practice.

Shuttleworth v Cox Bros & Co (Maidenhead) Ltd 1927

The facts: Expulsion of director appointed by the articles who had failed to account for funds was held to be valid.

Sidebottom v Kershaw, Leese & Co Ltd 1920

The facts: The articles were altered to enable the directors to purchase at a fair price the shareholding of any member who competed with the company in its business. The minority against whom the new article was aimed did carry on a competing business. They challenged the validity of the alteration on the ground that it was an abuse of majority power to 'expel' a member.

Decision: There was no objection to a power of 'expulsion' by this means. It was a justifiable alteration if made *bona fide* in the interests of the company as a whole. On the facts this was justifiable.

Brown v British Abrasive Wheel Co 1919

The facts: The company needed further capital. The majority who held 98 per cent of the existing shares were willing to provide more capital but only if they could buy up the 2 per cent minority. As the minority refused to sell, the majority proposed to alter the articles to provide for compulsory acquisition on a fair value basis. The minority objected to the alteration.

Decision: The alteration was invalid since it was merely for the benefit of the majority. It was not an alteration 'directly concerned with the provision of further capital' and therefore not for the benefit of the company.

> *Dafen Tinplate Co Ltd v Llanelly Steel Co (1907) Ltd 1920*
>
> *The facts:* The claimant was a minority shareholder which had transferred its custom from the defendant company to another supplier. The majority shareholders of the defendant company sought to protect their interests by altering the articles to provide for compulsory acquisition of the claimant's shares.
>
> The new article was not restricted (as it was in *Sidebottom's* case above) to acquisition of shares on specific grounds where benefit to the company would result. It was simply expressed as a power to acquire the shares of a member. The claimant objected that the alteration was invalid since it was not for the benefit of the company.
>
> *Decision:* The alteration was invalid because it 'enables the majority of the shareholders to compel any shareholder to transfer his shares'. This wide power could not 'properly be said to be for the benefit of the company'. The mere unexpressed intention to use the power in a particular way was not enough.

Therefore if the majority intend that the power to acquire the shares of a minority is to be restricted to specific circumstances for the benefit of the company, they should ensure that this restriction is included in the new article.

Question — Articles of Association

Explain the nature of the model articles of association under the Companies Act 2006.

Answer

The model articles are a single document containing model rules and regulations concerning the management and administration of a company. They can be amended by the company but do not need to be to have effect.

2.2.5 Filing of alteration

Whenever any alteration is made to the articles a copy of the altered articles must be delivered to the Registrar within **15 days after the amendment takes effect**, together with a copy of the special resolution making the alteration: s 26.

2.2.6 Interaction of statute and articles

There are two aspects to consider.

(a) The Companies Act may permit companies to do something **if** their **articles** also authorise it. For example a company may reduce its capital if its articles give power to do this. If, however, they do not, then the company must **alter** the articles to include the **necessary power** before it may exercise the statutory power.

(b) The Companies Act will **override** the articles:

  (i) If the Companies Act **prohibits something**.

  (ii) If something is permitted by the Companies Act **only** by a **special procedure** (such as passing a special resolution in general meeting).

3 Company objects and capacity

FAST FORWARD

A **company's objects** are its aims and purposes. If a company enters into a contract which is outside its objects, that contract is said to be *ultra vires*. However the rights of third parties to the contract are protected.

3.1 The objects

The objects are the '**aims**' and '**purposes**' of a company. Under previous companies legislation they were held in a specific clause within the old memorandum of association. This clause set out everything the company could do, including being a 'general commercial company', which meant it could pretty much do anything.

The Companies Act 2006 (TSO, 2006) changed matters. The objects could now be found in the **articles** but most articles will **not** mention any objects. This is because under the Act a company's objects are **completely unrestricted** (ie it can carry out any lawful activity). Only where the company wishes to restrict its activities is there an inclusion of those **restrictions** in the articles: s 31.

3.1.1 Alteration of the objects

As a company's objects are located in its articles it may, under s 21, alter its objects by **special resolution** for any reason. The procedure is the same as for any other type of alteration of the articles.

3.2 Contractual capacity and *ultra vires*

FAST FORWARD

Companies may only act in accordance with their **objects**. If the directors permit an act which is restricted by the company's objects then the act is *ultra vires*.

Key terms

Ultra vires is where a company exceeds its objects and acts outside its capacity.

Companies which have **unrestricted objects** are highly unlikely to act *ultra vires* since their constitution permits them to do anything. Where a company has restrictions placed on its objects and it breaches these restrictions then it would be acting *ultra vires*.

Ashbury Railway Carriage & Iron Co Ltd v Riche 1875

The facts: The company had an objects clause which stated that its objects were to make and sell, or lend on hire, railway carriages and wagons and all kinds of railway plant, fittings, machinery and rolling stock; and to carry on business as mechanical engineers. The company bought a concession to build a railway in Belgium, subcontracting the work to the defendant. Later the company repudiated the contract.

Decision: Constructing a railway was not within the company's objects so the company did not have capacity to enter into either the concession contract or the sub-contract. The contract was void for *ultra vires* and so the defendant had no right to damages for breach. The members could not ratify it and the company could neither enforce the contract nor be forced into performing its obligations.

The approach taken by the Companies Act 2006 is to give **security** to commercial transactions for **third parties**, while preserving the rights of shareholders to restrain directors from entering an *ultra vires* action.

S 39 provides as follows:

'*the validity of an act done by a company shall not be called into question on the ground of lack of capacity by reason of anything in the company's constitution.*'

S 40 provides as follows:

'in favour of a person dealing with a company in good faith, the power of the directors to bind the company, or authorise others to do so, shall be deemed to be free of any limitation under the company's constitution.'

There are a number of points to note about s 40.

(a) The section applies in favour of the **person dealing with the company**, it does not apply to the members.

(b) In contrast with s 39, **good faith** is required on the part of the third party. The company has, however, to prove lack of good faith in the third party and this may turn out to be quite difficult: s 40(2).

(c) The **third party** is not required to **enquire** whether or not there are any **restrictions** placed on the power of directors: s 40(2). They are free to assume the directors have any power they profess to have.

(d) The section covers not only acts beyond the capacity of the company, but acts beyond **'any limitation under the company's constitution'**.

While sections 39 and 40 deal with the company's transactions with **third parties**, the **members** may take action against the directors for permitting *ultra vires* acts. Their action will be based on the fact that the **objects specifically restricted** the particular act and under section 171, the **directors** must **abide** by the **company's constitution**.

The main problem for **members** is that they are most likely to be **aware** of the *ultra vires* act only **after** it has occurred. Therefore they are not normally in a position to prevent it, although in theory they could seek an **injunction** if they found out about the potential *ultra vires* act before it took place.

Question — Capacity to contract

Describe how a company's capacity to contract can be regulated and what third parties may assume when entering into a contract with the company.

Answer

A company's capacity to contract is regulated by its members passing resolutions which restrict its objects. Under section 40(2) of the Act, third parties can assume the directors have the necessary power to authorise the act.

Exam focus point

Make sure you understand how s 39 and s 40 protect third parties.

3.3 Transactions with directors

Section 41 of the Companies Act 2006 applies when the company enters into a contract with one of its **directors**, or its holding company, or any **person connected** with such a director. Contracts made between the company and these parties are **voidable** by the company if the director acts outside their capacity.

Whether or not the contract is avoided, the party and any authorising director is liable to repay any profit they made or make good any losses that result from such a contract.

4 The constitution as a contract

FAST FORWARD

The articles **constitute a contract** between:

- Company and members
- Members and the company
- Members and members

The articles **do not constitute** a contract between the **company** and **third parties**, or members in a **capacity** other than as **members** (the *Eley* case).

4.1 Effect

A company's constitution bind, under s 33 of the Companies Act 2006 (TSO, 2006):

- Members to company
- Company to members (but see below)
- Members to members

The company's constitution does **not** bind the company to third parties.

This principle applies only to rights and obligations which affect members **in their capacity as members**.

Hickman v Kent or Romney Marsh Sheepbreeders Association 1915

The facts: The claimant (H) was in dispute with the company which had threatened to expel him from membership. The articles provided that disputes between the company and its members should be submitted to arbitration. H, in breach of that article, began an action in court against the company.

Decision: The proceedings would be stayed since the dispute (which related to matters affecting H as a member) must, in conformity with the articles, be submitted to arbitration.

The principle that only rights and obligations of members are covered by s 33 applies when an outsider who is also a member seeks to rely on the articles in support of a claim made as an **outsider**.

Eley v Positive Government Security Life Assurance Co 1876

The facts: E, a solicitor, drafted the original articles and included a provision that the company must always employ him as its solicitor. E became a member of the company some months after its incorporation. He later sued the company for breach of contract in not employing him as its solicitor.

Decision: E could not rely on the article since it was a contract between the company and its members and he was not asserting any claim as a member.

The members are able to compel the company to obey the Articles: *Pender v Lushington 1877*.

4.2 Constitution as a contract between members

S 33 gives to the **constitution** the effect of a contract made between (a) the **company** and (b) its **members individually**. It can also impose a contract on the members in their dealings with each other.

Rayfield v Hands 1958

The facts: The articles required that (a) every director should be a shareholder and (b) the directors must purchase the shares of any member who gave them notice of his wish to dispose of them. The directors, however, denied that a member could enforce the obligation on them to acquire his shares.

Decision: There was 'a contract ... between a member and member-directors in relation to their holdings of the company's shares in its articles' and the directors were bound by it.

Articles and resolutions are usually **drafted** so that each stage is a dealing between the company and the members, to which s 33 clearly applies, so that:

(a) A member who intends to transfer his shares must, if the articles so require, give notice of his intention to the company.

(b) The company must then give notice to other members that they have an option to take up his shares.

4.3 Constitution as a supplement to contracts

FAST FORWARD

The constitution can be used to **establish the terms** of a contract existing elsewhere.

If an outsider makes a separate contract with the company and that contract contains no specific term on a particular point but the constitution does, then the contract is deemed to incorporate the constitution to that extent. One example is when services, say as a director, are provided under contract without agreement as to remuneration: *Re New British Iron Co, ex parte Beckwith 1898*.

If a contract incorporates terms of the articles it is subject to the company's **right** to **alter** its articles: *Shuttleworth v Cox Bros & Co (Maidenhead) Ltd 1927*. However a company's articles cannot be altered to deprive another person of a right already earned, say for services rendered **prior** to the alteration.

Attention!

Remember the articles only create contractual rights/obligations in relation to rights **as a member**.

4.4 Shareholder agreements

FAST FORWARD

Shareholders' agreements sometimes supplement a company's constitution.

Shareholder agreements are concerned with the **running of the company**; in particular they often contain terms by which the shareholders agree how they will vote on various issues.

They offer more protection to the interests of shareholders than do the articles of association. Individuals have a **power of veto** over any proposal which is contrary to the terms of the agreement. This enables a minority shareholder to protect his interests against unfavourable decisions of the majority.

Question
Constitution

State the parties who are bound by a company's articles.

Answer

The company is bound to the members, the members to the company and the members to the other members in their capacity as members.

5 Company name and registered office

FAST FORWARD

Except in **certain circumstances** a company's name must end with the words limited (Ltd), public limited company (plc) or the Welsh equivalents.

A company's name is its **identity**. There are a number of rules which restrict the choice of name that a company may adopt.

5.1 Statutory rules on the choice of company name

FAST FORWARD

No company may use a name which:
- Is the **same** as an existing company on the Registrar's index of company names.
- Is a **criminal offence, offensive,** or **'sensitive'**.
- Suggests a **connection** with the **government or local authority** (unless approved).

Under the Companies Act 2006 (TSO, 2006), the choice of name of a limited company must conform to the following rules.

(a) The name must **end** with the word(s):

    (i) **Public limited company** (abbreviated **plc**) if it is a public company.

    (ii) **Limited** (or Ltd) if it is a private limited company, unless permitted to omit 'limited' from its name.

    (iii) The **Welsh equivalents** of either (i) or (ii) may be used by a Welsh company.

(b) No company may have a name which is the **same** as any other company appearing in the statutory index at Companies House. For this purpose two names are treated as 'the same' in spite of minor or non-essential differences. For instance the word 'the' as the first word in the name is ignored. 'John Smith Limited' is treated the same as 'John Smith' (an unlimited company) or 'John Smith & Company Ltd'. Where a company has a name which is the same or too similar to another, the Secretary of State may direct the company to **change its name**.

(c) No company may have a name the use of which would be a **criminal** offence or which is considered **offensive** or **'sensitive'** (as defined by the Secretary of State).

(d) Official approval is required for a name which in the Registrar's opinion suggests a **connection** with the **government** or a **local authority** or which is subject to **control**.

A name which suggests some professional expertise such as 'optician' will only be permitted if the appropriate representative association has been consulted and raises no objection.

The general purpose of the rule is to **prevent** a company **misleading** the public as to its real circumstances or activities. Certain names may be approved by the Secretary of State on written application.

5.2 Omission of the word 'limited'

A private company which is a charity and a company limited by shares or guarantee and licensed to do so before 25 February 1982 may omit the word 'limited' from its name if the following conditions are satisfied.

(a) The objects of the company must be the **promotion** of either commerce, art, science, education, religion, charity or any profession (or anything incidental or conducive to such objects).

(b) The memorandum or articles must require that the **profits** or other income of the company are to be **applied to promoting** its objects and no dividends or return of capital may be paid to its members. Also on liquidation the **assets** (otherwise distributable to members) are to be **transferred** to another body with similar objects. The articles must not then be altered so that the company's status to omit 'Limited' is lost.

5.3 Change of name

A company may decide to change its name by:

(a) Passing a **special resolution**.

(b) **Any other means** provided for in the **articles** (in other words the company can specify its own procedure for changing its name).

Where a **special resolution** has been passed, the **Registrar** should be notified and a copy of the resolution sent. If the change was made by **any other procedure** covered by (b), the Registrar should be notified and a statement provided which states that the change has been made in accordance with the articles.

The change is effective from when a new **incorporation certificate is issued**, although the company is still treated as the same legal entity as before. The same limitations as above apply to adoption of a name by change of name as by incorporation of a new company.

5.4 Passing-off action

A person who considers that their rights have been infringed can apply for an injunction to restrain a company from using a name (**even if** the name has been duly registered). It can do this if the name suggests that the latter company is carrying on the business of the complainant or is otherwise connected with it.

A company can be **prevented** by an **injunction** issued by the court in a **passing-off action** from **using** its **registered name**, if in doing so it causes its goods to be confused with those of the claimant.

> *Ewing v Buttercup Margarine Co Ltd 1917*
>
> *The facts:* The claimant had since 1904 run a chain of 150 shops in Scotland and the north of England through which he sold margarine and tea. He traded as 'The Buttercup Dairy Co'. The defendant was a registered company formed in 1916 with the name above. It sold margarine as a wholesaler in the London area. The defendant contended that there was unlikely to be confusion between the goods sold by the two concerns.
>
> *Decision:* An injunction would be granted to restrain the defendants from the use of its name since the claimant had the established connection under the Buttercup name. He planned to open shops in the south of England and if the defendants sold margarine retail, there could be confusion between the two businesses.

If, however, the two companies' businesses are different, confusion is unlikely to occur, and hence the courts will refuse to grant an injunction: *Dunlop Pneumatic Tyre Co Ltd v Dunlop Motor Co Ltd 1907*.

The complaint will not succeed if the claimant lays claim to the exclusive use of a word which has a general use: *Aerators Ltd v Tollit 1902*.

5.5 Appeal to the Company Names Adjudicator

A company which feels that another company's name which is **too similar** to its own may object to the Company Names Adjudicator under the Companies Act. The Adjudicator will review the case and, within **90 days**, make their decision and provide their reasons for it in public. In most cases the Adjudicator will require the offending company to **change its name** to one which does not breach the rules. In some cases the **Adjudicator may determine** the new name.

An appeal against the decision may be made in Court. The Court may **reverse** the Adjudicator's decision, **affirm** it and may even **determine** a new name.

Question — Company name

Do It Yourself Ltd was incorporated on 1 September 20X7. On 1 October 20X7 the directors received a letter from DIY Ltd stating that it was incorporated in 19X4, that its business was being adversely affected by the use of the new company's name, and demanding that Do It Yourself Ltd change its name.

Advise Do It Yourself Ltd.

Answer

DIY Ltd may seek to bring a 'passing-off action'. This is a common law action which applies when one company believes that another's conduct (which may be the use of a company name) is causing confusion in the minds of the public over the goods which each company sells. DIY Ltd would apply to the court for an injunction to prevent Do It Yourself Ltd from using its name.

However, in order to be successful, DIY Ltd will need to satisfy the court that confusion has arisen because of Do It Yourself Ltd's use of its registered name and that it lays claim to something exclusive and distinctive and not something in general use: *Aerators Ltd v Tollit 1902*.

Appeal to Company Names Adjudicator

Alternatively DIY Ltd might object to the Company Names Adjudicator that the name Do It Yourself Ltd is too like its own name and is causing confusion, thus appealing to compel a change of name. In these circumstances, the Adjudicator would hear the case and make a decision. If they compel a name change Do It Yourself Ltd may appeal to the court.

5.6 Publication of the company's name

The company's name must appear legibly and conspicuously:

- **Outside** the **registered office** and all **places of business**.
- On all **business letters, order forms, notices** and **official publications**.
- On all **receipts** and **invoices** issued on the company's behalf.
- On all **bills of exchange, letters of credit, promissory notes, cheques** and **orders** for money or goods purporting to be signed by, or on behalf, of the company.
- On its **website**.

5.7 Business names other than the corporate name

Key term

> A **business name** is a name used by a company which is different from the company's corporate name or by a firm which is different from the name(s) of the proprietor or the partners.

Most companies trade under their own registered names. However a company may prefer to use some other name.

The rules require any person (company, partnership or sole trader) who carries on business under a different name from his own:

(a) To **state** its **name**, registered **number** and registered **address** on all **business letters (including emails)**, invoices, receipts, written orders for goods or services and written demands for payment of debts.

(b) To **display** its **name** and **address** in a **prominent position** in any **business premises** to which its customers and suppliers have access.

(c) On **request** from any **person** with whom it does business to give **notice** of its name and address.

5.8 Registered office

Section 86 of the Companies Act 2006 provides that a company must at all times have a **registered office** to which all communications and notices can be sent. It may **change its registered office** under s 87 by notifying the Registrar, but for a period of 14 days after notice is served any person may validly present documents to the previous address.

PART A INCORPORATION

Chapter roundup

- The memorandum is a **simple document** which states that the subscribers wish to form a company and become members of it.

- A **company's constitution** comprises the **articles of association** and any **resolutions and agreements** it makes which affect the constitution.

- The articles may be altered by a **special resolution**. The basic test is whether the alteration is for the **benefit of the company as a whole**.

- A **company's objects** are its aims and purposes. If a company enters into a contract which is outside its objects, that contract is said to be **ultra vires**. However the rights of third parties to the contract are protected.

- Companies may only act in accordance with their **objects**. If the directors permit an act which is restricted by the company's objects then the act is *ultra vires*.

- The articles **constitute** a **contract** between:

    – Company and members
    – Members and the company
    – Members and members

    The articles **do not constitute** a contract between the **company** and **third parties**, or members in a **capacity** other than as **members** (the *Eley* case).

- The constitution can be used to **establish the terms** of a contract existing elsewhere.

- **Shareholders' agreements** sometimes supplement a company's constitution.

- Except in **certain circumstances** the name must end with the words limited (Ltd), public limited company (plc) or the Welsh equivalents.

- No company may use a name which:

    – Is the **same** as an existing company on the Registrar's index of company names
    – Is a **criminal offence, offensive** or **'sensitive'**
    – Suggests a **connection** with the **government** or **local authority** (unless approved)

Quick quiz

1. Percy Limited has recently formed a contract with a third party which is restricted by the objects in the company's constitution.

   Which of the following statements is incorrect?

   - A The validity of the act cannot be questioned on the grounds of lack of capacity by reason of anything in the company's constitution.
   - B The act may be restrained by the members of Percy Ltd.
   - C The act may be enforced by the company and the third party.
   - D The directors have a duty to observe any limitation on their powers flowing from the company's constitution.

2. If a company wishes to restrict its objects, what kind of resolution is required?

   - A Special resolution
   - B Special resolution with special notice
   - C Ordinary resolution with special notice
   - D Ordinary resolution

3. A company has been formed within the last six months. Another long-established company considers that because of similarity there may be confusion between it and the new company. The only action the long-established company can take is to bring a passing-off action if it is to prevent the new company using its name.

   True ☐
   False ☐

4. Which of the following persons are NOT bound to one another by the constitution?

   - A Members to company
   - B Company to members
   - C Members to members
   - D Company to third parties

5. How long does a company have to file amended articles with the Registrar if they have been altered?

   - A 14 days
   - B 15 days
   - C 21 days
   - D 28 days

PART A   INCORPORATION

Answers to quick quiz

1. A, C and D are true. Members can only act before the contract is signed, so B is incorrect.
2. A. A special resolution is required to restrict the objects as with any alteration to the articles in general.
3. False. The long-established company can also complain to the Company Names Adjudicator.
4. A, B and C are correct: s 33. D is incorrect, illustrated by *Eley v Positive Government Security Life Assurance Co Ltd 1876*.
5. B. A company has 15 days to file amended articles with the Registrar.

End of chapter question

Articles

Explain the content and effect of a company's articles of association. **(10 marks)**

Capitalisation

Share capital

Topic list	Syllabus reference
1 Members	8.2
2 The nature of shares and capital	8.2
3 Types of share and class rights	8.2
4 Allotment of shares	8.2
5 Transfer of shares	8.2
6 Take-over procedures	8.5

Introduction

In this chapter, the nature of share capital is explained. You should note (and **not** confuse) the different types of capital that are important for company law purposes.

The rest of the chapter discusses procedural matters relating to the **issue** and **transfer** of shares. You will see that there are built-in safeguards to protect members' rights, **pre-emption rights** and the necessity for directors to be authorised to **allot** shares. There are also safeguards that ensure that a company receives **sufficient consideration** for its shares. This is an aspect of **capital maintenance**, which we discuss further in Chapter 6.

The **Companies Act 2006**, (TSO, 2006) and the **Small Business, Enterprise and Employment Act 2015**, (TSO, 2015) apply to this and all chapters unless otherwise stated.

PART B CAPITALISATION

1 Members

FAST FORWARD

A member of a company is a person who has **agreed to become a member**, and whose name has been **entered** in the **register of members**. This may occur by: subscription to the memorandum; applying for shares; presentation to the company of a transfer of shares to the prospective member applying as personal representative of a deceased member or as a trustee of a bankrupt.

1.1 Becoming a member

Key term

A **member** of a company is a person who has agreed to be a member and whose name has been entered in the register of members.

Entry in the register is **essential**. Mere delivery to the company of a transfer does not make the transferor a member until the transfer is entered in the register.

1.2 Subscriber shares

Subscribers to the memorandum are deemed to have agreed to become members of the company. As soon as the company is formed their names should be entered in the register of members.

Other persons may acquire shares and become members:

- By **applying** and being allotted shares.
- By presenting to the company for registration a **transfer** of shares to them.
- By applying as **personal representative** or **trustee** of a
  - Deceased member
  - Bankrupt member

1.3 Ceasing to be a member

FAST FORWARD

There are **eight** ways in which a member ceases to be so.

A member ceases to be a member in any of the following circumstances.

- He **transfers** all his shares to another person and the transfer is registered.
- The member **dies**.
- The **shares** of a bankrupt member are **registered** in the name of his trustee.
- A **member who is a minor repudiates his shares**.
- The **trustee** of a **bankrupt member disclaims** his shares.
- The **company forfeits** or **accepts** the **surrender of shares**.
- The **company** sells them in exercise of a lien.
- The **company is dissolved** and **ceases to exist**.

1.4 The number of members

FAST FORWARD

Public and **private companies** must have a minimum of **one** member (s 7). There is **no maximum** number.

(a) The **register of members** must contain a statement that there is **only one member** and give his or her address.

(b) **Quorum**. The Companies Act 2006 (TSO, 2006) **automatically permits** a **quorum of one** for general meetings.

2 The nature of shares and capital

> **FAST FORWARD**
>
> A **share** is a transferable form of property, carrying rights and obligations, by which the interest of a member of a company limited by shares is measured.

2.1 Shares

Key term

> A **share** is 'the interest of a shareholder in the company measured by a sum of money, for the purpose of a liability in the first place, and of interest in the second, but also consisting of a series of mutual covenants entered into by all the shareholders *inter se*': *Borland's Trustee v Steel Bros & Co Ltd 1901*.

The key points in this definition are:

- The share must be **paid for** ('liability'). The nominal value of the share fixes this liability, it is the base price of the share eg a £1 ordinary share.
- It gives a **proportionate entitlement** to dividends, votes and any return of capital ('interest').
- It is a form of **bargain** ('mutual covenants') between shareholders which underlies such principles as majority control and minority protection.

Key term

> A share's **nominal value** is its face value. So a £1 ordinary share for instance, has a nominal value of £1. No share can be issued at a value below its nominal value.

A share is a form of personal property, carrying rights and obligations. It is by its nature **transferable**.

A member who holds one or more shares is a **shareholder**. However some companies (such as most companies limited by guarantee) do not have a share capital. So they have members who are not also shareholders.

Information about any special rights attached to shares is obtainable from one of the following documents which are on the file at Companies House:

- The **articles**, which are the normal context in which share rights are defined.
- A **resolution** or agreement incidental to the creation of a new class of shares (copies must be delivered to the Registrar).
- A **statement of capital** given to the Registrar within one month of **allotment**, together with the return of allotment.

2.2 Types of capital

> **FAST FORWARD**
>
> The term **'capital'** is used in several senses in company legislation, to mean issued, allotted or called up share capital or loan capital.

2.2.1 Authorised share capital

Companies under previous company legislation had to specify a maximum authorised share capital that it could issue, although this could be increased by ordinary resolution of the members (Table A article 32). Under the Companies Act 2006 (TSO, 2006), the concept of authorised share capital was removed, so companies registered under this Act will not have to consider it. Furthermore, companies incorporated under earlier legislation are permitted by the 2006 Act to treat any limit on authorised capital as a provision in the company's articles of association which can therefore be altered or removed entirely, by ordinary rather than special resolution.

PART B   CAPITALISATION

2.2.2 Issued and allotted share capital

Key terms

> **Issued** and **allotted share capital** is the type, class, number and amount of the shares issued and allotted to specific shareholders, including shares taken on formation by the subscribers to the memorandum.

A company need not issue all its share capital at once. If it retains a part, this is **unissued share capital**.

Issued share capital can be **increased** through the allotment of shares (s 617), see Section 4.

Rights issues and the issue of **bonus shares** (see later) will also increase the amount of a company's capital.

2.2.3 Called up and paid up share capital

Key terms

> **Called up share capital** is the amount which the company has required shareholders to pay now or in the future on the shares issued.
>
> **Paid up share capital** is the amount which shareholders have actually paid on the shares issued and called up.

For example, a company has issued and allotted 70 £1 (nominal value) shares, has received 25p per share on application and has called on members for a second 25p. Therefore its issued and allotted share capital is £70 and its **called up** share capital is £35 (50p per share). When the members pay the call, the **'paid up'** share capital is then £35 also. Capital not yet called is **'uncalled capital'**. Called capital which is not yet paid is termed **'partly paid'**; the company therefore has an outstanding claim against its shareholders and this debt is transferred to the new shareholder if the share is transferred.

As we saw earlier, on allotment **public companies** must receive at least **one quarter** of the nominal value of the shares paid up, plus the **whole of any premium**.

2.2.4 Loan capital

Key term

> **Loan capital** comprises debentures and other long-term loans to a business.

Loan capital, in contrast with the above, is the term used to describe **borrowed money** obtained usually by the issue of debentures. **It is nothing to do with shares.**

Attention!

> We shall look at loan capital in detail in Chapter 5.

2.3 Market value of shares

Shares of a public company are freely transferable (providing the appropriate procedures are followed) and therefore may be subsequently sold by some or all of the shareholders. The sale price will not necessarily be the nominal value, rather it will reflect the prospects of the company and therefore may be greater or less than the nominal value.

3 Types of share and class rights

FAST FORWARD

> If the constitution of a company states no differences between shares, it is assumed that they are all **ordinary** shares with parallel rights and obligations. There may, however, be other types, notably **preference shares** and **redeemable shares**, which have different **class rights**.

3.1 Ordinary shares (equity)

If no differences between shares are expressed then all shares are equity shares with the **same rights**, known as ordinary shares.

4: SHARE CAPITAL

Key terms

> **Equity** is the residual interest in the assets of the company after deducting all its liabilities. It comprises issued share capital excluding any part that does not carry any right to participate beyond a specified amount in a distribution.
>
> **Equity share capital** is a company's issued share capital less capital which carries preferential rights.
>
> **Ordinary shares** are shares which entitle the holders to the remaining divisible profits (and, in a liquidation, the assets) after prior interests, eg creditors and prior charge capital, have been satisfied.

3.2 Class rights

Key term

> **Class rights** are rights which are attached to particular types of shares by the company's constitution.

A company may at its option attach special rights to different shares regarding:

- Dividends
- Return of capital
- Voting
- The right to appoint or remove a director

Any share which has different rights from others is grouped with the other shares carrying identical rights to form a **class**.

The most common types of share capital with different rights are **preference shares** and **ordinary shares**. There may also be ordinary shares with voting rights and ordinary shares without voting rights.

3.3 Preference shares

FAST FORWARD

> The most common right of preference shareholders is a **prior right** to receive a fixed dividend. This right is not a right to **compel payment** of a dividend, but it is **cumulative** unless otherwise stated. Usually, preference shareholders **cannot participate** in a dividend over and above their fixed dividend and **cease to be entitled to arrears of undeclared dividends** when the company goes into liquidation.

Key term

> **Preference shares** are shares carrying one or more rights such as a fixed rate of dividend or preferential claim to any company profits available for distribution.

A preference share may and generally will carry a **prior right** to receive an annual dividend of fixed amount, say a dividend of 6% of the share's nominal value.

Ordinary and preference shares are deemed to have identical rights. However, a company's articles or resolutions may create differences between them.

As regards the priority dividend entitlement, four points should be noted.

(a) **The right is merely to receive a dividend at the specified rate before any other dividend may be paid or declared**. It is **not** a right to compel the company to pay the dividend, *(Bond v Barrow Haematite Steel Co 1902)*. The company can decline to pay the dividend if it decides to transfer available profits to reserves instead of using the profits to pay the preference dividend.

(b) **The right to receive a preference dividend is deemed to be cumulative unless the contrary is stated**. If, therefore, a 6% dividend is not paid in Year 1, the priority entitlement is normally carried forward to Year 2, increasing the priority right for that year to 12% – and so on.

When arrears of cumulative dividend are paid, the holders of the shares at **the time when the dividend is declared** are entitled to the whole of it even though they did not hold the shares in the year to which the arrears relate.

An intention that preference shares should not carry forward an entitlement to arrears is usually expressed by the word **'non-cumulative'**.

(c) **If a company which has arrears of unpaid cumulative preference dividends goes into liquidation, the preference shareholders cease to be entitled to the arrears unless:**

 (i) A **dividend** has been **declared** though **not yet paid** when liquidation commences.
 (ii) The **articles** (or other terms of issue) **expressly provide** that in a liquidation arrears are to be paid in priority to return of capital to members.

(d) **Holders of preference shares have no entitlement to participate in any additional dividend over and above their specified rate.** If, for example, a 6% dividend is paid on 6% preference shares, the entire balance of available profit may then be distributed to the holders of ordinary shares.

 This rule also may be expressly overridden by the terms of issue. For example, the articles may provide that the preference shares are to receive a priority 6% dividend and are also to participate equally in any dividends payable after the ordinary shares have received a 6% dividend. Preference shares with these rights are called **participating preference shares**.

In all other respects preference shares carry the **same** rights as ordinary shares **unless otherwise stated**. If they do rank equally they carry the same rights, no more and no less, to return of capital, distribution of surplus assets and voting.

In practice, it is unusual to issue preference shares on this basis. More usually, it is expressly provided that:

(a) The preference shares are to carry a **right** to **return of capital,** to be paid in priority to the ordinary shareholders.
(b) They are **not to carry a right to vote, or voting is permitted only in specified circumstances**, for example failure to pay the preference dividend, variation of their rights or a resolution to wind up.

When preference shares carry a **priority right** to **return** of **capital** the result is that:

(a) The amount paid up on the preference shares, say £1 on each £1 share, is to be repaid in liquidation before anything is repaid to ordinary shareholders.
(b) Unless otherwise stated, the holders of the preference shares are **not** entitled to share in surplus assets when the share capital has been repaid. Instead this will all go to the ordinary shareholders.

3.3.1 Advantages and disadvantages of preference shares

The advantages of preference shares are **greater security of income** and (if they carry priority in repayment of capital) **greater security of capital**. However, in a period of persistent inflation, the benefit of entitlement to fixed income and to capital fixed in money terms is an illusion.

A number of other drawbacks and pitfalls, such as loss of arrears, poor rights on winding up and enforced payment, have been indicated above. Preference shares may be said to fall between the two stools of risk and reward (as seen in ordinary shares) and security (debentures).

3.4 Variation of class rights

FAST FORWARD

The holders of **issued** shares have **vested rights** which can only be varied by using a strict procedure. The standard procedure is by **special resolution** passed by at least **three quarters** of the votes cast at a **separate class meeting** or by written consent.

Key term

A **variation of class rights** is an alteration in the position of shareholders with regard to those rights or duties which they have by virtue of their shares.

The holders of issued shares have **vested rights** which can only be varied by the company with the consent of all the holders or with such consent of a majority as is specified (usually) in the articles.

The standard procedure for variation of class rights requires that a **special resolution** shall be passed by a **75% majority** cast either at a **separate meeting** of the class, or by **written consent**: s 630. If any other requirements are imposed by the company's articles then these must also be followed.

3.4.1 When variation rules apply

FAST FORWARD It is **not** a variation of class rights to issue shares to new members, to subdivide shares of another class, to return capital to preference shareholders, or to create a new class of preference shareholders.

It is only necessary to follow the variation of class rights procedure **if what is proposed amounts to a variation of class rights**. There are many types of transaction that do not actually constitute a variation of class rights.

3.4.2 Examples: Not a variation of class rights

(a) **To issue shares of the same class to allottees who are not already members of the class** (unless the defined class rights prohibit this).

> *White v Bristol Aeroplane Co Ltd 1953*
>
> *The facts:* The company made a bonus issue of new ordinary and preference shares to the existing ordinary shareholders who alone were entitled under the articles to participate in bonus issues. The existing preference shareholders objected. They stated that reducing their proportion of the class of preference shares (by issuing the bonus of preference shares) was a variation of class rights to which they had not consented.
>
> *Decision:* This was not a variation of class rights since the existing preference shareholders had the same number of shares (and votes at a class meeting) as before.

(b) **To subdivide shares of another class with the incidental effect of increasing the voting strength of that other class.**

> *Greenhalgh v Arderne Cinemas Ltd 1950*
>
> *The facts:* The company had two classes of ordinary shares, 50p shares and 10p shares. Every share carried one vote. A resolution was passed to subdivide each 50p share into five 10p shares, thus multiplying the votes of that class by five.
>
> *Decision:* The rights of the original 10p shares had not been varied since they still had one vote per share as before.

(c) **To return capital to the holders of preference shares**: *House of Fraser plc v ACGE Investments Ltd 1987.*

(d) **To create and issue a new class of preference shares with priority over an existing class of ordinary shares**: *Re John Smith's Tadcaster Brewery Co Ltd 1953.*

The cases cited in the preceding paragraph illustrate the principle that without a **'literal variation'** of class rights there is no alteration of rights to which the safeguards of proper procedure and appeal to the court apply. The fact that the **value** of existing rights may be affected will not concern the court if the rights are unchanged.

Exam focus point Knowledge of what does **not** constitute a variation of class rights is vital in this area.

3.4.3 Special situations

To deal with unusual special situations which in the past caused some difficulty, the following rules apply.

(a) If the class rights are set **by the articles and** they **provide** a **variation procedure**, that procedure must be followed for any variation even if it is less onerous than the statutory procedure.

(b) If class **rights** are **defined otherwise than by the articles** and there is **no variation procedure**, consent of a **three quarters majority** of the class is both necessary and sufficient.

PART B   CAPITALISATION

The rules on notice, voting, polls, circulation of resolutions and quorum relating to general meetings relate also to class meetings when voting on alteration of class rights. We shall come back to these in Chapter 8.

3.4.4 Minority appeals to the court for unfair prejudice

> **FAST FORWARD** A **dissenting minority** holding 15% or more of the issued shares may apply to the court within 21 days of class consent to have the variation cancelled as 'unfairly prejudicial'.

Under the Companies Act 2006 (TSO, 2006), whenever class rights are varied under a procedure contained in the constitution, a minority of holders of shares of the class may apply to the court to have the variation cancelled. The objectors together must:

- Hold **not less** than **15%** of the **issued shares** of the class in question.
- **Not** themselves have **consented** to or voted in favour of the variation.
- **Apply** to the court within **21 days** of the consent being given by the class: s 633.

The court can either approve the variation as made or cancel it as 'unfairly prejudicial'. It cannot, however, modify the terms of the variation.

To establish that a variation is 'unfairly prejudicial' to the class, the minority must show that the majority was seeking **some advantage** to themselves as **members** of a **different class** instead of considering the interests of the class in which they were then voting.

3.5 Redeemable shares

Redeemable shares, which are shares issued on terms that they may be bought back by a company either at a future specific date or at the shareholder's or company's option, are discussed further in Chapter 6.

Question — Types of share

Give brief definitions of the following types of share.

(a)   Equity share
(b)   Ordinary share
(c)   Preference share

Answer

(a)   An equity share is a share which gives the holder the right to participate in the company's surplus profit and capital. In a winding up the holder is entitled to a repayment of the nominal value plus a share of surplus assets. The term equity share embraces ordinary shares but also includes preference shares when the terms of issue include either the right to an additional dividend or the right to surplus assets in a winding up.

(b)   An ordinary share is the more common type of equity share, as discussed in (a) above. The dividend is payable only when preference dividends, including arrears, have been paid.

(c)   Preference shares carry a prior right to receive an annual dividend of a fixed amount, usually as a percentage of the share's nominal value. There are no other implied differences between preference and ordinary shares, although there may be express differences between them. For example, preference shares may carry a priority right to return of capital. Generally preference shares do not carry voting rights in the company other than those relating to their own class. Unless otherwise stated, dividends allocated to preference shares are assumed to be cumulative. This means that, if the company does not make sufficient profits to pay a dividend in one year, the arrears are carried forward to future years.

3.6 Treasury shares

Treasury shares are created when a **private** or **public limited company** legitimately **purchases its own shares** out of **cash** or **distributable profit**. The purchased shares are then held by the company 'in treasury' which means the company can re-issue them without the usual formalities. They can only be sold for cash and the company cannot exercise the **voting rights** which attach to them.

This type of share is a relatively **new innovation** which allows a company to purchase its own shares when previously it would have been unable to so because of the **rules on capital maintenance** (see Chapter 6).

3.7 Statement of capital

We have already seen, in Chapter 2 Section 3 (registration procedures) and above in Section 3.2 (rights of shares), that a return known as a **statement of capital** is required to be made to the **Registrar** in certain circumstances.

The statement of capital must give the following details in respect of the **share capital** of the company and be **up to date** as at the statement date.

(a) The **total number of shares** of the company.

(b) The **aggregate nominal value of the shares**.

(c) For **each class** of share:

   (i) The **prescribed particulars** of any rights attached.
   (ii) The **total number of shares** in the class.
   (iii) The **aggregate nominal value** of shares in the class.

(d) The **aggregate amount unpaid** on the **total number of shares**

(e) **Information that identifies the subscribers to the memorandum of association**.

(f) In respect of **each subscriber**, the **number, nominal value** and **class of shares** taken by them on formation and the **amount** to be **paid up**.

The statement of capital must include details of initial shareholdings when it is submitted on registration of the company.

4 Allotment of shares

FAST FORWARD

> Directors exercise the **delegated power** to allot shares, either by virtue of the articles or a resolution in general meeting.

4.1 Definition

Key term

> **Allotment of shares** is the issue and allocation to a person of a certain number of shares under a contract of allotment. Once the shares are allotted and the holder is entered in the register of members, the holder becomes a member of the company. The member is issued with a share certificate.

The allotment of shares is a **form of contract**. The intending shareholder applies to the company for shares, and the company accepts the offer.

The terms 'allotment' and 'issue' have slightly different meanings.

(a) A share is **allotted** when the person to whom it is allotted acquires an unconditional right to be entered in the register of members as the holder of that share. That stage is reached when the board of directors (to whom the power to allot shares is usually given) considers the application and formally resolves to allot the shares.

However, if the directors imposed a condition, for instance that the shares should be allotted only on receipt of the subscription money, the allotment would only take effect when payment was made.

(b) The **issue** of shares is not a defined term but is usually taken to be a later stage at which the allottee **receives** a **letter of allotment** or share certificate issued by the company.

4.2 Private company allotment of shares

The allotment of shares of a private company is a simple and immediate matter. As private companies cannot sell securities to the public the following procedure should be followed.

- An **application** to buy shares must be made to the directors directly. While a private company may not, as a general rule, offer its shares to the public it may, by private arrangement, issue shares to anyone it chooses.
- Shares are **allotted** and **issued**.
- The names of the allottees are entered in the **register of members** soon after, and as a direct consequence of the allotment of shares to them; they then become members (the allotment must be recorded in the register of members within two months).
- A **return of allotment of shares** must be sent within one month to the Registrar on Form SH01 containing prescribed particulars and a statement of capital.

4.3 Public company allotment of shares

The difference in procedure for **allotment of shares in a public company** only arises at the first stage. There are various methods for a public company to sell shares to the public.

- **Public offer**: members of the public subscribe for shares directly to the company. This is often associated with a public company's initial listing on a recognised investment exchange, when it offers a substantial number of new shares for sale (an initial public offering or IPO).
- **Offer for sale**: an offer to members of the public to apply for shares based on information contained in a prospectus.
- **Placing**: a method of raising share capital where shares are offered in a small number of large 'blocks', to persons or institutions who have previously agreed to purchase the shares at a predetermined price.

In order to encourage the public to buy shares in a public company, it may issue a **prospectus** which is a public advertisement for shares, and is thus an invitation to potential investors to make an offer for the shares. A company listed on the London Stock Exchange must issue a prospectus under the **Prospectus Rules** and the **Listing Rules** set down by the UK Listing Authority (part of the Financial Conduct Authority).

4.3.1 Allotment procedure

Public companies listed on the London Stock Exchange usually follow a two-stage procedure.

- They first issue a **renounceable allotment letter** which the original allottee may, for a limited period (up to six weeks), transfer to another person by signing a **form of renunciation** (included in the letter) and delivering it to the transferee. The original allottee, or the ultimate renouncee, sends in the allotment letter with a completed **application for registration** of the shares in their name.
- On receipt of an application for registration the company enters the name of the applicant in the register of members and delivers a **return of allotments** to the Registrar made up to show who is then on the register. The applicant **becomes a member by entry on the register** and receives a share certificate from the company.

Public companies face the further restriction that no allotment can be made unless:

- The shares offered are **subscribed for in full** (in which case money must be returned to applicants at the expiry of 40 days after the first issue of the prospectus), or
- The offer states that even if the capital is not subscribed in full, the amount of the capital subscribed for may be allotted in any event, or in the event of the conditions specified in the offer being satisfied.

4.4 Directors' powers to allot shares

Directors of **private companies** with **one class of share** have the **authority** to allot shares **unless restricted** by the articles: s 550.

Directors of **public companies** or **private companies with more than one class of share may not allot shares** (except to subscribers to the memorandum and to employees' share schemes) **can only allot shares if they have authority by ordinary resolution of the members contained either in the articles or a resolution: s 551**. Authority cannot be given for a period of more than five years.

4.5 Pre-emption rights: s 561

FAST FORWARD

If the directors propose to allot 'equity securities' wholly for cash, there is a general requirement to offer these shares to **holders** of **similar shares** in proportion to their holdings.

Key term

Pre-emption rights are the rights of existing ordinary shareholders to be offered new shares issued by the company *pro rata* to their existing holding of that class of shares.

If a company proposes to allot ordinary shares wholly for cash, it has a **statutory obligation** to offer those shares first to holders of similar shares in **proportion to their holdings** and on the same or more favourable terms as the main allotment. This is known as a **rights issue**.

4.6 Rights issues

Key term

A **rights issue** is a right given to a shareholder to subscribe for further shares in the company, usually *pro rata* to their existing holding in the company's shares.

A rights issue must be made **in writing** (hard copy or electronic) in the same manner as a notice of a general meeting is sent to members. It must specify a period of **not less than 21 days** during which the offer may be accepted but may not be withdrawn. If not accepted or renounced in favour of another person within that period the offer is deemed to be declined.

Equity securities which have been offered to members in this way but are **not accepted** may then be allotted on the same (or less favourable) terms to non-members.

If equity securities are allotted in breach of these rules the members to whom the offer should have been made may within the ensuing two years recover **compensation** for their loss from those in default. The allotment will generally be valid.

4.6.1 Exclusion of pre-emption rights: s 567

A **private** company may by its articles permanently exclude these rules so that there is no statutory right of first refusal.

4.6.2 Disapplication of pre-emption rights: s 570

Any company may, by special resolution, resolve that the statutory right of first refusal shall not apply: s 570. Such a resolution to 'disapply' the right must be sent to the Registrar and may either:

(a) Be combined with the grant to directors of authority to allot shares, or

(b) Simply permit an offer of shares to be made for cash to a non-member (without first offering the shares to members) on a particular occasion.

In case (b) the directors, in inviting members to 'disapply' the right of first refusal, must issue a circular. This sets out their reasons, the price at which the shares are to be offered direct to a non-member and their justification of that price.

4.7 Bonus issues

Key term

> A **bonus issue** is the capitalisation of the reserves of a company by the issue of additional shares to existing shareholders, in proportion to their holdings. Such shares are normally fully paid-up with no cash called for from the shareholders.

A bonus issue is more correctly but less often called a '**capitalisation issue**' (also called a 'scrip' issue). The articles of a company usually give it power to apply its reserves to paying up unissued shares wholly or in part and then to allot these shares as a bonus issue to members.

5 Transfer of shares

FAST FORWARD

> Once shares have been allotted they may be **transferred** by the allottee to a purchaser.

Under the Companies Act 2006 (TSO, 2006), shares are generally freely transferable in accordance with and subject to and restrictions contained in the company's articles (s 544).

5.1 Unlisted shares

Once the member-transferor and the transferee have reached an agreement, the transferor holds the shares as trustee for the transferee until the company registers the transfer but remains a member of the company with the right to vote as he chooses. Once the transferee pays for the shares the transferor must vote as directed by the transferee. Once the transferee's name is entered on the register of members, the transferor ceases to be a member and the transferee acquires all the member's rights.

The transferor executes a paper stock transfer form in the favour of the transferee and gives it to him with the share certificate. Both are sent to the company for registration. Once the company receives a proper instrument of transfer, it must either register the transfer and prepare a share certificate (certification) or give notice of refusal to the proposed transferee, with reasons for the refusal, **within two months.** Model articles and Table A articles contain no restrictions on the right to transfer fully paid shares but directors may refuse to register the transfer: Model article 26 (Table A article 24). Alterations to the articles could be made to specify for instance that directors could **refuse to register a transfer** to anyone except an existing shareholder, or to a family member. Where notice of refusal is given the transferee's beneficial interest is not affected (that is, he is still entitled to any dividend or the return of capital on winding up), but he cannot exercise all members' rights, including voting rights, until the transfer is registered and his name is entered on the register of members. He is also entitled to such information as he may reasonably require as to the reasons of refusal (but he is not entitled to minutes of directors' meetings). Where the company fails to comply with these provisions, it and its officers are guilty of an offence punishable by a fine.

There is no requirement for certification where shares are transmitted by operation of the law, for example where a bankrupt member's trustee in bankruptcy or a deceased member's personal representative become entitled to the member's shares.

Stamp duty of 0.5% is payable on purchases of shares over £1,000 using a stock transfer form.

5.2 Listed shares

Securities may be transferred paperlessly without a written instrument (stock transfer form), and this is the current situation where the shares are listed and traded on a recognised stock exchange.

A number of firms connected with all sections of the equities market operate the CREST system owned by Euroclear, a private company. CREST is a paperless electronic system which enables shareholders to hold and transfer their securities without the need for written instruments of transfer. Under the system a member appoints a custodian broker to hold his shares under a customer agreement, which provides for the broker to deal with the shares only in accordance with the shareholder's directions. Any transfer of shares is normally completed in three days.

Stamp Duty Reserve Tax at 0.5% is charged on paperless purchases of shares through a stockbroker.

Regulations under the Act may provide that companies may be **required**, rather than just permitted, to adopt such a paperless holding and transfer of shares (s 785). Such regulations might impose such a requirement in relation to particular types of company or security or provide for the company to pass an ordinary resolution to that effect.

You should be aware that there are very detailed rules for the disclosure of substantial interests in the relevant share capital (essentially voting shares) of public companies. For example, in the case of companies listed either on the Main Market or Alternative Investment Market (AIM), issuers are obliged to publish their total share capital and voting rights at the end of each calendar month in which a change has occurred. A shareholder must notify the issuer (by completing a notification form) where his or her percentage of voting rights reaches 3% of the total voting rights of the company, and each 1% thereafter. It follows that this threshold may be reached even where a shareholder does not actually deal in the shares. He or she is therefore obliged to make the notification within two trading days of when he or she became or should have become aware of the notifiable change. These provisions are set out in the Disclosure and Transparency Rules.

6 Take-over procedures

FAST FORWARD

> A take-over occurs when a bidder seeks to buy a company by acquiring all, or substantially all, its issued shares from its shareholders. If a very large proportion of the company – **90%** or more – is acquired then the acquirer may compulsorily acquire the remainder (**'squeeze-out'**). There are also provisions for the minority shareholders to demand to be bought out even if the acquirer does not really want to buy their shares (**'sell-out'**).

A **take-over** of a company (the **target company**) occurs when control (ownership) of the target is taken over by another company or individual (the **offeror** or **bidder**) by buying the shares from their current owners.

Take-overs are usually classed as either friendly or hostile:

- A **friendly take-over** (which is usually the situation in a private or unlisted public company, since the directors usually know the wishes of their shareholders quite well) occurs when the offeror:

    – Approaches the target's board with the terms of an offer the offeror wishes to make to the holders of all the target's shares that are not already owned by the offeror.

    – The target's board approves of the offer as being in the best interests of the shareholders and recommends it to the shareholders.

- A **hostile take-over** occurs when an offeror:

    – Approaches the target's board with the terms of an offer to the holders of all the target's shares not already owned by the acquirer.

    – The board rejects the offer as not being in the interests of shareholders.

    – The offeror announces its firm intention to make an offer, then goes ahead and makes the offer to shareholders.

The law on take-overs is contained in the Companies Act and, in relation to listed companies, the City Code on Take-overs and Mergers, known simply as the Take-over Code, published by the Take-over Panal. The aims of the regulations are principally to ensure that:

- Shareholders are treated fairly.
- Shareholders are not denied an opportunity to decide on the true merits of a take-over, so there are rules on what information companies must and cannot release publicly in relation to the bid.
- Shareholders of the same class are afforded equivalent treatment by an offeror.
- There is an orderly framework within which take-overs are conducted, for example there are timetables for certain aspects of the bid.

Under the Companies Act 2006 (TSO, 2006), a **take-over offer** is an offer to acquire either **all the allotted shares** in the target or, where there is more than one class of shares, all the shares of one or more classes, other than shares that at the date of the offer are already held by the offeror. The **terms of the offer must be the same** in relation to all the shares to which the offer relates or, where the shares to which the offer relates include shares of different classes, in relation to all the shares of each class: s 974.

A key aspect of the rules on take-overs is that if a **large majority of shareholders (90% or more** by nominal value and voting rights) like the terms of the offer and agree to sell their shares before the offer lapses, the offeror can then choose **to buy out the minority shareholders** by giving them a **'squeeze-out' notice** within a maximum of three months after the take-over offer lapsed: s 979. Any shares in the target that were already owned by the offeror at the date of the take-over offer are excluded when calculating the 90% threshold.

The squeeze-out notice **requires the shareholder to sell** their shares to the offeror on the terms of the take-over offer, and also **requires the offeror to buy them**: s 981.

If a shareholder believes the offer in the squeeze-out notice (ie the take-over offer terms) to be **unfair**, they may challenge the notice by application to the court within six weeks of being given the notice: s 986. The court may order that the offeror is not entitled and bound to acquire the shares to which the notice relates, or that the terms on which the shares can be acquired are to be determined by the court. As the offeror by definition has already managed to persuade 90% of the shareholders that the offer is fair, it can be difficult to argue this case, especially as the test for fairness relates to the shareholders as a whole rather than an individual shareholder in the target company. An application may be successful however if, for example:

- Insufficient information was given to shareholders about the offer: *Fiske Nominees Ltd v Dwyka Diamond Ltd 2002*, or
- There was a common interest between the offeror and the shareholders who accepted the offer: *Re Bugle Press Ltd 1961*.

Even if the take-over offer is accepted by a large number of shareholders there may still be a minority who did not accept at the time of the offer and so retain their shares. The offeror, which becomes the acquirer of those shares, may be happy to live with there being minority shareholders in the company and so may choose not to issue a squeeze-out notice for compulsory acquisition, even if it reached the 90% mark. However a **minority shareholder may compel the acquirer to buy their shares** in the target under the **'sell-out' provisions** of s 983, but only if:

- The offeror has acquired 90% of the shares (by value and voting rights) in the target before the period within which the offer can be accepted, and
- The shareholder writes to the acquirer requiring their shares to be purchased on the same terms as the original take-over offer or on such other terms as may be agreed: s 985.

Even if the acquirer is happy to live with minority shareholders, once it reaches the 90% threshold it must within one month give the minority shareholders **notice of their right to sell out** to the acquirer: s 984. Failure to give this notice is a criminal offence.

Note that, unlike for squeeze-out notices, any shares in the target that are already owned by the offeror at the date of the take-over offer are included when calculating the 90% threshold for sell-out.

Chapter roundup

- A member of a company is a person who has **agreed to become a member**, and whose name has been **entered** in the **register of members**. This may occur by: subscription to the memorandum; applying for shares; the presentation to the company of a transfer of shares to the prospective member; applying as personal representative of a deceased member or a trustee of a bankrupt.

- There are **eight** ways in which a member ceases to be so.

- **Public** and **private companies** must have a minimum of **one** member (s 7). There is **no maximum** number.

- A **share** is a transferable form of property, carrying rights and obligations, by which the interest of a member of a company limited by shares is measured.

- The term **'capital'** is used in several senses in company legislation, to mean issued, allotted or called up share capital or loan capital.

- If the constitution of a company states no differences between shares, it is assumed that they are all **ordinary** shares with parallel rights and obligations. There may, however, be other types, notably **preference shares** and **redeemable shares**, which have different **class rights**.

- The most common right of preference shareholders is a **prior right** to receive a fixed dividend. This right is not a right to **compel payment** of a dividend, but it is **cumulative** unless otherwise stated. Usually, preference shareholders **cannot participate** in a dividend over and above their fixed dividend and **cease to be entitled to arrears of undeclared dividends** when the company goes into liquidation.

- The holders of **issued** shares have **vested rights** which can only be varied by using a strict procedure. The standard procedure is by **special resolution** passed by at least **three quarters** of the votes cast at a **separate class meeting** or by written consent.

- It is **not** a variation of class rights to issue shares to new members, to subdivide shares of another class, to return capital to preference shareholders, or to create a new class of preference shareholders.

- A **dissenting minority** holding 15% or more of the issued shares may apply to the court within 21 days of class consent to have the variation cancelled as 'unfairly prejudicial'.

- Directors exercise the **delegated power** to allot shares, either by virtue of the articles or a resolution in general meeting.

- If the directors propose to allot 'equity securities' wholly for cash, there is a general requirement to offer these shares to **holders** of **similar shares** in proportion to their holdings.

- Once shares have been allotted they may be **transferred** by the allottee to a purchaser.

- A take-over occurs when a bidder seeks to buy a company by acquiring all, or substantially all, its issued shares from its shareholders. If a very large proportion of the company – **90%** or more – is acquired then the acquirer may compulsorily acquire the remainder (**'squeeze-out'**). There are also provisions for the minority shareholders to demand to be bought out even if the acquirer does not really want to buy their shares (**'sell-out'**).

PART B CAPITALISATION

Quick quiz

1   If a company fails to pay preference shareholders their dividend, they can bring a court action to compel the company to pay it.

    True ☐
    False ☐

2   Which two of the following are implied rights of preference shareholders?

    A   The right to receive a dividend is cumulative.
    B   If the company goes into liquidation, preference shareholders are entitled to claim all arrears of dividend from the liquidator.
    C   As well as rights to their preference dividends, preference shareholders can share equally in dividends payable to ordinary shareholders.
    D   Preference shareholders have equal voting rights to ordinary shareholders.

3   If a company issues new ordinary shares for cash, the general rule is that:

    A   The shares must first be offered to existing members in the case of a public but not a private company.
    B   The shares must first be offered to existing members whether the company is public or private.
    C   The shares must first be offered to existing members in the case of a private but not a public company.
    D   The shares need not be issued to existing members.

4   **Fill in the blanks** in the statements below.

    A .... issue is an allotment of additional shares to existing members in exchange for consideration payable by the members.

    A .... issue is an allotment of additional shares to existing members where the consideration is paid by using the company's reserves.

5   **Fill in the blanks** in the statements below.

    If there has been a variation of class rights, a minority of holders of shares of the class (who have not consented or voted in favour of the variation) may apply to the court to have the variation cancelled. The objectors must hold not less than .... of the issued shares of that class, and apply to the court within .... days of the giving of consent by that class.

6   What is the minimum number of members that a plc must have?

    A   One
    B   Two
    C   Three
    D   Four

7   Match the definitions to the correct type of capital.

    (a) Issued share capital
    (b) Called up share capital
    (c) Paid up share capital

    (i)   The amount which the company has required shareholders to pay on shares issued.
    (ii) The type, class, number and amount of the shares held by the shareholders.
    (iii) The amount which shareholders have actually paid on the shares issued and called up.

Answers to quick quiz

1. False. The company may decide not to pay any dividend, or may be unable to because it does not have any distributable profits. What the preference shareholders have is a right to receive their dividends before other dividends are paid or declared.

2. A and D are implied rights; the others have to be stated explicitly.

3. B. The shares must be first offered to existing members whether the company is public or private.

4. A **rights issue** is an allotment of additional shares to existing members in exchange for consideration payable by the members.

    A **bonus issue** is an allotment of additional shares to existing members where the consideration is effectively paid by using the company's reserves.

5. If there has been a variation of class rights, a minority of holders of shares of the class (who have not consented or voted in favour of the variation) may apply to the court to have the variation cancelled. The objectors must hold not less than **15%** of the issued shares of that class, and apply to the court within **21 days** of the giving of consent by that class.

6. A. All companies must have a minimum of one member (s 7).

7. (a) (ii)
   (b) (i)
   (c) (iii)

End of chapter question

Shares

(a) What is a company's share capital? **(5 marks)**

(b) Explain the meaning of the following:

  (i) Issued capital **(2 marks)**
  (ii) Paid up capital **(3 marks)**

  (Total = 10 marks)

PART B CAPITALISATION

Borrowing and loan capital

Topic list	Syllabus reference
1 Borrowing	8.2
2 Debentures and loan capital	8.2
3 Charges	8.2
4 Registration of charges	8.2
5 Debenture holders' remedies	8.2

Introduction

The last chapter was concerned with share capital. In this chapter on borrowing and **loan capital**, you should note that the interests and position of a lender is very different from that of a shareholder.

This chapter covers how loan capital holders protect themselves, specifically through taking out **fixed or floating charges**.

You need to understand the differences between fixed and floating charges, and also how they can protect loan creditors, for example by giving chargeholders the ability to appoint a **receiver**.

The **Companies Act 2006**, (TSO, 2006) and the **Small Business, Enterprise and Employment Act 2015**, (TSO, 2015) apply to this and all chapters unless otherwise stated.

1 Borrowing

> **FAST FORWARD**
>
> Companies have an **implied power** to borrow for purposes incidental to their trade or business.

All companies registered under the Companies Act 2006 (TSO, 2006) have an **implied power to borrow** for purposes **incidental to their trade or business**. A company formed under earlier Acts will have an implied power to borrow if its object is to carry on a trade or business.

In delegating the company's power to borrow to the directors it is usual, and essential in the case of a company whose shares are quoted on the Stock Exchange, to impose a **maximum limit** on the **borrowing** arranged by directors.

A contract to repay borrowed money may in principle be unenforceable if either:

- It is money borrowed for an *ultra vires* (or restricted) purpose, and this is known to the lender.
- The directors **exceed their borrowing powers** or have no powers to borrow.

However:

- In both cases the lender will probably be **able** to **enforce** the contract.
- If the contract is within the capacity of the company but beyond the delegated powers of the directors the company may **ratify** the **loan contract**.

Case law has determined that if a company has power to borrow, it also has power to **create charges** over the company's assets as **security** for the loan. *Re Patent File Co 1870.*

1.1 Personal guarantees

Some lenders may require directors and/or members to agree to repay a loan out of their personal wealth should the company default on the debt. This is known as requesting a **personal guarantee**, which is a promise by a person (the directors or shareholders) to assume a debt obligation in the event of non-payment by the borrower (the company). Personal guarantees are a means of protecting the lender by preventing the shareholders/members from hiding behind the protection of limited liability. It is commonly used where the lender is very powerful (such as a bank) and the borrower has no other source of funds available to it (such as a new or small company).

The main implication for directors or shareholders when giving personal guarantees to their company's creditors is that their liability will not be limited in respect to the amounts owing to the creditors. By giving a personal guarantee their personal assets will be used to repay the creditors should the company default on the loan, that is they cannot rely on the limited liability status of the company for any protection.

2 Debentures and loan capital

2.1 Loan capital

> **FAST FORWARD**
>
> **Loan capital** comprises all the longer term borrowing of a company. It is distinguished from share capital by the fact that, at some point, borrowing must be repaid. Share capital on the other hand is only returned to shareholders when the company is wound up.

A company's **loan capital** comprises all amounts which it borrows for the long-term, such as:

(a) Permanent overdrafts at the bank.
(b) Unsecured loans, from a bank or other party.
(c) Loans secured on assets, from a bank or other party.

Companies often issue long-term loans as capital in the form of **debentures**.

2.2 Debentures

FAST FORWARD

A **debenture** is a document stating the terms on which a company has borrowed money. There are three main types.

- A **single debenture**.
- **Debentures issued as a series** and usually registered.
- **Debenture stock** subscribed to by a large number of lenders. Only this form requires a **debenture trust deed**, although the others may often incorporate one.

Key term

A **debenture** is the written acknowledgement of a debt by a company, normally containing provisions as to payment of interest and the terms of repayment of principal. A debenture may be secured on some or all of the assets of the company or its subsidiaries.

A debenture may create a **charge** over the company's assets as security for the loan (see Section 3). However a document relating to an unsecured loan is also a debenture in company law.

2.3 Types of debenture

A debenture is usually a formal legal document, often in printed form. Broadly, there are three main types.

(a) **A single debenture**

If, for example, a company obtains a secured loan or overdraft facility from its bank, the latter is likely to insist that the company signs the bank's standard form of debenture creating the charge and giving the bank various safeguards and powers.

(b) **Debentures issued as a series and usually registered**

Different lenders may provide different amounts on different dates. Although each transaction is a separate loan, the intention is that the lenders should rank equally *(pari passu)* in their right to repayment and in any security given to them. Each lender therefore receives a debenture in identical form in respect of his loan.

The debentures are transferable securities.

(c) **The issue of debenture stock subscribed to by a large number of lenders**

Only a public company may use this method to offer its debentures to the public and any such offer is a prospectus; if it seeks a listing on The Stock Exchange then the rules on listing particulars must be followed.

Each lender has a right to be **repaid** his **capital** at the **due time** (unless they are perpetual) and to receive **interest** on it until **repayment**. This form of borrowing is treated as a single loan 'stock' in which each debenture stockholder has a specified fraction (in money terms) which they or some previous holder contributed when the stock was issued. Debenture stock is transferable in multiples of, say, £1 or £10.

A company must maintain a **register of all debenture holders** and register an allotment within two months.

One advantage of debenture stock over debentures issued as single and indivisible loan transactions is that the holder of debenture stock can sell part of his holding, say £1,000 (nominal), out of a larger amount.

Debenture stock must be created using a **debenture trust deed** though single and series debenture's may also use a debenture trust deed.

2.4 Debenture trust deed

Major elements of a debenture trust deed for debenture stock

The appointment usually of a trustee for prospective debenture stockholders. The trustee is usually a bank, insurance company or other institution but may be an individual.

The nominal amount of the debenture stock is defined, which is the maximum amount which may be raised then or later. The date or period of repayment is specified, as is the rate of interest and half-yearly interest payment dates.

If the debenture stock is secured **the deed creates a charge or charges** over the assets of the company.

The trustee is authorised to **enforce the security** in case of default and, in particular, to appoint a receiver with suitable powers of management.

The company enters into **various covenants**, for instance to keep its assets fully insured or to limit its total borrowings; breach is a default by the company.

There may be elaborate provisions for **transfer of stock** and **meetings** of debenture stockholders.

Advantages of a debenture trust deed for debenture stock

The **trustee** with appropriate powers can **intervene promptly** in case of default.

Security for the debenture stock in the form of charges over property can be **given to a single trustee**.

The **company** can **contact a representative of the debenture holders** with whom it can negotiate.

By calling a **meeting of debenture holders**, the trustee can consult them and obtain a decision binding on them all.

The **debenture holders** will be able to **enjoy the benefit of a legal mortgage** over the company's land.

2.5 Register of debenture holders

The Companies Act 2006 (TSO, 2006) does not specifically require a register of debenture holders be maintained. However, a company is normally required to maintain a register by the debenture or debenture trust deed when debentures are issued as a series or when debenture stock is issued.

When there is a register of debenture holders, the following regulations apply.

(a) The company is required by law to keep the **register** at its registered office, or at an **address** notified to the registrar: s 743.

(b) The register must be open to **inspection** by **any person** unless the constitution or trust deed provide otherwise. Any person may obtain a copy of the register or part of it for a fee. A holder of debentures issued under a trust deed may require the company (on payment) to supply them with a copy of the deed: s 749.

Under s 745 a company has **five working days** to respond to an inspection request or seek exemption to do so from the court.

(c) The register should be **properly kept** in accordance with the requirements of the Companies Act.

2.6 Rights of debenture holders

The position of debenture holders is best described by comparison with that of shareholders. At first sight the two appear to have a great deal in common.

- Both **own transferable company securities** which are usually long-term investments in the company.
- The **issue procedure** is much the same. An offer of either shares or debentures to the public is a prospectus as defined by the Act.
- The **procedure** for **transfer** of registered shares and debentures is the same.

But there are significant differences.

Differences	Shareholder	Debenture holder
Role	Is a proprietor or owner of the company	Is a creditor of the company
Voting rights	May vote at general meetings	May not vote
Cost of investment	Shares may not be issued at a discount to nominal value	Debentures may be offered at a discount to nominal value
Return	Dividends are only paid • Out of distributable profits • When directors declare them	Interest must be paid when it is due
Tax	Dividends are paid out of post-tax distributable profits	Interest is deducted from profits before tax is calculated
Redemption	Statutory restrictions on redeeming shares	No restriction on redeeming debentures
Liquidation	Shareholders are the last people to be paid in a winding up	Debentures must be paid back before shareholders are paid

From the investor's standpoint debenture stock is often **preferable to preference shares**. Although both yield a fixed income, debenture stock offers greater security.

2.6.1 Advantages and disadvantages of debentures (for the company)

Advantages	Disadvantages
Easily traded	May have to pay high interest rates to make them attractive
Terms clear and specific	Interest payments mandatory
Assets subject to a floating charge may be traded	Interest payments may upset shareholders if dividends fall
Popular due to guaranteed income	Debenture holder's remedies of liquidators or receivers may be disastrous for the company
Interest tax-deductible	Crystallisation of a floating charge can cause trading difficulties for a company
No restrictions on issue or purchase by a company	

Question — Rights of shareholders and debenture holders

Explain how the rights of the shareholders of a company differ from the rights of its debenture holders.

Answer

Rights of shareholders and debenture holders

Shareholders are members of the company. Debenture holders are creditors but not members of the company. Their relationships with the company differ in the following principal respects.

What governs the relationship

A company's relationship with its shareholders is governed by:

(a) Its articles which operate as a contract between them and between the shareholders and each other, and

(b) The Companies Act.

PART B CAPITALISATION

The relationship between a company and its debenture holders is regulated by:

(a) The terms of the trust deed or other formal document, and
(b) (Different) provisions of the Companies Act.

The major practical differences are set out below.

Voting

As members of the company, shareholders have the right to attend and vote at meetings. Debenture holders have no such automatic rights; they may however have votes if the articles and deed allow.

Income

A shareholder, even if he holds preference shares on which fixed dividends are due on specific days, can only receive dividends out of distributable profits. In addition he cannot force the company to pay dividends: *Bond v Barrow Haematite Steel Co 1902*.

By contrast interest at the agreed rate must be paid on debentures even if that interest has to be paid out of capital.

Rights on securities

The Companies Act confers pre-emption rights on shareholders, entitling them to first call on any new shares which are to be issued.

Debenture holders have no right of objection to further loans and debentures being taken out, unless the trust deed sets out restrictions. However there is no statutory restriction on debenture holders having debentures redeemed or purchased by the company. By contrast there are detailed rules regulating redemption or purchase of a company's own shares.

Rights if aggrieved

Shareholders have the right to complain to the court if directors are allowing *ultra vires* transactions or acting in a manner unfairly prejudicial to their interests. Shareholders can, by simple majority, remove directors from the board.

Debenture holders may have rights under the trust deed if the company breaches the agreement. These include:

(a) The right to appoint a receiver, or
(b) The right to enforce charges and sell the property under the charge to realise their debts.

Their consent may also be required before the company deals with certain of its assets, when the debenture holders have secured their loan by means of a fixed charge over those assets.

Rights on insolvency

In the event of the company's insolvency debenture holders must be repaid in full before anything is distributed to shareholders.

3 Charges

FAST FORWARD

A charge over the assets of a company gives a creditor a **prior claim** over other creditors to payment of their debt out of these assets.

Charges may be either **fixed**, which attach to the relevant asset on creation, or **floating**, which attach on 'crystallisation'. For this reason it is not possible to identify the assets to which a **floating** charge relates (until **crystallisation**).

3.1 Definition

Key term

A **charge** is an encumbrance upon real or personal property granting the holder certain rights over that property. They are often used as security for a debt owed to the charge holder. The most common form of charge is by way of legal mortgage, used to secure the indebtedness of borrowers in house purchase transactions. In the case of companies, charges over assets are most frequently granted to persons who provide loan capital to the business.

A charge **secured** over a company's assets gives to the creditor (called the 'chargee') a prior claim (over other creditors) to payment of their debt out of those assets. Charges are of two kinds, fixed and floating.

3.2 Fixed charges

Key term

A **fixed charge** is a form of protection given to secured creditors relating to specific assets of a company. The charge grants the holder the right of enforcement against the identified asset (in the event of default in repayment or some other matter) so that the creditor may realise the asset to meet the debt owed. Fixed charges rank first in order of priority in corporate insolvency.

Fixed (or specific) charges attach to the relevant asset as soon as the charge is created. By its nature a fixed charge is best suited to assets which the company is likely to retain for a long period. A mortgage is an example of a fixed charge.

If the company disposes of the charged asset it will either **repay the secured debt** out of the proceeds of sale so that the charge is discharged at the time of sale, or **pass the asset over to** the purchaser still subject to the charge.

3.3 Floating charges

Key term

A **floating charge** has been defined, in *Re Yorkshire Woolcombers Association Ltd 1903*, as:

(a) A charge on a class of assets of a company, present and future ...
(b) Which class is, in the ordinary course of the company's business, changing from time to time and ...
(c) Until the holders enforce the charge the company may carry on business and deal with the assets charged.

Floating charges do not attach to the relevant assets until the charge crystallises.

A floating charge is **not restricted** to assets such as **receivables** or **inventory**. A floating charge over 'the undertaking and assets' of a company (the most common type) applies to future as well as to current assets.

3.4 Identification of charges as fixed or floating

It is not always immediately apparent whether a charge is fixed or floating. Chargees often do not wish to identify a charge as being as it may get paid later than preferential debts in insolvency proceedings.

A charge contract may declare the charge as fixed, or fixed and floating, whether it is or not. **The label attached** by parties in this way is **not a conclusive statement of the charge's legal nature**.

The general rule is that a **charge over assets will not be registered as fixed if it envisages that the company will still be able to deal with the charged assets without reference to the chargee**.

R in Right of British Columbia v Federal Business Development Bank 1988

The facts: In this Canadian case the Bank had a charge over the company's entire property expressed as 'a fixed and specific mortgage and charge'. Another term allowed the company to continue making sales from stock in the ordinary course of business until notified in writing by the bank to stop doing so.

Decision: The charge was created as a floating, not a fixed, charge.

However, the courts have found **exceptions** to the general rule concerning permission to deal.

(a) In *Re GE Tunbridge Ltd 1995* it was held that as the three criteria stated in the *Yorkshire Woolcombers* case applied. The charge over certain fixed assets was a floating charge even though the company was required to obtain the chargee's permission before dealing with the assets.

(b) In *Re Cimex Ltd 1994* the court decided that the charge in dispute was a fixed charge. The assets did not in the ordinary course of business change from time to time. This was despite the company being able to deal with the assets without the chargee's permission.

3.4.1 Charges over receivables

Charges expressed to be fixed which cover **present and future receivables** (book debts) have historically been particularly tricky. Again the general rule applies. If the company is allowed to deal with money collected from customers without notifying the chargee, the courts have decided that the charge is floating. If the money collected must be paid in to a blocked account or to the chargee, say in reduction of an overdraft, the courts have determined that the charge is fixed over the proceeds: *Siebe Gorman & Co Ltd v Barclays Bank Ltd 1979*.

Following the decision by the House of Lords in *Re Spectrum Plus Ltd 2005* it will be unusual for fixed charges to be created over book debts, and such a charge will only be possible with very careful drafting.

3.5 Creating a floating charge

A **floating charge** is **often created by express words**. However no special form of words is essential. If a **company** gives to a chargee rights over its assets while **retaining freedom to deal with them in the ordinary course of business** until the charge crystallises, that will be a charge which 'floats'. The particular assets subject to a floating charge cannot be identified until the charge attaches by crystallisation.

3.6 Crystallisation of a floating charge

FAST FORWARD

Floating charges **crystallise** or harden (convert into a fixed charge) on the happening of certain relevant events.

Key term

Crystallisation of a floating charge occurs when it is converted into a fixed charge: that is, a fixed charge on the assets owned by the company at the time of crystallisation.

Events causing crystallisation
The **liquidation** of the company
Cessation of the company's **business**
Active intervention by the chargee, generally by way of appointing a receiver
If the **charge contract so provides**, when notice is given by the chargee that the charge is converted into a fixed charge (on whatever assets of the relevant class are owned by the company at the time of the giving of notice)
The **crystallisation** of **another floating charge** if it causes the company to cease business

Floating charge contracts sometimes make provision for 'automatic crystallisation'. This is where the charge is to crystallise when a **specified event** – such as a breach of some term by the company – occurs, regardless of whether:

- The chargee learns of the event.
- The chargee wants to enforce the charge as a result of the event.

Such clauses have been accepted by the courts if they state that, on the event happening, the floating charge is converted to a fixed one. Clauses which provide only that a company is to cease to deal with charged assets on the occurrence of a particular event have been rejected.

3.7 Comparison of fixed and floating charges

> **FAST FORWARD** Floating charges rank **behind** a number of other creditors on liquidation, in particular preferential creditors such as employees.

A **fixed charge** is normally the more satisfactory form of security since it **confers immediate rights** over identified assets. A **floating charge** has some advantage in being applicable to **current assets which may be easier to realise** than long term assets subject to a fixed charge. If for example a company becomes insolvent it may be easier to sell its inventory than its empty factory.

The principal disadvantages of floating charges
The **holder** of a floating charge **cannot be certain** until the charge crystallises which assets will form his security.
Even when a floating charge has crystallised over an identified pool of assets the **chargeholders** may find themselves **postponed** to the claim of **other creditors** as follows. (a) A **judgement creditor or landlord** who has seized goods and sold them may retain the proceeds if received before the appointment of the debenture holder's receiver or administrator: s 183 IA. (b) **Preferential debts** such as wages may be paid out of ring-fenced assets subject to a floating charge unless there are other uncharged assets available for this purpose: ss 40 and 175 IA. (c) The **holder** of a **fixed charge** over the same assets will usually have priority over a floating charge on those assets even if that charge was created before the fixed charge (see below). (d) A creditor may have sold goods and delivered them to the company on condition that he is to retain legal ownership until he has been paid (a **Romalpa** or retention of title clause).
A **floating charge** may become **invalid automatically** if the company creates the charge to secure an existing debt and goes into liquidation within a year thereafter (s 245 IA). The period is only six months with a fixed charge.

3.8 Priority of charges

> **FAST FORWARD** If more than one charge exists over the **same class of property** then legal rules must be applied to see which takes priority in the event the company goes into liquidation.

Different charges over the **same** property may be given to different creditors. It will be necessary in such cases to determine which party's claim has **priority**.

Illustration

If charges are created over the same property to secure a debt of £5,000 to X and £7,000 to Y and the property is sold yielding only £10,000, either X or Y is paid in full and the other receives only the balance remaining out of £10,000 realised from the security.

Priority of charges
Fixed charges rank according to the **order of their creation**. If two successive fixed charges over the same factory are created on 1 January and 1 February the earlier takes priority over the later one.
A **floating charge created before a fixed charge** will only take priority if, when the latter was created, the **fixed chargee** had **notice** of a clause in the floating charge that prevents a later prior charge.
A **fixed charge created before** a **floating charge** has **priority**.
Two floating charges take priority according to the **time of creation**.

PART B CAPITALISATION

If a floating charge is existing and a fixed charge over the same property is created later the fixed charge has priority. This is unless the fixed chargeholder knew of the floating charge. The **fixed** charge ranks **first** since it attached to the property at the time of **creation** but the **floating** charge attaches at the time of **crystallisation**. Once a floating charge has crystallised it becomes a fixed charge and a fixed charge created subsequently ranks after it.

A floating chargeholder may seek to protect himself against losing his priority by including in the terms of his floating charge a prohibition against the company creating a fixed charge over the same property (sometimes called a **'negative pledge clause'**).

If the company **breaks that prohibition** the creditor to whom the fixed charge is given nonetheless obtains priority, unless at the time when his charge is created he has **actual** knowledge of the prohibition.

If a company sells a charged asset to a **third party** the following rules apply.

- A chargee with a fixed charge still has recourse to the property in the hands of the third party – the **charge** is **automatically** transferred with the property.
- Property only remains charged by a floating charge if the **third party** had **notice** of it when he acquired the property.

Exam focus point

You should be aware of what fixed and floating charges are and what the implications are of the differences between them.

Question Registering charges

A floating charge is created on 1 January 20X1. A fixed charge over the same property is created on 1 April 20X1. Assuming both are registered within the prescribed time limits, which ranks first?

Answer

The fixed charge attaches to the asset on creation; the floating charge only attaches on crystallisation, and the effect of crystallisation is not retrospective. Therefore the fixed charge ranks first.

4 Registration of charges

FAST FORWARD

To be valid and enforceable, a charge needs to be **registered** by the Registrar within **21 days** of its creation.

Most charges created by a company **may be registered** with the Registrar within **21 days,** beginning with the day after the date of creation of the charge.

Excluded charges which may NOT be registered are:

- A charge in favour of a landlord on a cash deposit given as a security in connection with the lease of land.
- A charge created by a member of Lloyd's to secure the company's obligations in connection with its underwriting business at Lloyd's.
- A charge that any other Act specifically excludes from registration.

4.1 The registration process

Under the Companies Act 2006 (TSO, 2006), application for the charge **to be registered** may be made by the company or **by any other person** interested in the charge: s 859A.

To apply to register a charge a **statement of particulars relating to the charge must be delivered to the Registrar**. The statement of particulars sets out (s 859D):

- The registered name and number of the company.
- The date when the charge was created.
- Further particulars depending on whether or not there is an instrument creating or evidencing the charge.

Creation of a charge is usually effected by **execution of a instrument,** usually as a **deed**. Where the charge is created or evidenced by an instrument, the Registrar will only register the charge if a **certified copy of the instrument** is delivered along with the statement of particulars.

The Registrar allocates a unique reference code to the charge and places a note in the register recording that reference code. The certified copy of any instrument is also included in the register. The Registrar then issues a **certificate** which is **conclusive evidence** that the **charge had been duly registered**.

The 21 day period for registration runs from the day after the **creation** of the **charge**, or the acquisition of property charged, and not from the making of the loan for which the charge is security.

4.2 Failure to deliver particulars

The duty to deliver particulars falls upon the **company** creating the charge and, if no one delivers particulars within 21 days or any extension period, the **company and its officers are liable to a fine**: s 860.

Non-delivery in the original or any extended time period results in the **charge** being **void** against an administrator, liquidator or any creditor of a company: s 859H.

Non-delivery of the relevant documents relating to a charge means that the sum secured by it is **payable immediately**: s 859H.

4.3 Late delivery of particulars

A **court order** is required for registration of particulars after the 21 day deadline: s 859F.

A court will only allow an order for a charge to be registered late if the failure to deliver the documents was accidental or due to inadvertence or to some other sufficient cause, or it does not prejudice the creditors or shareholders of the company, or it is otherwise just and equitable to grant an extension. Therefore a correctly registered fixed charge has priority over a fixed charge created earlier but registered after it, if that charge is registered late. s 873.

4.4 Rectification of register

A mis-statement or omission in registered particulars on the register can be rectified by the Registrar on receipt of an order of the court, which itself must be registered: s 859M. The court will only make the order if the error or omission was accidental or due to inadvertence or to some other sufficient cause, or if it does not prejudice creditors or shareholders, or if it is just and equitable to do so.

4.5 Register of charges

As you already know, every company is under an obligation to keep a copy of instruments creating charges, and a register of charges, at its registered office or any other location permitted by regulations, so that they may be inspected. The Registrar must be notified of the place where the documents are available for inspection: s 859Q.

Question — Registering more charges

A company creates a charge over a property in favour of Margaret on 1 May 20X7. It creates a further charge of the same type in favour of Chris over the same property on 13 May 20X7. The company has Chris's charge registered on 25 May 20X7, and Margaret's charge on 29 May 20X7.

Whose charge ranks first, and why?

Answer

Margaret's charge would have taken precedence because it was created first, had it been registered within the allowed period of 21 days, up to 22 May. However it was not registered until 29 May, and Chris's charge was legitimately registered in the period between 22 and 29 May when Margaret's charge was void. The court would probably have allowed late registration of Margaret's charge but not at the expense of Chris's rights per s 873.

5 Debenture holders' remedies

5.1 Rights of unsecured debenture holders

FAST FORWARD

A debenture holder **without security** has the same rights as any other creditor.

Any debenture holder is a creditor of the company with the normal remedies of an unsecured creditor. He could:

- **Sue** the company for debt and seize its property if his judgement for debt is unsatisfied.
- Present a petition to the court for the **compulsory liquidation** of the company.
- Apply to the court for an **administration order**, that is, a temporary reprieve to try and rescue a company.

Attention! We shall look at liquidation and administration in Chapter 12.

5.2 Rights of secured debenture holders

FAST FORWARD

A **secured** debenture holder may enforce the security if the company defaults on payment of interest or repayment of capital. They may take possession of the asset subject to the charge and sell it or apply to the court for its transfer to their ownership by a foreclosure order. They may also appoint a receiver or administrator of it. A floating charge holder may place the company into administration.

A **secured** debenture holder (or the trustee of a debenture trust deed) may enforce the security. They may:

- Take **possession of the asset** subject to the charge if they have a fixed charge (if they have a floating charge they may only take possession if the contract allows).
- **Sell it** (provided the debenture is executed as a deed).
- Apply to the court for its **transfer** to their ownership by foreclosure order (rarely used and only available to a legal chargee).
- Appoint a **receiver** of it, provided an administration order is not in effect, or – in the case of floating chargeholders only – appoint an administrator without needing to apply to the court (see Chapter 12).

Exam focus point The last part of a question on charges may well ask what debenture holders can do if a company defaults.

Chapter roundup

- Companies have an **implied power** to borrow for purposes incidental to their trade or business.
- **Loan capital** comprises all the longer term borrowing of a company. It is distinguished from share capital by the fact that, at some point, borrowing must be repaid. Share capital on the other hand is only returned to shareholders when the company is wound up.
- A **debenture** is a document stating the terms on which a company has borrowed money. There are three main types.
    - A **single debenture**.
    - **Debentures issued as a series** and usually registered.
    - **Debenture stock** subscribed to by a large number of lenders. Only this form requires a **debenture trust deed**, although the others may often incorporate one.
- A charge over the assets of a company gives a creditor a **prior claim** over other creditors to payment of their debt out of these assets.
- Charges may be either **fixed**, which attach to the relevant asset on creation, or **floating**, which attach on 'crystallisation'. For this reason it is not possible to identify the assets to which a **floating** charge relates (until **crystallisation**).
- Floating charges **crystallise** or harden (convert into a fixed charge) on the happening of certain relevant events.
- Floating charges rank **behind** a number of other creditors on insolvency, in particular preferential creditors such as employees.
- If more than one charge exists over the **same class of property** then legal rules must be applied to see which takes priority in the event the company goes into liquidation.
- To be valid and enforceable, a charge needs to be **registered** by the Registrar within **21 days** of its creation.
- A debenture holder **without security** has the same rights as any other creditor.
- A **secured** debenture holder may enforce the security if the company defaults on payment of interest or repayment of capital. They may take possession of the asset subject to the charge and sell it or apply to the court for its transfer to their ownership by a foreclosure order. They may also appoint a receiver or administrator of it. A floating charge holder may place the company into administration.

PART B CAPITALISATION

Quick quiz

1. Which of the following are correct statements about the relationship between a company's ordinary shares and its debentures?

    A   Debentures do not confer voting rights, whilst ordinary shares do.
    B   The company's duty is to pay interest on debentures, and to pay dividends on ordinary shares.
    C   Interest paid on debentures is deducted from pre-tax profits, dividends are paid from net profits.
    D   A debenture holder takes priority over a member in liquidation.

2. A fixed charge

    A   Cannot be an informal mortgage
    B   Can be a legal mortgage
    C   Can only attach to land, shares or book debts
    D   Cannot attach to land

3. What are the elements of the definition of a floating charge?

4. Company law requires a company to maintain a register of charges, but not a register of debenture holders.

    True ☐
    False ☐

5. In which of the following situations will crystallisation of a floating charge occur?

    A   Liquidation of the company
    B   Disposal by the company of the charged asset
    C   Cessation of the company's business
    D   After the giving of notice by the chargee if the contract so provides

6. Certain types of charges need to be registered within 28 days of creation.

    True ☐
    False ☐

7. What steps can a fixed debenture holder take to enforce their security? (Max 30 words)

Answers to quick quiz

1. A, C and D are correct. Whilst the company has a contractual duty to pay interest on debentures, there is no duty on it to pay dividends on shares. B is therefore incorrect.

2. B. A mortgage is an example of a fixed charge. It can extend to, for instance, plant and machinery as well as land.

3. The charge is:

    (a) A charge on a class of assets, present and future

    (b) Which class is in the ordinary course of the company's business changing from time to time

    (c) Until the holders enforce the charge, the company may carry on business and deal with the assets charged

4. True. A register of charges must be kept, a register of debenture holders is not required to be kept by the Act (though if it is kept, Companies Act rules must be followed).

5. A, C and D are true. As the charge does not attach to the asset until crystallisation, B is untrue.

6. False. Certain charges such as charges securing a debenture issue and floating charges need to be registered within 21 days, not 28 days.

7. Take possession of the asset subject to the charge
    Sell it
    Apply to the court for a transfer to his ownership
    Appoint a receiver of it

End of chapter question

Debentures and charges

In relation to companies' loan capital explain the following terms.

(a)	Debenture	**(3 marks)**
(b)	Fixed charge	**(3 marks)**
(c)	Floating charge	**(4 marks)**
		(Total = 10 marks)

PART B CAPITALISATION

Capital maintenance and dividends

Topic list	Syllabus reference
1 Capital maintenance	8.2
2 Reduction of share capital	8.2
3 Redemption and purchase by a company of its own shares	8.2
4 Financial assistance for the purchase of shares	8.2
5 Issuing shares at a premium or at a discount	8.2
6 Distributing dividends	8.4

Introduction

The capital which a limited company obtains from its members as consideration for their shares is sometimes called **'the creditors' buffer'**. No one can prevent an unsuccessful company from losing its capital by trading at a loss. However, whatever capital the company does have must be held for the payment of the company's debts and may not be returned to members except under procedures which safeguard the interest of creditors. That is the price which members of a limited company are required to pay for the protection of limited liability. This principle has been developed in a number of detailed applications.

- Capital may only be distributed to members under the formal procedure of a **reduction** of **share capital** or a **winding up** of the company.
- A **premium** obtained on the allotment of shares and profits used to redeem or purchase shares of the company are statutory reserves subject to the basic rules on capital.
- **Dividends** may only be paid out of distributable profits.

The **Companies Act 2006**, (TSO, 2006) and the **Small Business, Enterprise and Employment Act 2015**, (TSO, 2015) apply to this and all chapters unless otherwise stated.

PART B CAPITALISATION

1 Capital maintenance

FAST FORWARD

The rules which dictate how a company is to manage and maintain its capital exist to maintain the delicate balance between the **members' enjoyment of limited liability** and the **creditors' requirements that the company shall remain able to pay its debts**.

Key term

Capital maintenance is a fundamental principle of company law, that limited companies should not be allowed to make payments out of capital to the detriment of company creditors. Therefore the Companies Act contains many examples of control upon capital payments. These include provisions restricting dividend payments, and capital reduction schemes.

Exam focus point

The rules affecting the possible threats to capital are complicated in certain areas. However, provided you know the rules, questions on capital maintenance tend to be straightforward.

2 Reduction of share capital

FAST FORWARD

Reduction of capital can be achieved by: **extinguishing/reducing liability on partly-paid shares**; **cancelling paid-up share capital**; or **paying off part of paid-up share capital**. Court confirmation is required for public companies. The court considers the interests of creditors and different classes of shareholder. There must be power in the articles and a special resolution.

Under the Companies Act 2006 (TSO, 2006), a limited company is permitted without restriction to cancel **unissued shares** as that change does not alter its financial position.

If a limited company with a share capital wishes to **reduce** its **issued share capital** it may do so if:

- It has **power** to do so in its articles. (If it does not have power in the articles, these may be amended by a **special resolution**.)
- It passes a **special resolution**. (If the articles have been amended, this is another special resolution.)
- It obtains **confirmation** of the reduction **from the court**.

2.1 Solvency statement

A private company need not apply to the court if it supports its special resolution with a solvency statement: s 643.

Key term

A **solvency statement** is a declaration by the directors, provided 15 days in advance of the meeting where the special resolution is to be voted on. It states there is no ground to suspect the company is currently unable or will be unlikely to be able to pay its debts for the next 12 months. All possible liabilities must be taken into account and the statement should be in the prescribed form, naming all the directors.

It is an **offence** for directors to deliver to the Registrar a solvency statement without having **reasonable grounds** for the opinions expressed in it.

2.2 Why reduce share capital?

A company may wish to reduce its capital for one or more of the following reasons.

- The company has suffered a **loss** in the **value** of its **assets** and it reduces its capital to reflect that fact.
- The company wishes to **extinguish** the **interests** of some members entirely.

- The capital reduction is part of a **complicated arrangement** of capital which may involve, for instance, replacing share capital with loan capital.

There are three basic methods of reducing share capital specified in s 641 of the Act.

Method	What happens	Effects
Extinguish or reduce liability on partly paid shares.	Eg Company has nominal value £1 shares 75p paid up. Either (a) reduce nominal value to 75p; or (b) reduce nominal value to a figure between 75p and £1.	Company gives up claim for amount not paid up (nothing is **returned** to shareholders).
Pay off part of paid-up share capital out of surplus assets.	Eg Company reduces nominal value of fully paid shares from £1 to 70p and repays this amount to shareholders.	Assets of company are reduced by 30p in £.
Cancel paid-up share capital which has been lost or which is no longer represented by available assets.	Eg Company has £1 nominal fully paid shares but net assets only worth 50p per share. Difference is a debit balance on reserves. Company reduces nominal value to 50p, and applies amount to write off debit balance.	Company can resume dividend payments out of future profits without having to make good past losses.

2.3 Role of the court in reduction of share capital

When the court receives an application for reduction of capital its **first concern** is the effect of the reduction on the company's ability to pay its debts, that is, that the creditors are protected.

If the reduction is by extinguishing liability or paying off part of paid-up share capital, the court requires that **creditors** shall be **invited** by advertisement to state their objections (if any) to the reduction. Where paid-up share capital is cancelled, the court **may** require an invitation to creditors.

Normally the company persuades the court to dispense with advertising for creditors' objections (which can be commercially damaging to the company).

Two possible approaches are:

- To **pay off** all **creditors** before application is made to the court; or, if that is not practicable.
- To produce to the court a **guarantee**, say from the company's bank, that its existing debts will be paid in full.

The **second** concern of the court, where there is more than one class of share, is whether the reduction is fair in its effect on different classes of shareholder.

If the reduction is, **in the circumstances**, a **variation of class rights** (for example removal of the right to an interest in the surplus on a winding-up) the **consent** of the class must be obtained under the variation of class rights procedure.

Within each class of share it is usual to make a uniform reduction of every share by the same amount per share, though this is **not** obligatory.

The court may also be concerned that the **reduction should not confuse or mislead people who may deal with the company in future**. It may insist that the company add 'and reduced' to its name or publish explanations of the reduction.

2.3.1 Confirmation by the court

If the court is satisfied that the reduction is in order, it confirms the reduction by making an order to that effect. A **copy of the court order** and a **statement of capital**, approved by the court, to show the altered share capital is delivered to the Registrar who issues a certificate of registration.

PART B   CAPITALISATION

Question: Reduction of share capital

What are the main methods for a public company to reduce its share capital? What procedures must it follow?

Answer

If a public company wishes to reduce its **issued** share capital it may do so provided that:

(a) It has power to do so in its articles.
(b) It passes a special resolution.
(c) It obtains confirmation of the reduction from the court: s 641.

Requirement (a) is simply a matter of procedure. Articles usually contain the necessary power. If not, the company in general meeting would first pass a special resolution to alter the articles appropriately. They would then proceed to pass a special resolution to reduce the capital.

There are three basic methods of reducing share capital under s 641:

(a) Extinguish or reduce liability on partly-paid shares.
(b) Cancel paid-up share capital which has been lost or which is no longer represented by available assets.
(c) Pay off part of the paid-up share capital out of surplus assets.

Although these are the methods specified in s 641, they are not the only possibilities.

If method (a) or (b) is used (or is part of a more complex scheme to reduce capital) creditors must be invited to object, and their consent must be granted. An alternative is that they are paid off, which will allow the court to confirm the reduction.

It should be remembered that public companies are subject to a minimum capital requirement, currently of £50,000. This means that any public company wishing to reduce its capital below this figure will only be allowed to do so by the court if it re-registers as a private company, which is not subject to the minimum capital requirement. This situation is relatively rare.

3 Redemption and purchase by a company of its own shares

FAST FORWARD — Specific rules govern the ability of private and public companies to **redeem** or **purchase** their own shares.

3.1 The basic rule

Under s 658 of the Companies Act 2006 (TSO, 2006), **a company cannot acquire its own shares** by purchase, subscription or other method. To do so is an **offence**, and the purported acquisition is **void**.

The prohibition is subject to exceptions in s 659. A company may:

- Purchase its own shares in compliance with a **court order.**
- Issue and redeem **redeemable** shares.
- **Purchase** (buyback) its **own shares** under certain specified procedures.
- Forfeit, or **accept** the **surrender** of, its shares.

3.2 Redeemable shares

Both ordinary and preference shares may be issued on terms which allow the company to redeem them. The expression 'redeemable shares' means only shares which are redeemable from the time of issue, so shares not issued as redeemable cannot later be made so.

Key term

> **Redeemable shares** are shares which are issued on terms which may require them to be bought back by the issuer at some future date, either at the discretion of the issuer or of the holder.

The conditions for the issue and redemption of redeemable shares are set out in ss 684 and 687. The rules for private and public companies differ slightly so you should read them carefully.

> The articles of a public company must give **authority** for the issue of redeemable shares. If the articles do not they must be altered before the shares are issued (public companies only). In private companies the directors have authority to allot redeemable shares unless restricted by the articles.

> Redeemable shares may only be issued if, at the time of issue, the company also has **issued shares** which are **not redeemable**. A company's capital may not consist entirely of redeemable shares.

> Redeemable shares may only be redeemed if they are **fully paid**.

> The terms of redemption must provide for **payment on redemption** or on a later date.

> The shares may be redeemed out of:
> - **Distributable profits**
> - The **proceeds of a new issue** of shares
> - **Capital** (if it is a **private** company)

> Any **premium payable on redemption** must generally be provided out of **distributable profits**.

> The company may redeem shares on such **terms** and in such manner as may be provide by the company's **articles** or company **resolution** subject only to the specific provisions set out in the Act.

When shares are redeemed they are cancelled and may not be reissued.

(a) The amount of the company's **issued** share capital is **reduced** by the nominal amount of the shares.

(b) Any new shares issued to raise money to redeem shares are treated as a **replacement** for them to the extent that the nominal value of the new shares does not exceed the nominal value of the shares redeemed.

(c) If shares are redeemed wholly out of profits an amount equal to the nominal value of shares redeemed must be transferred to a **capital redemption reserve** which is to be treated as if it were share capital, except that it may be applied in paying up issued shares as a bonus issue: s 733.

3.3 Purchase of own shares

Any company limited by shares may purchase or 'buyback' its own fully paid shares **out of distributable profits or the proceeds of an issue of new shares** under the redemption of shares rules: s 692(2).

A private company may in addition purchase its own fully paid shares:

- Out of capital using a 'permissible capital payment' (see Section 3.4) or

- With cash (if authorised to do so by its articles, which require a special resolution to be altered) at nominal value up to a 'de minimis' amount in a financial year not exceeding the lower of £15,000 or 5% of its share capital: s 692(1). The Act states that the company does not have to identify this cash amount as distributable profits, meaning that this is a payment out of capital to which the more extensive 'permissible capital payment' rules do not apply. Separate authority by ordinary resolution is required for the specific purchase (or multiple purchases) in question.

A company cannot, however, purchase ordinary shares if, as a result, only redeemable shares are left.

PART B CAPITALISATION

An **unlimited** company can reduce its share capital or purchase its own shares without statutory restriction.

There are two methods of carrying out the purchase: off-market or market purchase. Either can be used for any type of share, but only public companies can use the market method, as private companies will not have shares available on a public market.

- **Market purchase** is purchase by a public company under the normal market arrangements of a recognised investment exchange.
- **Off-market purchase** is any other purchase, usually by private treaty. This will apply to shares of private companies, but it can also apply to public companies.

Market purchase of own shares (s 701)	

Authority	The purchase must be authorised in advance by ordinary resolution specifying:
	• Maximum number of shares to be acquired.
	• Maximum and minimum prices to be paid
	  – By global sum, or
	  – By price formula.
	• A date (< five years after resolution) on which authority expires.

Filing	A return must be sent to the Registrar within 28 days.
Changes	The authority may be varied, revoked or renewed by ordinary resolution.
Off-market purchase of own shares (s 694)	
Authority	A contract for the purchase of shares must be approved in advance by ordinary resolution.
Inspection	A copy of the proposed contract must be available for inspection by members • At the registered office • For 15 days before the meeting for approval • At the meeting It must disclose the names of the sellers. If the resolution is a written one, a copy of the contract must be sent to all eligible members.
Voting	The members who intend to sell the shares should not vote. If they do vote and the resolution would not have been carried without their vote, it is invalid. They may cast votes attached to other shares which they are not selling.
Public company	A public company may only be given authority for a limited period (max five years).
Changes	The authority may be varied, revoked or renewed by ordinary resolution.

Question
Purchase of shares

A limited company may without restriction purchase its own shares providing the purchase is out of profits or an issue of new shares.

True or false?

Answer

False. Such an action is prevented if the purchase would leave only redeemable shares.

3.4 Payment for shares out of capital – private companies only

A private limited company which has a share capital may redeem or purchase its shares 'out of capital' by a '**permissible capital payment**' to which elaborate rules apply: s 709. These rules are designed to ensure that the company does not make itself insolvent by making a large return of capital to shareholders.

The conditions for a permissible capital payment are as follows.

(a) There must be **no restrictions** in the **articles** for redemption or purchase of shares out of capital.

(b) Capital may only be used to '**top up**' distributable profits and the proceeds of any issue of new shares in cases where those resources, fully used, do not suffice to make up the required amount.

Cost of redemption or purchase	=	Available distributable profits	+	Proceeds of fresh issue	+	Permissible capital payment

(c) A **capital redemption reserve** must be created where the amount of the permissible capital payment is less than the nominal amount of the shares redeemed or purchased: s 734.

If the payment is greater than the nominal amount then the capital redemption reserve, share premium account, share capital or revaluation reserve of the company may be reduced by the excess.

(d) A **statutory declaration of the directors** must be made and supported by a **report of the auditors** to the effect that after the payment is made the company will be able to pay its debts and to carry on its business for at least a year to come: s 714.

(e) Shareholders must approve the payment by passing a **special resolution s 716**. In this decision any vendor of shares may **not** use the votes attached to the shares which he is to sell to the company: s 717.

(f) A member who did not vote for the resolution and a creditor (for any amount) may **within five weeks apply to the court to cancel the resolution**, which may not be implemented until the five weeks have elapsed: s 721.

(g) A **notice** must be placed in the *London Gazette* and in an appropriate national newspaper, **or** every creditor must be informed: s 719.

If the company goes into insolvent liquidation within a year of making a payment out of capital the person who received the payment and the directors who authorised it may have to make it good to the company.

Note that different, less onerous rules apply where the payment out of capital relates to the purchase of own shares for the purposes of or pursuant to an **employees' share scheme**: s 720A. These rules require a special resolution supported by a solvency statement and statement of capital.

3.5 Subsidiary not to be a member of its holding company

The restrictions on acquisition by a company of its own shares are extended by a general prohibition against a subsidiary being a member of its holding company: s 136.

4 Financial assistance for the purchase of shares

FAST FORWARD

A **public** company may not give **financial assistance** to a third party to purchase shares in the company. A private company can do so.

PART B   CAPITALISATION

4.1 The rule against financial assistance

The general rules under the Companies Act 2006 (TSO, 2006), apply to all **public companies only**.

(a) A company is prohibited from giving any financial assistance for the purpose of the acquisition of shares either of the company or of its holding company or to discharge liabilities incurred in making the acquisition: s 678.

(b) 'Financial assistance' is elaborately defined to mean:
- A loan or gift
- A guarantee indemnity or security
- A realise from debt or a waiver
- 'Any other financial assistance given by a company which reduces to a material extent, its net assets': s 677.

Key term

> **Financial assistance** is the provision of benefit by a company to a person to put that person in funds so that s/he may purchase shares in the company.

A public company may give a person financial assistance if its principal purpose in doing so is not to reduce or discourage the person's liability, or if it is an incidental part of a larger purpose of the company, **and** if it is done in good faith: s 678(4). Two main tests have to be applied to any suspect transaction.

> What was its **purpose**? It is not objectionable if its **principal purpose** was **not** to give financial assistance for the purchase of the shares nor if it was an incidental part of some **larger purpose** of the company.
>
> What was the state of mind of the directors in approving the transaction? Did they act in **good faith** in what they deemed to be the interests of the company and not of a third party?

4.2 Group companies

Under the Act:

- A **private subsidiary** may give assistance to purchase its own shares and that of its parent (if it also is a private company).
- A **public subsidiary** may not give assistance to purchase its own shares or that of its parent (even if the parent is a private company).

4.3 Other exceptions from the financial assistance rules

Three other specific exceptions are also made. By s 682 a company is not prohibited from entering into any of the following transactions provided it is either a private company, or it is a public company and either its net assets are not reduced by giving the assistance, or it gives the assistance out of distributable profit.

(a) Making a loan if **lending is part of its ordinary business**, and the loan is made in the ordinary course of its business; this exception is restricted to money-lending companies.

(b) Providing money in good faith and in the best interests of the company for the purpose of an **employees' share scheme** or for other share transactions by *bona fide* employees or connected persons.

(c) **Making loans** or providing assistance to persons (other than directors) employed in good faith by the company with a view to those **persons acquiring fully paid shares** in the company or its holding company to be held by them as beneficial owners.

Exam focus point

> Do not confuse a company purchasing its own shares with a company providing financial assistance for **someone else** to purchase its shares.

Question: Financial assistance

Which of the following transactions for assistance to purchase a company's own shares are allowable under the Companies Act 2006?

Select all that apply.

A A private subsidiary can give assistance to a private parent.
B A public subsidiary can give assistance to a private parent.
C A private subsidiary can give assistance to a third party.
D A public company can give assistance to a third party company.

A and C. Public companies may never give assistance in these circumstances. Private companies can.

5 Issuing shares at a premium or at a discount

FAST FORWARD

In issuing shares, a company must fix a **price** which is **equal to** or **more than** the **nominal value of the shares**. It may not allot shares at a discount to the nominal value.

Under the Companies Act 2006 (TSO, 2006), every share has a **nominal value** and **may not be allotted at a discount** to that: s 580.

In allotting shares every company is required to obtain in money or money's worth, consideration of a value at least equal to the nominal value of the shares plus the whole of any premium. To issue shares **'at par'** is to obtain equal value, say, £1 for a £1 share.

> *Ooregum Gold Mining Co of India v Roper, 1892*
>
> *The facts:* Shares in the company, although nominally £1, were trading, at a market price 12.5p. In an honest attempt to refinance the company, new £1 preference shares were issued and credited with 75p already paid, so the purchasers of the shares were actually paying twice the market value of the ordinary shares. When, however, the company subsequently went into insolvent liquidation the holders of the new shares were required to pay a further 75p.

If shares are allotted at a discount to their nominal value, the allottee, if they agree to the issue, must nonetheless pay the **full nominal value** with **interest** at the appropriate rate. Any subsequent holder of such a share who knew of the underpayment must make good the shortfall: s 588.

Consideration for shares	
Partly-paid shares	The no-discount rule only requires that, in allotting its shares, a company shall not fix a price which is less than the nominal value of the shares. It may leave part of that price to be paid at some later time. Thus £1 shares may be issued partly-paid – 75p on allotment and 25p when called for or by instalment. The unpaid capital passes with the shares. If transferred, they are a debt payable by the holder at the time when payment is demanded.
Underwriting fees	A company may pay underwriting or other commission in respect of an issue of shares if so permitted by its Articles. This means that, if shares are issued at par the net amount received will be below par value. This is not a contravention of s 580 (prohibiting allotment of shares at a discount).
Bonus issue	The allotment of shares as a 'bonus issue' is for full consideration since reserves, which are shareholders' funds, are converted into fixed capital and are used to pay for the shares.

Consideration for shares	
Money's worth	The price for the shares may be paid in **money** or **'money's worth'**, including goodwill and know-how: s 582. It need not be paid in cash and the company may agree to accept a **'non-cash' consideration** of sufficient value. For instance, a company may issue shares in payment of the price agreed in the purchase of a property.

5.1 Private companies

FAST FORWARD

Private companies may issue shares for **inadequate consideration** provided the directors are behaving reasonably and honestly.

A private company may allot shares for **inadequate consideration** by acceptance of goods or services at an over-value. This loophole has been allowed to exist because in some cases it is very much a matter of opinion whether an asset is or is not of a stated value.

The **courts** therefore have **refused** to overrule directors in their valuation of an asset acquired for shares if it appears **reasonable** and **honest**: *Re Wragg 1897*. However a blatant and unjustified overvaluation will be declared **invalid**.

5.2 Public companies

FAST FORWARD

There are **stringent rules** on consideration for shares in public companies.

More stringent rules apply to public companies.

(a) The company must, at the time of allotment, receive **at least one quarter of the nominal value** of the shares and the **whole** of any premium: s 586.

(b) Any **non-cash consideration** accepted must be **independently valued** (see below).

(c) **Non-cash consideration** may **not** be accepted as payment for shares if an undertaking contained in such consideration is to be, or may be, **performed more than five years after the allotment**. This relates to, say, a property or business in return for shares. To enforce the five year rule the law requires that:

   (i) At the time of the allotment the **allottee** must **undertake** to **perform** his side of the agreement within a specified period which must not exceed five years. If no such undertaking is given the **allottee** becomes **immediately liable** to pay cash for his shares as soon as they are allotted.

   (ii) If the **allottee later fails** to **perform** his undertaking to transfer property at the due time he becomes liable to pay **cash** for his shares when he defaults.

(d) An **undertaking to do work or perform services is not to be accepted as consideration**. A public company may, however, allot shares to discharge a debt in respect of services already rendered.

If a public company does accept future services as consideration the holder must pay the company their **nominal value** plus any **premium** treated as paid-up, and **interest** at 5% on any such amount.

(e) Within **two years of receiving its trading certificate**, a public company **may not receive a transfer of non-cash assets from a subscriber** to the memorandum. This is unless its value is less than 10% of the issued nominal share capital and it has been independently valued and agreed by an ordinary resolution.

5.2.1 Valuation of non-cash assets

When a public company allots shares for a non-cash consideration the company must usually obtain a **report on its value** from an independent valuer.

6: CAPITAL MAINTENANCE AND DIVIDENDS

The valuation report must be made to the company within the six months before the allotment. On receiving the report the company must send a copy to the proposed allottee and later to the Registrar.

The independent valuation rule does not apply to an allotment of shares made in the course of a take-over bid.

5.3 Allotment of shares at a premium

FAST FORWARD

> If shares are issued at a premium, the **excess** must be credited to a **share premium** account.

Key term

> **Share premium** is the excess received, either in cash or other consideration, over the nominal value of the shares issued.

An established company may be able to obtain consideration for new shares in excess of their nominal value. The excess, called 'share premium', must be credited to a **share premium account**: s 610.

Exam focus point

> The prohibition on offer of shares at a discount on **nominal** value is often confused with a company issuing shares at a price below **market** value (which is not, provided there is no discount below nominal value, prohibited).

If a company obtains non-cash consideration for its shares which exceeds the nominal value of the shares the excess should also be credited to the **share premium account**.

5.3.1 Example: Using a share premium account

If a company allots its £1 (nominal) shares for £1.50 in cash, £1 per share is credited to the share capital account, and 50p to the share premium account.

Illustration

We will use the above example to illustrate the effects of the transaction on the balance sheet. The company has issued 100 shares.

	Before share issue £	After share issue £
Cash	100	250
Share capital	100	200
Share premium	–	50
	100	250

The general rule is that reduction of the share premium account is subject to the **same** restrictions as reduction of share capital. You should learn the fact that **a company cannot distribute any part of its share premium account as dividend**.

5.4 Uses of the share premium account

FAST FORWARD

> Use of the share premium account is limited. It is most often used for **bonus issues**.

According to s 610, the **permitted uses of share premium** are to pay:

- **Fully paid shares under a bonus issue** since this operation merely converts one form of fixed capital (share premium) into another (share capital).
- **Issue expenses** and **commission** in respect of a **new share issue**.

Additionally, under s 687, the share premium account may be used to finance any premium due when **redeemable shares** are redeemed.

Question — Increasing a company's share capital

Explain the rule concerning issuing shares at a discount to their nominal value.

Answer

Shares may not be issued at a discount to their nominal value: s 580. However shares may be issued 'partly paid' with, for example, 75p of a £1 share paid up. The 25p balance remains a liability that the shareholder must pay when demanded.

6 Distributing dividends

FAST FORWARD

Various rules have been created to ensure that dividends are only paid out of **available profits**.

Key term

A **dividend** is an amount payable to shareholders from profits or other distributable reserves.

6.1 Power to declare dividends

Under the Companies Act 2006 (TSO, 2006), a company may only pay dividends out of **profits available for the purpose**.

The power to declare a dividend is given by the articles which often include the following rules.

Rules related to the power to declare a dividend
The **company** in **general meeting** may declare dividends.
No dividend may exceed the **amount recommended** by the directors who have an implied power in their discretion to set aside profits as reserves.
The directors may declare such **interim dividends** as they consider justified.
Dividends are normally declared payable on the **paid up amount** of share capital. For example a £1 share which is fully paid will carry entitlement to twice as much dividend as a £1 share 50p paid.
A dividend may be paid **otherwise than in cash**.
Dividends may be paid by **cheque** or **warrant** sent through the post to the shareholder at his registered address. If shares are held jointly, payment of dividend is made to the first-named joint holder on the register.

Listed companies generally pay two dividends a year; an **interim dividend** based on interim profit figures, and a **final dividend** based on the annual accounts and approved at the AGM.

A **dividend becomes a debt** when it is **declared** and **due for payment**. A shareholder is not entitled to a dividend unless it is declared in accordance with the procedure prescribed by the articles and the declared date for payment has arrived.

This is so even if the member holds **preference shares** carrying a priority entitlement to receive a specified amount of dividend on a specified date in the year. The directors may decide to withhold profits and cannot be compelled to recommend a dividend.

If the articles refer to 'payment' of dividends this means **payment in cash**. A power to pay dividends **in specie** (otherwise than in cash) is not implied but may be expressly created. **Scrip dividends** are dividends paid by the issue of additional shares.

Any provision of the articles for the declaration and payment of dividends is subject to the overriding rule that **no dividend may be paid except out of profits distributable by law**.

6.2 Distributable profits

FAST FORWARD

Distributable profits may be defined as 'accumulated realised profits ... less accumulated realised losses'. **'Accumulated'** means that any losses of previous years must be included in reckoning the current distributable surplus. **'Realised'** profits are determined in accordance with generally accepted accounting principles.

Key term

Profits available for distribution are accumulated realised profits (which have not been distributed or capitalised) less accumulated realised losses (which have not been previously written off in a reduction or reorganisation of capital).

The word **'accumulated'** requires that any **losses** of **previous years** must be included in reckoning the current distributable surplus.

A profit or loss is deemed to be **realised** if it is treated as realised in accordance with generally accepted accounting principles. Hence, financial reporting and accounting standards in issue, plus generally accepted accounting principles (GAAP), should be taken into account when determining realised profits and losses.

Depreciation must be treated as a **realised loss**, and debited against profit, in determining the amount of distributable profit remaining.

However, a **revalued asset** will have deprecation charged on its historical cost and the increase in the value in the asset. The Companies Act allows the depreciation provision on the valuation increase to be treated also as a realised profit.

Effectively there is a cancelling out, and at the end **only depreciation that relates to historical cost will affect dividends**.

 Illustration

Suppose that an asset purchased for £20,000 has a 10 year life. Provision is made for depreciation on a straight line basis. This means an annual depreciation charge of £2,000 (£20,000/10 years) must be deducted in reckoning the company's realised profit less realised loss.

After five years the asset's written down value is £10,000 (£20,000 less £2,000 × 5 years). Suppose that the asset is then revalued to £50,000. The increase in the value of the asset (£40,000) is credited to the revaluation reserve.

The consequences of this revaluation are that the annual depreciation charge is raised to £10,000 (£50,000/5 remaining years of the asset's life) and £8,000 (£40,000/5 years) is transferred from the revaluation reserve to realised profit each year for the remaining life of the asset.

The net effect is that each year realised profits are still reduced by £2,000 (£10,000 – 8,000) in respect of depreciation.

If, on a general revaluation of all fixed assets, it appears that there is a diminution in value of any one or more assets, then any related provision(s) need **not** be treated as a realised loss.

The Act states that if a company shows **development expenditure** as an asset in its accounts it must usually be treated as a realised loss in the year it occurs. However it can be carried forward in special circumstances (generally taken to mean in accordance with accounting standards).

6.3 Dividends of public companies

FAST FORWARD

A public company may only make a distribution if its **net assets** are, at the time, **not less than the aggregate of its called-up share capital and undistributable reserves**. It may only pay a dividend which will leave its net assets at not less than that aggregate amount.

A public company may only make a distribution if its **net assets are**, at the time, **not less than the aggregate of its called-up share capital and undistributable reserves**. The dividend which it may pay is limited to such amount as will leave its net assets at not less than that aggregate amount: s 831.

Undistributable reserves in s 831 are defined as:

(a) **Share premium account**.
(b) **Capital redemption reserve**.
(c) Any **surplus** of **accumulated unrealised profits** over **accumulated unrealised losses** (known as a revaluation reserve). However a deficit of accumulated unrealised profits compared with accumulated unrealised losses must be treated as a realised loss.
(d) Any **reserve** which the company is **prohibited** from **distributing** by **statute** or by its constitution or any law.

Illustration

Suppose that a public company has an issued share capital (fully paid) of £800,000 and £200,000 on share premium account (which is an undistributable reserve). If its assets less liabilities are less than £1 million it may not pay a dividend. If however its net assets are say £1,250,000 it may pay a dividend but only of such amount as will leave net assets of £1 million or more, so its maximum permissible dividend is £250,000.

The dividend rules apply to every form of distribution of assets except the following:

- The **issue of bonus shares** whether fully or partly paid
- The **redemption** or **purchase** of the company's **shares** out of **capital** or **profits**
- A **reduction** of **share capital**
- A **distribution** of **assets** to members in a **winding up**

Exam focus point

You must appreciate how the rules relating to public companies in this area are more stringent than the rules for private companies.

Question
Distribution of profit

What are the main rules affecting a company's ability to distribute its profits as dividends?

Answer

Dividends may only be paid by a company out of profits available for the purpose. There is a detailed code of statutory rules which determines what are distributable profits. The profits which may be distributed as dividend are accumulated realised profits, so far as not previously utilised by distribution or capitalisation, less accumulated realised losses, so far as not previously written off in a reduction or reorganisation of capital duly made.

The above rules on distributable profits apply to all companies, private or public. A public company is subject to an additional rule which may diminish but cannot increase its distributable profit as determined under the above rules.

A public company may only make a distribution if its net assets are, at the time, not less than the aggregate of its called-up share capital and undistributable reserves. The dividend which it may pay is limited to such amount as will leave its net assets at not less than that aggregate amount.

6.4 Relevant accounts

FAST FORWARD

The profits available for distribution are generally determined from the **last annual accounts** to be prepared.

Whether a company has profits from which to pay a dividend is determined by reference to its **'relevant accounts'**, which are generally the last annual accounts to be prepared: s 836.

If the auditor has qualified their report on the accounts they must also state in writing whether, in their opinion, the subject matter of his qualification is **material** in determining whether the dividend may be paid. This statement must have been circulated to the members (for a private company) or considered at a general meeting (for a public company).

A company may produce **interim accounts** if the latest annual accounts do not disclose a sufficient distributable profit to cover the proposed dividend. It may also produce **initial accounts** if it proposes to pay a dividend during its first accounting reference period or before its first accounts are laid before the company in general meeting. These accounts may be unaudited, but they must suffice to permit a proper judgement to be made of amounts of any of the relevant items.

If a **public** company has to produce initial or interim accounts, which is unusual, they must be full accounts such as the company is required to produce as final accounts at the end of the year. They need not be audited. However the auditors must, in the case of initial accounts, satisfy themselves that the accounts have been 'properly prepared' to comply with the Act. A copy of any such accounts of a public company (with any auditors' statement) must be delivered to the Registrar for filing.

6.5 Infringement of dividend rules

FAST FORWARD

In certain situations the **directors** and **members** may be liable to make good to the company the amount of an **unlawful dividend**.

If a dividend is paid otherwise than out of distributable profits the company, the **directors and** the **shareholders** may be involved in making good the unlawful distribution.

The directors are held **responsible** since they either recommend to members in general meeting that a dividend should be declared or they declare interim dividends.

(a) **The directors are liable if they declare a dividend which they know is paid out of capital**.

(b) **The directors are liable if, without preparing any accounts, they declare or recommend a dividend which proves to be paid out of capital**. It is their duty to satisfy themselves that profits are available.

(c) **The directors are liable if they make some mistake of law or interpretation of the constitution which leads them to recommend or declare an unlawful dividend**. However in such cases the directors may well be entitled to relief as their acts were performed 'honestly and reasonably'.

The directors may however **honestly** rely on proper accounts which disclose an apparent distributable profit out of which the dividend can properly be paid. They are not liable if it later appears that the assumptions or estimates used in preparing the accounts, although reasonable at the time, were in fact unsound.

PART B CAPITALISATION

The position of members is as follows.

- A member may obtain an **injunction** to restrain a company from paying an unlawful dividend.
- Members voting in general meeting **cannot authorise** the payment of an unlawful dividend nor release the directors from their liability to pay it back.
- The company can **recover from members** an **unlawful dividend** if the **members knew** or had **reasonable grounds** to believe that it was unlawful, s 847.
- If the directors have to make good to the company an unlawful dividend they may claim **indemnity from members** who at the time of receipt knew of the irregularity.
- Members knowingly receiving an unlawful dividend may **not bring an action** against the directors.

If an unlawful dividend is paid by **reason of error** in the **accounts** the company may be unable to claim against either the directors or the members. The company might then have a claim against its **auditors** if the undiscovered mistake was due to negligence on their part.

Re London & General Bank (No 2) 1895

The facts: The auditor had drawn the attention of the directors to the fact that certain loans to associated companies were likely to prove irrecoverable. The directors refused to make any provision for these potential losses. They persuaded the auditor to confine his comments in his audit report to the uninformative statement that the value of assets shown in the balance sheet 'is dependent on realisation'. A dividend was paid in reliance on the apparent profits shown in the accounts. The company went into liquidation and the liquidator claimed from the auditor compensation for loss of capital due to his failure to report clearly to members what he well knew affecting the reliability of the accounts.

Decision: The auditor has a duty to report what he knows of the true financial position: otherwise his audit is 'an idle farce'. He had failed in this duty and was liable.

Chapter roundup

- The rules which dictate how a company is to manage and maintain its capital exist to maintain the delicate balance between the **members' enjoyment of limited liability** and the **creditors' requirements that the company shall remain able to pay its debts**.
- Reduction of capital can be achieved by: **extinguishing/reducing liability on partly-paid shares; cancelling paid-up share capital;** or **paying off part of paid up share capital**. Court confirmation is required for public companies. The court considers the interests of creditors and different classes of shareholder. There must be power in the articles and a special resolution.
- Specific rules govern the ability of private and public companies to **redeem** or **purchase** their shares.
- A **public** company may not give **financial assistance** to a third party to purchase shares in the company. A private company can do so.
- In issuing shares, a company must fix a **price** which is **equal** to or **more than** the **nominal value of the shares**. It may not allot shares at a discount to the nominal value.
- **Private** companies may issue shares for **inadequate consideration** provided the directors are behaving reasonably and honestly.
- There are **stringent rules** on consideration for shares in public companies.
- If shares are issued at a premium, the **excess** must be credited to a **share premium** account.
- Use of the share premium account is limited. It is most often used for **bonus issues**.
- Various rules have been created to ensure that dividends are only paid out of **available profits**.
- Distributable profits may be defined as 'accumulated realised profits ... less accumulated realised losses'. **'Accumulated'** means that any losses of previous years must be included in reckoning the current distributable surplus. **'Realised'** profits are determined in accordance with generally accepted accounting principles.
- A public company may only make a distribution if its **net assets** are, at the time, **not less than the aggregate of its called-up share capital and undistributable reserves**. It may only pay a dividend which will leave its net assets at not less than that aggregate amount.
- The profits available for distribution are generally determined from the **last annual accounts** to be prepared.
- In certain situations the **directors** and **members** may be liable to make good to the company the amount of an **unlawful dividend**.

PART B CAPITALISATION

Quick quiz

1. Where application is made to the court for confirmation of a reduction in capital, the court may require that creditors should be invited by advertisement to state their objections. In which of the following ways can the need to advertise be avoided?

    A Paying off all creditors before application to the court.
    B Producing a document signed by the directors stating the company's ability to pay its debts.
    C Producing a guarantee from the company's bank that its existing debts will be paid in full.
    D Renouncement by existing shareholders of their limited liability in relation to existing debts.

2. A share premium account can be used for bonus issues of shares or issue costs for new share issues.

    True ☐
    False ☐

3. **Fill in the blanks** in the statements below.

    Distributable profits may be defined as ……………….. ………..… profits less ……………….. …………. losses.

4. If a company makes an unlawful dividend, who may be involved in making good the distribution?

    A The company
    B The directors
    C The shareholders

5. Give four examples of undistributable reserves.

6. What normally are a company's relevant accounts in the context of payments of dividends?

Answers to quick quiz

1. A and C. The only guarantee that the courts will accept is from the company's bank.
2. True. Both are acceptable uses for the share premium account.
3. Distributable profits may be defined as **accumulated realised** profits less **accumulated realised** losses.
4. All three may be liable.
5. Share premium account

   Capital redemption reserve

   A surplus of accumulated unrealised profits over accumulated unrealised losses (revaluation reserve)

   Any reserve which the company is prohibited from distributing by statute or by its constitution or any law
6. The relevant accounts are the last accounts to have been prepared and laid in general meeting.

End of chapter question

Issuing shares

Explain the meaning of the following:

(a) The issue of shares at a premium (5 marks)
(b) The prohibition on the issue of shares at a discount (5 marks)

(Total = 10 marks)

PART B CAPITALISATION

Administration and control

Corporate governance

Topic list	Syllabus reference
1 What is corporate governance?	8.3
2 Governance structures	8.3
3 The UK Corporate Governance Code	8.3
4 Legal regulation of corporate governance	8.3, 8.5

Introduction

Corporate governance is about the direction and control of a company. In this chapter we shall start to look at the structures put in place to ensure that companies are managed well and in the best interests of the owners (the shareholders).

The law sets out basic principles. The **directors manage** the company. The **owners** are entitled to retain **ultimate control** over company strategy by exercising powers in **general meetings**.

In recent years, much attention has been focused on the issue of **corporate governance**. This is because **company failure** due to poor management or even fraud by management has had a significant impact on large numbers of people. The response to the need for better governance has been both extra-legal and statutory. We shall look in Section 3 at the UK's Corporate Governance Code (an extra-legal approach) and at the US Sarbanes-Oxley Act (a statutory approach).

The **Companies Act 2006**, (TSO, 2006) and the **Small Business, Enterprise and Employment Act 2015**, (TSO, 2015) apply to this and all chapters unless otherwise stated.

PART C ADMINISTRATION AND CONTROL

1 What is corporate governance?

> **FAST FORWARD**
>
> Corporate governance is simply a term used for **the way that companies** (corporate) **are managed** (governed).

Key term

> **Corporate governance** is the system by which companies are directed and controlled (Committee on the Financial Aspects of Corporate Governance, 1992) (The Cadbury Report).

1.1 A company's stakeholders

> **FAST FORWARD**
>
> There are many different **stakeholders** in most companies.

A company has **various interested parties**, known as **stakeholders**. Examples include:

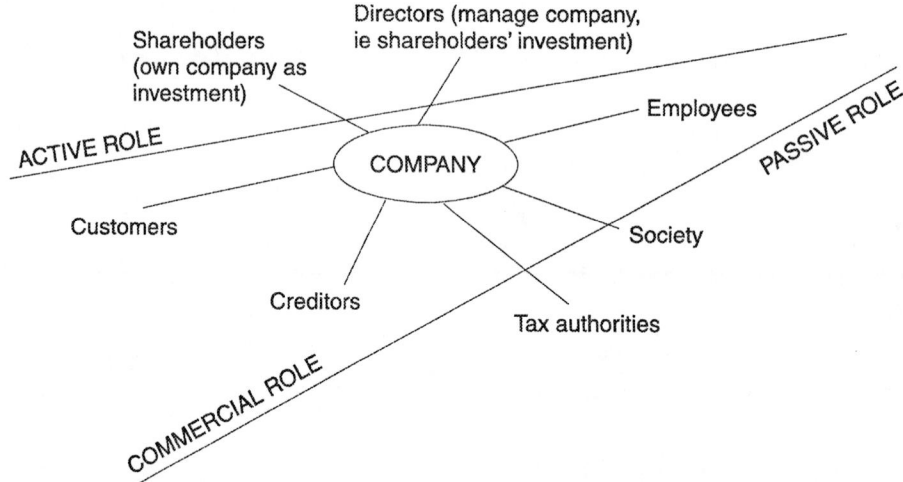

Each of the stakeholders has a **different role**, some of which are more passive than others. For example, **society** is a stakeholder in a company, but it is generally a **passive** participant. The tax authorities passively receive income from the company's profits. Customers, employees and creditors are more active, playing the 'commercial' role that keeps the company's operations going.

1.2 Shareholders and directors

> **FAST FORWARD**
>
> The stakeholders most closely involved in corporate governance are the **directors** (the managers of the company) and the **shareholders** (who have some ultimate controls in general meeting).

The key active stakeholders are **shareholders**, who **own the company**, and **directors**, who **manage the company**, and therefore, they manage the shareholders' investment.

Corporate governance is therefore all about **shareholders** (the owners) and **directors** (the management), as between them they direct and control the company. Sometimes, particularly in smaller businesses, companies are **owned and managed by the same people**. This is the situation where people form a company to carry out their own business, buy the shares and appoint themselves as directors. Such companies are known as 'owner-managed businesses'. The first diagram on the next page illustrates such a company.

7: CORPORATE GOVERNANCE

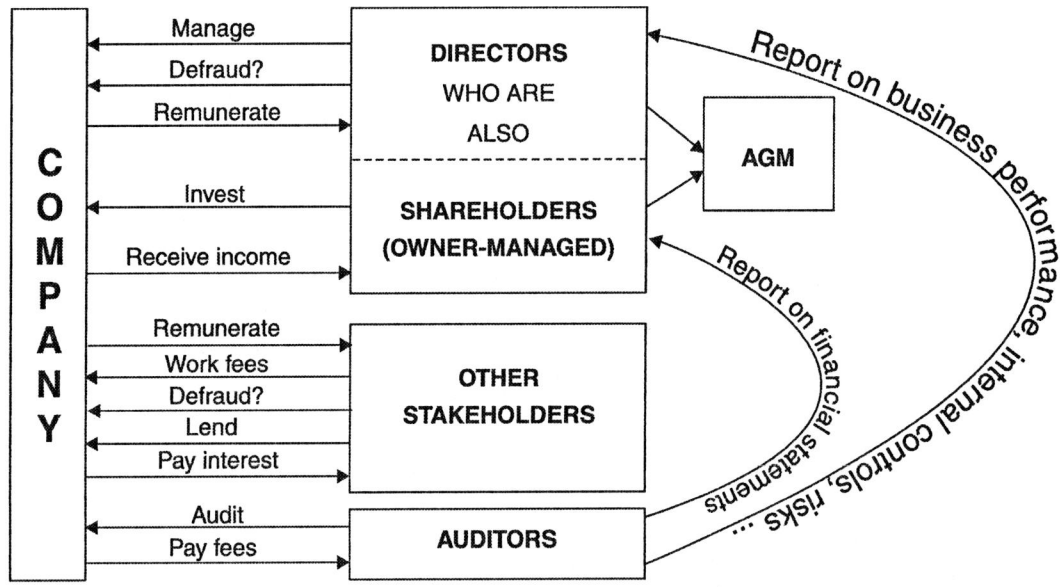

In other, often **bigger**, companies, the directors and shareholders are different sets of people. Often in larger companies quoted on stock exchanges, **shareholders** purchase shares as an investment and may have very little personal contact with the company. **Directors** are employed for their management expertise and have no other connection with the company. The diagram below illustrates such a company.

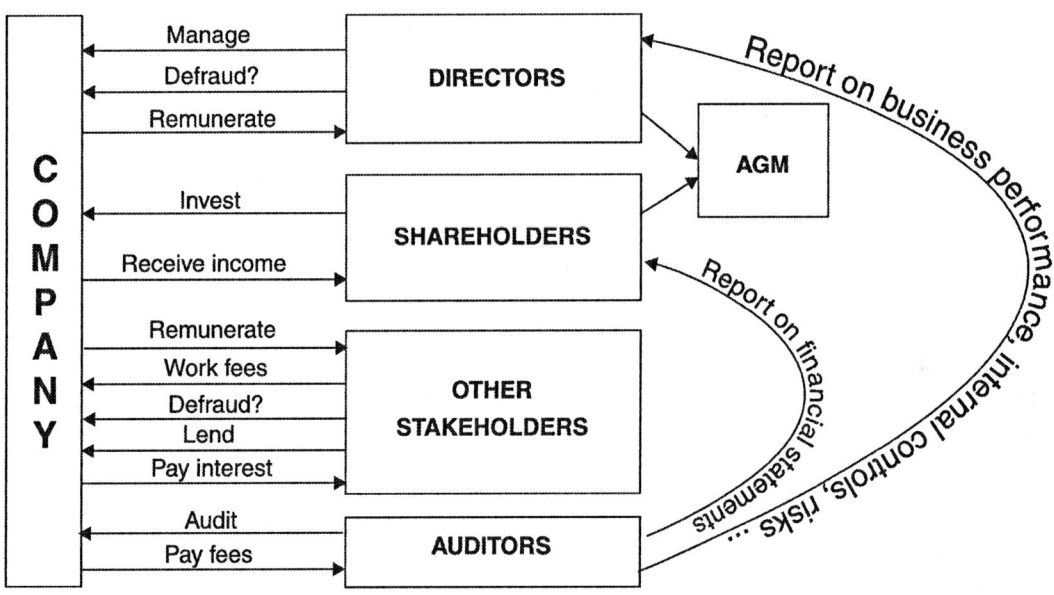

1.2.1 Knowledge gap

These two diagrams illustrate two positions between which there is a wide spectrum. They also illustrate a key difference between the two companies, which is a '**knowledge gap**'.

In the **owner-managed company**, as the directors and shareholders are the same people, they have **access to the same information** and are **in a position to direct company policy**. In the other company, the shareholders do not have access to day-to-day company management information.

This 'gap' in the shareholders' knowledge may cause difficulty for investors, who will want to be assured that their investment is being managed correctly and in accordance with their wishes, as owners. Company law and practice have adopted various measures to attempt to bridge the gap.

- Financial statements
- Annual general meetings
- Corporate governance codes

1.3 Financial statements

> **FAST FORWARD**
> Directors must prepare **financial statements** for shareholders annually, and these are independently audited to provide an objective check on the directors.

Directors are required by law to **report to members** on the **financial position** of the company on an annual basis. Company law requires that an independent professional **audits** these financial statements to ensure that they **give a true and fair view** as it gives an **objective check** on the stewardship of the directors.

1.4 Annual general meeting (AGM)

> **FAST FORWARD**
> At the AGM the shareholders can exercise their **ultimate control**.

The AGM is the **key shareholder meeting** for a **public company**. It gives **shareholders** an opportunity to **conduct dialogue with directors and to be heard by them**. There is also some **routine business** carried out at an AGM. For example, it is the meeting at which the financial statements are presented to the shareholders and the meeting at which directors and auditors are re-elected.

Although directors make day-to-day management decisions for the company, **shareholders retain control of the major company policy at company meetings**. Certain **key decisions and capabilities**, such as amending the object of the company or authorising additional share capital, are **retained by shareholders in general meetings**.

Despite the legal protection of the AGM for shareholders of public companies, they are often poorly attended by shareholders. Also, where shareholders invest in the largest of companies, there is often **apathy amongst shareholders** about decisions taken by management. This **reduces the effectiveness** of the statutory protection to shareholders given by the AGM and **can expose the company to poor management, and even fraud**.

1.5 Voluntary codes of corporate governance

> **FAST FORWARD**
> Following high-profile corporate failures, corporate governance codes set out **best practice**.

Although these interrelated issues have always been of concern in the way companies function, increased attention to corporate governance is a result of perceived **weaknesses** in company regulation. These became apparent from 2000 in notorious **scandals** involving large companies such as Enron and Worldcom in the US, and Marconi and Parmalat in Europe, and to some extent in the global financial crisis of 2008 and its aftermath.

In order to ensure an **effective corporate governance framework** it has been deemed necessary to set out defined rules and regulations, including voluntary codes. The UK **Corporate Governance Code** is the result of a number of reports into corporate governance since the 1990s. The various reports were amalgamated into the **Combined Code** in 1998, but in 2010 it was revised again and renamed the **UK Corporate Governance Code**, and it was subsequently updated in 2012 and 2014. The rules of this Code apply to listed companies by virtue not directly of statute but of the requirements of the UK Listing Authority's Disclosure Rules and Transparency Rules. Other companies are encouraged to follow the Code as well, as an example of best practice.

Listed companies (on the FTSE 100 or FTSE 350 indices of the Main Market of the London Stock Exchange) have either to confirm that they **comply** with the Code's provisions or, where they do not, to **provide an explanation** of their non-compliance.

Whilst listed companies are expected to comply with the Code's provisions most of the time, it is recognised that departure from its provisions may be justified in particular circumstances. Every listed company must review each provision carefully and give a considered explanation if it departs from the Code provisions.

1.5.1 Voluntary or prescriptive?

A feature of the UK Corporate Governance Code is that it is for many an entirely voluntary, 'extra-legal' code. As a condition of listing in the FTSE 350, a large company is required to apply the Code's main principles, and to include in their annual reports a **corporate governance statement** of compliance with the supporting principles and provisions of the Code, or an explanation of non-compliance (the 'comply or explain' basis). For smaller listed companies, for instance those on the Alternative Investment Market or AIM, there is more flexibility. For most companies the Code is a useful example of best practice, but its application is entirely voluntary.

An alternative approach would be for governments to make such corporate governance requirements **mandatory** for all companies. This approach is often shunned. Arguments in favour of keeping codes primarily voluntary include:

(a) The fact that all companies are different and the make-up of their stakeholders is different means that statutory standards might be **inflexible**. The **additional costs** and regulatory burdens **might not be** justified in all cases.

(b) In such cases, the result might be detrimental to shareholders (in terms of cost) who are the key stakeholders the regulation is seeking to protect.

(c) Statutory monitoring of compliance would be required, which again could add to the burden for the company.

(d) Some of the requirements of the codes are **subjective** (for example, in relation to non-executive directors) and it would be difficult to prescribe regulations in respect of them.

While codes are not mandatory, or legally required, they are **heavily encouraged**, particularly for listed companies, and **companies not complying with such requirements may find that they suffer in investment markets as a result**.

Question — Good corporate governance

Why is good corporate governance important?

Answer

Shareholders and managers are usually separate in a company and it is important that the management of a company deals fairly with the investment made by the owners.

2 Governance structures

FAST FORWARD

Whether their status is down to **voluntary** or **statutory** rules, there are certain aspects of governance, or 'governance structures', which are generally acceptable.

2.1 The split between executive and non-executive directors

One of the best forms of internal control is the **segregation of duties**, separating the roles of directors into those who have **executive** powers (the power to **manage** the company) and those who have **non-executive** powers (the power to **direct** and **control** the company).

PART C ADMINISTRATION AND CONTROL

2.2 Unitary board of directors

> **FAST FORWARD**
>
> Many companies have a **unitary board** system, where there is one board to run a company.

The UK and many other countries, including the US, follow a **single**, sometimes called a **unitary**, **board** structure. This is where the company is **managed by a single board of directors**.

This board may be formed of executive directors only, or a mixture of executive and non-executive directors. The UK Corporate Governance Code, which we shall look at shortly, gives significant guidance about the **composition of unitary boards**.

We shall consider the **advantages and disadvantages** of a unitary board structure later, as it will be easier to see the advantages and disadvantages in comparison to the other major type of board structure, used internationally, the supervisory board structure.

2.2.1 Composition of the unitary board

There are **very few legal requirements** relating to the composition of a unitary board. As we have discussed above, there are requirements concerning the **number of directors** a company has and there are requirements concerning **quorum**. There are also requirements about **who is allowed to be a director**. The law is otherwise silent on the composition of the board.

2.3 Supervisory board structure

> **FAST FORWARD**
>
> In Germany and some other countries, a supervisory (or dual) board system is used. This means that there is a **management board to run the company** plus a **supervisory board to oversee** the management board.

Some countries, notably **Germany** and **Holland**, use a different board structure to the UK. The type of board structure used in Germany, is known as the **supervisory board structure**, sometimes called the **two-tier or dual system**.

The supervisory board system involves the use of two boards, **management** and **supervisory**. The management board is loosely comparable to the UK unitary board, and it has general responsibility to **manage** the company. The supervisory board is an **independent, separate board**.

2.3.1 Composition of the supervisory board

The supervisory board consists of **members elected by the shareholders and by employees of the company**. Usually, a third of the board is elected by the employees and the remainder by the shareholders. If the company has more than a certain number of employees, half the members of the board must be representatives of the employees of the company.

2.3.2 Role of the supervisory board

The **supervisory board** has an advisory role in relation to the business. It has the following key powers:

- Appoints members of the management board
- May request information from members of the management board
- Must be formally reported to about matters of policy
- Must be formally reported to about profit and loss
- Must be formally reported to about the state of the company's affairs
- Must be formally reported to in exceptional circumstances
- Approves the financial statements and dividends
- Inspects the books and accounts
- May set up committees and delegate jobs to them
- May initiate independent investigations
- May convene shareholder meetings
- May remove management board members (as a last resort and on legitimate grounds)

However, this power is limited in that it does not have power to manage the company, only to **supervise the managers**. It is not entitled to make **policy decisions** and cannot represent the company in **legal action**.

2.4 Unitary board and supervisory board compared

FAST FORWARD

In practice, the principles of **independence** and **verification** behind both the **unitary** and the **dual systems** are increasingly growing closer. Both systems face **similar problems** in terms of finding **suitably qualified people** to undertake supervisory roles and to be an **independent** voice in a company.

2.5 Advantages of the unitary board structure

The fact that all participants in the management of the company are given responsibility for management of the company suggests a **more involved approach** by those directors who are non-executive directors and therefore act in an independent and 'supervisory' capacity.

If all the directors attend the same meetings, the **independent directors are less likely to be effectively excluded from decision-making and given restricted access to information**. The **presence of non-executive directors** to question the actions and decisions of executive directors as they are taking place **should lead to better decisions being made**.

2.5.1 Criticisms of the unitary board structure

Asking an 'external' or 'independent' director to be **both manager and supervisor** may be **too awkward and demanding a task**.

Criticism has also been made of the requirement to have as many **independent non-executive directors** as **executive directors** on the board. Who are these non-executive directors? Where are people with such expertise and time-availability to be found?

The criticism is intensified when the **independence requirement** is considered. It raises questions such as: How can people who fulfil the independence requirement be expected to have sufficient knowledge about the company to properly fulfil their management capacity?

The supervisory board system takes account of the needs of stakeholders other than shareholders, specifically **employees**, who are clearly important stakeholders in practice. The unitary board system makes no specific provision for employees to be represented on the management board, other than by the people who employ them.

The unitary board **emphasises the divide between the shareholders and the directors** as there is no crossover between them. It **puts pressure on the annual general meeting** as the only place where shareholder grievance or concern can be heard.

2.5.2 Advantages of the supervisory board structure

The formal supervisory role given to the members of this board has the **capacity** to be an **effective guard** against management inefficiency or worse. Indeed its very existence may be a **deterrent** to fraud or irregularity in a similar way to the independent audit.

The system actively **encourages transparency within the company**, between the boards and, through the supervisory board, to the employees and the shareholders. This is in sharp contrast to the closed doors policy of UK boards.

It also **actively involves the shareholders and employees** in the supervision and appointment of directors.

2.5.3 Criticisms of the supervisory board structure

The main criticism of the system centres around the fact that in practice, the supervisory board may not be as effective as it seems in theory:

- The **management board may restrict the information passed on** to the supervisory board.
- In practice, the boards may only liaise **infrequently**.

The supervisory board may not be as **independent** as would be wished, depending on how rigorous the appointment procedures are. In addition, members of the supervisory board can be shareholder representatives, and this could detract from the legal requirement that shareholders should not instruct directors how to manage.

2.5.4 Board committees

Whether a unitary or a supervisory board system is used, the effective operation of the board is often facilitated by the creation of **board committees**. Authority of the board as a whole is delegated to these committees with respect to certain defined areas, such as audit, directors' remuneration and nominations/appointments to the board.

3 The UK Corporate Governance Code

Guidance on corporate governance in the UK is given in the UK **Corporate Governance Code**. This code contains principles and supporting provisions which should be followed by listed companies. Where the rules have not been followed, this should be explained in the financial statements.

We shall now briefly look at the principles of the **UK Corporate Governance Code** (FRC, 2018) which are grouped into five areas.

3.1 Board leadership and company purpose

3.1.1 Principles

A successful company is led by an effective and entrepreneurial board, whose role is to promote the long-term sustainable success of the company, generating value for shareholders and contributing to wider society.

The board should establish the company's purpose, values and strategy, and satisfy itself that these and its culture are aligned. All directors must act with integrity, lead by example and promote the desired culture.

The board should ensure that the necessary resources are in place for the company to meet its objectives and measure performance against them. The board should also establish a framework of prudent and effective controls, which enable risk to be assessed and managed.

In order for the company to meet its responsibilities to shareholders and stakeholders, the board should ensure effective engagement with, and encourage participation from, these parties.

The board should ensure that workforce policies and practices are consistent with the company's values and support its long-term sustainable success. The workforce should be able to raise any matters of concern.

3.2 Division of responsibilities

3.2.1 Principles

The chair leads the board and is responsible for its overall effectiveness in directing the company. They should demonstrate objective judgement throughout their tenure and promote a culture of openness and debate. In addition, the chair facilitates constructive board relations and the effective contribution of all non-executive directors, and ensures that directors receive accurate, timely and clear information.

The board should include an appropriate combination of executive and non-executive (and, in particular, independent non-executive) directors, such that no one individual or small group of individuals dominates the board's decision-making. There should be a clear division of responsibilities between the leadership of the board and the executive leadership of the company's business.

Non-executive directors should have sufficient time to meet their board responsibilities. They should provide constructive challenge, strategic guidance, offer specialist advice and hold management to account.

The board, supported by the company secretary, should ensure that it has the policies, processes, information, time and resources it needs in order to function effectively and efficiently.

3.3 Composition, succession and evaluation

3.3.1 Principles

Appointments to the board should be subject to a formal, rigorous and transparent procedure, and an effective succession plan should be maintained for board and senior management. Both appointments and succession plans should be based on merit and objective criteria and, within this context, should promote diversity of gender, social and ethnic backgrounds, cognitive and personal strengths.

The board and its committees should have a combination of skills, experience and knowledge. Consideration should be given to the length of service of the board as a whole and membership regularly refreshed.

Annual evaluation of the board should consider its composition, diversity and how effectively members work together to achieve objectives. Individual evaluation should demonstrate whether each director continues to contribute effectively.

3.4 Audit, risk and internal control

3.4.1 Principles

The board should establish formal and transparent policies and procedures to ensure the independence and effectiveness of internal and external audit functions and satisfy itself on the integrity of financial and narrative statements.

The board should present a fair, balanced and understandable assessment of the company's position and prospects.

The board should establish procedures to manage risk, oversee the internal control framework, and determine the nature and extent of the principal risks the company is willing to take in order to achieve its long-term strategic objectives.

3.5 Remuneration

3.5.1 Principles

Remuneration policies and practices should be designed to support strategy and promote long-term sustainable success. Executive remuneration should be aligned to company purpose and values, and be clearly linked to the successful delivery of the company's long-term strategy.

A formal and transparent procedure for developing policy on executive remuneration and determining director and senior management remuneration should be established. No director should be involved in deciding their own remuneration outcome.

Directors should exercise independent judgement and discretion when authorising remuneration outcomes, taking account of company and individual performance, and wider circumstances.

Exam focus point

Exam questions are likely to focus on the key principles of the Code rather than the tiny details.

3.6 Compliance with the Code

The **UK Corporate Governance Code** requires listed companies (and encourages others) to include in their accounts:

(a) A narrative statement of how they **applied** the **principles** set out in the UK Corporate Governance Code. This should provide explanations which enable their shareholders to assess how the principles have been applied.

(b) A statement as to whether or not they **complied throughout** the **accounting period** with the provisions set out in the UK Corporate Governance Code. Listed companies that did not comply throughout the accounting period with all the provisions must **specify the provisions with which they did not comply**, and give **reasons** for **non-compliance**.

4 Legal regulation of corporate governance

> **FAST FORWARD**
>
> Much of the law we have studied so far has involved to some extent the **regulation** of corporate governance through statute.

Other than aspects of the Companies Act there is currently **no legal regulation** of corporate governance in the UK that is comparable to the UK Corporate Governance Code. However you have already studied aspects of the Companies Act aimed at tightening up corporate governance. These are summarised below.

4.1 Company law

Some provisions of the Companies Act 2006 (TSO, 2006) cover the same or similar ground as the UK Corporate Governance Code.

(a) **Members' agreement** is required for directors' notice periods under service contracts of more than two years. In the UK Corporate Governance Code, any such period longer than one year initially must reduce quickly to one year or less.

(b) A general meeting is required to remove an auditor or a director.

(c) At least 21 days' notice must be given to shareholders of a listed company's AGM.

(d) Listed companies can put the results of a poll at a meeting on their **websites**.

In terms of **clarifying relations** between directors, shareholders and auditor, the Companies Act also seeks to support good corporate governance in quoted companies by:

(a) **Ensuring** that a **company's constitution** is contained just in the articles plus company resolutions. There are different model articles available for different types of company so this should help to avoid confusion.

(b) Providing that company directors must be at least 16 years of age.

(c) Providing that companies must have at least one natural person as a director.

(d) Codifying directors' duties to their company.

(e) Revising and clarifying rules on loans to directors.

(f) Making directors' service agreements available to members.

(g) Extending and clarifying the definition of the people a director is deemed to be 'connected' to.

(h) Clarifying the procedure by which members may bring actions against a director or former director for breach of duty.

(i) Allowing shareholders with at least 5% of a company's shares to call for an independent report on a poll vote.

(j) Requiring auditors to disclose fees paid for non-audit services.

(k) Allowing the auditor of a listed company to **report** on the reasons for their resignation.

4.2 Other regulation of corporate behaviour

FAST FORWARD

The Financial Conduct Authority (FCA) is part of the system of regulation **of the financial services industry, company markets** and **share exchanges** in the UK.

In the UK, regulation of corporate behaviour is effected through a regime consisting of:

- The Financial Policy Committee of the Bank of England.
- The Prudential Regulation Authority, which aims to support the soundness of financial services firms so as to ensure the stability of the UK's financial system as a whole.
- The Financial Conduct Authority (FCA), which regulates the conduct of individual firms in financial services, plus company markets and share exchanges in the UK.

The FCA is **not a government agency**. It is a private company limited by guarantee and is financed by the financial services industry.

The FCA incorporates the **UK Listing Authority** (UKLA). This means that it supervises the rules which listed companies are required to follow. We are also interested in the role the FCA and government agencies play in relation to **company investigations**, particularly regarding **market abuse, insider dealing** and **money laundering**.

4.3 Company investigations

FAST FORWARD

The FCA has a wide remit to monitor companies and market participants with respect to offences such as **money laundering** and **insider dealing**, and to protect markets against **market abuse**.

The FCA regulates and if necessary investigates relevant financial services firms in relation to:

- Market abuse
- Breaches of the Listing Rules
- Misleading adverts, statements and practices
- Money laundering
- Insider dealing
- Regulatory failure

It **shares power** to investigate companies with the Department for Business, Innovation and Skills and other government agencies, which also carry out investigations in relation to both trading companies and the **liquidation of companies**.

Exam focus point

Exam questions often focus on the offences of insider dealing and money laundering which we shall look at in the final chapter of this Study Text.

4.4 Market abuse

FAST FORWARD

Market abuse relates to behaviour which amounts to abuse of a person's position regarding the stock market. Market abuse in relation to qualifying investments is a crime.

The main source of regulation of market abuse is the EU Market Abuse Regulation (MAR) which seeks to increase market integrity and create a common rulebook across Europe. It extended the existing UK rules under the Financial Services and Markets Act 2000 (TSO, 2000) to a wider range of financial instruments, although the actual rules on market abuse are very similar to existing legislation.

4.4.1 Market abuse offences

The **Market Abuse Regulations** apply to activities conducted over regulated markets and other organised trading facilities both inside and outside of the EU. The following **market abuse offences** were created:

- **To engage or attempt to engage in insider dealing** – when an insider deals, or tries to deal, on the basis of inside information. For example, this would include knowingly buying shares in a takeover target before a general disclosure of the proposed takeover.

- **To recommend or induce another party to engage or attempt to engage in insider dealing** – simply where one party seeks to convince another to commit an insider dealing offence.

- **To unlawfully disclose inside information** – where an insider improperly discloses inside information to another person. However, the regulations provide for a "market soundings" safe harbour protection that allow disclosures to potential investors in order to gauge their interest in a possible investment (for example in regards to investment size or price).

- **To engage or attempt to engage in "market manipulation"**. Market manipulation may take many forms. The following examples (taken from existing UK legislation) are indicative of the types of activity that would be covered by this offence.

Activity	Description
Misuse of information	Behaviour based on information that is not generally available but would affect an investor's decision about the terms on which to deal.
Manipulating transactions	Trading, or placing orders to trade, that gives a false or misleading impression of the supply of, or demand for, one or more investments, raising the price of the investment to an abnormal or artificial level.
Manipulating devices	Trading, or placing orders to trade, which employs fictitious devices or any other form of deception or contrivance.
Dissemination	Giving out information that conveys a false or misleading impression about an investment or the issuer of an investment where the person doing this knows the information to be false or misleading.
Distortion and misleading behaviour	Behaviour that gives a false or misleading impression of either the supply of, or demand for, an investment; or behaviour that otherwise distorts the market in an investment. An example of such distortion might be dealing on an exchange just prior to the exchange closing with the purpose of positioning the share price at a distorted level in order to avoid having to pay out on a derivatives transaction. An example of misleading behaviour might be posting an inaccurate story on an internet bulletin board.
Manipulation of benchmarks	Making of a false or misleading statement, or the creation of a false or misleading impression, in connection with the setting of a relevant benchmark.

4.5 The Sarbanes-Oxley Act 2002

The some jurisdictions, most notably the **US**, the approach taken to corporate governance has been overwhelming statutory rather than being based on extra-legal codes of practice. In 2002 the Public Company Accounting Reform and Investor Protection Act, commonly called **Sarbanes-Oxley, SOX** or **SarbOx**, was passed in response to several major failures of corporate governance and accounting, including Enron and WorldCom, which led to a serious loss of public trust in accounting and reporting practices in particular.

The most common transgressions of good corporate governance in the US before SarBox can be identified as follows:

- Directors' remuneration being grossly disproportionate to the company's results.
- Promotion of share issues on the basis of questionable or unproven business concepts.
- Misuse of company funds.
- Insider dealing in company shares, particularly by managers exercising share options that reward short-termism (that is, acting to achieve good results in the short term at the expense of long-term success).
- Misrepresentation of the true earnings and financial contribution of some companies.
- Obstructing justice by concealing activities or destroying evidence.

The people who could be identified as being to blame for these transgressions were:

- Passive, non-independent boards of directors.
- Chief executives and senior managers with serious conflicts of interest between their own and their company's interests.
- Biased and non-independent investment analysts and fund managers.
- Non-independent audit firms.
- Regulators not paying enough attention to the systemic conflicts of interest at the core of poor corporate governance.

The core problem was that non-performing managers, directors and auditors, acting in a **fiduciary position** as agents, were not being held accountable to the shareholders as principals. Corporate governance should aim to guarantee performance excellence by management and the board of directors when performing their agency duties for shareholders, in particular by avoiding conflicts of interest.

The Act established **new** or **enhanced standards** for all US public company boards and senior managers, and for audit firms.

The Act:

- Established a new quasi-public agency, the Public Company Accounting Oversight Board (PCAOB).
- Required that public companies evaluate and disclose the effectiveness of their internal controls as they relate to financial reporting in the form of an internal control report.
- Required that independent auditors for public companies 'attest' or agree to such disclosure.
- Required that certain financial information concerning material changes in the company's financial condition or operations should be disclosed more quickly.
- Required that financial reports should be personally certified by chief executive officers (CEOs) and chief financial officers (CFOs) as being free from misrepresentation.
- Banned external auditors from undertaking certain types of work for audit clients.
- Required the company's audit committee to pre-certify all other types of non-audit work to be undertaken by the external audit firm.

- Required that companies listed on stock exchanges should have fully independent audit committees overseeing the relationship between the company and its auditor.
- Banned most personal loans to any executive officer or director.
- Accelerated reporting of dealing by insiders.
- Prohibited deals by insiders during certain reporting periods.
- Enhanced criminal and civil penalties for violations of the law on share issues.
- Enhanced criminal penalties for altering, destroying, mutilating or concealing any document with the intent of impairing its use in an official proceeding.
- Set longer maximum jail sentences and larger fines for executives who knowingly and wilfully misstate financial statements.
- Protected employees who 'blow the whistle' on problems in the company, allowing corporate fraud whistleblowers to be compensated for loss of office and so on.
- Allowed for clawback of executive compensation where there has been misconduct.

Chapter roundup

- Corporate governance is simply a term used for **the way that companies** (corporate) **are managed** (governed).
- There are many different **stakeholders** in most companies.
- The stakeholders most closely involved in corporate governance are the **directors** (the managers of the company) and the **shareholders** (who have some ultimate controls in general meeting).
- Directors must prepare **financial statements** for shareholders annually, and these are independently audited to provide an objective check on the directors.
- At the AGM the shareholders can exercise their **ultimate control**.
- Following high-profile corporate failures, corporate governance codes set out **best practice**.
- Whether their status is down to **voluntary** or **statutory** rules, there are certain aspects of governance, or 'governance structures', which are generally acceptable.
- Many companies have a **unitary board** system, where there is one board to run a company.
- In Germany and some other countries, a supervisory (or dual) board system is used. This means that there is a **management board to run the company** plus a **supervisory board to oversee** the management board.
- In practice, the principles of **independence** and **verification** behind both the **unitary** and the **dual systems** are increasingly growing closer. Both systems face **similar problems** in terms of finding **suitably qualified people** to undertake supervisory roles and to be an **independent** voice in a company.
- Guidance on corporate governance in the UK is given in the UK **Corporate Governance Code**. This code contains principles and supporting provisions which should be followed by listed companies. Where the rules have not been followed, this should be explained in the financial statements.
- Much of the law we have studied so far has involved to some extent the **regulation** of corporate governance through statute.
- The Financial Conduct Authority (FCA) is one of the **regulators of the financial services industry, company markets** and **share exchanges** in the UK.
- The FCA has a wide remit to monitor companies and market participants with respect to offences, such as **money laundering**, **insider dealing** and to protect markets against **market abuse**.
- **Market abuse** relates to behaviour which amounts to abuse of a person's position regarding the stock market. Market abuse in relation to qualifying investments is a crime.

PART C   ADMINISTRATION AND CONTROL

Quick quiz

1. Complete the definition.

   The system by which companies are directed or controlled is the definition of ....

2. Which of the following criteria might indicate that a director was not independent?

   - Being an employee of the group in the previous five years
   - Being a qualified accountant
   - Having been employed by the company's audit firm 10 years ago
   - Representing a significant shareholder
   - Having served on the board for six years

3. Name three criticisms of the unitary board approach.

   (1) ....

   (2) ....

   (3) ....

4. According to the UK Corporate Governance Code, executive remuneration should be aligned to:

   (1) ....

   (2) ....

7: CORPORATE GOVERNANCE

Answers to quick quiz

1 Corporate governance.

2 Being an employee in the last five years, representing a significant shareholder.

3 (1) Being both a manager and a supervisor is too awkward a task for non-executives
   (2) The independence criteria is too difficult to meet
   (3) The system does not properly account for representing the needs of employees

4 Executive remuneration should be aligned to:

   (1) Company purpose
   (2) Company values

End of chapter question

Boards

In the context of company law, explain:

(a)	Non-executive director	**(2 marks)**
(b)	Executive director	**(2 marks)**
(c)	Single board	**(3 marks)**
(d)	Supervisory board	**(3 marks)**
		(Total = 10 marks)

PART C ADMINISTRATION AND CONTROL

Meetings and resolutions

Topic list	Syllabus reference
1 The importance of meetings	8.3
2 General meetings	8.3
3 Types of resolution	8.3
4 Calling a general meeting	8.3
5 Proceedings at meetings	8.3
6 Class meetings	8.3
7 Single member private companies	8.3

Introduction

In this chapter we consider the **procedures** by which companies are controlled by the shareholders, namely general meetings and resolutions. These afford members a measure of protection of their investment in the company. There are many transactions which, under the Act, cannot be entered into without a **resolution** of the company.

Moreover, a general meeting at which the annual accounts and the auditors' and directors' reports will be laid must normally be held by public companies annually. This affords the members an opportunity of questioning the directors on their **stewardship**.

The **Companies Act 2006**, (TSO, 2006) and the **Small Business, Enterprise and Employment Act 2015**, (TSO, 2015) apply to this and all chapters unless otherwise stated.

1 The importance of meetings

> **FAST FORWARD**
>
> Although the management of a company is in the hands of the directors, the **decisions which affect the existence of the company**, its structure and scope are **reserved to the members** in general meeting.

Under the Companies Act 2006 (TSO, 2006), the decision of a general meeting is only valid and binding if the meeting is **properly convened** by notice and if the **business** of the meeting is **fairly** and **properly conducted**. Most of the rules on company meetings are concerned with the issue of notices and the casting of votes at meetings to carry resolutions of specified types.

1.1 Control over directors

The members in general meeting can exercise control over the directors, though only to a limited extent.

(a) Under normal procedure **one third** of the **directors retire** at each annual general meeting though they may offer themselves for re-election. The company may remove directors from office by **ordinary resolution**: s 168. (Note that the UK Corporate Governance Code is more onerous: it requires **all** directors of listed companies to be re-elected **every** year.)

(b) Member approval in general meeting is required if the directors wish to:
   (i) **Exceed their delegated power** or to use it for other than its given purpose.
   (ii) **Allot shares** (unless private company with one class of shares).
   (iii) **Make a substantial contract** of sale or purchase with a director.
   (iv) Grant a director a **long-service agreement**.

(c) The **appointment and removal of auditors** is done in general meeting.

1.2 Resolution of differences

In addition, general meetings are the means by which **members resolve differences** between themselves by voting on resolutions.

2 General meetings

> **FAST FORWARD**
>
> There are two kinds of general meeting of members of a company:
> - Annual general meeting (AGM)
> - General meetings at other times

2.1 Annual general meeting (AGM)

The **AGM** plays a major role in the life of a public company although often the business carried out seems fairly routine. It is a statutorily protected way for members to have a regular assessment and discussion of their company and its management.

Under the Companies Act 2006 (TSO, 2006), **private companies** are **not required** to have an **AGM** each year and therefore their business is usually conducted through **written resolutions**. However, members holding sufficient shares or votes can request a general meeting or written resolution.

8: MEETINGS AND RESOLUTIONS

Rules for directors calling an AGM	
Timing s 336	• Public companies must hold an AGM within **six months** of their year end.
Notice s 337	• Must be in **writing** and in **accordance** with the **articles**. • May be in **hard** or **electronic form** and may also by means of a **website** (s 308). • At least **21 days' notice** should be given; a longer period may be specified in the articles. • Shorter notice is only **valid** if all members agree. • The notice must specify the **time**, **date** and **place** of the meeting and that the meeting is an AGM. • Where notice is given on a **website** it must be available from the **date of notification** until the **conclusion of the meeting** (s 309).

The business of an annual general meeting usually includes:

- Considering the accounts
- Receiving the directors' report, the directors' remuneration report and the auditors' report
- Dividends
- Electing directors
- Appointing auditors

2.2 General meetings at other times

2.2.1 Directors

The **directors** may have power under the articles to convene a general meeting whenever they see fit.

2.2.2 Members

The directors of **public and private** companies may be required to convene a general meeting by **requisition of the members:** s 303.

Rules for members requisitioning a general meeting (s 303)	
Shareholding	• The requisitioning members must hold at least **5%** of the **paid up share capital** holding **voting rights**.
Requisition	• They must deposit a **signed requisition** at the registered office or make the request in electronic form. • This must state the 'objects of the meeting': the **resolutions proposed** (s 303(4)).
Date	• A notice conveying the meeting must be sent out within **21 days** of the requisition. • It must be held within **28 days** of the notice calling to a meeting being sent out. • If the directors have not called the meeting within 21 days of the requisition, the **members may convene** the meeting for a date within three months of the deposit of the requisition.
Quorum	• If **no quorum** is present, the meeting is **adjourned**.

2.2.3 Court order

The court, on the application of a director or a member entitled to vote, may order that a meeting shall be held and may give instructions for that purpose including fixing a quorum of one: s 306.

This is a method of last resort to resolve a deadlock such as the refusal of one member out of two to attend (and provide a quorum) at a general meeting.

2.2.4 Auditor requisition

An auditor who gives a statement of circumstances for their resignation or other loss of office in their written notice may also requisition a meeting to receive and consider their explanation: s 518.

2.2.5 Loss of capital by public company

The directors of a public company must convene a general meeting if the net assets fall to half or less of the amount of its called-up share capital: s 656.

3 Types of resolution

FAST FORWARD

A meeting can pass two types of resolution. **Ordinary resolutions** are carried by a simple majority (more than 50%) of votes cast and require 14 days' notice to be given to members. **Special resolutions** require a 75% majority of votes cast and also 14 days' notice to members.

Under the Companies Act 2006 (TSO, 2006), a meeting reaches a decision by passing a resolution (either by a show of hands or a poll). There are **two major kinds** of resolution, and an additional one for **private** companies.

Types of resolution	
Ordinary (s 282)	For most business. Requires simple (50%+) majority of the votes cast by those entitled to vote. 14 days' notice.
Special (s 283)	For major changes. Requires 75% majority of the votes cast by those entitled to vote. 14 days' notice.
Written (for private companies)	Can be used for all general meeting resolutions except for removing a director or auditor before their term of office expires. Either a simple (50%+) or 75% majority of total voting rights of eligible members is required depending on the business being passed.

3.1 Differences between ordinary and special resolutions

Apart from the required size of the majority, the main differences between the types of resolution are as follows.

(a) The **text** of **special resolutions** must be **set out** in **full** in the notice convening the meeting, and it must be described as a special resolution. This is not necessary for an ordinary resolution if it is routine business.

(b) A **signed copy** of every **special resolution** must be **delivered** to the **Registrar** for filing. Although **some ordinary resolutions**, particularly those relating to share capital, have to be **delivered** for filing, many do not.

3.2 Special resolutions

A special resolution is required for **major changes** in the company such as the following.

- A change of name
- Restriction of the objects or other alteration of the articles
- Reduction of share capital
- Winding up the company
- Presenting a petition by the company for an order for a compulsory winding up

Question — Notice period

The period of notice for a general meeting (not an AGM) at which a special resolution is proposed is:

A 14 days
B 21 days
C 28 days
D 42 days

Answer

A A general meeting at which a special resolution is proposed requires 14 days' notice.

3.3 Written resolutions

FAST FORWARD

A private company can pass any decision needed by a **written resolution**, except for removing a director or auditor before their term of office has expired.

As we saw earlier, a private company is **not** required to hold an **AGM**. Therefore the Act provides a mechanism for directors and members to conduct business solely by **written resolution**.

3.3.1 Written resolutions proposed by directors

Copies of the resolution proposed by directors must be sent to **each member** eligible to vote by hard copy, electronically or by a website. Alternatively, the same copy may be sent to each member in turn.

The resolution should be accompanied by a statement informing the member:

- How to **signify their agreement** to the resolution.
- The **date** the resolution must be passed by.

3.3.2 Written resolutions proposed by members

Members holding 5% (or lower if authorised by the articles) of the **voting rights** may request a written resolution providing it:

- **Would be effective** (not prevented by the articles or law).
- Is **not defamatory, frivolous** or **vexatious**.

A **statement** containing no more than **1,000 words** on the subject of the resolution may accompany it.

Copies of the resolution, and statements containing information on the subject matter, how to agree to it and the date of the resolution must be sent to each member within **21 days** of the request for resolution.

Expenses for circulating the resolution **should be met by the members** who requested it unless the company resolves otherwise.

The company may **appeal to the court** not to circulate the 1,000 word statement by the members if the rights provided to the members are being abused by them.

3.3.3 Agreement

The members may indicate their agreement to the resolution in **hard copy** or **electronically**.

If no **period for agreement** is specified by the articles, then the default period is **28 days** from the date the resolution was circulated. Agreement after this period is ineffective.

Once agreed, a member **may not revoke** their decision.

PART C ADMINISTRATION AND CONTROL

Either a **simple** (50%+) or **75% majority** is required to pass a written resolution depending on the nature of the business being decided.

Three further points should be noted concerning written resolutions.

(a) Written resolutions can be used **notwithstanding any provisions** in the company's **articles**.

(b) A written resolution **cannot** be **used to remove a director or auditor** from office, since such persons have a right to **speak** at a **meeting**.

(c) **Copies of written resolutions** should be **sent to auditors** at or before the time they are sent to shareholders. Auditors do not have the right to object to written resolutions. If the auditors are not sent a copy, the resolution remains valid; however the directors and secretary will be liable to a fine. The purpose of this provision is to ensure auditors are kept informed about what is happening in the company.

Question
Resolutions

Briefly explain the main features of the following types of resolution which may be passed at a general meeting of a company:

(a) An ordinary resolution
(b) A special resolution

Answer

(a) Ordinary resolutions require a simple majority of votes cast (ie over 50%). 14 days' notice is sufficient. Ordinary resolutions of a routine nature need not be set out in full in the notice of an annual general meeting, and most ordinary resolutions need not be filed with the Registrar.

(b) Special resolutions require a 75% majority of votes cast and also require 14 days' notice of the intention to propose such a resolution. The full text of the resolution should be set out in the notice.

4 Calling a general meeting

FAST FORWARD

A meeting cannot make valid and binding decisions until it has been properly convened. Notice of general meetings must be given at least **14 days** in advance of the meeting. The notice should contain **adequate information** about the meeting.

Meetings must be called by a **competent person** or authority.

Under the Companies Act 2006 (TSO, 2006), a meeting cannot make valid and binding decisions until it has been properly convened according to the company's articles, though there are also statutory rules.

(a) The meeting must generally be **called by** the **board of directors** or other competent person or authority.

(b) The notice must be issued to members in advance of the meeting so as to give them **14 days'** 'clear notice' of the meeting. The members may agree to waive or increase this requirement (see below).

(c) The **notice** must be sent to every member (or other person) entitled to receive the notice.

(d) The notice must include any information **reasonably necessary** to enable shareholders to know in advance what is to be done.

(e) As we saw earlier members may require the directors to call a meeting if:

(i) They hold at least **5% of the voting rights**.

(ii) They provide a **statement of the general business** to be conducted and the text of any proposed resolution.

The directors must within **21 days call a meeting** to be held no later than **28 days from the date of the notice** they send calling the meeting.

An example of a rule in the articles as opposed to statute is contained in Table A article 38, which states that 21 days' notice must be given of a general meeting called for the purpose of considering the board's appointment of a director, or at which a special resolution is being considered.

In most cases the notice need **not** be sent to a member whose only shares do not give him a right to attend and vote (as is often the position of **preference shareholders**).

4.1 Electronic communication

We have already seen that **notice** may be given by means of a **website** and in **electronic form** (s 308). Section 333 extends this by deeming that where a company gives an **electronic address** in a notice calling a meeting, any information or document relating to the meeting may be sent to that address.

4.2 Timing of notices

> **FAST FORWARD** — **Clear notice** must be given to members. **Notice** must be **sent to all members** entitled to receive it.

Members may – and in small private companies often do – waive the required notice. For **short notice** to be effective:

(a) **All members** of a public company must consent in respect of an **AGM**.
(b) In **any other case**, a **majority of members** in a private company who hold at least **90%** of the **issued shares** or voting rights must consent. 95% is required by a public company: s 307.

The following specific rules by way of exception should be remembered.

- When **special notice** of a resolution is given to the company in the two circumstances mentioned in Section 4.3 below, it must be given **28 days** in advance as prescribed.
- In a **creditors' voluntary winding up** there must be at least **7 days' notice** of the **creditors' meeting** (to protect the interests of creditors). The members may shorten the period of notice down to 7 days but that is all: s 98 Insolvency Act.

The **clear days rule** in s 360 provides that the day of the meeting and the day the notice was given are **excluded** from the required notice period.

4.3 Special notice of a resolution

> **FAST FORWARD** — **Special notice of 28 days** of intention to propose certain resolutions (removal of directors/auditors) must be given.

Key term — **Special notice** is notice of 28 days which must be given to a company of the intention to put certain types of resolution at a company meeting.

Special notice must be given **to the company** of the intention to propose a resolution for any of the following purposes.

- To **remove** an **auditor** or to **appoint** an **auditor other** than the **auditor** who was **appointed** at the **previous year's meeting**.
- To **remove a director from office** or to appoint a substitute in their place after removal.

A member may request a resolution to be passed at a particular meeting. In this case, the **member must give special notice** of their intention **to the company** at **least 28 days** before the date of the meeting. If, however, the company calls the meeting for a date less than 28 days after receiving the special notice that notice is deemed to have been **properly given.**

On receiving special notice a **public company may be obliged** to **include the resolution** in the **AGM notice** which it issues.

If the company gives notice to members of the resolution it does so by a **21 day notice** to them that special notice has been received and what it contains. If it is not practicable to include the matter in the notice of meeting, the company may give notice to members by newspaper advertisement or any other means permitted by the articles.

Where special notice is received of intention to propose a resolution for the removal of a director or to change the auditor, the company must send a copy to the **director** or **auditor**. This is to allow them to exercise their statutory right to defend themself by issuing a memorandum and/or addressing the meeting in person.

The essential point is that a **special notice is given to the company**; it is **not a notice from the company to members** although it will be followed (usually) by such notice.

4.4 Members requisitioning a resolution

FAST FORWARD

> **Members** rather than directors may be able to requisition resolutions. This may be achieved by requesting the directors call a meeting, or proposing a resolution to be voted on at a meeting already arranged.

The directors normally have the **right to decide** what resolutions shall be included in the notice of a meeting. However, apart from the requisition to call a general meeting, members can also take the initiative to requisition certain resolutions be considered at the AGM.

Rules for members requisitioning a resolution at the AGM	
Qualifying holding s 338	• The members must represent 5% of the voting rights, or • Be at least 100 members holding shares with an average paid up of £100, per member.
Request s 338	• Must be in hard copy or electronic form, identify the resolution and be delivered at least six weeks in advance of an AGM or other general meeting.
Statement s 314	• Members may request a statement (<1,000 words) be circulated to all members by delivering a **requisition**. Members with a qualifying holding may request a statement regarding their own resolution or any resolution proposed at the meeting. • The company must send the statement with the notice of the meeting or as soon as practicable after.

In either instance, the **requisitionists** must bear the incidental costs unless the company resolves otherwise.

Exam focus point

> The right of members to have resolutions included on the agenda of AGM or other meetings is asked frequently in law assessments. It is an **important consideration if some of the members disagree with the directors.**

4.5 Content of notices

FAST FORWARD

> The **notice** convening the meeting must give certain details. The **date, time** and **place** of the meeting, and identification of AGM and special resolutions. Sufficient information about the business to be discussed at the meeting should be provided to enable shareholders to know what is to be done.

The notice of a general meeting must contain adequate information on the following points.

(a) The **date**, **time** and **place** of the meeting must be given.
(b) An **AGM** or a **special resolution** must be described as such.
(c) Information must be given of the business of the meeting **sufficient** to enable members (in deciding whether to attend or to appoint proxies) to **understand what will be done** at the meeting.

4.5.1 Routine business

In issuing the notice of an AGM it is standard practice merely to list the **items of ordinary or routine business** to be transacted, such as the following.

- Declaration of dividends (if any)
- Election of directors
- Appointment of auditors and fixing of their remuneration

The articles usually include a requirement that members shall be informed of any intention to **propose** the **election** of a director, other than an existing director who retires by rotation and merely stands for re-election.

Question — Removal of a director

How can members remove a director from office? What is the significance of special notice in this context?

Answer

A company may by ordinary resolution remove any director from office, notwithstanding any provision to the contrary in the articles or in a contract such as a director's service agreement.

However, this procedure requires that special notice shall be given to the company at least 28 days before the meeting of the intention to propose such a resolution. Moreover, the directors are not required to include the resolution in the notice of the meeting unless the person who intends to propose it has a sufficient shareholding.

If a company receives special notice it must send a copy to the director concerned who has the right to have written representations of reasonable length circulated to members. They may also speak before the resolution is put to the vote at the meeting.

Question — General meeting

When is a public company compelled to call a general meeting?

Answer

Members of a company who hold not less than 5% of the company's paid up share capital carrying voting rights, or members representing 5% of the voting rights, may requisition the holding of a general meeting. The directors are then required within 21 days to issue a notice convening the meeting to transact the business specified in the requisition. This must be within 28 days.

An auditor who resigns giving reasons for his resignation may requisition a general meeting so that he may explain to members the circumstances of his resignation.

If the net assets of a public company are reduced to less than half in value of its called-up share capital, the directors must convene a general meeting to consider what, if any, steps should be taken.

The court has statutory power in certain circumstances to direct that a meeting shall be held.

5 Proceedings at meetings

5.1 How a meeting proceeds

> **FAST FORWARD**
> Company meetings need to be properly run if they are to be **effective** and within the **law**.

Under the Companies Act 2006 (TSO, 2006), a meeting can only reach binding decisions if:

- It has been properly **convened** by notice.
- A **quorum is present**.
- A **chairman presides**.
- The **business** is **properly transacted** and **resolutions** are **put to the vote**.

There is no obligation to allow a member to be present if their shares do not carry the right to attend and vote. However **full general meetings** and **class meetings** can be held when shareholders not entitled to vote are present.

Each **item of business** comprised in the notice should be taken separately, discussed and **put to the vote**.

Members may propose **amendments** to any resolutions proposed. The chairman should reject any amendment which is outside the limits set by the notice convening the meeting.

If the relevant business is an **ordinary resolution** it may be possible to amend the resolution's wording so as to **reduce its effect** to something less (provided that the change does not entirely alter its character). For example, an ordinary resolution authorising the directors to borrow £100,000 might be amended to substitute a limit of £50,000 (but not to increase it to £150,000 as £100,000 would have been stated in the notice).

5.2 The chairman

> **FAST FORWARD**
> The meeting should usually be chaired by the **chairman** of the board of directors. They do not necessarily have a casting vote.

The articles usually provide that the **chairman** of the board of directors **is to preside** at general meetings; in their absence another director chosen by the directors shall preside instead. In the last resort a member chosen by the members present can preside.

The chairman derives their authority from the articles and they have **no casting vote unless** the **articles give them one**. Their duties are to **maintain order** and to **deal** with the **agenda** in a methodical way so that the business of the meeting may be properly transacted.

The chairman:

- **May dissolve** or **adjourn** the **meeting** if it has become disorderly or if the members present agree.
- Must **adjourn** if the meeting **instructs** them to do so.

5.3 Quorum and proxies

> **FAST FORWARD**
> The **quorum** for meetings may be two or more (except for single member private companies). **Proxies** can attend, speak and vote on behalf of members.

Key term

> A **quorum** is the minimum number of persons required to be present at a particular type of (company) meeting. In the case of shareholders' meetings, the figure is usually two, in person or by proxy, but the articles may make other provisions.

There is a legal principle that a 'meeting means a coming together of more than one person'. Hence it follows that as a matter of law **one person generally cannot be a meeting**.

The rule that at least two persons must be present to constitute a 'meeting' does not require that both persons must be members. Every member has a **statutory right to appoint a proxy** to attend as their representative.

In theory, **ultimate control** over a company's business lies with the **members** in a **general meeting**. One would obviously conclude that a meeting involved more than one person, and indeed there is authority to that effect in *Sharp v Dawes 1876*. In this case a meeting between a lone member and the company secretary was held not to be validly constituted. It is possible, however, for a meeting of only one person to take place and we shall consider this shortly.

5.3.1 Proxies

Key term

> A **proxy** is a person appointed by a shareholder to vote on behalf of that shareholder at company meetings.

Any member of a company which has a share capital, provided they are entitled to attend and vote at a general or class meeting of the company, has a statutory right (s 324) to appoint an **agent**, called a **'proxy'**, to attend and vote for them.

Rules for appointing proxies	
Basic rule	• Any **member** may appoint a proxy. • The proxy **does not** have to be a member. • Proxies **may speak** at the meeting. • A member may **appoint more than one proxy** provided each proxy is appointed in respect of a different class of share held by the member.
Voting	• Proxies **may vote** on **poll** and on a **show of hands**. • Proxies may **demand a poll** at a meeting. • Most companies provide **two-way proxy cards** that the member can use to instruct a proxy how to vote, either for or against a resolution.
Notice	• Every notice of a meeting must **state** the member's right to a proxy. • **Notice** of a proxy appointment should be given to the company at least 48 hours before the meeting (excluding weekends and bank holidays).

Hence one member and another member's proxy may together provide the quorum (if it is fixed, as is usual, at 'two members present in person or by proxy'). However one member who is also the proxy appointed by another member cannot by themselves be a meeting, since a **minimum of two individuals** present is required.

There may, however, be a meeting attended by one person only, if:

(a) It is a **class meeting** and all the **shares** of that class are **held** by **one member**.
(b) The **court**, in exercising a power to order a general meeting to be held, **fixes** the **quorum** at one. This means that in a two-member company, a meeting can be held with one person if the other deliberately absents themself to frustrate business.
(c) The company is a **single member private company**.

The articles usually fix a **quorum** for general meetings which may be as low as two (the minimum for a meeting) but may be more – though this is unusual.

If the articles do fix a quorum of two or more persons present, the meeting lacks a quorum (it is said to be an 'inquorate' meeting) if either:

- The **required number** is **not present** within a **stipulated time** (usually half an hour) of the appointed time for commencing a meeting.
- The **meeting begins** with a **quorum** but the **number present dwindles** to less than the quorum – unless the articles provide for this possibility.

The articles usually provide for automatic and compulsory **adjournment of an inquorate meeting**.

The articles can provide that a meeting which begins with a quorum may continue despite a reduction in numbers present to less than the quorum level. However, there must still be **two or more persons present**.

5.4 Voting and polls

FAST FORWARD

Voting at general meetings may be on a **show of hands** or a **poll**.

The **rights of members** to **vote** and the **number of votes** to which they are entitled in respect of their shares are fixed by the **articles**.

One vote per share is normal but some shares, for instance preference shares, may carry no voting rights in normal circumstances. To shorten the proceedings at meetings the procedure is as follows.

5.4.1 Voting on a show of hands

Key term

A **show of hands** is a method of voting for or against a resolution by raising hands. Under this method each member has one vote irrespective of the number of shares held, in contrast to a poll vote.

On putting a resolution to the vote the chairman calls for a show of hands. One vote may be given by each member present in person, including proxies.

Unless a poll is then demanded, the chairman's declaration of the result is **conclusive**. However, it is still possible to challenge the chairman's declaration on the grounds that it was fraudulent or manifestly wrong.

5.4.2 Voting on a poll

Key term

A **poll** is a method of voting at company meetings which allows a member to use as many votes as their shareholding grants them.

If a **real test of voting strength** is required a poll may be demanded. The result of the previous show of hands is then disregarded. On a poll every member and also proxies representing absent members may cast the full number of votes to which they are entitled. A poll need not be held at the time but may be postponed so that arrangements to hold it can be made.

A poll may be **demanded** by:

- Not **less than five members** having the right to vote on the resolution.
- Member(s) **representing** not less than **10%** of the **total voting rights**.
- Member(s) **holding shares** which **represent** not less than **10%** of the **paid-up capital**.

Any provision in the articles is **void** if it seeks to prevent such members demanding a poll or to exclude the right to demand a poll on any question other than the election of a chairman by the meeting or an adjournment: s 321.

When a poll is held it is usual to appoint **'scrutineers'** and to ask members and proxies to sign voting cards or lists. The votes cast are checked against the register of members and the chairman declares the result.

Members of a quoted company may require the directors to obtain an **independent report** in respect of a poll taken, or to be taken, at a general meeting if:

- They represent at least 5% of the voting rights, or
- Are at least 100 in number holding at least £100 of paid up capital: s 342.

5.4.3 Result of a vote

In voting, either by show of hands or on a poll, the **number of votes cast determines the result**. Votes which are not cast, whether the member who does not use them is present or absent, are simply disregarded. Hence the majority vote may be much less than half (or three quarters) of the total votes which could be cast.

Results of quoted company polls of must be made available on a **website**. The following information should be made available as soon as **reasonably practicable**, and should remain on the website for at least **two years**.

- Meeting date
- Text of the resolution or description of the poll's subject matter
- Number of votes for and against the resolution

5.5 Minutes of company meetings

FAST FORWARD

> Minutes must be kept of all **general, directors'** and **management meetings**, and members can inspect those of general meetings.

Key term

> **Minutes** are a record of the proceedings of meetings. Company law requires minutes to be kept of all company meetings including general, directors' and managers' meetings.

Every company is **required to keep minutes** which are a formal written record of the proceedings of its general meetings for ten years: s 355. These minutes are usually kept in **book form**. If a loose-leaf book is used to facilitate typing there should be safeguards against falsification, such as sequential prenumbering.

The chairman **normally signs** the minutes. If he does so, the signed minutes are admissible evidence of the proceedings, though evidence may be given to contradict or supplement the minutes or to show that no meeting at all took place.

Members of the company have the **right to inspect** minutes of general meetings. The minutes of general meetings must be held at the **registered office** or the **single alternative inspection location (SAIL)** and be available for inspection by members, who are also entitled to demand copies.

5.6 The assent principle

A unanimous decision of the members is often treated as a substitute for a formal decision in general meeting properly convened and held, and is equally binding.

6 Class meetings

FAST FORWARD

> **Class meetings** are held where the interests of different groups of shareholders may be affected in different ways.

6.1 Types of class meeting

Under the Companies Act 2006 (TSO, 2006), class meetings are of two kinds.

(a) If the company has more than one class of share, for example if it has 'preference' and 'ordinary' shares, it may be necessary to call a meeting of the holders of one class of shares, to approve a proposed **variation** of the **rights** attached to their shares.

(b) Under a **compromise** or **arrangements with creditors** (s 895), the holders of shares of the same class may nonetheless be divided into **separate** classes if the scheme proposed will affect each group differently.

When separate meetings of a class of members are held, the same procedural rules as for general meetings apply (but there is a different rule on quorum).

6.2 Quorum for a class meeting

The standard general meeting rules, on issuing notices and on voting, apply to a class meeting.

However, the **quorum** for a class meeting is fixed at two persons who hold, or represent by proxy, at least **one third** in nominal value of the issued shares of the class (unless the class only consists of a single member).

If no quorum is present, the meeting is **adjourned** (under the standard adjournment procedure for general meetings). When the meeting resumes, the quorum is **one** person (who must still hold at least one third of the shares).

7 Single member private companies

> **FAST FORWARD**
> There are **special rules** for **private companies** with only **one shareholder**.

Under the Companies Act 2006 (TSO, 2006), if the sole member takes any decision that could have been taken in general meeting, that member shall (unless it is a written resolution) provide the company with a **written record** of it. This allows the sole member to conduct members' business informally without notice or minutes.

Filing requirements still apply, for example, in the case of alteration of articles.

Written resolutions **cannot** be used to remove a director or auditor from office as these resolutions require special notice.

Chapter roundup

- Although the management of a company is in the hands of the directors, the **decisions which affect the existence of the company**, its structure and scope are **reserved to the members** in general meeting.
- There are two kinds of general meeting of members of a company:
    - **Annual general meeting (AGM)**
    - **General meetings at other times**
- A meeting can pass two types of resolution. **Ordinary resolutions** are carried by a simple majority (more than 50%) of votes cast and require 14 days' notice to be given to members. **Special resolution**s require a 75% majority of votes cast and also 14 days' notice to members.
- A private company can pass any decision needed by a **written resolution**, except for removing a director or auditor before their term of office has expired.
- A meeting cannot make valid and binding decisions until it has been properly convened. Notice of general meetings must be given **14 days'** in advance of the meeting. The notice should contain adequate information about the meeting.
- Meetings must be called by a **competent person** or authority.
- **Clear notice** must be given to members. **Notice** must be **sent to all members** entitled to receive it.
- **Special notice of 28 days** of intention to propose resolutions for removal of directors/auditors must be given.
- **Members** rather than directors may be able to requisition resolutions. This may be achieved by requesting the directors call a meeting, or proposing a resolution to be voted on at a meeting already arranged.
- The **notice** convening the meeting must give certain details. The **date**, **time** and **place** of the meeting, and identification of AGM and special resolutions. Sufficient information about the business to be discussed at the meeting should be provided to enable shareholders to know what is to be done.
- Company meetings need to be properly run if they are to be **effective** and within the **law**.
- The meeting should usually be chaired by the **chairman** of the board of directors. They do not necessarily have a casting vote.
- The **quorum** for meetings may be two or more (except for single member private companies). **Proxies** can attend, speak and vote on behalf of members.
- Voting at general meetings may be on a **show of hands** or a **poll**.
- **Minutes** must be kept of all **general, directors'** and **management meetings**, and members can inspect those of general meetings.
- **Class meetings** are held where the interests of different groups of shareholders may be affected in different ways.
- There are **special rules** for **private companies** with only **one shareholder.**

PART C   ADMINISTRATION AND CONTROL

Quick quiz

1. Which of the following decisions can only be taken by the members in general meeting?

    A   Alteration of articles
    B   Change of name
    C   Reduction of capital
    D   Appointment of a managing director

2. Before a private company can hold a general meeting on short notice, members holding a certain percentage of the company's shares must agree. Which one of the following percentages is correct?

51%	90%
75%	95%

3. A plc must hold its AGM within six months of its year end.

    True ☐
    False ☐

4. Minutes of company meetings must be kept for

    A   One year
    B   Five years
    C   Ten years
    D   Fifteen years

5. A member of a public company may only appoint one proxy, but the proxy has a statutory right to speak at the meeting.

    True ☐
    False ☐

Answers to quick quiz

1. A, B and C. The board can appoint someone to be managing director, so D is incorrect.
2. 90%.
3. True. A plc must hold its AGM within six months of its year end.
4. C. Under s 355, minutes must be kept for ten years.
5. False. Public company members can appoint more than one proxy. They have a statutory right to speak.

End of chapter question

Hydrangea

The directors of Hydrangea plc, a company selling garden furniture, wishes to call an AGM at which the accounts will be approved and all the directors re-elected. It also wishes to change the name of the company to Motormowers plc.

Required

(a) The directors seek your advice on the statutory requirements which apply to the calling of the meeting and the notice of the meeting, to ensure the resolutions gain legal effect when passed.

(5 marks)

(b) Provide advice to the directors on how the votes of members and proxies should be taken and counted at the meeting. **(5 marks)**

(Total = 10 marks)

Company directors and other company officers

Topic list	Syllabus reference
1 The role of directors	8.3
2 Appointment of directors	8.3
3 Remuneration of directors	8.3
4 Vacation of office	8.3
5 Disqualification of directors	8.3
6 Powers of directors	8.3
7 Powers of the Chief Executive Officer (Managing Director)	8.3
8 Powers of an individual director	8.3
9 Duties of directors	8.3
10 The company secretary	8.3

Introduction

In this chapter, we turn our attention to the **appointment** and **removal**, and the **powers and duties, of the directors**.

The important principle to grasp is that the **extent of directors' powers is defined by the articles**.

If **shareholders** do not approve of the directors' acts they must either **remove them** under s 168 or **alter the articles** to regulate their future conduct. However, they **cannot** simply **take over** the functions of the directors.

In essence, the directors act as **agents of the company**. This ties in with the **agency** part of your law studies also discussed in connection with partnerships. The different types of authority a director can have (implied and actual) are important in this area.

We also consider the **duties** of directors under statute and **remedies for the breach of such duties**.

Statute also imposes some duties on directors, specifically concerning openness when transacting with the company.

Finally, we look at the duties and powers of the **company secretary**.

The **Companies Act 2006**, (TSO, 2006) and the **Small Business, Enterprise and Employment Act 2015**, (TSO, 2015) apply to this and all chapters unless otherwise stated.

PART C   ADMINISTRATION AND CONTROL

1 The role of directors

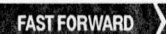

Any person who occupies the position of director is treated as such, the test being one of **function**.

Key term

> A **director** is a person who is responsible for the overall direction of the company's affairs. In company law, director means any person occupying the position of director, by whatever name called.

Any person who occupies the position of director is treated as such. The test is one of **function**. The directors' function is to take part in **making decisions** by **attending meetings** of the board of directors. Anyone who does that is a director whatever they may be called.

A person who is given the title of director, such as 'sales director' or 'director of research', to give them status in the company structure is not a director in company law. This is unless by virtue of their appointment they are a **member** of the **board** of **directors**, or they carry out functions that would be properly discharged only by a director.

1.1 De jure and de facto directors

Most directors are **expressly appointed** by a company and are known as **de jure** directors. A **de facto** director is **anyone** who is **held out by a company** as a director, **performs the functions** of a director and is **treated by the board** as a director although they have **never been validly appointed**.

1.2 Shadow directors

A person might seek to **avoid the legal responsibilities of being a director** by avoiding appointment as such but using his power, say as a major shareholder, to manipulate the acknowledged board of directors. In other words they seek the **power** and **influence** that come with the position of director, but **without the legal obligations** it entails.

The **Small Business Enterprise and Employment Act 2015** (TSO, 2015) includes measures aimed at increasing transparency around who controls UK companies, and as a consequence, statutory rules relating to directors are extended to **shadow directors**. Shadow directors are directors for legal purposes if the board of directors are accustomed to act in **accordance with their directions** and **instructions**. This rule does **not** apply to **professional advisers** merely acting in that capacity.

1.2.1 Shadow directors and de facto directors

Shadow directors differ from de facto directors because the **public** (and the **authorities**) are **rarely aware of their existence**. Whereas a **de facto director performs the everyday tasks that a director would** (dealing with suppliers and customers and being present at general meetings), the shadow director exerts their influence away from the day-to-day running of the business.

1.3 Alternate directors

A director may, if the articles permit, appoint an **alternate director** to attend and vote for them at board meetings which they are unable to attend. Such an alternate may be another director, in which case they have the vote of the absentee as well as their own. More usually they are an outsider. Company articles could make specific provisions for this situation.

1.4 Executive directors

Key term

> An **executive director** is a director who performs a specific role in a company under a **service contract** which requires a regular, possibly daily, involvement in management.

A director may also be an **employee** of his company. Since the company is also his **employer** there is a potential conflict of interest which, in principle, a director is required to avoid.

To allow an individual to be **both a director and employee** the articles usually make express provision for it, but prohibit the director from voting at a board meeting on the terms of their own employment.

Directors who have additional management duties as employees may be distinguished by **special titles**, such as 'Finance Director'. However **any such title does not affect their personal legal position**. They have two distinct positions as:

- A member of the board of directors; and
- A manager with management responsibilities as an **employee**.

1.5 Non-executive directors

Key term

A **non-executive director** does not have a function to perform in a company's management but is involved in its governance.

In **listed companies**, good corporate governance suggests that boards of directors are more likely to be fully effective if they comprise both **executive directors** and strong, independent **non-executive directors**. The main tasks of the NEDs are as follows:

- **Contribute** an **independent view** to the board's deliberations.
- **Help the board provide** the company with **effective leadership**.
- **Ensure** the **continuing effectiveness** of the **executive directors** and management.
- **Ensure high standards** of **financial probity** on the part of the company.

Non-executive and shadow directors are subject to the same duties as executive directors. Duties are discussed in Section 9.

1.6 The Chief Executive Officer (Managing Director)

Key term

A **Chief Executive Officer** (also commonly known as a **Managing Director**) is one of the directors of the company appointed to carry out overall day-to-day management operations.

Boards of directors usually appoint one director to be **Chief Executive Officer** (this position is also commonly known as **Managing Director**). A Chief Executive Officer (CEO) or Managing Director (MD) has a special position and has wider apparent powers than any director who is not appointed to that position.

1.7 Number of directors

Every company must have at least **one director**; for a **public company the minimum is two**. There is no statutory maximum in the UK, but the articles usually impose a limit. All directors must be a natural person, not a body corporate.

1.8 The board of directors

Companies are run by the directors collectively, in a **board of directors**.

Key term

The **board of directors** is the elected representative of the shareholders acting collectively in the management of a company's affairs.

One of the basic principles of company law is that the **powers** which are delegated to the directors under the articles are given to them as a **collective body**. The **board meeting** is the **proper place for the exercise of the powers**, unless they have been validly passed on, or 'sub-delegated', to committees or individual directors. In the event of deadlock at a board meeting, the Chairman of the meeting has the casting vote (Model article 13, also found in Table A).

1.9 The Chairman

As we have already seen, according to the **UK Corporate Governance Code**, a company's Chairman is responsible for leading the board and ensuring its effectiveness. This is a very distinct role from that of the CEO/MD, who is responsible for leading the company's operations. In addition, the company Chairman has a key role in relation to chairing company meetings, as we have also seen.

2 Appointment of directors

> **FAST FORWARD**
>
> The method of appointing directors, along with their rotation and co-option is **controlled** by the **articles**.

2.1 Appointment of first directors

The **application for registration** delivered to the Registrar to form a company includes particulars of the first directors, with their consents. On the formation of the company those persons become the first directors.

2.2 Appointment of subsequent directors

Under the Companies Act 2006 (TSO, 2006), once a company has been formed further directors can be appointed, either to **replace** existing directors or as **additional** directors.

Appointment of further directors is carried out **as the articles provide**. Most company articles allow for the appointment of directors:

- By **ordinary resolution** of the shareholders (eg Model article 17, Table A article 78), and
- By a **decision** of the directors (eg Model article 17, Table A article 79).

However the articles do not have to follow these provisions and may impose **different methods** on the company.

Table A provided that a director appointed by the board only holds office until the next annual general meeting (AGM). The Companies Act 2006 allowed private companies to dispense with AGMs, so the board of a private company with Table A articles which has dispensed with AGMs can appoint a director indefinitely.

When the appointment of directors is proposed at a general meeting of a public company a **separate** resolution should be proposed for the election of **each director**. However the rule may be waived if a resolution to that effect is first carried without any vote being given against it.

2.3 Publicity

In addition to giving notice of the first directors, every company must within **14 days** give **notice** to the **Registrar** of any change among its directors. This includes any changes to the register of directors' residential addresses.

2.4 Age limit

The **minimum age** limit for a director is **16** and, unless the articles provide otherwise, there is no upper limit.

3 Remuneration of directors

> **FAST FORWARD**
>
> Directors are entitled to **fees** and **expenses** as directors as per the articles, and **emoluments** (and compensation for loss of office) as per their service contracts (which can be inspected by members). Some details are published in the directors' remuneration report along with accounts.

3.1 Directors' service contracts

Details of directors' remuneration is usually contained within their **service contract**. This is a contract where the director agrees to personally perform services for the company. **Written service contracts** set out their entitlement to emoluments and expenses. Under the Companies Act 2006 (TSO, 2006), where service contracts **guarantee employment** for longer than **two years** then an **ordinary resolution** must be passed by the members of the company that the contract is with: s 188.

3.2 Directors' expenses

Most articles state that directors are entitled to **reimbursement** of **reasonable expenses** incurred while carrying out their duties or functions as directors.

3.3 Compensation for loss of office

Any director may receive **non-contractual** compensation for loss of office paid to him voluntarily. Any such compensation is lawful **only if** approved by members of the company in general meeting after proper disclosure has been made to all members, whether voting or not: s 217.

This only applies to uncovenanted payments; approval is not required where the company is contractually bound to make the payment.

Compensation paid to directors for loss of office is distinguished from any payments made to directors **as employees**, for example to settle claims arising from the premature termination of the service agreements. These are contractual payments which do not require approval in general meeting.

3.4 Directors' remuneration report

Quoted companies are required to include a **directors' remuneration report** as part of their annual report, part of which is subject to audit: s 420. Failure to produce the report is an offence. The report must cover:

- The details of each **individual directors' remuneration package**.
- The company's **remuneration policy**.
- The **role** of the **board** and **remuneration committee** in deciding the **remuneration** of **directors**.

Under s 421(3), it is the duty of the directors (including those who were a director in the preceding five years) to provide any information about themselves that is necessary to produce this report.

Quoted companies are required to allow a vote by members on the directors' remuneration report. The vote is purely advisory and does not mean the remuneration should change if the resolution is not passed. A negative vote would be a strong signal to the directors that the members are unhappy with remuneration levels.

Items not subject to audit

- Consideration by the directors (remuneration committee) of matters relating to directors' remuneration
- Statement of company's policy on directors' remuneration
- Performance graph (share performance)
- Directors' service contracts (dates, unexpired length, compensation payable for early termination)

Items subject to audit

- Salary/fees payable to each director
- Bonuses paid/to be paid
- Expenses
- Compensation for loss of office paid
- Any benefits received
- Share options and long term incentive schemes – performance criteria and conditions
- Pensions
- Excess retirement benefits
- Compensation to past directors
- Sums paid to third parties in respect of a director's services

3.5 Inspection of directors' service agreements

A company must make available for inspection by members a copy or particulars of **contracts of employment** between the company or a subsidiary with a director of the company. Such contracts must cover all services that a director may provide, including services outside the role of a director, and those made by a third party in respect of services that a director is contracted to perform.

Contracts must be **retained** for **one year** after expiry and must be available either at the **registered office**, or any other location permitted by the Secretary of State.

Prescribed particulars of **directors' emoluments** must be given in the accounts and also particulars of any **compensation for loss of office** and directors' **pensions**.

4 Vacation of office

> **FAST FORWARD**
>
> A director may vacate office as director due to: **resignation**; **not going** for **re-election**; **death**; **dissolution** of the company; **removal**; **disqualification**.

A director may leave office in the following ways.

- **Resignation**
- Not **offering themselves for re-election** when their term of office ends
- **Death**
- **Dissolution of the company**
- Being **removed** from office
- Being **disqualified**

A form should be filed with the Registrar whenever and however a director vacates office.

4.1 Retirement and re-election of directors

The Model articles for public companies provide the following rules for the **retirement and re-election** of all directors ('rotation') at AGMs.

(a) At the **first AGM** of the company **all directors shall retire**.
(b) At every subsequent AGM any **directors appointed by the other directors** since the **last AGM** shall retire.
(c) Directors who were **not appointed** or **re-elected at one of the preceding two AGMs** shall retire.

Directors who are **retired by rotation** are eligible to offer themselves for **re-election**. This mandatory retirement of directors provides another **control over their performance**. Rather than having to go through the process of seeking a resolution to remove a director, members have the opportunity every three years to dispose of an underperforming director by **simply not electing** them.

4.2 Removal of directors

In addition to provisions in the articles for removal of directors, under the Companies Act 2006 (TSO, 2006), a director may be removed from office by **ordinary** resolution at a meeting of which **special notice** to the company has been given by the person proposing it: s 168.

On receipt of the special notice the company must send a copy to the director who may require that a **memorandum of reasonable length** shall be issued to members. They also have the **right to address the meeting** at which the resolution is considered.

The articles and the service contract of the director **cannot override the statutory power**. However, the articles can **permit dismissal without the statutory formalities** being observed, for example dismissal by a resolution of the board of directors.

The power to remove a director is **limited** in its effect in four ways.

9: COMPANY DIRECTORS AND OTHER COMPANY OFFICERS

Restrictions on power to remove directors	
Shareholding qualification to call a meeting	In order to propose a resolution to remove a director, the shareholder(s) involved must call a general meeting. To do this they must hold 5% of the paid up share capital: s 303.
Shareholding to request a resolution	Where a meeting is already convened, 100 members holding an average £100 of share capital each may request a resolution to remove a director: s 338.
Weighted voting rights	A director who is also a member may have weighted voting rights given to them under the constitution for such an eventuality, so that they can automatically defeat any motion to remove them as a director: *Bushell v Faith 1970*.
Class right agreement	It is possible to draft a shareholder agreement stating that a member holding each class of share must be present at a general meeting to constitute quorum. If so, a member holding shares of a certain class could prevent a director being removed by not attending the meeting.

Exam focus point

The courts have stressed that the s 168 power of members to remove directors is an important right, but you should remember the ways in which members' intentions might be frustrated.

The dismissal of a director may also entail payment of a **substantial sum** to settle their claim for breach of contract if they have a service contract. Under s 168(5), no resolution may deprive a removed director of any compensation or damages related to their termination to which they are entitled to.

Southern Foundries (1926) Ltd v Shirlaw 1940

The facts: In 1933 S entered into a written agreement to serve the company as Managing Director for ten years. In 1936 F Co gained control of the company and used their votes to alter its articles to confer on F Co power to remove any director from office. In 1937 F Co exercised the power by removing S from his directorship and thereby terminated his appointment as Managing Director (which he could only hold so long as he was a director).

Decision: The alteration of the articles was not a breach of the service agreement but the exercise of the power was a breach of the service agreement for which the company was liable.

Question — Resolution for removal of director

A company has three members who are also directors. Each holds 100 shares. Normally the shares carry one vote each, but the articles state that on a resolution for a director's removal, the director to be removed should have three votes per share. On a resolution for the removal of Jeremy, a director, Jeremy casts 300 votes against the resolution and the other members cast 200 votes for the resolution. Has Jeremy validly defeated the resolution?

Answer

Yes. This was confirmed in a case called *Bushell v Faith 1970*.

5 Disqualification of directors

FAST FORWARD

Directors may be required to vacate office because they have been disqualified on grounds dictated by the articles. Directors **may** be disqualified from a wider range of company involvements under the Company Directors Disqualification Act 1986 (CDDA).

A person cannot be appointed as a director or continue in office if they are or become **disqualified** under the articles or statutory rules (such as the Company Directors Disqualification Act 1986 (HMSO, 1986) and the Small Business Enterprise and Employment Act 2015 (TSO, 2015)).

5.1 Disqualification under model articles

Model articles under the Companies Act 2006 (TSO, 2006), include a number of grounds for disqualification. These include where:

- A person **ceases to be a director** by virtue of any **provision of the Companies Act 2006**, or is prohibited from being a director by law;
- A **bankruptcy order** is made against that person;
- A composition is made with that **person's creditors** generally in satisfaction of that person's debts;
- A **registered medical practitioner**, who is treating that person, gives a written opinion to the company stating that that person has become physically or mentally incapable of acting as a director and may remain so for more than three months;
- Notification is received by the company from the director that the **director is resigning from office**, and such resignation has taken effect in accordance with its terms.

Unless the court approves it, an **undischarged bankrupt** cannot act as a director nor be concerned directly or indirectly in the management of a company. If they do continue to act, they become personally liable for the company's relevant debts.

In addition to the main grounds of disqualification, the articles may provide that **a director shall automatically vacate office** if they are **absent** from **board meetings** (without obtaining the leave of the board) for a **specified period** (say six months). The effect of this disqualification depends on the words used.

- If the articles refer merely to 'absence' this includes involuntary absence due to illness.
- The words 'if they shall absent himself' restrict the disqualification to periods of voluntary absence.

The **specified period** is reckoned to begin from the **last meeting** which the absent director did attend. The normal procedure is that a director who foresees a period of absence, applies for leave of absence at the last board meeting which they attend; the leave granted is duly minuted. They are not then absent 'without leave' during the period.

If they fail to obtain leave but later offer a reasonable explanation the other directors may let the matter drop by simply not resolving that they shall vacate office. The general intention of the rule is to **impose a sanction against slackness**; a director has a duty to attend board meetings when they are able to do so.

5.2 Disqualification under statute

The **Company Directors Disqualification Act 1986** (HMSO, 1986) (CDDA 1986) provides that a **court may** formally **disqualify a person from being a director** or in any way directly or indirectly being concerned or taking part in the promotion, formation or management of a company: s 1. To avoid the need for court proceedings, a director may give a disqualification undertaking, which has the same effect as a disqualification order.

The terms of the disqualification order are very wide, and include acting as a consultant to a company. The Act, despite its title, is not limited to the disqualification of people who have been directors. **Any person** may be disqualified if they fall within the appropriate grounds. These are discussed later in the chapter, in the context of directors' duties.

In addition to the grounds of disqualification described above, the articles may provide that **a director shall automatically vacate office** if they are **absent** from **board meetings** (without obtaining the leave of the board) for a **specified period** (three months is usual). The effect of this disqualification depends on the words used.

- If the articles refer merely to 'absence' this includes involuntary absence due to illness.
- The words 'if they shall absent himself' restrict the disqualification to periods of voluntary absence.

The period of **three months** is reckoned to begin from the **last meeting** which the absent director did attend. The normal procedure is that a director who foresees a period of absence, applies for leave of absence at the last board meeting which they attend; the leave granted is duly minuted. They are not then absent 'without leave' during the period.

If they fail to obtain leave but later offer a reasonable explanation the other directors may let the matter drop by simply not resolving that they shall vacate office. The general intention of the rule is to **impose a sanction against slackness**; a director has a duty to attend board meetings when they are able to do so.

The Registrar keeps a **register of disqualification orders and undertakings** at Companies House.

Question — Vacation of office

The articles of Robert Ltd provide that if a director should 'absent himself' for a period exceeding three months from board meetings, the director shall automatically vacate office. Miles, a director, obtains a twelve month leave of absence to go abroad. Whilst abroad, he contracts a rare illness; on his return he is rushed to hospital and remains there for nine months. On the day of his release, there is a board meeting which he does not attend, and he resolves not to attend board meetings again. After a further two months he has a relapse and dies a fortnight later. At what point does he cease to be a director?

A   After three months of his holiday
B   After three months of hospitalisation
C   At the point where he decides not to attend board meetings again
D   When he dies

Answer

D   The board can grant leave of absence, and 'absenting himself' does not include forced hospitalisation. The period of three months **begins** on his release from hospital, and has not been completed when he dies.

5.3 Grounds for disqualification of directors

FAST FORWARD

Directors may be **disqualified** from acting as directors or being involved in the management of companies in a number of circumstances. They must be disqualified if the company is insolvent, or the director is found to be unfit to be concerned with management of a company, especially in relation to breach of competition law.

Under the CDDA 1986 the court **may** make a disqualification order on any of the following grounds.

(a) **Where a person is convicted of an indictable offence (either in the UK or overseas) in connection with the promotion, formation, management or liquidation of a company or with the receivership or management of a company's property (s 2).**

An indictable offence is an offence which may be tried at a crown court; it is therefore a serious offence. It need not actually have been tried on indictment but if it was the maximum period for which the court can disqualify is 15 years, compared with only five years if the offence was dealt with summarily (at the Magistrates' court).

(b) **Where it appears that a person has been persistently in default in relation to provisions of company legislation (s 3).**

This legislation requires any return, account or other document to be filed with, delivered or sent or notice of any matter to be given to the Registrar. Three defaults in five years are conclusive evidence of persistent default.

The maximum period of disqualification under this section is five years.

(c) **Where it appears that a person has been guilty of fraud or fraudulent trading.** This means carrying on business with intent to defraud creditors or for any fraudulent purpose whether or not the company has been, or is in the course of being, wound up (see Chapter 11).

The person does not actually have to have been convicted of fraudulent trading. The legislation also applies to anyone who has otherwise been guilty, of any fraud in relation to the company or of any breach of their duty as an officer (s 4).

The maximum period of disqualification under this section is 15 years.

(d) **Where a person has three or more indictable or summary convictions for breaches of companies legislation in relation to returns and accounts in the previous five years (s 5).**

(e) **Where the Secretary of State, acting on a report made by the inspectors or from information or documents obtained under the Companies Act, applies to the court for an order believing it to be expedient in the public interest.**

If the court is satisfied that the person's conduct in relation to the company makes that person unfit to be concerned in the management of a company, then it may make a disqualification order (s 8). Again the maximum is 15 years.

(f) **Where a director of an insolvent company has participated in wrongful trading (s 10)** (see Chapter 11). Maximum – 15 years.

The court **must** make an order where it is satisfied that the following apply:

(a) A person has been a director of a company which has at any time become **insolvent** (whether while they were a director or subsequently).

(b) Their conduct as a director of that company makes them **unfit** to be **concerned** in the **management** of a company, particularly as a result of a breach of competition law (in which case a **competition disqualification order** will be made: s 9A). The courts may also take into account their conduct as a director of other companies, whether or not these other companies are insolvent. Directors can be disqualified under this section even if they take no active part in the running of the business.

When determining **unfitness**, the following factors should be taken into account (the company concerned may be based in the UK or overseas):

- The extent to which the person was responsible for the company breaking the law
- The extent to which the person was responsible for causing the company to become insolvent
- The nature and extent of the loss or damage caused by the person's conduct

In such cases the **minimum** period of disqualification is two years.

Illustration

Offences for which directors have been disqualified include the following.

(a) **Insider dealing**: *R v Goodman 1993*

(b) **Failure** to **keep proper accounting records**: *Re Firedart Ltd, Official Receiver v Fairall 1994*

(c) **Failure to read the company's accounts**: *Re Continental Assurance Co of London plc 1996*

(d) **Loans** to another company for the purposes of purchasing its own shares with **no grounds for believing the money would be repaid**: *Re Continental Assurance Co of London plc 1996*

(e) **Loans** to associated companies on **uncommercial terms** to the detriment of creditors: *Re Greymoat Ltd 1997*

5.4 Disqualification periods

In *Re Sevenoaks Stationers (Retail) Ltd 1991* the Court of Appeal laid down certain 'disqualification brackets'. The appropriate period of disqualification which should be imposed was a **minimum of two to five years** if the conduct was not very serious, **six to ten years** if the conduct was serious but did not merit the maximum penalty, and **over ten years** only in particularly serious cases.

Disqualification as a director need not mean disqualification from all involvement in management: (*Re Griffiths 1997*), and it may mean that the director can continue to act as an **unpaid director** (*Re Barings plc 1998*), but only if the court gives leave to act.

5.4.1 Mitigation of disqualification

Examples of circumstances which have led the court to imposing a lower period of disqualification include the following.

- **Lack of dishonesty**: *Re Burnham Marketing Services Ltd 1993*
- **Loss of director's own money** in the company: *Re GSAR Realisations Ltd 1993*
- **Absence of personal gain**, for example excessive remuneration: *Re GSAR Realisations Ltd 1993*
- **Efforts to mitigate** the situation: *Re Burnham Marketing Services Ltd 1993*
- **Likelihood of re-offending**: *Re Grayan Building Services Ltd 1995*
- **Proceedings hanging over director** for a long time: *Re Aldermanbury Trust 1993*

5.5 Procedures for disqualification

Company administrators, receivers and liquidators all have a statutory duty to report directors to the Government where they believe the conditions for a disqualification order have been satisfied.

The Secretary of State then decides whether to apply to the court for an order, but if they do decide to apply they must do so within two years of the date on which the company became insolvent.

5.6 Acting as a director whilst disqualified

Acting as a director whilst disqualified is a **serious offence** and where it is committed, **directors are personally liable for the debts of the company**.

Question — Disqualification

In what circumstances can a court make a disqualification order against a director of a company?

Answer

The provisions for disqualification of directors are contained in the Company Directors Disqualification Act 1986. A court may, by order, disqualify a person from being a director, liquidator, administrator, receiver or manager of a company, and from being concerned in the promotion or management of any company.

The order may be made in any one of the following circumstances.

(a) The director concerned is convicted of an indictable offence in connection with a company.

(b) The director concerned has been persistently in default in relation to company law requirements requiring the delivery to the Registrar of annual accounts, the annual return and other documents. A previous decision of a court on three previous occasions in five years that the person concerned has been in default in compliance with these requirements is conclusive evidence of 'persistent' default.

(c) The director concerned has been guilty of fraudulent trading.

(d) The Secretary of State applies for disqualification in the public interest. This would arise from an investigation by Government inspectors or documents obtained under the Companies Act.

(e) The director has been found to be in breach of certain aspects of competition law.

(f) The director has participated in wrongful trading in insolvency.

In general, disqualification may be ordered for up to 15 years. But the maximum is 5 years in case (b) above or when the order is made by a magistrates' court. A person subject to disqualification may apply to the court for remission of the order.

Bankruptcy

An undischarged bankrupt may not, without leave of the court, act as a director of a company or be concerned in the management or promotion of a company.

Here the disqualification is the automatic result of the bankruptcy order made against him by the court.

6 Powers of directors

> **FAST FORWARD** The **powers** of the directors are **defined** by the **articles**.

The powers of the directors are **defined by the articles**. The directors are usually authorised 'to manage the company's business' and 'to exercise all the powers of the company for any purpose connected with the company's business'.

Therefore they may take **any decision which is within the capacity** of the company **unless** either **the Act** or **the articles** themselves **require** that the **decision shall be taken by the members in general meeting**.

6.1 Restrictions on directors' powers

> **FAST FORWARD** Directors' powers may be restricted by statute or by the articles. The directors have a duty to exercise their powers in what they honestly believe to be the **best interests** of the company and for the **purposes** for which the powers are given.

6.1.1 Statutory restrictions

Under the Companies Act 2006 (TSO, 2006), many transactions, such as an alteration of the articles or a reduction of capital, must by law be effected by passing a **special resolution**. If the directors propose such changes they must secure the passing of the appropriate resolution by shareholders in a general meeting.

6.1.2 Restrictions imposed by articles

As an example, the articles often set a maximum amount which the directors may borrow. If the directors wish to exceed that limit, they should **seek authority** from a **general meeting**.

When the directors clearly have the necessary power, their decision may be challenged if they exercise the power in the wrong way. They must exercise their powers:

- In what they **honestly believe to be the interests of the company**: *Re Smith v Fawcett Ltd 1942*
- For a **proper purpose**, being the purpose for which the power is given: *Bamford v Bamford 1969*.

We shall come back to these points when we consider directors' duties.

6.1.3 Members' control of directors

There is a **division of power** between the board of directors who manage the business and the members who as owners take the major policy decisions at general meetings. How, then, do the owners seek to 'control' the people in charge of their property?

- The members **appoint** the directors and may **remove** them from office under s 168, or by other means.
- The members can, by **altering the articles** (special resolution needed), re-allocate powers between the board and the general meeting.
- Articles may allow the members to pass a **special resolution ordering** the **directors to act** (or **refrain from acting**) in a **particular way**. Such special resolutions cannot invalidate anything the directors have already done.

Directors are not agents of the members. They cannot be instructed by the members in general meeting as to how they should exercise their powers. **The directors' powers are derived from the company as a whole** and are to be exercised by the directors as they think best in the **interests of the company**.

6.1.4 Control by the law

Certain powers must be exercised **'for the proper purpose'** and all powers must be exercised *bona fide* **for the benefit of the company**. Failure by the directors to comply with these rules will result in the **court setting aside their powers** unless the shareholders **ratify** the directors' actions by **ordinary resolution** (50% majority).

7 Powers of the Chief Executive Officer (Managing Director)

FAST FORWARD

The CEO or MD has **apparent authority** to make business contracts on behalf of the company. Their **actual authority** is whatever the board gives them.

In their dealings with outsiders the CEO or MD has **apparent authority** as agent of the company to **make business contracts**. No other director, even if they work full time, has that **apparent** authority as a director, though if they are employed as a manager they may have apparent authority at a slightly lower level.

The CEO or MD's **actual authority** is whatever the board gives them.

Although appointment as CEO or MD has special status, it may be **terminated** just like that of any other director (or employee); they then revert to the position of an ordinary director. Alternatively the company in general meeting may **remove them from their office of director** and they immediately cease to be CEO or MD since being a director is a necessary qualification for holding the post.

7.1 Agency and the CEO/MD

The directors are **agents of the company, not the members**. Where they have **actual or usual** authority they can **bind the company**. In addition a director may have **apparent authority** by virtue of **holding out**.

Holding out is a basic rule of the law of agency. It means that if the principal (the company) holds out a person as its authorised agent they are estopped from denying that they are its **authorised agent**. They are bound by a contract entered into by them on the company's behalf.

Key term

Apparent authority is the authority which an agent appears to have to a third party. A contract made within the scope of such authority will bind the principal even though the agent was not following their instructions.

Therefore if the board of directors **permits a director** to behave as if they were a CEO or MD duly appointed when in fact they are not, the company may be bound by their actions.

A CEO or MD has, by virtue of their position, **apparent authority** to make commercial contracts for the company. Moreover if the board allows a director to enter into contracts, being aware of their dealings and taking no steps to disown them, the company will usually be bound.

PART C ADMINISTRATION AND CONTROL

> *Freeman & Lockyer v Buckhurst Park Properties (Mangal) Ltd 1964*
>
> *The facts:* A company carried on a business as property developers. The articles contained a power to appoint a Managing Director but this was never done. One of the directors of the company, to the knowledge but without the express authority of the remainder of the board, acted as if he were Managing Director. He found a purchaser for an estate and also engaged a firm of architects to make a planning application. The company later refused to pay the architect's fees on the grounds that the director had no actual or apparent authority.
>
> *Decision:* The company was liable since by its acquiescence it had represented that the director was a Managing Director with the authority to enter into contracts that were normal commercial arrangements, and which the board itself would have been able to enter.

Exam focus point

> Situations where the facts are similar to the *Freeman & Lockyer* case often occur in law exams so be prepared to spot them.

There are four conditions which must be satisfied in claiming under the principle of **holding out**. The claimant must show that:

(a) A **representation** was made to them that the **agent had** the **authority** to enter on behalf of the company into the contract of the kind sought to be enforced.

(b) Such **representation** was **made by a person** who had **'actual' authority** to **manage** the **business** of the company.

The board of directors would certainly have actual authority to manage the company. Some commentators have also argued that the CEO/MD has actual or apparent authority to make representations about the extent of the actual authority of other company agents. (However, a third party cannot rely on the representations a CEO/MD makes about their own actual authority.)

(c) They were **induced** by the **representation** to enter into the contract; they had in fact relied on it.

(d) There must be **nothing** in the **articles** which would prevent the company from giving valid authority to its agent to enter into the contract.

Question — Directors' powers

Under the articles of association of Recycle Ltd the directors of the company need the consent of the general meeting by ordinary resolution to borrow sums of money in excess of £50,000. The other articles are all standard model articles.

Mary has been appointed CEO of the company and she holds 1% of the issued shares of the company. Early in May 20X5 Mary entered into two transactions for the benefit of Recycle Ltd. First, she arranged to borrow £100,000 from Conifer Bank Ltd, secured by a floating charge on the company's assets. She had not sought the approval of the members as required by the articles. Secondly, she placed a contract worth £10,000 with Saw Ltd to buy some agricultural machinery.

Advise the directors of Recycle Ltd whether they are bound by the agreements with Conifer Bank Ltd and Saw Ltd.

Answer

The enforceability of the loan agreement and floating charge by Conifer Bank Ltd against Recycle Ltd is determined by reference to s 40. The transaction is *intra vires* the company, but beyond the authority of the CEO. Mary failed to obtain an ordinary resolution of the company as required by its articles of association.

S 40 provides that, in favour of a person dealing in good faith with a company, the power of the board of directors to bind the company or (importantly in this case) to authorise others to do so, shall be deemed to be free of any limitation under the company's constitution.

There is no suggestion that Conifer Bank Ltd has not acted in good faith and it will be presumed that it has in fact acted in good faith unless the contrary is proved by the company.

The articles allow the board to appoint a CEO. In that position, Mary has apparent authority as agent of the company to make business contracts including the type of transaction entered into with Saw Ltd.

Under the Act, the restriction placed on her actual authority (by the article requiring an ordinary resolution) shall be deemed not to exist in favour of the third party, Conifer Bank Ltd. The power of the board to authorise Mary to bind the company is deemed to be free of any constitutional limitation.

In conclusion, Recycle Ltd will be bound to the contracts with both Conifer Bank Ltd and Saw Ltd.

8 Powers of an individual director

The position of any other individual director (not an MD) who is also an employee is that:

(a) They **do not have the apparent authority to make general contracts** which attaches to the position of MD, but they have **whatever apparent authority attaches** to their **management position**.

(b) **Removal** from the office of director may be a **breach** of their **service contract** if that agreement stipulates that they are to have the status of director as part of the conditions of employment.

9 Duties of directors

FAST FORWARD

The Companies Act 2006 sets out the **seven principal duties** of **directors**.

The Companies Act 2006 (TSO, 2006) sets out the **principal duties** that directors owe to their company. Many of these duties developed over time through the operation of **common law** and **equity**, or are **fiduciary duties** which have now been codified to make the law clearer and more accessible.

Attention!

> When deciding whether a duty has been broken, the courts will consider the Companies Act primarily. All case law explained in this section applied before the 2006 Act and is included here to help you understand the types of situation that arise and how the law will be interpreted and applied by the courts in the future.

Key term

> **Fiduciary duty** is a duty imposed upon certain persons because of the position of trust and confidence in which they stand in relation to another. The duty is more onerous than generally arises under a contractual or tort relationship. It requires full disclosure of information held by the fiduciary, a strict duty to account for any profits received as a result of the relationship, and a duty to avoid conflict of interest.

Broadly speaking directors must be **honest** and **not allow their personal interests to conflict with their duties as directors**. The directors are said to hold a **fiduciary position** since they make contracts as **agents** of the company and have control of its property.

The duties included in the Companies Act 2006 effectively form a **code of conduct** for directors. They do not tell them what to do but rather create a framework that sets out how they are expected to **behave** generally. This code is important as it addresses situations where:

- A director may put their **own interests** ahead of the company's, and
- A director may be **negligent** and liable to an action under tort.

9.1 Who are the duties owed to?

Section 170 makes it clear that directors owe their duties to the company, **not** the members. This means that the **only company itself can take action against a director** who breaches them. However, it is possible for a member to bring a derivative claim against the director on behalf of the company.

The effect of the **duties are cumulative**, in other words, a director owes **every duty** to the company that could apply in any given situation. The Act provides guidance for this. Where a director is offered a bribe for instance they will be breaking the duty not to accept a benefit from a third party and they will also not be promoting the company for the benefit of the members.

When deciding whether or not a director has breached a duty, the court should consider their actions in the context of **each individual duty** in turn.

9.2 Who are the duties owed by?

Every person who is **classed as a director** under the Act owes the duties that are outlined below. Certain aspects of the duties regarding conflicts of interest and accepting benefits from third parties also apply to **past directors**. This is to prevent directors from exploiting a situation for their own benefit by simply resigning. The courts are directed to apply duties to **shadow directors** where they are capable of applying.

Directors must at all times continue to **act in accordance with all other laws**; no authorisation is given by the duties for a director to breach any other law or regulation.

9.3 The duties and the articles

The articles may provide more onerous regulations than the Act, but they may not reduce the level of duty expected unless it is in the following circumstances:

- If a director has **acted in accordance with the articles** they cannot be in breach of the duty to exercise independent judgement.
- Some **conflicts of interest by independent directors** are permissible by the articles.
- Directors will not be in breach of duty concerning **conflicts of interest** if they follow any **provisions in the articles for dealing with them** as long as the provisions are lawful.
- The company may **authorise anything** that would otherwise be a breach of duty.

9.4 The duties of directors

The **statutory duties** owed by directors are to:

- Act within their powers
- Promote the success of the company
- Exercise independent judgement
- Exercise reasonable skill, care and diligence
- Avoid conflicts of interest
- Not to accept benefits from third parties
- Declare an interest in a proposed transaction or arrangement

We shall now consider the duties placed on directors by the Act. Where cases are mentioned it is to **demonstrate** the previous common law or equitable principle that courts will follow when interpreting and applying the Act.

9.4.1 Duty to act within powers (s 171)

The directors owe a duty to act in accordance with the company's constitution, and only to exercise powers for the purposes for what they were conferred. They have a **fiduciary duty to the company to exercise their powers bona fide in what they honestly consider to be the interests of the company**:

Re Smith v Fawcett Ltd 1942. This honest belief is effective even if, in fact, the interests of the company were not served.

This duty is owed **to the company** and **not generally to individual shareholders**. The directors will not generally be liable to the members if, for instance, they purchase shares without disclosing information affecting the share price: *Percival v Wright 1902.*

In exercising the powers given to them by the articles the directors have a fiduciary duty not only to act bona fide but also only to use their powers for a proper purpose: *Bamford v Bamford 1969.*

The powers are restricted to the **purposes for which they were given**. If the directors infringe this rule by exercising their powers for a collateral purpose the transaction will be invalid **unless the company** in **general meeting authorises it, or subsequently ratifies it**.

Most of the directors' powers are found in the **articles**, so this duty means that the directors must not act outside their power or the capacity of the company (in other words *ultra vires*).

If the irregular use of directors' powers is in the **allotment of shares** the votes attached to the new shares may not be used in reaching a decision in general meeting to sanction it.

Howard Smith Ltd v Ampol Petroleum Ltd 1974

The facts: Shareholders who held 55% of the issued shares intended to reject a takeover bid for the company. The directors honestly believed that it was in the company's interest that the bid should succeed. The directors therefore allotted new shares to the prospective bidder so that the shareholders opposed to the bid would then have less than 50% of the enlarged capital and the bid would succeed.

Decision: The allotment was invalid. 'It must be unconstitutional for directors to use their fiduciary powers over the shares in the company purely for the purpose of destroying an existing majority or creating a new majority which did not previously exist'.

Any **shareholder** may **apply to the court** to declare that a transaction in breach of s 171 should be set aside. However the practice of the courts is generally to **remit the issue** to the **members in general meeting** to see if the members wish to confirm the transaction. If the majority approve what has been done (or have authorised it in advance) that decision is treated as a proper case of **majority control** to which the minority must normally submit.

Hogg v Cramphorn 1966

The facts: The directors of a company issued shares to trustees of a pension fund for employees to prevent a takeover bid which they honestly thought would be bad for the company. The shares were paid for with money belonging to the company provided from an employees' benevolent and pension fund account. The shares carried 10 votes each and as a result the trustees and directors together had control of the company. The directors had power to issue shares but not to attach more than one vote to each. A minority shareholder brought the action on behalf of all the other shareholders.

Decision: If the directors act honestly in the best interests of the company, the company in general meeting can ratify the use of their powers for an improper purpose, so the allotment of the shares would be valid. But only one vote could be attached to each of the shares because that is what the articles provided.

Bamford v Bamford 1969

The facts: The directors of Bamford Ltd allotted 500,000 unissued shares to a third party to thwart a takeover bid. A month after the allotment a general meeting was called and an ordinary resolution was passed ratifying the allotment. The holders of the newly-issued shares did not vote. The claimants (minority shareholders) alleged that the allotment was not made for a proper purpose.

Decision: The ratification was valid and the allotment was good. There had been a breach of fiduciary duty but the act had been validated by an ordinary resolution passed in general meeting.

These cases can be distinguished from the *Howard Smith* case (where the allotment was invalid) in that in the *Howard Smith* case the original majority would not have sanctioned the use of directors' powers. In the *Bamford* case the decision could have been sanctioned by a vote which excluded the new shareholders.

Ratification is not effective when it attempts to validate a transaction when

- It constitutes **fraud on a minority**.
- It involves **misappropriation of assets**.
- The transaction **prejudices creditors' interests** at a time when the company is insolvent.

Under s 239, any resolution which proposes to ratify the acts of a director which are negligent in default or in breach of duty or trust regarding the company must exclude the director or any members connected with them from the vote.

Most of the cases discussed above concern the **duty of directors** to exercise their power to allot shares. This is only one of the powers given to directors that are subject to this **fiduciary duty**.

Others include:

- Power to borrow
- Power to give security
- Power to refuse to register a transfer of shares
- Power to call general meetings
- Power to circulate information to shareholders

9.4.2 Duty to promote the success of the company (s 172)

An overriding theme of the Companies Act 2006 is the principle that the **purpose of the legal framework** surrounding companies should be **to help companies do business**. Their main purpose is to create wealth for the shareholders.

This theme is evident in the **duty of directors to promote the success of a company**. During the development of the Act, the independent Company Law Review recommended that company law should consider the interests of those who companies are run for. It decided that the new Act should embrace the principle of **'enlightened shareholder value'**.

In essence, this principle means that the law should encourage **longtermism** and **regard for all stakeholders** by directors and that **stakeholder interests** should be **pursued** in an **enlightened** and **inclusive** way.

To achieve this, a duty of directors to act in a way, which, in **good faith**, promotes the success of the company for the benefit of the members as a whole, was created.

The requirements of this duty are difficult to define and possibly problematic to apply, so the Act provides directors with a **non-exhaustive list** of issues to keep in mind.

When exercising this duty directors should consider:

- The **consequences of decisions** in the long term.
- The **interests of** their **employees**.
- The need to **develop good relationships** with **customers** and **suppliers**.
- The **impact of the company** on the **local community** and the **environment**.
- The desirability of **maintaining high standards of business conduct** and a **good reputation**.
- The need to **act fairly as between all members** of the company.

The list identifies areas of **particular importance** and **modern day expectations** of **responsible business behaviour**. For example the interests of the company's employees and the impact of the company's operations on the community and the environment.

The **Act does not define** what should be regarded as the **success of a company**. This is down to a director's judgement in good faith. This is important as it ensures that business decisions are for the directors rather than the courts.

No guidance is given for what the **correct course of action** would be where the various s 172 **duties are in conflict**. For example a decision to shut down an office may be in the long term best interests of the company but it is certainly not in the interests of the employees affected, nor the local community in which they live. Conflicts such as this are inevitable and could potentially leave directors open to breach of duty claims by a wide range of stakeholders if they do not deal with them carefully.

According to the **FRC's Revised Guidance on the Strategic Report** (FRC, 2018) company strategic reports provide important information to shareholders and can help them to assess how the directors have performed their duty, under section 172.

Such reports reflect the directors view of the company and provide context for the related financial statements. Their contents are derived from the Companies Act 2006, and include a description of the business' strategy, objectives and business model. In addition, they also include an explanation of the main trends and factors affecting the entity, principal risks and uncertainties and an analysis of the development and performance of the business. Other elements that are associated with the section 172 duty include disclosures about the environment, employees, social, community, human rights, and anti-corruption and anti-bribery matters when material. There is also a requirement to include disclosures on gender diversity.

9.4.3 Duty to exercise independent judgement (s 173)

This is a simple duty that states directors must **exercise independent judgement. This means they should** remain independent and open-minded when exercising their discretion. They should **not delegate** their powers of decision-making or be **swayed by the influence of others**. It is sometimes said the directors must not 'fetter their discretion'. However unless a decision is expressly reserved to directors, a director can delegate his functions to any person he thinks fit.

The Companies Act 2006 does recognise that a director's **future discretion** may legitimately be restricted on account of a contract entered into between the company and a third party. The duty to exercise independent judgement is not infringed therefore by acting in accordance with any agreement by the company that restricts the exercise of discretion by directors, or by acting in a way authorised by the company's constitution.

9.4.4 Duty to exercise reasonable skill, care and diligence (s 174)

Directors have a **duty of care** to show **reasonable skill, care and diligence**.

Section 174 provides that a director 'owes a duty to his company to exercise the same standard of 'care, skill and diligence that would be exercised by a reasonably diligent person with:

(a) The general knowledge, skill and experience that may reasonably be expected of a person carrying out the functions carried out by the director in relation to the company; and

(b) The general knowledge, skill and experience that the director has.

There is therefore a **reasonableness test** consisting of two parts:

(a) An **objective test**

Did the director act in a manner reasonably expected of a person performing the same role?

A director, when carrying out his functions, must show such **care** as could **reasonably** be expected from a **competent person** in that role. If a 'reasonable' director could be expected to act in a certain way, it is no defence for a director to claim, for example, lack of expertise.

(b) A **subjective test**

Did the director act in accordance with the skill, knowledge and experience that they actually have?

In the case of *Re City Equitable Fire and Insurance Co Ltd 1925* it was held that a director is expected to show the **degree of skill** which may **reasonably be expected** from a person of his knowledge and experience. The standard set is personal to the person in each case. An accountant who is a director of a mining company is not required to have the expertise of a mining engineer, but they should show the expertise of an accountant.

The duty to be competent extends to **non-executive directors**, who may be liable if they fail in their duty.

PART C   ADMINISTRATION AND CONTROL

> *Dorchester Finance Co Ltd v Stebbing 1977*
>
> *The facts:* Of all the company's three directors S, P and H, only S worked full-time. P and H signed blank cheques at S's request who used them to make loans which became irrecoverable. The company sued all three; P and H, who were experienced accountants, claimed that as non-executive directors they had no liability.
>
> *Decision:* All three were liable, P's and H's acts in signing blank cheques being negligent and not showing the necessary objective or subjective skill and care.

In other words, the **standard of care** is an objective 'competent' standard, plus a higher 'personal' standard of application. If the director actually had particular expertise that leads to a higher standard of competence being reasonably expected.

The company may recover damages from its directors for loss caused by their negligence. However something more than imprudence or want of care must be shown. It must be shown to be a case of **gross negligence**. This was defined in *Overend Gurney & Co v Gibb 1872* as conduct such that 'no men with any degree of prudence, acting on their own behalf, would have entered into such a transaction as they entered into'.

Therefore, in the absence of fraud it was difficult to control careless directors effectively. The statutory provisions on disqualification of directors of insolvent companies and on liability for wrongful trading therefore both set out how to judge a director's competence, and provide more effective enforcement (discussed below).

The company by decision of its members in general meeting decides whether to sue the directors for their negligence. Even if it is a case in which they could be liable **the court has discretion under s 1157 to relieve directors of liability** if it appears to the court that:

- The directors acted **honestly** and **reasonably**.
- They **ought**, having regard to the circumstances of the case, **fairly to be excused**.

> *Re D'Jan of London Ltd 1993*
>
> *The facts:* D, a director of the company, signed an insurance proposal form without reading it. The form was filled in by D's broker. An answer given to one of the questions on the form was incorrect and the insurance company rightly repudiated liability for a fire at the company's premises in which stock worth some £174,000 was lost. The company became insolvent and the liquidator brought this action under s 212 of the Insolvency Act 1986 alleging D was negligent.
>
> *Decision:* In failing to read the form D was negligent. However, he had acted honestly and reasonably and ought therefore to be partly relieved from liability by the Court under s 727 of the Companies Act 1985, (now s 1157 under the Companies Act 2006).

In the absence of **fraud**, **bad faith** or **ultra vires** the members may vote unanimously to forgive the director's negligence, even if it is those negligent directors who control the voting and exercise such forgiveness: *Multinational Gas & Petrochemical Co v Multinational Gas and Petrochemical Services Ltd 1983*. Where there is no fraud on the minority, a majority decision is sufficient: *Pavlides v Jensen 1956*.

9.4.5 Duty to avoid conflicts of interest (s 175)

Directors have a **duty to avoid circumstances** where their **personal interests conflict**, or may possibly conflict, **with the company's interests**. It may occur when a director makes personal use of information, property or opportunities belonging to the company, whether or not the company was able to take advantage of them at the time.

Therefore directors must be careful not to breach this duty when they **enter into a contract** with their company or if they **make a profit in the course of being a director**.

This duty does not apply to a conflict of interest in relation to a transaction or arrangement with the company, provided the director declared an interest (see Section 9.4.7 below).

As **agents,** directors have a **duty to avoid a conflict of interest**. In particular:

- The directors must **retain their freedom of action** and **not fetter their discretion** by agreeing to vote as some other person may direct.
- The directors owe a fiduciary duty to **avoid a conflict of duty and personal interest.**
- The directors **must not obtain any personal advantage** from their position as directors **without the consent of the company** for whatever gain or profit they have obtained.

The following cases are important in the area of conflict of interest.

Regal (Hastings) Ltd v Gulliver 1942

The facts: The company owned a cinema. It had the opportunity of acquiring two more cinemas through a subsidiary to be formed with an issued capital of £5,000. However the company could not proceed with this scheme since it only had £2,000 available for investment in the subsidiary.

The directors and their friends therefore subscribed £3,000 for shares of the new company to make up the required £5,000. The chairman acquired his shares not for himself but as nominee of other persons. The company's solicitor also subscribed for shares. The share capital of the two companies (which then owned three cinemas) was sold at a price which yielded a profit of £2.80 per share of the new company in which the directors had invested. The new controlling shareholder of the company caused it to sue the directors to recover the profit which they had made.

Decision:

(a) The directors were **accountable** to the company for their profit since they had obtained it from an opportunity which came to them as directors.

(b) It was **immaterial** that the **company** had **lost nothing** since it had been unable to make the investment itself.

(c) The directors might have kept their profit if the company had **agreed** by resolution passed in general meeting that they should do so. The directors might have used their votes to approve their action since it was not fraudulent (there was no misappropriation of the company's property).

(d) The chairman was not accountable for the profit on his shares since he did not obtain it for himself. The solicitor was not accountable for his profit since he was **not a director** and so was not subject to the rule of accountability as a director for personal profits obtained in that capacity.

Industrial Development Consultants Ltd v Cooley 1972

The facts: C was Managing Director of the company which provided consultancy services to gas companies. A gas company was unlikely to award a particular contract to the company but C realised that, acting personally, he might be able to obtain it. He told the board of his company that he was ill and persuaded them to release him from his service agreement. On ceasing to be a director of the company C obtained the contract on his own behalf. The company sued him to recover the profits of the contract.

Decision: C was accountable to his old company for his profit.

Directors will not be liable for a breach of this duty if:

- The **members** of the company **authorised** their actions.
- The **situation cannot reasonably be regarded** as likely to give rise to a conflict of interest.
- The **actions have been authorised by the other directors**. This only applies if they are genuinely independent from the transaction and:
    - If the company is private – the articles do not restrict such authorisation, or
    - If it is public – the articles expressly permit it.
- The company explicitly rejected the opportunity they took up: *Peso Silver Mines v Cropper.*

9.4.6 Duty not to accept benefits from third parties (s 176)

This duty **prohibits the acceptance of benefits** (including bribes) from third parties conferred by reason of them being director, or doing, (or omitting to do) something as a director. Where a director accepts a benefit that may also create or potentially create a conflict of interest, they will also be in breach of their s 175 duty (see above).

Unlike s 175, an act which would potentially be in breach of this duty **cannot be authorised** by the **directors**, but **members do have the right to authorise it**.

Directors will not be in breach of this duty if the acceptance of the benefit **cannot reasonably** be regarded as likely to give rise to a conflict of interest.

9.4.7 Duty to declare interest in proposed transaction or arrangement (s 177)

Directors are required to disclose to the other directors the nature and extent of any interest, direct or indirect, that they have in relation to a **proposed transaction** or **arrangement** with the **company** (this is also required by Table A article 85). Even if the director is not a party to the transaction, the duty may apply if they are aware, or ought reasonably to be aware, of the interest. For example, the interest of another person in a contract with the company may require disclosure under this duty if that other person's interest is a direct or indirect interest on the part of the director.

Directors are required to disclose their interest in any transaction **before** the company enters into the transaction. Disclosure can be made by:

- Written notice
- General notice
- Verbally at a board meeting

Disclosure to the **members** is **not** sufficient to discharge the duty. Directors must declare the **nature** and **extent** of their interest to the **other directors** as well.

If the declaration becomes **void** or **inaccurate**, a **further declaration** should be made.

No declaration of interest is required if the director's interest in the transaction **cannot reasonably** be regarded as likely to give rise to a conflict of interest.

A director in a company with Table A articles is also prevented, by articles 94 and 95, from voting on any board resolutions related to a proposed transaction in which they have declared an interest.

9.5 Consequences of breach of duty

Breach of duty comes under the **civil law** rather than criminal law and, as mentioned earlier, the company itself must take up the action. This usually means the other directors starting proceedings.

Consequences for breach include:

- **Damages** payable to the company where it has suffered loss.
- **Restoration** of company property.
- **Repayment of any profits** made by the director.
- **Rescission of contract** (where the director did not disclose an interest).

9.6 Declaration of an interest in an existing transaction or arrangement (s 182)

Directors have a statutory obligation to declare any direct or indirect interest in an existing transaction entered into by the company. This obligation is almost identical to the duty to disclose an interest in a **proposed** transaction or arrangement under s 177 (see above). However, this section is relevant to transactions or arrangements that have **already occurred**.

A declaration under s 182 is **not** required if:

- It has **already been disclosed** as a proposed transaction under s 177.
- The director is **not aware** of either
  - **The interest** they have in the transaction, or
  - In **the transaction** itself.
- The director's interest in the transaction **cannot reasonably** be regarded as likely to give rise to a conflict of interest.
- The **other directors are aware** (or reasonably should be aware) of the situation.
- It concerns the **director's service contract** and it has been considered by a board meeting or special board committee.

Where a declaration is required it should be made as soon as **reasonably practicable** either:

- By written notice
- By general notice
- Verbally at a board meeting

If the declaration becomes **void** or **inaccurate**, a **further declaration** should be made.

9.7 Dealings between the company and its directors

The table below summarises other statutory controls over dealings between directors and their companies included in the Companies Act 2006.

CA06 Ref	Control
188	**Long service contracts:** directors' service contracts lasting more than two years must be approved by the members.
190	**Substantial property transactions:** directors or any person connected to them (see below) may not acquire a 'substantial' non-cash asset from the company without approval of the members. An asset's value is substantial if it is more than £5,000, or more than 10% of the company's asset value. All sales of assets with a value exceeding £100,000 must be approved.
197	Any loans given to directors, or guarantees provided as security for loans provided to directors, must be approved by members by ordinary resolution at a meeting or by written resolution. Persons connected to public company directors are also covered. Members should have been given information as to the nature of the transaction, the amount and purpose of the loan and the extent of the company's liability: s 197(4). This information must be in a memorandum circulated at the same time as a written resolution. If the general meeting procedure is used, the memorandum must be made available to members at the company's registered office for at least 15 days prior to the meeting, as well as at the meeting itself.
198	Expands section 197 to prevent unapproved **quasi-loans** to directors and connected persons (public companies only).
201	Expands section 197 to prevent unapproved **credit transactions** by the company for the benefit of a director (public companies only).
217	**Non-contractual payments to directors for loss of office** must be approved by the members.

Loans etc made without shareholder approval are voidable at the instance of the company and the director would be liable to account for any gain made as a result of the transaction, or indemnify the company for any loss: s 213.

Transactions under s 197, s 198 and s 201 do not require shareholder approval if they are to meet expenditure in the company's business where the total value does not exceed £50,000: s 204.

9.7.1 Connected persons

For the purpose of s 190 (substantial property transactions), s 197 (loans by public companies) and s 198 (quasi-loans by public companies) a person is connected with a director if:

- They are a member of the director's **family** (spouse, civil partner, long-term partner, child, step-child, parent – not grandparent or grandchild, sister, brother, aunt or uncle, or nephew or niece).
- They are a **body corporate** with which the director is connected (the director has an interest in 20% or more of the equity capital or voting rights).
- They act as a **trustee** of a trust which includes the director or a connected person as a beneficiary, or which requires the person to act for the director's or a connected person's benefit.
- They are a **partner** of the director or a connected person.
- They are a **firm** that is a legal person in which the director or a connected person is a partner: s 252.

9.8 Examples of remedies against directors

Remedies against directors for breach of duties include accounting to the company for a **personal gain**, **indemnifying the company**, and **rescission of contracts** made with the company.

The type of remedy varies with the breach of duty.

(a) The director may have to **account for a personal gain**: *Regal (Hastings) Ltd v Gulliver 1942*.

(b) They may have to **indemnify the company** against loss caused by their negligence such as an unlawful transaction which they approved.

(c) If they contract with the company in a conflict of interest the **contract may be rescinded by the company**. However under common law rules the company cannot both affirm the contract and recover the director's profit: *Burland v Earle 1902*.

(d) The court may declare that a transaction is *ultra vires* or unlawful: *Re Lee Behrens & Co 1932*.

A company may, either by its **articles** or by **passing a resolution** in general meeting, **authorise or ratify** the conduct of directors in breach of duty. There are some limits on the power of members in general meeting to **sanction a breach of duty** by directors or to release them from their strict obligations.

(a) If the directors **defraud** the company and vote in general meeting to approve their own fraud, their votes are invalid (*Cook v Deeks 1916*).

(b) If the directors **allot shares** to alter the balance of votes in a general meeting the votes attached to those shares may not be cast to support a resolution approving the issue (see *Bamford's* case above).

9.9 Directors' liability for acts of other directors

A director is **not liable** for acts of fellow directors. However if they become aware of serious breaches of duty by other directors, they may have a duty to inform members of them or to take control of assets of the company without having proper delegated authority to do so.

In such cases the director is **liable for their own negligence** in what they allow to happen and not directly for the misconduct of the other directors.

9.10 Directors' personal liability

As a general rule a director has no personal liability for the debts of the company. But there are certain exceptions.

- Personal liability **may arise** by **lifting the veil** of incorporation.
- A **limited company** may by its articles or by **special resolution** provide that its directors shall have unlimited liability for its debts.
- A director may be **liable** to the **company's creditors** in certain circumstances.

Can a director be held personally liable for **negligent advice** given by his company? The case below shows that they can, but only when they assume responsibility in a personal capacity for advice given, rather than simply giving advice in their capacity as a director.

Williams and Another v Natural Life Health Foods Ltd 1998

The facts: The director was sued personally by claimants who claimed they were misled by the company's brochure. The director helped prepare the brochure, and the brochure described him as the source of the company's expertise. The claimants did not however deal with the director but with other employees.

Decision: The House of Lords overruled the Court of Appeal, and ruled that the director was not personally liable. In order to have been liable, there would have had to have been evidence that the director had assumed personal responsibility. Merely acting as a director and advertising his earlier experience did not amount to assumption of personal liability.

9.11 Fraudulent and wrongful trading

In cases of **fraudulent or wrongful trading** liquidators can apply to the court for an order that those responsible (usually the directors) are liable to repay all or some specified part of the **company's debts**.

The liquidator should also report the facts to the Director of Public Prosecutions so that the DPP may **institute criminal proceedings**. We shall come back to these points in Chapter 13.

10 The company secretary

> **FAST FORWARD**
>
> Every public company must have a **company secretary**, who is one of the officers of a company and may be a director. Private companies are not required to have a secretary.

Under the Companies Act 2006 (TSO, 2006), every public company must have a **company secretary**, who is one of the officers of a company and may be a director: s 271. Private companies are not required to have a secretary: s 270. In this case the roles normally done by the company secretary may be done by one of the directors, or an approved person. The Secretary of State may require a public company to appoint a secretary where it has failed to do so.

10.1 Appointment of a company secretary

To be appointed as a company secretary to a plc, the directors must ensure that the candidate should be qualified (s 273) by virtue of:

- **Employment** as a plc's secretary for **three out of the five years** preceding appointment.
- **Membership** of one of a list of **qualifying bodies**: the ACCA, CIMA, ICAEW, ICAS, ICAI or CIPFA.
- **Qualification** as a **solicitor**, **barrister** or **advocate** within the UK.
- **Employment** in a position or **membership** of a professional body that, in the opinion of the directors, **appears to qualify that person** to act as company secretary.

They should also have the **'necessary knowledge and experience'** as deemed by the directors.

A **sole director** of a private company cannot also be the company secretary, but a company can have **two** or more joint secretaries. A **corporation** can fulfil the role of company secretary. A register of secretaries must be kept.

Under the **UK Corporate Governance Code**, the appointment of the company secretary is a matter for the board as a whole.

10.2 Duties of a company secretary

The specific **duties** of each company secretary are **determined by the directors** of the company. As a company officer, the company secretary is responsible for ensuring that the company complies with its statutory obligations. In particular, this means:

- **Establishing** and **maintaining** the company's **statutory registers**
- **Filing accurate returns** with the Registrar on time
- **Organising** and **minuting** company and **board meetings**
- **Ensuring** that **accounting** records meet **statutory requirements**
- **Ensuring** that **annual accounts** are **prepared** and **filed** in accordance with **statutory requirements**
- **Monitoring statutory requirements** of the company
- **Signing company documents** as may be required by law

Under the UK Corporate Governance Code, the company secretary must:

- **Ensure good information flows** within the board and its committees
- **Facilitate induction of board members** and assist with professional development
- **Advise** the **chairman** and the **board** on all **governance issues**

10.3 Powers and authority of a company secretary

The powers of the company secretary have historically been very limited. However, the common law increasingly recognises that they may be able to act as agents to exercise apparent or **ostensible authority**, therefore, they may enter the company into contracts connected with the administrative side of the company.

> *Panorama Developments (Guildford) Ltd v Fidelis Furnishing Fabrics Ltd 1971*
>
> *The facts:* B, the secretary of a company, ordered cars from a car hire firm, representing that they were required to meet the company's customers at London Airport. Instead he used the cars for his own purposes. The bill was not paid, so the car hire firm claimed payment from B's company.
>
> *Decision:* B's company was liable, for he had apparent authority to make contracts such as the present one, which were concerned with the administrative side of its business. The decision recognises the general nature of a company secretary's duties.

Chapter roundup

- Any person who occupies the position of director is treated as such, the test being one of **function**.
- The method of appointing directors, along with their rotation and co-option is **controlled** by the **articles**.
- Directors are entitled to **fees** and **expenses** as directors as per the articles, and **emoluments** (and compensation for loss of office) as per their service contracts (which can be inspected by members). Some details are published in the directors' remuneration report along with the accounts.
- A director may vacate office as director due to: **resignation**; **not going** for **re-election**; **death**; **dissolution** of the company; **removal**; **disqualification**.
- Directors may be required to vacate office because they have been disqualified on grounds dictated by the articles. Directors **may** be disqualified by court order or via a voluntary disqualification undertaking from a wider range of company involvements under the Company Directors Disqualification Act 1986 (CDDA).
- Directors may be **disqualified** from acting as directors or being involved in the management of companies in a number of circumstances. They must be disqualified if the company is insolvent, or the director is found to be unfit to be concerned with management of a company, especially in relation to breach of competition law.
- The **powers** of the directors are **defined** by the **articles**.
- Directors' powers may be restricted by statute or by the articles. The directors have a duty to exercise their powers in what they honestly believe to be the **best interests** of the company and for the **purposes** for which the powers are given.
- The CEO or MD has **apparent authority** to make business contracts on behalf of the company. Their **actual authority** is whatever the board gives them.
- The Companies Act 2006 sets out the **seven principal duties** of **directors**.
- The **statutory duties** owed by directors are to:
    - Act within their powers
    - Promote the success of the company
    - Exercise independent judgement
    - Exercise reasonable skill, care and diligence
    - Avoid conflicts of interest
    - Not accept benefits from third parties
    - Declare an interest in a proposed transaction or arrangement
- Every public company must have a **company secretary**, who is one of the officers of a company and may be a director. Private companies are not required to have a secretary.

PART C ADMINISTRATION AND CONTROL

Quick quiz

1. A person who is held out by a company as a director and performs the duties of a director without actually being validly appointed is a

    A Shadow director
    B De facto director
    C Non-executive director
    D Executive director

2. **Fill in the blanks** in the statements below.

    Under model articles directors are authorised to m……………….. the b……………….. of the company, and e…………. the p………………..of the company.

3. Under which of the following grounds may a director be disqualified if he is guilty, and under which must a director be disqualified?

    A Conviction of an indictable offence in connection with a company.

    B Persistent default with the provisions of company legislation.

    C Wrongful trading.

    D Director of an insolvent company whose conduct makes him unfit to be concerned in the management of the company.

4. What is the extent of a CEO's actual authority?

5. What are the two principal ways by which members can control the activities of directors?

6. A public company must have two directors, a private company only needs one.

    True ☐
    False ☐

7. The directors of a company are in breach of the rule requiring them to act for a proper purpose. A general meeting can

    A Do nothing that will authorise the transaction.
    B Authorise the transaction by ordinary resolution.
    C Authorise the transaction by special resolution only.
    D Relieve the directors of any liability under the transaction by special resolution only.

8. Describe the subjective test that directors must pass in order to meet their duty of care.

9. A private company with a sole director is not legally required to have a company secretary, but if it does, the sole director cannot also be the company secretary.

    True ☐
    False ☐

Answers to quick quiz

1. B. The description is of a de facto director.
2. Under model articles directors are authorised to **manage** the **business** of the company, and **exercise all** the **powers** of the company.
3. A to C are grounds under which a director may be disqualified; D is grounds under which a director must be disqualified.
4. The actual authority is whatever the board gives them.
5. Appointing and removing directors in general meeting

   Reallocating powers by altering the articles
6. True. Private companies only need one director.
7. B. This was the decision in *Bamford v Bamford 1969*.
8. A director is expected to show the degree of skill, knowledge and expertise that he or she actually has in order to meet the subjective test.
9. True. Sole directors cannot be company secretaries. Private companies are not legally required to have a company secretary.

End of chapter question

Statutory duties

Briefly explain any FIVE of the statutory duties owed by directors to their companies. **(10 marks)**

Majority control and minority protection

Topic list	Syllabus reference
1 Majority control: the rule in *Foss v Harbottle*	8.3
2 Minority protection: fraud on the company	8.3
3 Minority protection: s 994	8.3
4 Derivative claims	8.3
5 'Just and equitable' winding up	8.3
6 Other statutory rights of minorities	8.3

Introduction

Every member of a company is bound by the articles to the company and to his fellow members as we saw in an earlier chapter. By implication, a member agrees to be bound by the decisions of the **majority** as expressed at a general meeting. This principle of majority rule was established in the UK in the case of *Foss v Harbottle*.

However, while **directors** must exercise their power *bona fide* for the benefit of the company and for a proper purpose, shareholders are under no such obligation. Clearly shareholders may exercise their votes in their own interests and not those of the company. There must, therefore, be some restraint on the power of those able to command a majority vote. Minorities are therefore protected by **common law** and **statute**, and the various rules are all covered in this chapter.

The **Companies Act 2006**, (TSO, 2006) and the **Small Business, Enterprise and Employment Act 2015**, (TSO, 2015) apply to this and all chapters unless otherwise stated.

PART C   ADMINISTRATION AND CONTROL

1 Majority control: the rule in *Foss v Harbottle*

FAST FORWARD

The majority ultimately control the company, though the minority may need to be protected. It is the company which should bring actions to recover goods etc, not the shareholders individually.

Attention!

Foss v Harbottle confirmed the rule that the **majority shareholders control the company** and therefore established the **need** for minority protection. It did not establish a right to minority protection.

Members voting in general meeting have **ultimate control of a company**, and therefore its directors.

A problem arises if a person or number of people who are directors denominate the general meeting (that is, they hold more than 75% of the shares) and **behave unfairly** to minority shareholders or improperly to the company who are powerless to do anything about it. This is illustrated by the following case.

Foss v Harbottle 1843

The facts: A shareholder (Foss) sued the directors of the company alleging that the directors had defrauded the company by selling land to it at an inflated price. The company was by this time in a state of disorganisation and efforts to call the directors to account at a general meeting had failed.

Decision: The action must be dismissed.

- The company as a personal separate from its members is the only proper plaintiff in an action to protect its rights or property (see the Fischer case below).
- The company in general meeting must decide whether to bring such legal proceedings.

A shareholder in a company may be entitled to recover damages for the diminution of the value of his shareholding, where such diminution was the result of loss inflicted on the company by the actions of the controlling majority. If the company successfully sues the wrongdoers then the company's losses are made good and the shares should not lose value. If a shareholder suffers losses which are simply a reflection of the company's losses (eg dividends not paid because of the losses), he cannot recover losses from the wrongdoers: *Johnson v Gore Wood 2002.*

In laying down the general principles of procedure the court did nonetheless recognise that 'the **claims of justice**' must prevail over '**technical rules**'.

The protection of a minority in various situations is provided by making **exceptions to the rule in** *Foss v Harbottle*.

2 Minority protection: fraud on the company

FAST FORWARD

A minority can bring proceedings to prevent a **fraud** on the company or minority shareholders. Fraud can mean misappropriation of property or discrimination against a minority.

There is an exception to the rule (in *Foss v Harbottle*) over fraud by a controlling majority. It aims to **protect the company** (by a member's action) **since the company cannot protect itself**. It must be shown that:

- What was taken **belonged to the company**.
- It **passed to those against** who the claim is made.
- Those who **appropriated the company's property are in control** of the company.

A member may bring an action to **enforce the company's rights** (a derivative action). Any remedy awarded goes to the company.

2.1 Majority control and minority protection

Diverting profitable contracts away from the company is to deprive it of its 'property'.

Cook v Deeks 1916

The facts: The directors who were also controlling shareholders negotiated a contract in the name of the company. They took the contract for themselves and passed a resolution in general meeting declaring that the company had no interest in the contract. A minority shareholder sued them as trustees for the company of the benefit of the contract.

Decision: The contract 'belong in equity to the company' and the directors could not, by passing a resolution in general meeting, bind the company to approving this action of defrauding it.

2.2 Passing of property to controlling shareholders

Passing property to **controlling shareholders** (though **not** to **third parties**) may well be equivalent to fraud even though no dishonesty is shown.

Daniels v Daniels 1978

The facts: The company was controlled by its two directors, husband and wife. It bought land for £4,250 (probate value) from the estate of a deceased person and alter resold it at the same price to the lady director. She re-sold it for £120,000. A minority shareholder sued the directors but did not allege fraud. Objection was raised that a member could not sue the directors on the company's behalf for negligence (Pavlides' case above) but only for fraud.

Decision: The circumstances required investigation and a member might sue the directors and controlling shareholders for negligence if one of them secured a benefit form the company by reason of it.

In particular those directors who are also managers of the company's business are able to **control the flow of information** to the full board and to a general meeting. If the information is inaccurate or incomplete it may result in a wrong decision by the independent majority.

2.3 Discrimination against minority

The courts have taken **fraud** to mean not just misappropriation of company property but **discrimination against** the minority in some cases.

Clemens v Clemens Bros Ltd 1976

The facts: A and B (who were aunt and niece) held 55% and 45% respectively of the shares with voting rights. A proposed to vote in favour of ordinary resolutions to increase the authorised share capital and to approve the allotment of new shares to or for the benefit of employees of the company. No more shares would be allotted to A or B but the effect of the scheme would be to reduce B's shareholding from 45% to 24.5% with the object of depriving B of her power to block a special resolution to alter the articles as A desired. B sought a declaration that A could not use her votes in this way.

Decision: A should be restrained from using her votes to deprive B of her 'negative control' (her ability to block an alteration of the articles to which B objected).

---

3 Minority protection: s 994

> **FAST FORWARD**
>
> S 994 offers a statutory remedy to a minority if **unfairly prejudicial conduct** has occurred. Unfairly prejudicial conduct generally involves **discrimination against a minority** or **exclusion of a director** from a **quasi-partnership company**, and includes removal of the company's auditor from office on grounds of divergence of opinions on accounting treatments or audit procedures, or on any other improper grounds.

Statute law also gives protection to minority shareholders.

Any member may apply to the court for relief under s 994 Companies Act 2006 (TSO, 2006) on the grounds that the company's affairs are being or have been conducted in a manner which is **unfairly prejudicial** to the interests of the members **generally or of some part** of the members. Application may also be made in respect of a single prejudicial act omission.

3.1 Definition of unfairly prejudicial conduct

Unfair prejudice to some of the members includes **removal of the company's auditor** from office on grounds of divergence of opinions on accounting treatments or audit procedures, or on any other improper grounds: s 994(1A).

There is **no** other statutory definition of what constitutes unfairly prejudicial conduct. Applications against unfairly prejudicial conduct often arise from:

(a) **Exclusion of a director** from participation in the management of a quasi-partnership company when he could legitimately have expected to be involved in management. A **'quasi-partnership' company** is a small, generally private and often family-owned company where essentially the relationship between the directors and members is equivalent to partners in a partnership.

(b) **Discrimination against minority shareholders**.

Whatever the reason for the application, the complaint must be based on prejudice to the **member as a member** and not as an employee, nor as an unpaid creditor. The complaint must relate to **breach of the terms by which it has been agreed the company should be run**, and not to private acts of shareholders.

Courts will have regard to the **expectations** of members when considering whether conduct is unfairly prejudicial, particularly in quasi-partnership cases where the 'partner' expects to be involved in management. It is therefore unfairly prejudicial for the members to ignore that expectation and expel him.

> *Re Bird Precision Bellows 1986*
>
> *The facts:* A minority with 26% of the shares suspected the MD of this 'quasi-partnership' company of concealing bribes paid to secure contracts. When the DTI refused to investigate the minority was removed from the board. They claimed unfair prejudice under s 994.
>
> *Decision:* The claim was allowed as it was a 'quasi-partnership'.

3.2 Limits to unfair prejudice claims

The courts have established **limits** to claims under s 994.

(a) There has to have been an **actual act** by the company, for example a breach in the terms on which it was agreed the company would be run. A minority shareholder will not be able to obtain relief just because he has lost trust or confidence in the way the company is being run.

(b) The court will take into account the **contents** of the company's **constitution** in deciding whether the minority had legitimate expectations: *Re Tottenham Hotspur plc 1994*. It is unlikely that 'expectations' can override the terms of the memorandum and articles whether company is a plc.

(c) In **public companies**, shareholders are unlikely to have a reasonable expectation of being involved in management.

The courts may also take the **petitioner's conduct into account** when deciding whether certain actions are unfairly prejudicial.

> *Re R A Noble & Sons (Clothing) Ltd 1983*
>
> *The facts:* B had provided the capital but left the management in the hands of N, the other director, on the understanding that N would consult B on major company matters. N did not do so and B confined himself to enquiries to N on social occasions; he accepted N's vague assurances that all was well. The petition followed from a breakdown of the relationship.

10: MAJORITY CONTROL AND MINORITY PROTECTION

Decision: B's exclusion from discussion of company management questions was largely the result of his own lack of interest. The petition was dismissed.

Re London School of Electronics 1985

The facts: The other shareholders had removed the petitioner from his directorship after he had alleged that they were diverting business form the company to themselves. He then setup a rival business and took part of the company's connections with him.

Decision: He had a right to relief even though he did not have 'clean hands'. The majority had to buy out the minority without any discount for the fact that his were minority shareholders and therefore of less value.

Unfairly prejudicial conduct need not be **illegal**, nor need it be intention nor discriminatory. It is the effect of the conduct that is considered.

The courts will not generally intervene in cases of disputes about **management** (even bad management).

Re A Company 1983

The facts: The petitioners' grievance was the directors' refusal to put forward a scheme of reconstruction or a proposal to purchase their shares (by the company). The directors were preoccupied with plans for diversification of the business.

Decision: The directors' duty was to manage the company to its advantage as they saw it. It was not a case of 'unfair prejudice'.

In *Re Five Minute Car Wash Service Ltd 1966*, the complaint was of incompetent management causing loss but tolerated by the controlling shareholder. The petition failed.

3.3 Examples: Unfairly prejudicial contract

- **Exclusion** and **removal** from the **board**. When the company was one in which the director had legitimate expectations of being involved in management: *Re Bird Prediction Bellows Ltd 1986*.
- **Improper allotment** of shares.

Re DR Chemicals Ltd 1989

The facts: The majority shareholder allotted further shares to himself to increase his holding.

Decision: The allotment was a blatant case of unfair prejudicial conduct (and also, incidentally, a breach of the Companies Act pre-emption rules).

- **Failure** to **call a meeting**: *Re McGuinness and Another 1988*
- **Making an inaccurate statement to shareholders.**

Re A Company 1986

The facts: The petitioners complained that the directors had misled them in recommending acceptance of a bid by another company which the directors owned.

Decision: The directors' conduct was unfairly prejudicial since it affected members' rights to sell their shares at the best price.

- A managing director using **assets** for his own **personal benefit** and the personal benefit of his family and friends: *Re Elgindata Ltd 1991*.
- **Diversion of a company's business** to a director-controlled company: *Re Cumana 1986*.
- Making a **rights issue** which minority shareholders could not take up: *Re Cumana 1986*.

- Payment of **excessive directors' bonuses** and **pension contributions**: *Re Cumara 1986*.
- **Continued mismanagement** caused serious financial damage to the company and the minority's interests: *Re Macro (Ipswich) Ltd 1994*.

3.4 Examples: Not unfairly prejudicial conduct

- **Late presentation** of **accounts**: *Re Ringtower Holdings plc 1989*
- **Failure** by a parent company **to pay** the **debts** of a **subsidiary**: *Nicholas v Soundcraft Electronics Ltd 1993*
- **Non-compliance** with **Stock Exchange rules** and the UK Corporate Governance Code: *Re Astec (BSR) plc 1998*

The limits on the application of s 994 remain under debate and are determined on a case by case basis. It has been argued for example that a s 994 action could be used as a check on excessive board remuneration packages. *Re Cumana 1986* laid down the principle that excessive directors' remuneration can be conduct that is unfairly prejudicial to numbers' interests.

Maidment v Attwood and Others 2012

A shareholder petitioned for relief from unfair prejudice under s 994 on the grounds that the company's sole director paid himself excessive remuneration in the years prior to the company going into insolvency

Held: the director had breached his duties by fixing his remuneration by reference to his own interests, contrary to his duty as a director, which subsequently amounted to unfairly prejudicial conduct under s 994 CA 2006.

In *O'Neill v Phillips 1999* it was stressed that the relationship between shareholders is primarily governed by the **constitution**, so if this has been complied with, or any breach is only minor, the courts will not rush to find unfair prejudice. It is only where there is an equitable consideration of unfairness that the constitution **does not represent the understandings** on which the members are associated that an act which actually complies with the document may be found to be **unfairly prejudicial**.

3.5 Court order where there is unfair prejudice

FAST FORWARD
> Courts may take whatever orders they deem fit, most often **purchase of a dissenting minority's shares**.

When a petition is successful the court may make **whatever order** it deems fit.

- An order regulating the **future conduct** of the company's affairs, for example that a controlling shareholder shall conform to the decisions taken at board meetings.
- An authorisation to any person to bring **legal proceedings** on behalf of the company; the company is then responsible for the legal costs.
- An order requiring the company to **refrain** from doing or continuing an act complained of.
- An order for the wrongdoer to account to the company for its losses.
- Provision for the **purchase of shares** of the **minority**.
- **Inclusion in the articles** of provisions which may only be altered or removed thereafter by leave of the court.

Where the issue is a **minority objecting to a take-over**, a common relief is an order that either the controlling shareholder or the company shall **purchase the petitioner's shares at a fair price**. This ends a relationship which has probably broken down beyond repair.

- The shares should be valued on the basis of their **worth before** the controlling shareholders' conduct had diminished it.
- The **court** may determine what is **fair**; in particular no allowance need be made because the shares to be brought are only a minority holding and do not give control.
- When the articles provide a method for valuing shares this should be used unless it would be unfair to the petitioners.

10: MAJORITY CONTROL AND MINORITY PROTECTION

 **Question** — S 994

James is the majority shareholder in Elan Ltd, holding 52% of the issued shares. The other shareholders are Chris, Martin, Jennifer and Henry, each of whom holds 12% of the shares. The minority shareholders feel that James has been abusing his position as majority shareholder and have lost confidence in him. They approach you for general advice.

Advise them on the nature of the action available under s 994 Companies Act 2006 on the basis of unfair prejudice to the minority.

Answer

Under s 994, any member may now apply to the court for relief on the grounds that the company's affairs are being or have been conducted in a manner which is unfairly prejudicial to the interests of the members generally or some part of the members or in respect of a particular act or omission which has been or will be prejudicial. Applications are commonly made in cases of discrimination against a minority or exclusion of a director in a quasi-partnership company.

The prejudice complained of must affect the complainant-member in his capacity as member and not as an employee or unpaid creditor. The member need not prove bad faith or even an intention to discriminate.

The court will take into account the surrounding circumstances including the parties' conduct and may make such orders as it deems fit. It might regulate the company's future affairs in some way, order the purchase of the minority's shares by the majority or by the company itself (*SCWS v Meyer 1958*), authorise some person to bring proceedings on the company's behalf, order the company to refrain from doing the act complained of or include in the company's constitution provision which could then only be altered by the court.

Loss of confidence in itself will rarely be found to be unfair prejudice.

Examples of the types of conduct that have been held to be unfairly prejudicial include:

(a) Exclusion and removal from the board where there was a legitimate expectation of participation: *Re Bird Precision Bellows Ltd 1985*

(b) Where a managing director uses assets for his own personal benefit and the personal benefit of his family and friends: *Re Elgindata Ltd 1991*

(c) Where a majority shareholder transfers sources of profit into another company owned by the majority shareholder: *Re London School of Electronics Ltd 1986*

(d) The diversion of a company's business to a director-controlled company or the making of a rights issue which minority shareholder were not permitted to take up or the payment of excessive directors' bonuses and pension contributions: *Re Cumana 1986*

(e) The improper allotment of shares: *Re D R Chemicals Ltd 1989*

(f) The failure to call a meeting as requisitioned by the petitioner-minority: *Re McGuinness and Another 1988*

(g) The late presentation of accounts (Re Ringtower Holdings plc 1989) and failure by a parent company to pay the debts of a subsidiary: *Nicholas v Spendcroft Electronics Ltd 1993*

(h) Failure to increase dividends at a time when directors' remuneration was sharply increased: *Re Sam Weller 1989*

(i) Payment of excessive remuneration: *Maidment v Attwood 2012*

Exam focus point

A shareholder who is unhappy about the conduct of the company's affairs will often try to obtain a remedy under s 994, so remember to include it in any answer on this area.

4 Derivative claims

As we saw when considering the law governing directors under section 170 of the Act, directors owe their **general duties** to the company as a whole rather than to an individual member and therefore the company is the only proper claimant which can enforce them.

Under English common law members may, under certain circumstances, bring an action on behalf of a company that they are a member of. This is known as a **derivative claim**. The purpose of such claims is to enforce liability for breach of duty by one of the directors. After all, if the company itself is the only proper claimant and the directors claim for negligence, default, breach of trust or breach of duty against a director or other person, even if the director has not benefitted personally.

Sections 260 to 269 of the Companies Act 2006 (TSO, 2006) provide a **statutory basis** for deciding whether or not a member has a right to bring a **derivative claim**. They do not replace the rule in *Foss v Harbottle*, but instead set out new rules that allow a derivative claim for negligence, default, breach of trust or breach of duty against a director or other person, even if the director has not benefitted personally.

The sections introduce a two-stage procedure for derivative claims.

(a) The applicant presents a *prima facie* case for their claim and the court considers the issues on the basis of the evidence filed by the applicant only. At this stage courts can dismiss applications if the applicant cannot establish a *prima facie* case.

(b) If a *prima facie* case is established then the court shall consider a range of other matters before giving permission for a substantive claim.

Under a substantive claim, the claimant brings an action on behalf of the company to **enforce the company's rights** or to recover its property. Any **benefits** received from the claim will **accrue to the company** and not to the member.

The claimant would usually combine the derivative action with a **representative action** (on behalf of the other members who are not defendants) and a **personal claim** for damages.

5 'Just and equitable' winding up

A dissatisfied member may get the court to wind the company up on the just and equitable ground.

A member who is dissatisfied with the directors or controlling shareholders over the management of the company may petition the court for the company to be wound up (liquidated) on the **just and equitable ground**.

For such a petition to be successful, the member must show that no other remedy is available. It is not enough for a member to be **dissatisfied** to make it just and equitable that the company should be wound up, since winding up what may be an otherwise healthy company is a **drastic step**.

5.1 Examples: When companies have been wound up

(a) **The substratum of the company has gone** – the only main object(s) of the company (its underlying basis or substratum) cannot be or can no longer be achieved.

> *Re German Date Coffee Co 1882*
>
> *The facts:* The objects clause specified very pointedly that the sole object was to manufacture coffee from dates under a German patent. The German government refused to grand a patent. The company manufactured coffee under a Swedish patent for sale in Germany. A contributory petitioned for compulsory winding up.
>
> *Decision:* The company existed only to 'work a particular patent' and as it could not do so it should be wound up.

(b) **The company was formed for an illegal or fraudulent purpose or there is a complete deadlock in the management of its affairs.**

> *Re Yenidje Tobacco Co Ltd 1916*
>
> *The facts:* Two sole traders merged their businesses in a company of which they were the only directors and shareholders. They quarrelled bitterly and one sued the other for fraud. Meanwhile they refused to speak to each other and conducted board meetings by passing notes through the hands of the secretary. The defendant in the fraud action petitioned for compulsory winding up.
>
> *Decision:* 'In substance these two people are really partners' and by analogy with the law of partnership (which permits dissolution if the partners are really unable to work together) it was just and equitable to order liquidation.

(c) **The understandings between members or directors which were the basis of the association have been unfairly breached by lawful action.**

> *Ebrahimi v Westbourne Galleries Ltd 1973*
>
> *The facts:* E and N carried on business together for 25 years, originally as partners and for the last 10 years through a company in which each originally had 500 shares. E and N were the first directors and shared the profits as directors' remuneration; no dividends were paid. When N's son joined the business he became a third director and E and N each transferred 100 shares to N's son. Eventually there were disputes; N and his son used their voting control in general meeting (600 votes against 400) to remove E from his directorship under the power of removal given by the Companies Act (removal by ordinary resolution).
>
> *Decision:* The company should be wound up. N and his son were within their legal rights in removing E from his directorship, but the past relationship made it 'unjust or inequitable' to insist on legal rights and the court could intervene on equitable principles to order liquidation.

> *Re A Company 1983*
>
> *The facts:* The facts were similar in essentials to those in Ebrahimi's case but the majority offered and the petitioner agreed that they would settle the dispute by a sale of his shares to the majority. This settlement broke down however because they could not agree on the price. The petitioner then petitioned on the just and equitable ground.
>
> *Decision:* An order for liquidation on this ground may only be made 'in the absence of any other remedy'. As the parties had agreed in principle that there was an alternative to liquidation the petition must be dismissed.

(d) **The directors deliberately withheld information so that the shareholders have no confidence in the company's management.**

6 Other statutory rights of minorities

We have noted a number of rights for minority shareholders as we have worked through this company law Study Text. Here is a summary.

Minority rights	
Subject	**Required**
Variation of class rights	Holders of 15%+ of class of shares can apply to court for cancellation
Alteration of objects	Holders of 15%+ of issued shares can apply to court for cancellation
Company meeting	Can be requisitioned by holders of 5% of company's voting capital
Notice of members' resolution	Must be given by company on requisition of members holding 5%+ of voting rights/100 or more members holding shares in the company on which an average sum of £100+ per member has been paid up
Full notice of special resolution	Must be given if members with 5%+ of voting capital insist
Conversion of public company to private	50+ members or members holding 5%+ of issued share capital can apply to court for cancellation
Purchase of own shares out of capital by private company	Holders of 10%+ of shares/any class of shares can apply to court to prohibit the transaction
Financial assistance by private company	Any member can apply to court to prohibit the transaction
Poll	Can be demanded by at least 5 members/members holding 10%+ of voting rights or have 10%+ of total of all paid up shares
Off-market purchase of own shares	Poll can be demanded by individual members
Full notice of AGM	Can be demanded by individual members
Registration of limited company as unlimited	Can be prevented by individual members
Department for Business, Innovation and Skills investigation into affairs/ownership of company	Can be requested by 200+ members/members holding 10%+ of issued shares
Public company investigation into membership of company	Can be demanded by holders of 10%+ of company's voting capital

10: MAJORITY CONTROL AND MINORITY PROTECTION

Chapter roundup

- The majority ultimately control the company, though the minority may need to be protected. It is the company which should bring actions to recover goods etc, not shareholders individually.
- A minority can bring proceedings to prevent a **fraud** on the company or minority shareholders. Fraud can mean misappropriation of property or discrimination against a minority.
- S 994 offers a statutory remedy to a minority if **unfairly prejudicial conduct** has occurred. Unfairly prejudicial conduct generally involves **discrimination against a minority** or **exclusion of a director** from a **quasi-partnership company** and includes removal of the company's auditor from office on grounds of divergence of opinions on accounting treatments or audit procedures, or on any other improper grounds.
- Courts may make whatever orders they deem fit, most often **purchase of a dissenting minority's shares**.
- A dissatisfied member may get the court to wind the company up on the just and equitable ground.

Quick quiz

1. *Foss v Harbottle* established the rights of minority shareholders to obtain relief from oppressive acts by the majority.

    True ☐   False ☐

2. The three conditions to succeed in a claim for a fraud on the company are:

    (1) ....

    (2) ....

    (3) ....

3. Give four examples of remedies a court may provide for unfairly prejudicial conduct.

4. **Fill in the blanks** in the statements below.

    S 994 gives relief on the grounds that the company's affairs are being or have been conducted in a manner that is .... to the interests of .... or ....

5. Which of the following are statutory rights of individual members?

    A   To demand full notice of an AGM

    B   To prevent re-registration of a limited company as unlimited

    C   To apply for a cancellation of a variation of class rights

    D   To demand a poll on a resolution for an off market purchase of own shares

    E   To require the Department of Business, Innovation and Skills to investigate a company's membership

    F   To insist on full notice for a special resolution

6. **Fill in the blanks** in the statements below.

    Petitions under s 994 often arise from exclusion of a director from participation in the management of a .... company, or .... against a minority.

7. Give four examples of instances where the court has ordered a company to be wound up on the just and equitable grounds.

PART C   ADMINISTRATION AND CONTROL

Answers to quick quiz

1   False. *Foss v Harbottle* emphasised the principle of majority rule. (It was thus evident that the minority needed protection.)

2   (1)   What was taken belonged to the company
    (2)   It passed to those against whom the claim is made
    (3)   Those who appropriated the company's property are in control of the company

3   An order regulating the future conduct of the company's affairs
    Authorising the company to bring legal proceedings
    Ordering the company to refrain from actions
    Providing for the purchase of shares of the minority

4   S 994 gives relief on the grounds that the company's affairs are being or have been conducted in a manner that is **unfairly prejudicial** to the interests of **members generally** or **some part of the members**.

5   A, B and D represent individual rights. C requires application by holders of at least 15% of the shares of the class. E requires 200 members or the holders of at least 10% of issued shares. F requires members holding at least 5% of voting shares.

6   Petitions under s 994 often arise from exclusion of a director from participation in the management of a **quasi-partnership** company, or **discrimination** against a minority.

7   The substratum of the company has gone.

    The company was formed for an illegal or fraudulent purpose, or there is complete deadlock in its affairs.

    The understandings between members or directors which were the basis of association have been unfairly breached.

    The directors deliberately withhold information so that the shareholders have no confidence in the company's management.

End of chapter question

Frank

Frank is managing director of Good plc, a company listed on the London Stock Exchange. The constitution of Good plc states that the company's areas of business operation is to be restricted to the production and sale of non-alcoholic soft drinks, and that any contract above £50,000 requires the prior approval of the full board of directors. In January, Frank entered into a contract on behalf of Good plc to purchase £100,000 worth of a new type of alcoholic drink for sale in Good plc's shops. He did not inform the board of directors of his intentions. The alcoholic drinks were hugely successful and increased Good plc's profits substantially. A few weeks before the declaration of the company's improved results Frank secretly bought more shares in it.

Required

Advise Henry, who is a shareholder in Good plc, as to whether any action can be taken against Frank, and if so, what action can be taken. **(20 marks)**

Accounts and audit

Topic list	Syllabus reference
1 Accounting records and annual accounts	8.4
2 The company auditor	8.4
3 The auditor's independence	8.4
4 Auditors' liability	8.4

Introduction

This chapter deals with the statutory requirements for companies to

- Keep accounting records
- Prepare accounts and file them with the Registrar
- Appoint auditors (unless exempt)

and then covers the vital role of the auditor which has now increased in weighting in the syllabus. As well as appointment, resignation and removal of auditors we look at eligibility and ineligibility for office, the auditors' independence and their duties and rights.

Finally this chapter summarises the position regarding auditors' liability which is covered in more detail in your Auditing syllabus.

The **Companies Act 2006**, (TSO, 2006) and the **Small Business, Enterprise and Employment Act 2015**, (TSO, 2015) apply to this and all chapters unless otherwise stated.

PART C ADMINISTRATION AND CONTROL

1 Accounting records and annual accounts

1.1 Accounting records

FAST FORWARD

Companies must keep **sufficient accounting records** to explain the company's transactions and its financial position, in other words so that accurate financial statements can be prepared.

Under the Companies Act 2006 (TSO, 2006), a company is required to keep accounting records sufficient to **show and explain** the company's transactions. At any time, it should be possible:

- To **disclose** with reasonable accuracy the **company's financial position** at intervals of not more than six months.
- For the directors to ensure that any accounts required to be prepared **comply** with the **Act** and **International Accounting Standards**.

Certain specific records are required by the Act.

(a) Daily entries of **sums paid** and **received**, with details of the source and nature of the transactions.

(b) A **record** of **assets** and **liabilities**.

(c) **Statements of stock** held by the company at the end of each financial year.

(d) **Statements of stocktaking** to back up the records in (c).

(e) **Statements of goods bought and sold** (except retail sales), together with details of buyers and sellers sufficient to identify them.

The requirements (c) to (e) above apply only to businesses involved in dealing in goods.

Accounting records must be kept for **three** years (in the case of a **private** company), and **six** years in that of a **public** one.

Accounting records should be kept at the company's **registered office** or at some other place thought fit by the directors. Accounting records should be open to **inspection** by the **company's officers**. Shareholders have **no statutory rights** to inspect the records, although they may be granted the right by the articles.

Failure in respect of these duties is an offence by the officers in default.

1.2 Annual accounts

FAST FORWARD

A registered company must prepare **annual accounts** showing a true and fair view, lay them and various reports before members, and file them with the Registrar following directors' approval.

For each **accounting reference period** (usually 12 months) of the company the directors must prepare accounts for the members, and deliver or file them with the Registrar of Companies. Where they are prepared in Companies Act format they must include a **balance sheet** and **profit and loss account** which, for the accounting reference period up to the **accounting reference date,** give a **true and fair view** of the individual company's and the group's

- Assets
- Liabilities
- Financial position
- Profit or loss

The accounts can either be in **Companies Act format** or prepared in accordance with **International Accounting Standards**. Where international accounting standards are followed a note to this effect must be included in the notes to the accounts. After a financial year in which the directors of a company prepare IAS accounts for the company, the directors may change to preparing Companies Act accounts for a

190

reason other than a relevant change of circumstance provided they have not changed to Companies Act individual accounts in the period of five years preceding the first day of that financial year: s 395(4A).

The accounts can be prepared for a different period than 12 months if the company changes its accounting reference date. There is no restriction on how often a company can change the date if it means the accounting reference period is 12 months or less, but it cannot be extended beyond 12 months more than once in five years except in limited circumstances.

1.2.1 Approving, laying and filing accounts

The company's board of directors must **approve** the **annual accounts** and they must be signed by a director on behalf of the board. When directors approve annual accounts that do not comply with the Act or IAS they are **guilty** of an **offence**.

A public company is required to **lay its accounts**, and the **directors' report**, before **members** in **general meeting**. A quoted company must also lay the **directors' remuneration report** before the general meeting.

A company must **file** its annual accounts and its report with the **Registrar** within a maximum period reckoned from the accounting reference date, to which the accounts are made up. The standard permitted interval between the end of the accounting reference period and the filing of accounts is **six months** for a **public** and **nine months** for a **private company.**

1.2.2 Auditing accounts

The accounts must be **audited** (unless the company is exempt). The **auditors' report** must be attached to the copies issued to members, filed with the Registrar or published. Exemptions apply to **small and dormant companies,** though members may require an audit. The accounts must also be accompanied by a **directors' report** giving information on a number of prescribed matters. These include (where an audit was necessary) a statement that there is no relevant information of which the auditors are unaware, and another statement from the directors that they exercised due skill and care in the period. Quoted companies must submit the **directors' remuneration report**.

1.2.3 Abridged accounts

Most private companies are permitted to file **abridged accounts with the Registrar.** This right to prepare abbreviated accounts for Companies House does NOT affect the company's obligations to prepare full accounts for its members.

An entity is classed as 'micro' if it meets at least two of the following conditions:

- Annual turnover must be not more than £632,000
- The balance sheet total must be not more than £316,000
- The average number of employees must be not more than 10.

A private company is classed as 'small' if it meets at least two of the following conditions:

- Annual turnover must be not more than £10.2 million
- The balance sheet total must be not more than £5.1 million
- The average number of employees must be not more than 50.

A private company is classed as 'medium-sized' if it meets at least two of the following conditions:

- Annual turnover must be not more than £36 million
- The balance sheet total must be not more than £18 million
- The average number of employees must be not more than 250.

Public companies and certain types of organisation, such as banks, cannot benefit from the micro-entity and small and medium-sized company disclosure exemptions.

A **micro-entity** has to option to take advantage of certain accounting exemptions. These include using **simple profit and loss accounts** and **balance sheets** and only providing a minimum of accounting information (referred to in the regulations as **minimum accounting terms**). No notes to the accounts are required and the entity can apply the small company rules (see below) in relation to other aspects such as the directors' report.

A **small company** can either choose to file a copy of the full accounts which it prepared for its members, or to file **an abridged balance sheet but no directors' report or profit and loss account**: s 444. They must be filed with a special auditor's report unless the company is also exempt from audit (see 1.3 below).

A **medium-sized company** must deliver its annual accounts and directors' report to the Registrar, plus a copy of the auditor's report (unless the company is exempt from audit). The accounts must include **a balance sheet plus a profit and loss account in which certain items are combined**, that is a different form of abridged accounts to small companies: s 445. Again a special auditor's report is required: s 449.

1.2.4 Recipients of annual accounts

Each **member** and **debentureholder** is entitled to be sent a copy of the **annual accounts**, together with the directors' and auditor's reports. In the case of public companies, they should be sent at least 21 days before the meeting at which they shall be laid. In the case of private companies they should be sent at the same time as the documents are filed, if not earlier.

Anyone else entitled to **receive** notice of a general meeting, including the company's auditor, should **also be sent** a copy. At any other time any member or debentureholder is entitled to a copy free of charge within **seven days** of requesting it.

All companies may prepare a **summary financial statement** to be circulated to members instead of the full accounts, subject to various requirements as to form and content being met. However, members have the right to receive full accounts should they wish to.

Quoted companies must make their annual accounts and reports available on a website which is maintained on the company's behalf and which identifies it. The documents must be made available as soon as reasonably practicable and access should not be conditional on the payment of a fee or subject to other restrictions.

Where the company or its directors **fail to comply** with the Act, they may be subject to a **fine**.

1.2.5 Late filing of accounts with Companies House

Late filing of accounts will result in a fine being due.

1.3 Exemption from audit

> **FAST FORWARD**
> Certain companies are **exempt from audit** provided that certain conditions are fulfilled.

These conditions are as follows:

(a) A small company is totally exempt from the annual audit requirement in a financial year if its turnover for that year is **not more** than **£10.2 million**, and its **balance sheet total** is **not more than £5.1 million**: s 477.

(b) The exemptions do not apply to **public companies**, **banking** or **insurance companies** or those subject to a **statute-based regulatory regime**.

(c) **Members** holding **10%** or more of the capital of any company can veto the exemption: s 476.

(d) **Dormant companies** also qualify for exemption from an audit.

2 The company auditor

> **FAST FORWARD**
>
> Every company (apart from certain small companies) must appoint appropriately qualified **auditors**. An audit is a check on the stewardship of the directors.

Under the Companies Act 2006 (TSO, 2006), **every company** (except a dormant private company and certain small and subsidiary companies) must **appoint auditors** for each financial year: s 475.

2.1 Appointment of auditors

The **first auditors** may be appointed by the directors, to hold office until the **first general meeting** at which their appointment is considered.

Subsequent auditors may not take office until the previous auditor has ceased to hold office. They will hold office until the end of the next financial period (private companies) or the next accounts meeting (public companies) unless re-appointed.

Appointment of auditors	
Members	• Usually appoint auditor in general meeting by ordinary resolution. • Auditors hold office from 28 days after the meeting in which the accounts are laid until the end of the corresponding period the next year. This is the case even if the auditors are appointed at the meeting where the accounts are laid. • May appoint in general meeting to fill a casual vacancy.
Directors	• Appoint the first ever auditors. They hold office until the end of the first meeting at which the accounts are considered. • May appoint to fill a casual vacancy.
Secretary of State	• May appoint auditors if members fail to do so. • Company must notify Secretary of State within 28 days of the general meeting where the accounts were laid.

2.2 Eligibility as auditor

> **FAST FORWARD**
>
> Membership of a **Recognised Supervisory Body** is the main prerequisite for eligibility as an auditor.

Membership of a **Recognised Supervisory Body** is the main prerequisite for eligibility as an auditor. An audit firm may be either a body corporate, a partnership or a sole practitioner.

The Act requires an auditor to hold an **'appropriate qualification'**. A person holds an 'appropriate qualification' if they:

- Have satisfied **existing criteria** for appointment as an auditor.
- Hold a **recognised qualification** obtained in the UK.
- Hold an **approved overseas qualification**.

2.3 Ineligibility as auditor

> **FAST FORWARD**
>
> Under the Companies Act 2006, a person may be ineligible on the grounds of **'lack of independence'**.

A person is ineligible for appointment as a company auditor if they are:

- An **officer** or **employee** of the company being audited
- A **partner** or **employee** of such a person

- A **partnership** in which such a person is a partner
- **Ineligible** by virtue of the above for appointment as auditor of any parent or subsidiary undertaking where there exists a **connection** of any description as may be specified in regulations laid down by Secretary of State.

2.4 Effect of lack of independence or ineligibility

No person may act as auditor if they become ineligible or lack independence. If during their term of office an auditor loses their independence or eligibility they must **resign** with immediate effect, and **notify** their client of their resignation, giving the reason.

A person continuing to act as auditor despite losing their independence or becoming ineligible is **liable to a fine**. However it is a defence if they can prove they were not aware that they lost independence or became ineligible.

The legislation does **not** disqualify the following from being an auditor of a limited company:

- A shareholder of the company
- A debtor or creditor of the company
- A close relative of an officer or employee of the company

However, the **regulations** of the **accountancy bodies** applying to their own members are **stricter than statute in this respect**.

2.5 Re-appointing auditors of a private company

As private companies are not required to hold annual general meetings, auditors of **private companies** are normally deemed **automatically re-appointed** each year.

The rules on appointment make reference to a **meeting** where the accounts are laid. This is not always relevant for private companies as under the Act they are not required to hold an AGM or lay the accounts before the members at a meeting. Therefore **auditors of private companies are deemed automatically re-appointed** unless one of the following circumstances applies.

- The auditor was **appointed by the directors** (most likely when the first auditor was appointed).
- The **articles require formal re-appointment**.
- **Members holding 5% of the voting rights** serve notice that the auditor should not be reappointed s 488.
- A **resolution** (written or otherwise) has been passed that prevents reappointment.
- The **directors have resolved that auditors should not be appointed** for the forthcoming year as the company is likely to be exempt from audit.

In the first case – where auditors have been appointed by the directors - there will have to be a members' meeting at an early stage so that they can be appointed by the members.

2.6 Auditors' remuneration

Whoever appoints the auditors has power to **fix their remuneration** for the period of their appointment. It is usual when the auditors are appointed by the general meeting to leave it to the directors to fix their remuneration (by agreement at a later stage). The auditors' remuneration must be **disclosed** in a **note to the accounts**.

2.7 Duties of auditors

The **statutory duty** of auditors is to report to the members whether the accounts give a **true and fair view** and have been properly prepared in accordance with the Companies Act.

11: ACCOUNTS AND AUDIT

They must also:

- **State** whether or not the **directors' report** is **consistent** with the **accounts**.
- For **quoted companies**, **report** to the members on the **auditable** part of the **directors' remuneration report** including whether or not it has been properly prepared in accordance with the Act: s 497.
- For listed companies, state in his report whether, in his opinion, the information given in the **corporate governance statement** about internal control and risk management systems in relation to financial reporting processes, and about share capital structures, is consistent with those accounts: s 497A.
- Be **signed** by the **auditor**, stating their **name**, and **date**. Where the auditor is a firm, the **senior auditor** must sign in their **own name** for, and on behalf, of the auditor.

If the directors of the company have prepared accounts in accordance with the **small companies regime**, or have taken advantage of small companies exemption in preparing the directors' report, and in the auditor's opinion they were not entitled to do so, the auditor shall state that fact in his report: s 497(5).

To fulfil their statutory duties, the auditors **must carry out such investigations as are necessary** to form an opinion as to whether:

(a) **Proper accounting records** have been kept and proper returns adequate for the audit have been received from branches.

(b) The **accounts** are in **agreement** with the **accounting records**.

(c) The **information** in the **directors' remuneration report** is consistent with the **accounts**.

The auditors' report must be **read** before any general meeting at which the accounts are considered and must be open to inspection by members. Auditors have to make disclosure of other services rendered to the company and the remuneration received.

Where an auditor **knowingly** or **recklessly** causes their report to be **materially misleading**, **false** or **deceptive**, they commit a criminal offence and may be liable to a **fine**: s 507.

2.8 Rights of auditors

FAST FORWARD The Companies Act provides **statutory rights** for auditors to enable them to carry out their duties.

The **principal rights** of auditors, excepting those dealing with resignation or removal, are set out in the table below, and the following are notes on more detailed points.

Access to records	A right of access at all times to the books, accounts and vouchers of the company: s 499 (1)
Information and explanations	A right to require from the company's officers, employees or any other relevant person, such information and explanations as they think necessary for the performance of their duties as auditors: s 499 (1)
Attendance at/notices of general meetings	A right to attend any general meetings of the company and to receive all notices of and communications relating to such meetings which any member of the company is entitled to receive: s 502 (2)
Right to speak at general meetings	A right to be heard at general meetings which they attend on any part of the business that concerns them as auditors: s 502 (2)
Rights in relation to written resolutions	A right to receive a copy of any written resolution proposed: s 502 (1)

If auditors have **not received** all the information and explanations they consider necessary, they should state this fact in their audit report. The Act makes it an **offence** for a company's officer knowingly or recklessly to make a statement in any form to an auditor which:

- Conveys or purports to convey any information or explanation required by the auditor and
- Is materially misleading, false or deceptive.

The **penalty** is a maximum of two years' imprisonment, a fine or both.

2.9 Termination of auditors' appointment

FAST FORWARD

Auditors may leave office in the following ways: **resignation**; **removal from office** by an ordinary resolution with special notice passed before the end of their term; **failing** to **offer themselves** for **re-election**; and **not being re-elected** at the general meeting at which their term expires.

Departure of auditors from office can occur in the following ways.

(a) Auditors may **resign** their appointment by giving notice in writing to the company delivered to the registered office.

(b) Auditors may **decline reappointment**.

(c) Auditors may be **removed** from office before the expiry of their appointment by the passing of an ordinary resolution in general meeting. Special notice is required and members and auditors must be notified. **Private companies cannot remove an auditor by written resolution;** a meeting must be held.

(d) Auditors **do not have to be reappointed** when their term of office expires, although in most cases they are. Special notice must be given of any resolution to appoint auditors who were not appointed on the last occasion of the resolution, and the members and auditor must be notified.

Where a private company resolves to **appoint** a replacement auditor by **written resolution**, copies of the resolution must be sent to the proposed and outgoing auditor. The outgoing auditor may circulate a **statement of reasonable length** to the members if they notify the company within 14 days of receiving the copy of the written resolution.

2.10 Procedure for resignation of auditors

FAST FORWARD

However auditors leave office they must either: state there are **no circumstances** which should be brought to **members' and creditors' attention**; or list **those circumstances**. Auditors who are resigning can also: **circulate a statement** about their resignation to members; **requisition a general meeting'**, **or speak** at a general meeting.

	Procedures for resignation of auditors
Statement of circumstances	Auditors must deposit a statement at the registered office with their resignation stating: • For quoted companies – the circumstances around their departure. • For non-quoted public companies and all private companies – there are no circumstances that the auditor believes should be brought to the attention of the members or creditors. • If there are such circumstances the statement should describe them. • Statements should also be submitted to the appropriate audit authority.
Company action	• The company must send notice of the resignation to the Registrar. Failure to do so is an offence: s 521. • The company must **send** a copy of the statement of circumstances to **every person entitled to receive a copy of the accounts.**
Auditors' rights	If the auditors have deposited a statement of circumstances, they may: • Circulate a statement of reasonable length to the members. • Requisition a general meeting to explain their reasons: s 518. • Attend and speak at any meeting where appointment of successors is to be discussed.

11: ACCOUNTS AND AUDIT

If the auditors decline to seek reappointment at an AGM, they must nevertheless fulfil the requirements of a **statement of the circumstances** just as if they had resigned during the year.

The reason for this provision is to prevent auditors who are unhappy with the company's affairs keeping their suspicions secret. The statement must be deposited not less than **14 days** before the time allowed for next appointing auditors. It is an offence on the part of the auditor to fail to deposit the statement of circumstances: s 518.

2.11 Removal of auditors from office

Procedures for removal from office	
Auditor representations	If a resolution is proposed either to: • Remove the auditors before their term of office expires; or • Change the auditors when their term of office is complete the auditors have the right to make representations of reasonable length to the company.
Company action	The company must: • Notify members in the notice of the meeting of the representations. • Send a copy of the representations in the notice. • If it is not sent out, the auditors can require it is read at the meeting.
Attendance at meeting	Auditors removed before expiry of their office may: • Attend the meeting at which their office would have expired. • Attend any meeting at which the appointment of their successors is discussed.
Statement of circumstances	If auditors are removed at a general meeting they must: • Make a statement of circumstances for members and creditors as above.

Exam focus point

Remember that:

(a) A statement of circumstances/no circumstances must be deposited **however** the auditors leave office.

(b) The auditors have **additional rights** depending on how they leave office.

In the exam you **must** read any question on this area carefully to ensure you answer it correctly.

3 The auditor's independence

3.1 The problems of independence

FAST FORWARD

Independence is a key attribute of any auditor, and the reason for the provisions in the Companies Act for ineligibility for office.

From the above it is clear that **independence** is a key attribute of any auditor, and the reason for the provisions in the **Companies Act** on ineligibility for office, set out in 2.3 above. This topic is dealt with in detail elsewhere in your syllabus, but the position can be summarised briefly here.

Any link to a client, whether personal or financial, has the potential **to cloud auditors' judgement** when arriving at their opinion on the company's accounts.

Ethical standards (see 3.2 below) list **six threats** to an auditor's independence:

- **Self-interest threat** – a member of the audit team has financial or other personal interests in a client which threaten objectivity.
- **Self-review threat** – accounting records are prepared and audited by the same person.

- **Management threat** – auditors take executive decisions which should be the responsibility of management.
- **Advocacy threat** – the auditors support the client in an adversarial situation, eg in litigation.
- **Familiarity or trust threat** – close personal relationships inhibit questioning of a client.
- **Intimidation threat** – auditors are influenced by fear or threats, eg of removal.

There is general agreement that if auditors are not independent from their clients, the audit is **devalued** or even worthless. For the great majority, this is a matter of professionalism, and their independence and judgement are not in doubt. But **the threats are very real** and cannot be ignored.

3.2 Ethics and the auditor

> **FAST FORWARD**
>
> The most effective way in which professionals can combat the threats outlined above is by adherence to the **Ethical Standards** issued by the **Auditing Practices Board (APB)**.

The **APB Ethical Standards** (APB, 2010, 2011) have been drawn up to ensure consistency with the accounting bodies' own **codes of professional ethics**.

These Standards (again dealt with elsewhere in your syllabus) are:

ES1 Integrity, objectivity and independence
ES2 Financial, business, employment and personal relationships
ES3 Long association with the audit engagement
ES4 Fees, remuneration and evaluation policies, litigation, gifts and hospitality
ES5 Non-audit services provided to audited entities

ES2 to 5 essentially provide specific rules which ensure the objectives set out in ES1. By following the requirements of these standards, auditors are able to avoid the factors which threaten independence.

4 Auditors' liability

4.1 Nature of auditors' liability

> **FAST FORWARD**
>
> Auditors may be liable for **negligence** to anyone to whom they owe a **duty of care**.
>
> The Companies Act allows companies and their auditors to make agreements which limit the auditors' **liability** to a 'fair and reasonable amount'.
>
> The accounting bodies require all members in practice to have **professional indemnity insurance**.

The development (by means of case-law) of the liability of auditors for negligence is covered elsewhere in the syllabus. The current position, in summary, is that auditors may be liable for negligence to anyone to whom they owe a **duty of care** – namely:

- The company
- The members as a whole
- Anyone who they know, at the time of signing the audit report, is likely to rely on that report; to be liable they also must be aware of the reasons for that reliance.

4.2 Liability limitation agreements

Under the Companies Act 2006 (TSO, 2006), s 532 any **agreement** between an auditor and a company that seeks to **indemnify the auditor** for their own negligence, default, or breach of duty or trust is **void**. However, under s 534, an agreement can be made which **limits the auditor's liability** to the company. Such **liability limitation agreements** (LLAs) can only stand for **one financial year** and must therefore be replaced annually.

Liability can only be **limited** to what is **fair and reasonable** having regard to the auditor's responsibilities, their contractual obligations and the professional standards expected of them. Such agreements must be approved by the members and **publicly disclosed** in the **accounts** or **directors' report**. The Financial Reporting Council (FRC) has issued guidance on these agreements.

Perhaps not surprisingly, companies are not rushing to sign up to liability limitation agreements, and they may never become widespread.

4.3 Professional indemnity insurance

Professional indemnity insurance (PII) provides cover for professionals against **claims for professional negligence** or loss through fraud or dishonesty.

AIA members in practice must obtain at least **a minimum level** of PII cover depending on their total fee income for the previous accounting year. The AIA advises its practising members to consider the **risk profile** of their work and their clients, and decide whether, and by how much, they need to hold PII cover **in excess** of the minimum requirements.

Increasing amounts of claims for professional negligence in recent years have resulted in ever-**increasing PII premiums**. The accountancy profession in the UK has **lobbied successive governments** in attempts to have a **'cap'** set to auditors' liability: these have always been **unsuccessful**, and the provisions for **liability limitation agreements** as described in 4.2 above are unlikely to make a great deal of difference.

Chapter roundup

- Companies must keep **sufficient accounting records** to explain the company's transactions and its financial position, in other words so that accurate financial statements can be prepared.

- A registered company must prepare **annual accounts** showing a true and fair view, lay them and various reports before members, and file them with the Registrar following directors' approval.

- Certain companies are **exempt from audit** provided that certain conditions are fulfilled.

- Every company (apart from certain small companies) must appoint appropriately qualified **auditors**. An audit is a check on the stewardship of the directors.

- Membership of a **Recognised Supervisory Body** is the main prerequisite for eligibility as an auditor.

- Under the Companies Act 2006 a person may be ineligible for office as auditor on the grounds of **'lack of independence'**.

- As private companies are not required to hold AGMs, auditors of **private companies** are normally deemed **automatically re-appointed** each year.

- The Companies Act provides **statutory rights** for auditors to enable them to carry out their duties.

- Auditors may leave office in the following ways: **resignation**; **removal from office** by an ordinary resolution with special notice passed before the end of their term; **failing** to **offer themselves** for **re-election**; and **not being re-elected** at the general meeting at which their term expires.

- However auditors leave office they must either: state there are **no circumstances** which should be brought to **members' and creditors' attention**; or provide a **statement of circumstances**. Auditors who are resigning can also: **circulate a statement** about their resignation to members; **requisition a general meeting**; or **speak** at a general meeting.

- **Independence** is a key attribute of any auditor, and the reason for the provisions in the Companies Act for ineligibility for office.

- The most effective way in which professionals can combat the threats outlined above is by adherence to the **Ethical Standards** issued by the **Auditing Practices Board (APB)**.

- Auditors may be liable for **negligence** to anyone to whom they owe a **duty of care**.

- The Companies Act allows companies and their auditors to make liability limitation agreements which limit the auditors' **liability** to a **'fair and reasonable amount'**.

- The accounting bodies require all members in practice to have **professional indemnity insurance**.

11: ACCOUNTS AND AUDIT

Quick quiz

1. What are the minimum specific accounting records required by the Companies Act for a company that does NOT deal in goods?

2. What is the maximum period after a company's year-end within which its accounts must be filed?

   Private company...............

   Public company...............

3. Blandings plc has turnover of £5 million for the current year and its balance sheet total is £3 million. Can the company be exempt from audit?

4. When may directors appoint auditors, and for how long may auditors so appointed hold office?

5. State two reasons a person would be ineligible to be an auditor under Companies Act 2006.

   (1) ....

   (2) ....

6. When an auditor resigns, to whom must they supply a statement of circumstances?

7. List the threats to auditors' independence set out in the APB Ethical Standards.

8. If a company does not need an audit, its accounts are not required to give a true and fair view.

   True ☐

   False ☐

9. To whom do auditors currently owe a duty of care?

10. Against what is professional indemnity insurance protecting professionals?

PART C   ADMINISTRATION AND CONTROL

Answers to quick quiz

1   (a)   Daily entries of sums paid and received, with details of the source and nature of the transactions.
    (b)   A record of assets and liabilities

2   Public companies six months; private companies nine months.

3   No, because it is a public company.

4   The first auditors may be appointed by the directors, to hold office until the first general meeting at which their appointment is considered. Directors may also appoint auditors to fill a casual vacancy.

5   Any of:
    (1)   Is an officer/employee of the company being audited
    (2)   A partner or employee of a person in (1)
    (3)   A partnership in which (1) is a partner
    (4)   Ineligible by (1), (2) and (3) to be auditor of any of the entity's subsidiaries

6   To the company at its registered office, and to the appropriate audit authority.

7   Self-interest, self-review, management, advocacy, familiarity, intimidation.

8   False. All companies' statutory accounts are required to give a true and fair view.

9   Auditors owe a duty of care to:
    - The company
    - The members as a whole
    - Anyone who they know, at the time of signing the audit report, is likely to rely on that report; to be liable they also must be aware of the reasons for that reliance

10 Claims for professional negligence or loss through fraud or dishonesty.

End of chapter question

Parsloe Ltd

Parsloe Ltd owns a minority of the shares of Matchingham plc and, on the basis of encouraging results and growth potential shown in Matchingham's latest annual accounts, Parsloe Ltd wishes to buy a controlling interest in Matchingham plc.

The directors of Parsloe Ltd wait for the accounts to be approved at Matchingham plc's annual general meeting, and then purchase the shares.

Within six months of this investment the board of Matchingham plc make moves to wind up the company on the basis of its insolvency. Enquiries by the directors of Parsloe Ltd reveal that the accounts laid before the AGM were wildly inaccurate and contained numerous misleading statements.

Required

Produce notes for a report to the directors of Parsloe Ltd, explaining what success they might have if they were to sue the auditors of Matchingham plc.   **(20 marks)**

Insolvency

Insolvency

Topic list	Syllabus reference
1 What is liquidation?	8.6
2 Voluntary liquidation	8.6
3 Compulsory liquidation	8.6
4 Differences between compulsory and voluntary liquidation	8.6
5 Increasing the assets available to creditors	8.6
6 Revision: insolvency situations	8.6

Introduction

A **company in difficulty** or **in crisis** (an **insolvent** company) basically has a choice of two alternatives:

(1) To carry on with the business, using statutory methods to help remedy the situation.

(2) To stop.

A company which is heading towards insolvency can often be **saved**, using a variety of **legal protections** from creditors until the problem is sorted out. As we shall see in Chapter 13, the **directors** of a company can get into a lot of trouble if they carry on trading through a company in serious financial difficulties, and their actions result in **creditors** being **defrauded**.

However, alternative 1 does not have to mean carrying on as if everything is normal. It can mean **seeking help** from the **court** or a **qualified insolvency practitioner** to put a plan together to **save the company** and get it out of its bad financial position.

Unfortunately, many companies cannot be saved, and the members and directors are forced to take alternative 2, **to stop** operating the business through the company. Liquidation, sometimes called 'winding up', is **when a company is formally dissolved** and ceases to exist.

Various methods of achieving liquidation are covered in the first three sections of this chapter. Note though that a company **does not have to be in financial difficulty to be liquidated**.

The **Insolvency Act 1986**, (HMSO, 1986) applies to this chapter unless otherwise stated.

PART D INSOLVENCY

1 What is liquidation?

FAST FORWARD

Liquidation is the dissolution or 'winding up' of a company.

Key terms

Liquidation means that the company must be dissolved and its affairs 'wound up', or brought to an end. It is often referred to as **winding up**.

The assets are realised, debts are paid out of the proceeds, and any surplus amounts are returned to members. Liquidation leads on to **dissolution** of the company.

1.1 Who decides to liquidate?

FAST FORWARD

There are three different methods of **liquidation: compulsory, members' voluntary** and **creditors' voluntary**. Compulsory liquidation and creditors' voluntary liquidation are proceedings for insolvent companies which cannot pay their debts, and members' voluntary liquidation is for solvent companies.

The parties most likely to be involved in the decision to liquidate are:

- The directors
- The creditors
- The members

The **directors** are best placed to know the financial position and difficulty that the company is in. The **creditors** may become aware that the company is in financial difficulty when their invoices do not get paid on a timely basis, or at all.

The **members** are likely to be the last people to know that the company is in financial difficulty, as they rely on the directors to tell them. In public companies, there is a rule that the directors must call a general meeting of members if the net assets of the company fall to half or less of the amount of its called-up share capital. There is no such rule for private companies.

As we shall see in the next two sections, there are three methods of winding up. They depend on **who has instigated the proceedings**. Directors cannot formally instigate proceedings for winding up, they can only make recommendations to the members.

However, if the **members refuse** to put the company in liquidation and the directors feel that to continue to trade will prejudice creditors, they could resign their posts. This prevents them from committing the offences we shall see in Chapter 13.

In any case, if the company was in such serious financial difficulty for this to be an issue, it is likely that a **creditor** would have commenced proceedings against it.

1.1.1 Creditors

If a creditor has grounds (we shall discuss these in Section 2) they may **apply to the court** for the **compulsory winding up** of the company.

Creditors may also be closely involved in a **creditors' voluntary winding up**, if the company is **insolvent** when the **members** decide to wind the company up.

1.1.2 Members

The members may decide to wind the company up (probably on the advice of the directors). If they do so, the company is **voluntarily wound up**. This can lead to two different types of members' winding up:

- Members' voluntary winding up (if the company is solvent)
- Creditors' voluntary winding up (if the company is insolvent)

1.2 Role of the liquidator

FAST FORWARD A **liquidator** must be an authorised, qualified insolvency practitioner.

Once the decision to liquidate has been taken, the company goes under the **control of a liquidator** who must be a **qualified** and **authorised insolvency practitioner**.

We shall look at the procedures that the liquidator carries out in the next two sections. However, the liquidator also has a statutory duty to **report** to the Secretary of State where he feels that any **director** of the insolvent company is **unfit** to be involved in the management of a company. This may lead to disqualification of directors, as we saw in Chapter 9.

1.3 Common features of liquidations

FAST FORWARD Once **insolvency procedures** have commenced, share trading must cease, the company documents must state that the company is in liquidation and the directors' power to manage ceases.

Regardless of what method of liquidation is used, similar **legal problems** may arise in each of them. In addition, the following factors are true at the start of any liquidation:

- **No share dealings** or **changes in members** are allowed.
- All company documents (eg invoices, letters, emails) and the website must **state the company is in liquidation**.
- The **directors' power to manage ceases**.

2 Voluntary liquidation

FAST FORWARD A **winding up** is **voluntary** where the decision to wind up is taken by the company's members, although if the company is insolvent, the creditors will be heavily involved in the proceedings.

As we discussed in Section 1, there are two types of voluntary liquidation under the Insolvency Act 1986 (HMSO, 1986):

- A **members' voluntary winding up**, where the company is **solvent** and the members merely decide to 'kill it off'.
- A **creditors' voluntary winding up**, where the company is **insolvent** and the members resolve to wind up in consultation with creditors.

The main differences between a members' and a creditors' voluntary winding up are set out below.

Function	Winding up	
	Members' voluntary	Creditors' voluntary
(1) Appointment of liquidator	By members	Nominated by members, creditor approval required
(2) Approval for liquidator's actions	General meeting of members	Liquidation committee
(3) Liquidation committee	None	Up to five representatives of creditors

The effect of the voluntary winding up being a creditors' one is that the **creditors** have a **decisive influence** on the conduct of the liquidation.

In both kinds of voluntary winding up, the **court has the power to appoint a liquidator** (if for some reason there is none acting) or to remove one liquidator and appoint another: s 108.

PART D INSOLVENCY

2.1 Members' voluntary liquidation

FAST FORWARD

In order to be a members' winding up, the directors must make a **declaration of solvency**. It is a criminal offence to make a declaration of solvency without reasonable grounds.

Type of resolution to be passed	
Ordinary	This is **rare, but** if the **articles** specify liquidation at a certain point, only an ordinary resolution is required.
Special	A company may resolve to be **wound up** by special resolution.

The winding up **commences** on the passing of the resolution. A signed copy of the resolution must be delivered to the Registrar within 15 days. A **liquidator** is usually appointed by the same resolution (or a second resolution passed at the same time).

2.1.1 Declaration of solvency

A voluntary winding up is a members' voluntary winding up **only** if the directors make and deliver to the Registrar a **declaration of solvency**: s 89.

This is a **statutory declaration** that the directors have made full enquiry into the affairs of the company and are of the opinion that it will be able to pay its debts, within a specified period not exceeding 12 months.

(a) The declaration is made by all the directors or, if there are more than two directors, by a **majority** of them.

(b) The declaration includes a **statement of the company's assets and liabilities** as at the latest practicable date before the declaration is made.

(c) The declaration must be:
   (i) Made not more than five weeks before the resolution to wind up is passed, and
   (ii) Delivered to the Registrar within 15 days after the meeting.

If the liquidator later concludes that the company will be unable to pay its debts they must call a meeting of creditors and lay before them a **statement of assets and liabilities**: s 95.

Exam focus point

It is a **criminal offence** punishable by fine or imprisonment for a director to make a declaration of solvency without having **reasonable grounds** for it. If the company proves to be insolvent they will have to justify their previous declaration or be punished.

In a members' voluntary winding up the **creditors play no part** since the assumption is that their debts will be paid in full. The liquidator calls special and annual general meetings of contributories (members) to whom they report:

(a) Within three months after each anniversary of the commencement of the winding up the liquidator must call a meeting and lay before it an account of his transactions during the year.

(b) When the liquidation is complete the liquidator calls a meeting to lay before it his final accounts.

After holding the final meeting the liquidator sends a **copy of his accounts** to the Registrar who dissolves the company three months later by removing its name from the register: s 201.

2.2 Creditors' voluntary liquidation

FAST FORWARD

When there is no declaration of solvency there is a **creditors' voluntary winding** up.

If no declaration of solvency is made and delivered to the Registrar the liquidation proceeds as a creditors' voluntary winding up **even if** in the end the company pays its debts in full.

The **meeting of members** is held first and its business is as follows:

- To resolve to wind up, and
- To nominate a liquidator.

Creditor approval is required for the nomination of the liquidator. This is achieved through the deemed consent procedure or by a virtual meeting. If the creditors nominate a different person to be liquidator, **their choice prevails** over the nomination by the members.

Of course, the creditors may decide **not to appoint a liquidator** at all. They cannot be compelled to appoint a liquidator, and if they do fail to appoint one it will be the members' nominee who will take office.

In the past, the presence of the members' nominee as liquidator has been exploited for the purpose known as **'centrebinding'**.

Re Centrebind Ltd 1966

The facts: The directors convened a general meeting, without making a statutory declaration of solvency, but failed to call a creditors' meeting for the same or the next day. The penalty for this was merely a small default fine. The liquidator chosen by the members had disposed of the assets before the creditors could appoint a liquidator. The creditors' liquidator challenged the sale of the assets (at a low price) as invalid.

Decision: The first liquidator had been in office when he made the sale and so it was a valid exercise of the normal power of sale.

In a 'centrebinding' transaction the assets are sold by an **obliging liquidator** to a new company formed by the members of the insolvent company. The purpose is to defeat the claims of the creditors at minimum cost and enable the same people to continue in business until the next insolvency supervenes.

The Government has sought to limit the abuses during the period between the members' and creditors' meetings. The **powers of the members' nominee as liquidator are now restricted** to:

- Taking control of the company's property,
- Disposing of perishable or other goods which might diminish in value if not disposed of immediately, and
- Doing all other things necessary for the protection of the company's assets.

If the members' liquidator wishes to perform any act other than those listed above, he will have to **apply to the court for leave**.

Question — Voluntary liquidation

What are the key differences between a creditors' voluntary liquidation and a members' voluntary liquidation?

Answer

Creditors' voluntary liquidation	Members' voluntary liquidation
Company is insolvent	Company is solvent
Creditors approve members' nominee for liquidator	Members appoint liquidator
Liquidation committee approve liquidator's action	Members approve liquidator's actions in general meeting

3 Compulsory liquidation

> **FAST FORWARD**
>
> A creditor may apply to the court to wind up the company, primarily if the company is **unable to pay its debts**. There are statutory tests to prove that a company is unable to pay its debts.

Under the Insolvency Act 1986 (HMSO, 1986) a **creditor** may apply to the court for a compulsory winding up. There are seven statutory reasons he can give, which can all be found in s 122. We shall consider the two most important here.

Statutory reasons for compulsory liquidation	
s 122(1)(f)	Company is unable to pay its debts
s 122(1)(g)	It is just and equitable to wind up the company

The **Government** may petition for the compulsory winding up of a company:

- If a public company has not obtained a, **trading certificate** within one year of incorporation.
- Following a report by Government inspectors that it is in the **public interest** and **just and equitable** for the company to be wound up.

3.1 Company unable to pay its debts

A creditor who petitions on the grounds of the company's insolvency must show that the company is unable to pay its debts. There are three permitted ways to do that: s 123.

(a) A **creditor owed more than £750 serves** the company at its registered office a **written demand** for payment and the **company neglects** either to **pay the debt** or to offer reasonable security for it within **21 days**.

 If the company denies it owes the amount demanded on apparently reasonable grounds, the court will dismiss the petition and leave the creditor to take legal proceedings for debt.

(b) A creditor obtains **judgement** against the company for debt, and attempts to enforce the judgement. However, they are **unable to obtain payment** because no assets of the company have been found and seized.

(c) A creditor satisfies the court that, taking into account the contingent and prospective liabilities of the company, it is **unable to pay its debts**. The creditor may be able to show this in one of two ways:

 (i) By proof that the company is not able to pay its debts as they fall due – the **commercial insolvency test**

 (ii) By proof that the company's assets are less than its liabilities – the **balance sheet test**

 This is a residual category. Any suitable evidence of actual or prospective insolvency may be produced.

> **Exam focus point**
>
> In Chapter 5, we outlined that a secured creditor might appoint a receiver to control secured assets for the purpose of realising the creditor's loan. If the receiver appointed under a floating charge cannot find any assets to realise, the creditor can appoint an administrator, or file for compulsory liquidation under (a) (if the debt is for more than £750) or (b) (if they obtain a court judgement).

3.2 The just and equitable ground

> **FAST FORWARD**
>
> A **dissatisfied member** may get the court to wind the company up on the **just and equitable ground**.

A member who is dissatisfied with the directors or controlling shareholders over the management of the company may petition the court for the company to be wound up on the **just and equitable ground**.

For such a petition to be successful, the member must show that **no** other remedy is available. It is not enough for a member to be **dissatisfied** to make it just and equitable that the company should be wound up, since winding up what may be an otherwise healthy company is a **drastic step**.

3.2.1 Examples: When companies have been wound up

(a) **The substratum of the company has gone – the only or main object(s) of the company (its underlying basis or substratum) cannot be or can no longer be achieved.**

Re German Date Coffee Co 1882

The facts: The objects clause specified very pointedly that the sole object was to manufacture coffee from dates under a German patent. The German government refused to grant a patent. The company manufactured coffee under a Swedish patent for sale in Germany. A member petitioned for compulsory winding up.

Decision: The company existed only to 'work a particular patent' and as it could not do so it should be wound up.

(b) **The company was formed for an illegal or fraudulent purpose or there is a complete deadlock in the management of its affairs.**

Re Yenidje Tobacco Co Ltd 1916

The facts: Two sole traders merged their businesses in a company of which they were the only directors and shareholders. They quarrelled bitterly and one sued the other for fraud. Meanwhile they refused to speak to each other and conducted board meetings by passing notes through the hands of the secretary. The defendant in the fraud action petitioned for compulsory winding up.

Decision: 'In substance these two people are really partners' and by analogy with the law of partnership (which permits dissolution if the partners are really unable to work together) it was just and equitable to order liquidation.

(c) **The understandings between members or directors which were the basis of the association have been unfairly breached by lawful action.**

Ebrahimi v Westbourne Galleries Ltd 1973

The facts: E and N carried on business together for 25 years, originally as partners and for the last 10 years through a company in which each originally had 500 shares. E and N were the first directors and shared the profits as directors' remuneration; no dividends were paid. When N's son joined the business he became a third director and E and N each transferred 100 shares to N's son. Eventually there were disputes. N and his son used their voting control in general meeting (600 votes against 400) to remove E from his directorship under the power of removal given by what is now s 168 of the Companies Act 2006 (removal by ordinary resolution).

Decision: The company should be wound up. N and his son were within their legal rights in removing E from his directorship, but the past relationship made it 'unjust or inequitable' to insist on legal rights and the court could intervene on equitable principles to order liquidation.

Re A company 1983

The facts: The facts were similar in essentials to those in *Ebrahimi's case* but the majority offered and the petitioner agreed that they would settle the dispute by a sale of his shares to the majority. This settlement broke down however because they could not agree on the price. The petitioner then petitioned on the just and equitable ground.

Decision: An order for liquidation on this ground may only be made 'in the absence of any other remedy'. As the parties had agreed in principle that there was an alternative to liquidation the petition must be dismissed.

3.3 Other circumstances for compulsory liquidation

As mentioned previously, there are a **number of other circumstances** where compulsory liquidation may be commenced. These are:

- The **company passed a special resolution** that it should be wound up by the court
- The company registered as a **public limited company** more than a year previously but has not yet been issued with a **trading certificate**
- The company is an **'old' public company**
- The company has **not begun trading within a year** of its incorporation or **has suspended its trading** for a whole year
- A **moratorium for a voluntary arrangement** for the company has passed and no voluntary arrangement is in place

3.4 Proceedings for compulsory liquidation

When a petition is presented to the **court** a copy is delivered to the **company** in case it objects. It is advertised so that other creditors may intervene if they wish.

The petition **may** be presented by a member. If the petition is presented by **a member** he **must show** that:

(a) The company is **solvent** or alternatively refuses to supply information of its financial position, and

(b) He has been a **registered shareholder** for at least 6 of the 18 months up to the date of his petition. However this rule is not applied if the petitioner acquired his shares by allotment direct from the company or by inheritance from a deceased member or if the petition is based on the number of members having fallen below two.

Attention!

> The court will not order compulsory liquidation on a member's petition if he has nothing to gain from it. If the company is insolvent he would receive nothing since the creditors will take all the assets.

Once the court has been petitioned, a **provisional liquidator** may be appointed by the **court**. The **Official Receiver** is usually appointed, and his powers are conferred by the court. These usually extend to taking control of the company's property and applying for a special manager to be appointed.

Key term

> The **Official Receiver** is an officer of the court. They are appointed as liquidator of any company ordered to be wound up by the court, although an insolvency practitioner may replace them.

3.5 Effects of an order for compulsory liquidation

The effects of an **order** for compulsory liquidation are:

(a) The **Official Receiver** (an official of the Government whose duties relate mainly to bankruptcy of individuals) **becomes liquidator**: s 136.

(b) The liquidation is **deemed to have commenced at the time** (possibly several months earlier) **when the petition was first presented**.

(c) Any **disposition** of the **company's property** and any transfer of its shares subsequent to the commencement of liquidation is **void** unless the court orders otherwise: s 127.

(d) Any **legal proceedings** in progress against the company are halted (and none may thereafter begin) unless the court gives leave. Any seizure of the company's assets after commencement of liquidation is void: ss 130 and 128.

(e) The **employees** of the company are **automatically dismissed**. The liquidator assumes the powers of management previously held by the directors.

(f) Any **floating charge crystallises**.

The assets of the company may remain the company's legal property but **under the liquidator's control** unless the court by order **vests** the assets in the liquidator. The business of the company may continue but it is the liquidator's duty to continue it with a view only to realisation, for instance by sale as a going concern.

Within 21 days of the making of the order for winding up a **statement of affairs** must be delivered to the liquidator verified by one or more company officers (and possibly by other persons). The statement shows the assets and liabilities of the company and includes a list of creditors with particulars of any security: s 131.

The liquidator may require that any **officers or employees** concerned in the recent management of the company shall join in submitting the statement of affairs.

3.5.1 Investigations by the Official Receiver

The Official Receiver **must investigate** (s 132)

- The **causes of the failure** of the company, and
- Generally the **promotion, formation, business dealings** and **affairs** of the company.

The Official Receiver **may report** to the court on the results.

(a) The Official Receiver may require the **public examination** in open court of those believed to be implicated (a much-feared sanction).

(b) The Official Receiver may apply to the court for public examination where half the **creditors** or three-quarters of the **shareholders** (in value in either case) so request. Failure to attend, or reasonable suspicion that the examinees will abscond, may lead to arrest and detention in custody for contempt of court.

3.5.2 Meetings of contributories and creditors

Key term

> **Contributories** are **members** of a company.
>
> At winding up, the member may have to make payments to the company in respect of any unpaid share capital or guarantees.

The Official Receiver has 12 weeks to decide whether or not to convene **separate meetings** of creditors and contributories. The meetings provide the creditors and contributories with the opportunity to appoint their own nominee as permanent liquidator to replace the Official Receiver, and a **liquidation committee** to work with the liquidator.

If the Official Receiver believes there is little interest and that the creditors will be unlikely to appoint a liquidator he can **dispense with a meeting**, informing the court, the creditors and the contributories of the decision. He can always be required to call a meeting if at least 25% in value of the creditors require him to do so: s 136.

If no meeting is held, or one is held but no liquidator is appointed, the Official Receiver continues to act as liquidator. If the creditors do hold a meeting and **appoint their own nominee** this person automatically becomes liquidator subject to a right of objection to the court. Any person appointed to act as liquidator must be a qualified insolvency practitioner.

At any time after a winding up order is made, **the Official Receiver may ask the Secretary of State to appoint a liquidator**. Similarly, he may request an appointment if the creditors and members fail to appoint a liquidator: s 137.

If separate meetings of creditors and contributories are held and different persons are nominated as liquidators, it is the **creditors' nominee** who **takes precedence**.

Notice of the order for compulsory liquidation and of the appointment of a liquidator is given to the Registrar and in the *London Gazette*.

If, while the liquidation is in progress, the liquidator decides to call meetings of contributories or creditors he may arrange to do so under powers vested in the court.

3.6 Order of payments on liquidation

In a compulsory liquidation (and often in a voluntary one) the liquidator distributes the assets that remain after any fixed charge-holder has satisfied its secured debt following appointment of a receiver, as follows:

Order		Explanation
1	Costs	These include the costs of selling the assets, the liquidator's remuneration and all costs incidental to the liquidation procedure.
2	Preferential debts	• Employees' wages (subject to a statutory maximum) • Accrued holiday pay • Contributions to an occupational pension fund • Money borrowed by the company to enable it to pay wages
3	Debts secured by floating charges	Subject to the ring-fenced 'prescribed part' (see below).
4	Debts owed to unsecured ordinary creditors	A proportion of assets (known as the 'prescribed part') is 'ring-fenced' for unsecured creditors. This proportion (which is subject to a statutory maximum) is calculated as 50% of the first £10,000 of realisations of debts secured by floating charge and 20% of the floating charge realisations thereafter (subject to a prescribed maximum of £600,000).
5	Members	Any surplus (unlikely in compulsory and creditors' voluntary liquidations since the company is solvent if it has a surplus) is distributed to members according to their rights under the articles or the terms of issue of their shares.

It is important to remember that secured **creditors with fixed charges may appoint a receiver** to sell a charged asset, passing any surplus on to the liquidator. Floating charge-holders with charges created before 15 September 2003 can appoint administrative receivers to manage and sell the charged asset. However those with charges created on/after that date may only appoint an administrator. In the event of a shortfall secured creditors become unsecured creditors for the balance. However, a floating charge-holder who faces a shortfall on his secured debt (which is therefore treated as unsecured) cannot share in the ring-fenced part available to unsecured creditors.

3.7 Completion of compulsory liquidation

When the liquidator completes his task he reports to the Government, which **examines his accounts**. He may apply to the court for an order for dissolution of the company.

An Official Receiver may also apply to the Registrar for an **early dissolution** of the company if its realisable assets will not cover his expenses and further investigation is not required: s 202.

Question — Compulsory liquidation order

What are the six effects of a compulsory liquidation order?

Answer

- Official Receiver appointed as liquidator
- Liquidation deemed to have commenced at time when petition first presented
- Disposition of company property since commencement of liquidation deemed void
- Legal proceedings against the company are halted
- Employees are dismissed
- Any floating charge crystallises

4 Differences between compulsory and voluntary liquidation

FAST FORWARD

The differences between compulsory and voluntary liquidation are associated with **timing**, the **role** of the **Official Receiver**, **stay of legal proceedings** and the **dismissal of employees**.

The main differences in **legal consequences** between a compulsory and a voluntary liquidation up are:

	Differences
Control	Under a members' voluntary liquidation the members control the liquidation process. Under a creditors' voluntary liquidation the creditors control the process. The court controls the process under a compulsory liquidation.
Timing	A voluntary winding up commences on the day when the **resolution to wind up is passed**. It is not retrospective. A compulsory winding up, once agreed to by the court, commences on the day the **petition was presented**.
Liquidator	The **Official Receiver** plays **no role** in a **voluntary winding up**. The members or creditors select and appoint the liquidator and he is not an officer of the court.
Legal proceedings	In a **voluntary winding up** there is **no automatic stay of legal proceedings** against the company, nor are previous dispositions or seizure of its assets void. However the liquidator has a general right to apply to the court to make any order which the court can make in a compulsory liquidation. He would do so, for instance, to prevent any creditor obtaining an unfair advantage over the other creditors.
Management and staff	In any **liquidation the liquidator replaces the directors** in the management of the company (unless he decides to retain them). However, the employees are **not automatically dismissed by commencement of voluntary liquidation**. Insolvent liquidation may amount to repudiation of their employment contracts (provisions of the statutory employment protection code apply).

5 Increasing the assets available to creditors

5.1 Avoidance of floating charges

Under the Insolvency Act 1986 (HMSO, 1986) s 245, liquidation automatically renders void any floating charge created within the period of 12 months (or in the case where the charge was created in favour of a 'connected person', two years) subject to the following exceptions.

(a) The charge is **valid** if the company was **solvent** at the time when the charge was created, unless as a result of the transaction under which the charge was created the company became unable to pay its debts. This exception does not apply where the charge was created in favour of a '**connected person**'. Note that a company is not solvent unless it can pay its **debts in full** as they fall **due**.

(b) If the company was not solvent at the time the charge was created, the floating charge is still valid to the extent of **money paid** or **goods and services** received by the company at the same time or after the charge is created, or discharge or reduction of the company's liability.

Only the charge (as security), not the debt, becomes void: s 247.

5.2 Transactions at an undervalue and preferences

When a company goes into liquidation the court may avoid transactions at an undervalue and preferences. A transaction '**at an undervalue**' is a gift or a transaction in the two years previous to liquidation (or administration), by which the company gives consideration of greater value than its receives, for instance a sale at less than full market price: s 238.

However, such a transition does not become void if the company enters into it:

- In **good faith**.
- For the **purpose of carrying on its business**.
- **Believing on reasonable grounds** that it will benefit the company.

A company '**gives preference**' to a creditor or guarantor of its debts if it does anything by which this position will be benefited if the company goes into insolvent liquidation and the company does this with the intention of producing that result: s 239.

If at the time of the undervalue or preference the company was unable to pay its debts, or became so by reasons of the transaction, and the company later goes into liquidation or administration, the liquidator or the administrator can apply to the court for an order to restore the position to what it would have been if no such transaction had taken place.

The relevant period which brings the avoidance powers into operation in relation to a transaction are as follows.

- **Undervalues two years** before the commencement of liquidation.
- **Preferences**
    - With a person **unconnected** with the company **six months** before the commencement of liquation.
    - With a person **connected** with the company **two years** prior to commencement.

Unless the person in whose favour the undervalue or preference operates is connected with the company, the company must be **insolvent** at the time of entering into the disputed transaction, or must have become so in consequence of it, if it is to be disputed by the court.

If the court is satisfied that a preference has been given it can (under s 241):

- **Order return** of **property** or of the proceeds of its sale
- **Discharge any security** given
- **Order payment** in respect of benefit to the liquidator
- **Renew guarantee obligations** discharged by the preference
- **Charge property**

The term 'connected persons' appears in the law both in the context of preferences and transactions at an undervalue and also in relation to floating charges. A person is '**connected**' with the company if he is:

- A **director** or **shadow director** (see chapter on directors) of the company.
- An **associate** of a director, shadow director or the company itself.

These provisions are summarised below.

Transaction with		Transactions at an undervalue	Preference
Unconnected person	Time period before commencement	2 years	6 months
	Company insolvent at that time?	Yes	Yes
Connected person	Time period before commencement	2 years	2 years
	Company insolvent at that time?	Yes	No

5.2.1 Transactions defrauding creditors

If the transaction at an undervalue was **intended to defraud creditors**, that is the transaction was undertaken with the intention of putting assets beyond the reach of creditors, there is **no statutory time limit**.

12: INSOLVENCY

> *Sands v Clitheroe 2006*
>
> *The facts*: Mr Clitheroe, a practising solicitor, gifted his interest in his home to his wife in 1988. At the time he was solvent and a partner in a fairly secure practice, but he effected the transfer specifically in order to protect the family home in the event of the financial collapse of the partnership. He was made bankrupt 15 years later and the trustee in bankruptcy sought an order that the transaction should be overturned and the half-share treated as Mr Clitheroe's assets when the bankruptcy order was made.
>
> *Decision*: as the intent of the transaction had been to put assets beyond creditors' reach, even though the debtor was not engaging in 'risky business' and none of the bankruptcy debts existed at the time, the transaction fell within s 423, for which there is no time limit. Notably, s 423 applies equally to companies as to individuals.

5.3 Corporate rescue procedures

FAST FORWARD — Corporate rescue procedures include **company voluntary arrangements (CVAs)** and **administration**.

5.4 Company voluntary arrangement (CVA)

Under a **company voluntary arrangement** a company makes an agreement with its creditors for the settlement of its debts (known as a **composition in satisfaction of its debt** or a **scheme of arrangement of its affairs**) then gets court approval for it.

The CVA process is as follows:

- A CVA is proposed by an **administrator**, a **liquidator** or, if there is no administration order or insolvency proceeding, the **directors**, and court approval is sought.

- The court may decide the company is eligible for a **moratorium** from other proceedings for debts, which will normally last for a period of 28 days and will be managed by a nominee, who may or may not be a registered insolvency practitioner. At the end of a moratorium a company may (or may not) proceed to a corporate voluntary arrangement.

- Where the proposal is made by the directors then either immediately, or following a moratorium, a **nominee** is appointed to supervise the implementation of the proposal, reporting to the court within 28 days on whether, in their opinion, meetings of the company and of its creditors should be called.

- Where there is a **liquidator or administrator** in post they become the nominee and proceed straight to summoning meetings (see below).

- The **company and creditors meetings** summoned by the nominee decide whether to approve the proposal either with or without modifications. The arrangement is then binding on all creditors who had notice of the meeting and were entitled to vote. The nominee of the proposal or a replacement then becomes the **supervisor** of the arrangement.

- At least once every 12 months the supervisor must send a **report** on the progress and prospects for the full implementation of the voluntary arrangement to all interested parties including the Registrar.

- When the arrangement is **suspended or revoked** the Registrar must be notified.

- When the arrangement is **completed**, that is the debts are settled in line with the agreement, or when it is terminated the supervisor must notify the Registrar within 28 days.

5.5 Administration

FAST FORWARD — An **administrator** is appointed primarily to try to rescue the company as a going concern. A company may go into administration to carry out an established plan to save the company.

PART D   INSOLVENCY

Key term

> **Administration** puts an insolvency practitioner in control of the company with a defined programme for rescuing the company from insolvency as a going concern.

The rules on administration are contained in the Enterprise Act 2002 (TSO, 2002). Its purpose is to **insulate** the company **from its creditors while it seeks:**

- To save itself as a going concern, or failing that
- To achieve a better result for creditors than an immediate winding up would secure, or failing that
- To realise property so as to make a distribution to creditors.

Administration orders and liquidations are **mutually exclusive**. Once an administration order has been passed by the court, it is **no longer possible to petition the court** for a **winding up** order against the company. Similarly, however, once an order for winding up has been made, an administration order cannot be granted (except when appointed by a floating chargeholder, see Section 6.2).

Administration can be initiated with or without a court order.

5.6 Appointment of an administrator without a court order

FAST FORWARD

> Some parties – **secured creditors with a floating charge** and **directors** and the **members** by resolution – can appoint an administrator without a court order.

It is possible to appoint an administrator **without reference to the court**. There are three sets of people who might be able to do this:

- Floating chargeholders
- Directors
- Company

Attention!

> Floating chargeholders were introduced in Chapter 5. Revise them now if you are not sure.

5.6.1 Floating chargeholders

Floating chargeholders have the right to appoint an administrator without reference to the court even if there is no actual or impending insolvency. They may also **appoint an administrator even if the company is in compulsory liquidation**. This enables steps to be taken to save the company before its financial situation becomes irreversible.

In order to qualify for this right, the **floating charge must entitle the holder to appoint an administrator**. This would be in the terms of the charge. It must also be over all, or substantially all, the company's property.

Attention!

> In practice, such a floating chargeholder with a charge over all or substantially all the company's property is likely to be a **bank**.

However, the floating chargeholder may only appoint an administrator if:

- They have given **two business days'** written notice to the holder of any prior floating charge where that person has the right to appoint an administrator.
- Their floating charge is **enforceable**.

After any relevant two business day notice period (see above), the floating chargeholder will file the following **documents** at court:

- A **notice of appointment** in the prescribed form identifying the administrator.
- A **statement by the administrator** that he **consents to the appointment**.
- A **statement by the administrator** that, in his **opinion**, the **purpose of the administration** is likely to be **achieved**.
- A **statutory declaration** that he **qualifies** to make the appointment.

Once these documents have been filed, the **appointment is valid**. The appointer must notify the administrator and other people prescribed by regulations of the appointment as soon as is reasonably practicable.

5.6.2 Company and directors

The process by which a company commences appointing an administrator will depend upon its **articles of association**. A company or its directors may appoint an administrator if:

- The company has not done so in the last 12 months or been subject to a **moratorium** as a result of a voluntary arrangement with its creditors in the last 12 months.
- The company is, or is likely to be, **unable to pay its debts**.
- **No petition for winding up** nor any **administration order** in respect of the company has been presented to the court and is outstanding.
- The company is **not in liquidation**.
- **No administrator** is already in office.

The company or its directors must give notice to any floating chargeholders entitled to appoint an administrator. This means that the **floating chargeholders may** appoint their own administrator within this time period, and so **block the company's choice of administrator**.

5.7 Appointment of an administrator through the court

> **FAST FORWARD** Various parties can apply for **administration** through the court.

There are four sets of parties that may apply to the court for an administration order:

- The **company** (that is, a majority of the members by (ordinary) resolution)
- The **directors** of the company
- One or more **creditors** of the company
- The **Justice** and **Chief Executive of the Magistrates' Court** following non-payment of a fine imposed on the company

> **Exam focus point** **Individual** members **cannot** apply to the court for an administration order.

The court will grant the administration order if it is satisfied that:

- The company is, or is likely to be, **unable to pay its debts**, and
- The administration order is reasonably likely to **achieve the purpose of administration**.

The application will name the person whom the applicants want to be the **administrator**. Unless certain interested parties object, this person is appointed as administrator.

5.8 The effects of appointing an administrator

> **FAST FORWARD** The **effects** of administration depend on whether it is effected by the **court** or by a **floating chargeholder**, to some degree.

PART D INSOLVENCY

Effects of an administrator appointment

A **moratorium** over the company's debts commences (that is, no creditor can enforce their debt during the administration period without the court's permission). This is the advantageous aspect of being in administration.

The court must give its permission for:
- **Security** over company property to be **enforced**
- Goods held under hire purchase to be **repossessed**
- A landlord to conduct **forfeiture** by peaceable entry
- Commencement/continuation of any **legal process** against the company

The **powers of management** are subjugated to the authority of the administrator and managers can only act with his consent.

All outstanding **petitions for winding-up** of the company are **dismissed**.

5.9 Duties of the administrator

> **FAST FORWARD**
>
> The administrator has **fiduciary duties** to the company as its agent, plus some legal duties.

The administrator is an **agent of the company** and the **creditors as a whole**. He therefore owes fiduciary duties to them and has the following legal duties.

Legal duties of the administrator

As soon as **reasonably practicable** after appointment he must:

- **Send notice** of appointment to the company.
- **Publish notice** of appointment.
- Obtain a list of **company creditors** and sent notice of appointment to each.
- Within seven days of appointment, send notice of appointment to **Registrar**.
- Require certain relevant people to provide a **statement of affairs** of the company.
- Ensure that every **business document** of the company **bears the identity** of the administrator and a statement that the affairs, business and property of the company are being managed by him.
- Consider the **statements of affairs** submitted to him and set out his **proposals** for achieving the aim of administration. The proposals must be **sent to the Registrar** and the company's **creditors**, and be made available to **every member of the company** as soon as is reasonably practicable, and **within eight weeks**.
- While preparing their proposals, the administrator must **manage the affairs** of the company.

The **statement of affairs** must be provided by the people from whom it is requested within 11 days of it being requested. It is in a prescribed form, and contains:

- Details of the **company's property**
- The company's **debts** and **liabilities**
- The **names** and **addresses** of the **company's creditors**
- Details of any **security** held by any **creditor**

Failing to provide a statement of affairs, or providing a statement in which the writer has no reasonable belief of truth, is a **criminal offence** punishable by fine.

5.10 Administrator's proposals

> **FAST FORWARD**
>
> The administrator must either **propose a rescue plan**, or state that the **company cannot be rescued**.

Having considered all information the administrator must within 8 weeks (subject to possible extension) either:

- Set out his **proposals for achieving the aim of the administration**; or
- Set out why it is not **reasonable and practicable** that the company be rescued. In this case he will also set out why the creditors as a whole would benefit from winding up.

The proposal must be sent to all members and creditors he is aware of. It must not

- Affect the right of a **secured creditor** to enforce his security
- Result in a non-preferential debt being paid in priority to a preferential debt
- Result in one preferential creditor being paid a smaller proportion of his debt than another.

5.10.1 Creditors' meeting

The administrator must call a **meeting of creditors** within **10 weeks** of their appointment to approve the proposals. The creditors may either accept or reject them. Once the proposals have been agreed, the administrator cannot make any substantial amendment without first gaining the creditors' consent.

5.11 Administrator's powers

FAST FORWARD | The administrator takes on the **powers** of the directors.

The powers of the administrator are summed up as follows:

> 'The administrator of a company may do **anything necessarily expedient** for the management of the affairs, business and property of the company.'

The administrator **takes on the powers previously enjoyed by the directors** and the following specific powers to:

- Remove or appoint a **director**
- Call a **meeting of members or creditors**
- **Apply to court for directions** regarding the carrying out of his functions
- Make payments to **secured or preferential creditors**
- With the permission of the court, **make payments to unsecured creditors**

The administrator usually requires the permission of the court to make payments to unsecured creditors. However, this is not the case if the administrator feels that paying the unsecured creditor will assist the **achievement of the administration**. For example, if the company has been denied further supplies by a major supplier unless payment is tendered.

Any creditor or member of the company may **apply to the court** if they feel that the administrator has acted or will act in a way that has harmed or will harm his interest. The court may take various actions against the administrator.

5.12 End of administration

FAST FORWARD | Administration can last up to **12 months**.

The administration period **ends** when:

- The administration has been successful
- Twelve months have elapsed from the date of the appointment of administrator
- The administrator applies to the court to end the appointment
- A creditor applies to the court to end the appointment
- An improper motive of the applicant for applying for the administration is discovered

The administrator automatically vacates office after **12 months of his appointment**. This time period can be extended by court order or by consent from the appropriate creditors.

Alternatively, the administrator may **apply to the court** when he thinks:

- The purpose of administration cannot be achieved
- The company should not have entered into administration
- The administration has been successful (if appointed by the court)

He must also apply to the court if required to by the **creditors' meeting**.

Where the administrator was appointed by a chargeholder or the company/its directors, and he feels that the purposes of administration have been achieved, he must file a **notice** with the court and the Registrar.

5.13 Advantages of administration

Administration has been found to have many advantages for the **company**, the **members** and the **creditors**.

Advantages of administration	
To the company	The company does not necessarily cease to exist at the end of the process, whereas liquidation will always result in the company being wound up.
	It provides temporary relief from creditors to allow breathing space to formulate rescue plans.
	It prevents any creditor applying for compulsory liquidation.
	It provides for past transactions to be challenged.
To the members	They will continue to have shares in the company which has not been wound up. If the administration is successful, regenerating the business should enhance share value and will restore any income from the business.
To the creditors	Creditors should obtain a return in relation to their past debts from an administration.
	Unsecured creditors will benefit from asset realisations.
	Any creditor may apply to the court for an administration order, while only certain creditors may apply for other forms of relief from debt. For example, the use of receivers or an application for winding up.
	Floating chargeholders may appoint an administrator without reference to the court.
	It may also be in the interests of the creditors to have a continued business relationship with the company once the business has been turned around.

Exam focus point

You may be asked to consider the advantages of administration as opposed to liquidation from the point of view of all the parties involved.

6 Revision: insolvency situations

As we have discussed, various situations could arise when a company gets into financial difficulties.

Exam focus point

It is vital that you do not confuse the various implications for a company of getting into financial difficulties. This can be a difficult area to keep clear in your head, particularly given that many of the terms introduced in this chapter and the personnel involved sound very similar to each other.

Given the possibility of confusion arising in this area, the following scenarios are given for you to work through using the Insolvency Act 1986 (HMSO, 1986) and the Enterprise Act 2002 (TSO, 2002), to ensure that you understand the implications for the company in each situation.

6.1 Company defaults on secured debt

When the company defaults on secured debt, the creditor can usually take one of four steps under the terms of his security:

- Take **possession of the asset** subject to the charge if they have a fixed charge (if they have a floating charge they may only take possession if the contract allows).
- **Sell it** (provided the debenture is executed as a deed).
- Apply to the court for its **transfer** to their ownership by foreclosure order (rarely used).
- Appoint a **receiver** of it, provided an administration order is not in effect, or — in the case of floating chargeholders only — appoint an administrator without needing to apply to the court.

The most common result is that a receiver, or an administrator, is appointed. The next two scenarios will outline this in relation to both fixed and floating charges.

Illustration

Fixed charge

X Ltd has a mortgage with ABC Bank which is secured by a fixed charge over the building to which it relates. X Ltd fails to keep up its payments to ABC Bank. Under the terms of its security, ABC Bank appoints a receiver of the building, who sells the building and realises the debt.

Once the bank had realised its debt, the receiver would leave and the business would be left to continue (as best it could without its premises). In such a situation, liquidation might follow this act of the receiver if the business could no longer operate (see Illustration below on the petition for compulsory liquidation).

Illustration

Floating charge

Y Ltd has a loan from EFG Bank which is secured by a fixed and floating charge over all the company's assets. Y Ltd defaults on the loan. EFG Bank demands in writing that the repayment be made. Y Ltd continues to default on the loan. Under the terms of its security, EFG Bank appoints a receiver to take control of the company's assets.

The receiver's purpose is to realise the debt for the bank. He may achieve this by selling the business as a going concern or by breaking up the business and realising individual assets.

Unsecured creditors may apply for a petition for a compulsory winding up (see Illustration below) during the course of a receivership. The two can run simultaneously.

If the terms of the floating charge so provided, EFG Bank could instead have appointed an administrator of the company, without referring to the court

6.2 Company defaults on unsecured debt

An unsecured creditor has the following rights against a company who has defaulted on a debt:

- Sue the company for the debt/seize the asset if his judgement is not satisfied.
- Petition the court for the compulsory liquidation of the company.
- Petition the court for an administration order.

It is important to note that a secured creditor also has these remedies open to him. However, a secured creditor has more to gain from appointing a receiver or administrator as discussed above than commencing liquidation proceedings.

Illustration

Petition for compulsory liquidation

A has sold goods worth £29,567 to B on credit. B Ltd has exceeded the credit terms extended and A has presented B Ltd with a written demand to their registered office, which B Ltd has not responded to after a month. B Ltd have sold on the goods which they purchased from A and do not dispute the value of the invoice.

A can apply to the court for the compulsory winding up of the company because the company has not paid its debts.

The court appoints the Official Receiver to be the provisional liquidator until it gives an order for compulsory liquidation.

Illustration

Petition for administration order

A has sold goods worth £29,567 to B Ltd on credit. B Ltd has exceeded the credit terms extended. A has discovered that the management of B Ltd is experiencing difficulties, but believes that the business is sound and that the debt could be paid if the business was managed properly. A is also aware that B Ltd has a loan from the bank which is secured by a floating charge.

A suspects that if the bank exercises its right to bring in a receiver, the business will be wound up and the unsecured debts might not be paid. It therefore applies to the court of an administration order so that debt collection will be frozen while an action plan is undertaken to ensure that debts can be paid. However, if the terms of the floating charge allow the bank to appoint an administrator, this can be done by the bank without reference to the court so the bank's choice of administrator would prevail.

An unsecured creditor would benefit from an administration order over a compulsory liquidation as once an administration order has been granted, secured creditors are barred from appointing receivers to realise their debts without the court's permission.

Remember that 'in receivership' and in liquidation, the priority of claims is as follows:

- Costs of selling assets
- Receiver's expenses
- Preferential debts
- Debts secured under a floating charge
- (By implication) any other unsecured debt (with rights over a 'ring-fenced' element)

The administration order can represent a good alternative to liquidation to the unsecured creditor.

6.3 Actions of members

The only way that a company can be wound up is if its members determine that this should be so. In this case, a voluntary winding up would take place.

Exam focus point

The following are issues which as a minimum you must learn and remember:

- Distinction between liquidator/receiver/Official Receiver/administrator.
- A company can have a receiver and be in liquidation at the same time.
- Once an administration **order** has been made, no receiver can be appointed or liquidation proceedings started (although they can until the court grants the petition).

- A secured creditor will usually enforce his security and appoint a receiver, where possible, or an administrator.
- A voluntary liquidation is always instigated by the members.

You should consider the advantages of administration as opposed to liquidation from the point of view of all the parties involved.

Advantages of administration	
To the company	It does not necessarily cease to exist at the end of the process. Liquidation will always result in the company being wound up. It also provides temporary relief from creditors to allow breathing space to formulate rescue plans.
To the members	They will continue to have shares in the company which has not been wound up. If the administration is successful, regenerating the business should enhance share value and will restore any income from the business (dividends or any salary for owner-managed business).
To the creditors	Creditors should obtain a return in relation to their past debts from an administration. Unsecured creditors will benefit from the 'prescribed part' of asset realisations. Any creditor may apply to the court for an administration order, while only certain creditors may apply for other forms of relief from debt, for example, the use of receivers or an application for winding up. Floating chargeholders may appoint an administrator without reference to the court if the terms of the charge so provides. It may also be in the interests of the creditors to have a continued business relationship with the company once the business has been turned around.

Chapter roundup

- **Liquidation** is the **dissolution** or 'winding up' of a company.
- There are three different methods of **liquidation: compulsory, members' voluntary** and **creditors' voluntary**. Compulsory liquidation and creditors' voluntary liquidation are proceedings for insolvent companies, and members' voluntary liquidation is for solvent companies.
- A **liquidator** must be an authorised, qualified insolvency practitioner.
- Once **insolvency procedures** have commenced, share trading must cease, the company documents must state that the company is in liquidation and the directors' power to manage ceases.
- A **winding** up is **voluntary** where the decision to wind up is taken by the company members in general meeting, although if the company is insolvent, the creditors will be heavily involved in the proceedings.
- In order to be a members' winding up, the directors must make a **declaration of solvency**. It is a criminal offence to make a declaration of solvency without reasonable grounds.
- When there is no declaration of solvency there is a **creditors' voluntary** winding up.
- A creditor may apply to the court to wind up the company, primarily if the company is **unable to pay its debts**. There are statutory tests to prove that a company is unable to pay its debts.
- A **dissatisfied member** may get the court to wind the company up on the **just and equitable ground**.
- The differences between compulsory and voluntary liquidation are associated with **timing**, the **role** of the **Official Receiver, stay of legal proceedings** and the **dismissal of employees**.
- Corporate rescue procedures include **company voluntary arrangements (CVAs)** and **administration**.
- An **administrator** is appointed primarily to try to rescue the company as a going concern. A company may go into administration to carry out an established plan to save the company.
- Some parties – **secured creditors with a floating charge** and **directors** and the **company** by resolution of the members – can appoint an administrator without a court order.
- Various parties can apply for **administration** through the court.
- The **effects** of administration depend on whether it is effected by the **court** or by a **floating chargeholder**, to some degree.
- The administrator has **fiduciary duties** to the company as its agent, plus some legal duties.
- The administrator must either **propose a rescue plan**, or state that the **company cannot be rescued**.
- The administrator takes on the **powers** of the directors.
- Administration can last up to **12 months**.
- Administration has been found to have many advantages for the **company**, the **members** and the **creditors**.

Quick quiz

1. Complete the following definition.

    Liquidation means that a company must be .... and its affairs wound up.

2. Name three common effects of liquidations.

    (1) ....
    (2) ....
    (3) ....

3. What are the two most important grounds for **compulsory liquidation**?

    (1) ....
    (2) ....

4. A members' voluntary winding up is where the members decide to dissolve a healthy company.

    True ☐
    False ☐

5. Complete the following definition, using the words given below.

    An (1) .... is an arrangement which puts an (2) .... (3) .... in control of the business to attempt to save it.

    | (1) | insolvency | (2) | practitioner | (3) | administration |

6. Name two advantages of administration.

    (1) ....
    (2) ....

PART D INSOLVENCY

Answers to quick quiz

1. Dissolved

2. (1) No further changes in membership permitted
   (2) All documents must state prominently that company is in liquidation
   (3) Directors' power to manage ceases

3. (1) Company is unable to pay its debts
   (2) It is just and equitable to wind up the company

4. True. Members can decide to wind up a healthy company.

5. Administration, insolvency, practitioner

6. (1) It does not necessarily result in the dissolution of the company
   (2) It prevents creditors applying for compulsory liquidation

   Subsidiary advantages are

   (3) All creditors can apply for an administration order
   (4) The administrator may challenge past transactions of the company

End of chapter question

Liquidation

Explain the meaning of compulsory and voluntary liquidation and the main differences between them.

(10 marks)

Criminal law

Criminal law

Topic list	Syllabus reference
1 Financial crime	8.5
2 Insider dealing	8.5
3 Money laundering	8.3, 8.5
4 Bribery	8.3, 8.5
5 Criminal activity relating to companies	8.5, 8.6

Introduction

Criminal law is the law governing the behaviour of people within society and towards the state. In a criminal case, the state prosecutes the accused and, if he is found guilty, a penalty can be imposed. In this chapter, we shall look specifically at some **financial crimes** and the **measures** that have been put into place to combat them.

Insider dealing is a criminal offence. It has proved difficult to convict people of the crime of insider dealing, hence the introduction of the civil wrong of market abuse, which covers both insider dealing and market manipulation, plus related criminal offences of making misleading statements and creating misleading impressions, discussed in Chapter 7.

Money laundering is a serious criminal offence that is often related to other types of organised crime and is highly topical. Money laundering is the process of 'legalising' funds raised through crime. Money laundering crosses national boundaries and it can be difficult to enforce the related laws. Accountants in particular are key to efforts to prosecute money launderers

Finally we shall look at **bribery offences** and offences in relation to **companies**, especially **insolvent companies**.

1 Financial crime

> **FAST FORWARD**
>
> Crime is **conduct prohibited by the law**. Financial crime can be international in nature, and there is a need for international cooperation to prevent it.

Crime is **conduct prohibited by the law**.

Law tends to be organised on a **national basis**. However, as we shall see later in this chapter, some crime, particularly money laundering, is perpetrated **across national borders**. Indeed the international element of the crime contributes to its success.

Particularly with regard to money laundering, international bodies are having to **co-operate** with one another in order to control financial crimes which spreads across national boundaries.

1.1 Example: international financial crime

Suppose money laundering is a crime in Country A but not in Country B. Money laundering can be effected legally in Country B and the proceeds returned to Country A. Hence Country A cannot prosecute for the crime of money laundering, which has not been committed within its national boundaries.

2 Insider dealing

> **FAST FORWARD**
>
> Insider dealing is the criminal offence of **dealing** in securities while in **possession** of **inside information** as an insider, the securities being price affected by the information.

The **Criminal Justice Act 1993** (HMSO 1993) (CJA) contains the rules on **insider dealing**. It was regarded and treated as a crime since a few people are enriched at the expense of the reputation of the stock market and the interests of all involved in it.

2.1 What is insider dealing?

Key term

> **Insider dealing** is dealing in securities while in possession of inside information as an insider, the securities being **price-affected** by the information.

To prove insider dealing, the prosecution must prove that the possessor of inside information (under s 52 CJA):

- **Dealt** in **price-affected securities** on a regulated market, or
- **Encouraged another** to **deal** in them on a regulated market, or
- **Disclosed** the **information** other than in the proper performance of their employment, office or profession.

2.1.1 Dealing

Dealing is **acquiring or disposing** of or **agreeing** to **acquire** or **dispose** of relevant securities whether **directly** or **through an agent** or nominee or a person acting according to direction: s 55 CJA.

2.1.2 Encouraging another to deal

An offence is also committed if an individual, having information as an insider, **encourages another person** to deal in price-affected securities in relation to that information. They must **know** or have reasonable cause to believe that **dealing** would **take place**.

It is irrelevant whether:

- The person encouraged realises that the securities are **price-affected** securities.
- The **inside information is given** to that person. For example, a simple recommendation to the effect that 'I cannot tell you why but now would be a good time to buy shares in Bloggs plc' would infringe the law.
- **Any dealing takes place**, the offence being committed at the time of encouragement.

2.2 Securities covered by the Act

Securities include shares, debt securities and warranties: s 54 CJA.

2.3 Inside information

Key term

> **Inside information** is **'price sensitive information'** relating to a **particular issuer** of **securities** that are price-affected and not to securities generally: s 56 CJA.

Inside information must, if made public, be likely to have a **significant effect on price** and it must be **specific or precise**. Specific would, for example, mean information that a takeover bid would be made for a specific company; precise information would be details of how much would be offered for shares.

2.4 Insiders

Under s 57 a person has information as a **primary insider** if it is (**and** they **know** it is) inside information, and if they have it (**and know** they have) from an inside source:

- Through being a **director**, **employee** or **shareholder** of an issuer of securities.
- Through access because of **employment**, **office** or **profession**.

If the direct or indirect source is a person within these two previous categories then the person who has inside information from this source is a **secondary insider**.

2.5 General defences

Under s 53, the individual has a defence regarding dealing and encouraging others to deal if they prove that:

- They did **not expect** there to be a **profit** or avoidance of loss.
- They had **reasonable grounds** to **believe** that the information had been **disclosed widely** enough to ensure that those taking part in the dealing would be prejudiced by having the information.
- They would have **done** what they did **even** if they did not have the **information**, for example, where securities are sold to pay a pressing debt.

Defences to disclosure of information by an individual are that:

- They **did not expect** any person to deal.
- Although dealing was expected, **profit** or **avoidance of loss** was **not expected**.

2.6 'Made public'

This term is not exhaustively defined by the statute, leaving final determination to the Court. Information **is** made public if:

- It is **published** under the rules of the regulated market, such as the Stock Exchange.
- It is in **public records**, for example, notices in the *London Gazette*.
- It can **readily be acquired** by those likely to deal.
- It is **derived** from **public information**.

Information **may** be treated as made public even though:

- It can **only** be **acquired** by **exercising diligence** or expertise (thus helping analysts to avoid liability).
- It is **communicated only** to a **section** of the **public** (thus protecting the 'brokers' lunch' where a company informs only selected City sources of important information).
- It can be **acquired** only by **observation**.
- It is **communicated** only on a **payment of a fee** or is published outside the UK.

2.7 Penalties

Maximum penalties given by the statute are **seven years' imprisonment** and/or an **unlimited fine**. Contracts remain valid and enforceable at civil law.

2.8 Territorial scope

The offender or any professional intermediary must be **in the UK** at the time of the offence or the market must be a UK regulated market.

2.9 Problems with the laws on insider dealing

> **FAST FORWARD**
>
> The law on insider dealing has had some **limitations**, and new offences, such as market abuse, have been brought in to reduce security related crime.

The courts may have problems deciding whether information is **specific** or **precise**.

The statute states that information shall be treated as relating to an issuer of securities not only when it is **about the company** but also where it may **affect the business prospects** of the company.

The requirement that price-sensitive information has a **significant effect on price** limits the application of the legislation to fundamental matters. These include an impending takeover, or profit or dividend levels which would be out of line with market expectations.

As a result, the concept of **'market abuse'** was introduced in the UK in 2000 (see Chapter 7) and made more rigorous in 2012. This was partly in response to the perceived ineffectiveness of the insider dealing provisions in the Criminal Justice Act 1993.

> **Exam focus point**
>
> Future exam questions may be set on insider dealing and market abuse. If this is the case, remember that while insider dealing is primarily a criminal offence, market abuse also covers insider dealing and market manipulation as civil matters. Furthermore, there are criminal market abuse offences concerning making misleading statements and creating misleading impressions.

3 Money laundering

3.1 What is money laundering?

> **FAST FORWARD**
>
> Money laundering is the attempt to **make money from criminal activity appear legitimate**, by disguising its original source.

> **Key term**
>
> **Money laundering** is the term given to attempts to make the proceeds of crime appear respectable.
>
> It covers any activity by which the apparent source and ownership of money representing the proceeds of income are changed so that the money appears to have been obtained legitimately.

Money laundering is a **crime** that is **against the interests of the state**, and it is associated with drug and people trafficking in particular, and with organised crime in general.

Money laundering is primarily found in:

- Proceeds of Crime Act 2002 (PCA) (TSO, 2002)
- Money Laundering Regulations 2017 (TSO, 2017)

3.2 Categories of criminal offence

FAST FORWARD

In the UK, there are various offences relating to **money laundering**, including **tipping off** a money launderer (or suspected money launderer) and **failing to report** reasonable suspicions.

There are **three categories of criminal offences** in the Proceeds of Crime Act.

- **Laundering**: acquisition, possession or use of the proceeds of criminal conduct, or assisting another to retain the proceeds of criminal conduct and concealing, disguising, converting, transferring or removing criminal property. This relates to its nature, source, location, disposition, movement or ownership of the property. Money laundering includes possession of the proceeds of one's own crime, and facilitating any handling or possession of criminal property, which may take any form, including in money or money's worth, securities, tangible property and intangible property. There is no *de minimis* limit, so a money laundering offence may be committed in respect only to £1.
- **Failure to report** by an individual: failure by an accountant or other 'relevant person' to disclose knowledge or suspicion of money laundering (suspicion is more than mere speculation, but falls short of proof or knowledge).
- **Tipping off**: an accountant or other relevant person disclosing information to any person if disclosure may prejudice an investigation into drug trafficking, drug money laundering, terrorist related activities, or laundering the proceeds of criminal conduct.

For the purposes of laundering, 'criminal property' is defined by s 340 PCA as property which constitutes a person's benefit from criminal conduct and which the person knows or suspects constitutes or represents such a benefit.

In relation to **laundering**, a person may have a **defence** if they make disclosure to the authorities:

- As soon as possible after the transaction.
- Before the transaction takes place.

Alternatively, they may have a defence if they can show there was a **reasonable excuse** for not making a disclosure.

In relation to **failure to report**, the person who suspects money laundering and who forms this suspicion in the course of his or her activities in the 'regulated sector' (for example as an accountant) must disclose the suspicion to a nominated officer within their organisation, or directly to the National Crime Agency (NCA) – in the form of a Suspicious Activity Report (SAR). NCA has responsibility in the UK for collecting and disseminating information related to all forms of serious organised crime, including money laundering and related activities. The nominated officer in an organisation acts as a filter and notifies NCA.

In relation to **tipping off**, this covers the situation when a person making a disclosure to the nominated officer or NCA also tells the person at the centre of their suspicions about the disclosure. There is a **defence** to the effect that the person did not know that tipping off would prejudice an investigation.

3.3 Penalties

The law sets out the following penalties in relation to money laundering:

(a) 14 years' imprisonment and/or a fine, for knowingly assisting in the **laundering** of criminal funds.
(b) 5 years' imprisonment and/or a fine, for **failure to report knowledge** or the **suspicion** of money laundering and for **tipping off** a suspected launderer.

Question: Money laundering

Why should a professional adviser not give a warning to a client whom he suspects of money laundering?

Answer

Tipping off a suspected money launderer is an offence. Alerting the suspect would be likely to hamper any subsequent investigation by the authorities.

The money laundering process usually involves three phases:

- **Placement** – this is the initial disposal of the proceeds of the initial illegal activity into apparently legitimate business activity or property.
- **Layering** – this involves the transfer of monies from business to business or place to place to conceal the original source.
- **Integration** – having been layered, the money has the appearance of legitimate funds.

For accountants, the most onerous aspect of the law on money laundering relates to the offence of '**failing to disclose**'. It is relatively straightforward to identify actual 'knowledge' of money laundering, and therefore of the need to disclose it, but the term 'suspicion' of money laundering is not defined. The nearest there is to a definition is that suspicion is more than mere speculation but falls short of proof or knowledge. It is a question of judgement.

3.4 The Money Laundering Regulations 2017

The **Money Laundering Regulations 2017** (TSO, 2017) require **organisations** to **establish internal systems** and **procedures** which are designed to deter criminals from using the organisation to launder money or finance terrorism. Such systems also assist in detecting the crime and prosecuting the perpetrators.

These regulations apply to all '**relevant persons**', a term which covers a wide range of organisations, including banking and investment businesses, accountants and auditors, tax advisers, lawyers, estate agents and casinos. They set out a prescriptive approach in the form of a firm-wide written risk assessment that includes a number of factors that must be taken into account.

As each organisation is different, **systems** should be designed which are **appropriate and tailored to each business**.

These include:

(a) **Risk management practices**
The business should take a 'whole firm' approach to assessing the money laundering risks faced by the business. The business should also assess the risk of clients being involved in money laundering or terrorist financing. The risk management approach adopted will depend on the size of the business and the nature of its activities. The overall objective for any business is to properly identify and assess the risk of money laundering, or terrorist financing, and to document the assessment.

(b) **Internal controls**
Businesses are required to have a number of internal controls in place. These should include:

- Appointing a Money Laundering Compliance Principal (MLCP) who must sit on the board of directors.
- Appointing a nominated officer to receive internal reports of suspected money laundering and, where appropriate, to report them to the NCA.

- Assessing the skills, knowledge, conduct and integrity of employees responsible for identifying, mitigating, preventing or detecting money laundering and terrorist financing.
- Establishing an independent audit function whose role is to assess the adequacy and effectiveness of anti-money laundering policies, controls and procedures.

(c) **Customer due diligence**

Businesses are required to perform customer due diligence before establishing the business relationship. They must also identify instances where factors relevant to the risk assessment change.

Customer due diligence work includes, for example, identifying and independently verifying customers and their agents and monitoring the business relationship or transaction according to the level of risk of money laundering. There are two levels of due diligence, **simplified** and **enhanced**.

Simplified due diligence is permitted where the risk assessment indicates that the business relationship or transaction presents a low risk of money laundering or terrorist financing. Customer due diligence should still be performed, but at a level that reflects the low-level of risk.

Enhanced due diligence measures are required to be applied in a number of circumstances. Such circumstances include where a transaction or business relationship involves a person established in a 'high risk third country', if they are, or if a family member is a 'politically exposed person' or is a known associate of one, and any other situation that presents a higher risk of money laundering or terrorist financing.

Examples of **enhanced due diligence measures** include:

- Understanding the background and purpose of transactions.
- Increased monitoring of the business relationship or transaction to determine whether there is any reason to be suspicious about them.
- Obtaining additional independent, reliable verification of information provided by the customer.
- Taking additional measures to obtain satisfaction that customer transactions are consistent with the purpose and nature of their business relationship.
- Placing transactions under greater scrutiny and increased monitoring of the business relationship.

(d) **Reliance and record-keeping procedures**

Businesses should have policies, controls and procedures in place to prevent activities related to money laundering and terrorist financing. A written record of these procedures, as well as employee training on them (see below), must be maintained. Such procedures may include, for example, retaining copies of customer identity details such as passports. These procedures are important in proving compliance with the regulations.

(e) **Monitoring and management of compliance**

Businesses should continuously monitor and manage compliance with the policies, controls and procedures that they have in place. Employees should receive appropriate training concerning the law relating to money laundering and the business's policies and procedures in dealing with it. Employee training records should also be monitored to ensure compliance and that the employees are up-to-date as requirements develop over time.

Should a business fail to implement these measures a criminal offence, punishable with a maximum sentence of **two years' imprisonment and/or an unlimited fine**, is committed irrespective of whether money laundering has taken place.

3.5 The role of the Financial Conduct Authority

In addition to the Money Laundering Regulations 2017, there are other rules which apply to **investment firms** (that is firms which sell financial services or shares).

The **FCA** and the **Joint Money Laundering Steering Group (JMLSG)** provide similar guidance, and therefore parallel but separate rules. Investment firms are required to have:

(a) **Control systems** in place to monitor possible money laundering activities.

(b) A **Money Laundering Reporting Officer (MLRO)** who is responsible for the oversight of the anti-money laundering activities.

(c) **Internal reporting procedures.** Staff must be able to identify suspicious transactions, understand reporting procedures, and be able to notify the MLRO of any person who they suspect of engaging in money laundering.

(d) **Adequate records** such as:

  (i) A copy of the evidence of identity obtained

  (ii) A record of where a copy of the identity evidence can be obtained

  (iii) Procedures for internal and external reporting

  (iv) Evidence of an applicant's identity must be retained for five years from the end of the firm's relationship with the client, or

  (v) Money laundering training given to all staff who handle transactions (or who manage others who are responsible for handling transactions) that may involve money laundering.

Although investment firms may be particularly at risk of being involved with clients who are seeking to launder money, **methods used** for laundering such dirty money **can be extremely complex**. They may involve **trusts, companies** (both offshore and onshore) and could involve the use of relatively complex bank instruments.

Therefore **all companies**, their **managers** and their **advisers need to be aware** of the issue of money laundering and not fall foul of the regulations.

There is a **legal requirement** for organisations to take the following actions.

- To set up procedures and establish accountabilities for senior individuals to take action to prevent money laundering.
- To educate staff and employees about the potential problems of money laundering.
- To obtain satisfactory evidence of identity where a transaction is for more than £10,000.
- To report suspicious circumstances (according to the established procedures).
- Not to alert persons who are or might be investigated for money laundering.
- To keep records of all transactions for five years.

Exam focus point: You must be clear of how this guidance seeks to prevent or minimise money laundering.

4 Bribery

FAST FORWARD — Bribery is a serious offence which often relates to the **offering** and **receiving** of **gifts** or **hospitality**.

The **Bribery Act 2010** (TSO, 2010) came into effect in July 2011. The Act brought together, and is intended to simplify the previous law on bribery and corruption which was contained in both common law and statute.

4.1 Bribery offences

The **Bribery Act** created **four main offences**, the first three of which are committed by **individuals** while the fourth is a **corporate** offence. The offences are:

- Bribing another person
- Being bribed
- Bribing a foreign public official
- Corporate failure to prevent bribery

4.1.1 Bribing another person

This offence is committed where a person **offers, promises or gives financial** or **other advantages** to another person with the intention of inducing that person to **perform improperly** a **relevant function** or **activity**, or to **reward** them for such **improper performance**.

It does not matter whether or not the person being bribed is the **same person** as the one who would **usually perform** the function or whether the offer is made **directly** or via a **third party**. This offence can also be committed where **acceptance of an advantage** itself **constitutes improper performance** of a function or activity.

4.1.2 Being bribed

This offence is committed where a person requests or accepts a financial or other advantage improperly, or as a reward for improper performance of a relevant function or activity, or intending that improper performance should result. It does not matter whether the advantage is received directly or through a third party. The offence also applies if a person receives a benefit on behalf of another person.

4.1.3 Relevant function or activity

Both of the above offences make reference to a '**relevant function or activity**' and it is important to be aware of what this means. In terms of the Act, a relevant function or activity includes any function of **a public nature** or any **activity connected with business** or **carried out in the course of employment**. It applies to individuals who perform that function or activity from a **position of trust** or are otherwise expected to perform it in **good faith** or **impartially**.

It is irrelevant whether the **function** or **activity** has a **connection with the UK** – for example, if it is performed outside the UK. 'Improper' performance means performance which does not meet the **standard** that a **reasonable person** in the UK would expect.

4.1.4 Bribing a foreign public official

This offence is similar to that of **bribing another person**, but is committed where the bribe is offered to a **foreign public official** (FPO). It is committed where a person offers financial or other advantages to an **FPO** or a **third party** with the intention of influencing the FPO in that capacity and to obtain or retain business or an advantage in the conduct of business, where that official is not permitted or required by the written law applicable to him to be so influenced.

An **FPO** is any individual who holds a **legislative**, **administrative** or **judicial position** of any kind outside the UK, or who exercises a **public function** outside the UK, or who is an **official** or **agent** of a **public international organisation**.

4.1.5 Defences and penalties for individual offences

It is a **defence** for an individual charged with a bribery offence if they can prove that their **conduct was necessary for the proper exercise of any function of an intelligence service or the proper exercise of any function of the armed forces when engaged on active service**.

The maximum **penalty** for bribery under the Act is **10 years' imprisonment** and/or an **unlimited fine**.

4.1.6 Corporate failure to prevent bribery

The offence of corporate failure to prevent bribery is **committed by an organisation** that **fails to prevent** a **bribery offence** being committed by a **person who performs services** for it in any capacity — such as an agent, employee or subsidiary. Under the Act, an **organisation** includes **companies** and **partnerships** based in the UK or doing business in the UK.

4.1.7 Defence and penalties for corporate offences

An organisation has a **defence** to this offence if it can prove that it had in place '**adequate procedures**' designed to prevent persons associated with it from committing bribery.

'**Adequate procedures**' are not defined by the Act, but the Secretary of State's non-prescriptive published guidance on adequate procedures is based around six principles:

(a) **Proportionate procedures** – organisations should have procedures in place aimed at preventing bribery. The scale and complexity of the procedures should be proportionate to the size of the organisation. The procedures expected of a small organisation will differ from that of a large one.

(b) **Top-level commitment** – an organisation's senior management should be committed to preventing bribery and should foster a culture in the organisation that sees bribery as unacceptable.

(c) **Risk assessment** – organisations should assess the nature and extent of their exposure to bribery from both inside and outside the organisation. Some industries and some overseas markets are seen as, by their nature, more susceptible to bribery and therefore risk assessments in these areas should be even more stringent.

(d) **Due diligence** – organisations should perform due diligence procedures in respect of those who perform services for the organisation or on its behalf, to mitigate the risk of bribery.

(e) **Communication** – anti-bribery policies and procedures should be embedded in the fabric of the organisation and communicated both internally and externally. This is likely to include relevant training if proportionate to the risk.

(f) **Monitoring and review** – the anti-bribery policies and procedures should be regularly monitored and reviewed. Amendments and improvements must be made as appropriate. This is because the risks an organisation faces will change so adaptation is necessary.

Whether an organisation had **adequate procedures is a matter for the courts** who will look at the particular circumstances an organisation is faced with. However, the onus is on the organisation to prove that its procedures were adequate.

Reasonable and **proportionate hospitality** is **not prohibited,** although what is reasonable and proportionate will be determined in future cases.

The **maximum penalty** that may be imposed on a guilty organisation is an **unlimited fine**. However, it is likely that its **business will suffer** too as a consequence of **loss of reputation** and **compensation payable** for civil claims against the directors for failure to maintain adequate procedures.

5 Criminal activity relating to companies

We have already seen a number of potential crimes in relation to the operation and management of companies, and the way in which these can be investigated.

With regard to the **operation and management of companies**, a company as a legal person may be prosecuted for many different types of crime. However, this is nearly always in conjunction with the directors and/or managers of the company. Companies have been prosecuted for manslaughter (unsuccessfully), fraud, and breaches of numerous laws for which fines are stated as being punishment, such as health and safety laws.

Prosecutions are often brought against directors of **insolvent** companies for **fraudulent trading** and **wrongful trading**.

5.1 Criminal offences in relation to winding up

Criminal offences in relation to winding up include: making a declaration of solvency without reasonable grounds; fraudulent trading; wrongful trading.

The law seeks to **protect creditors** who may be disadvantaged by the company being liquidated. **Directors** can be found guilty of various criminal offences if they try to **deceive** creditors, and, in some cases, even if they do not attempt to deceive creditors, but the effect is the same as if they had.

5.2 Declaration of solvency

As discussed in Chapter 12, a winding up can only be a members' voluntary winding up if the company is solvent. If the company is not solvent, the creditors are far more involved in the winding up process. In order to carry out a members' voluntary winding up, the directors have to file a **declaration of solvency**.

It is a **criminal offence** punishable by fine or imprisonment for a director to make a **declaration of solvency without** having **reasonable grounds** for it. If the company proves to be insolvent, they will have to justify their previous decision, or be punished.

5.3 Fraudulent trading

This **criminal offence** occurs under the **Companies Act 2006** (TSO, 2006) where the business of a company in liquidation or administration has been carried on with **intent to defraud creditors** or for any fraudulent purpose. Offenders are liable to imprisonment for up to 10 years or a fine (s 993).

There is also a **civil offence** of the same name under s 213 of the Insolvency Act 1986. Under this offence courts may declare that **any persons** who were knowingly parties to carrying on the business in this fashion shall be liable for the debts of the company.

Various rules have been established to determine **what is fraudulent trading**:

(a) Only persons who **take the decision** to carry on the company's business in this way or play some active part are liable.

(b) **'Carrying on business'** can include a single transaction and also the mere payment of debts as distinct from making trading contracts.

(c) It relates not only to **defrauding creditors**, but also to carrying on a business for the purpose of any kind of fraud: *R v Kemp 1988*.

If the liquidator considers that there has been fraudulent trading they should apply to the court for an order that those responsible are liable to make good to the company all or some specified part of the **company's debts**.

5.4 Wrongful trading

The problem which faced the creditors of an insolvent company before the introduction of **'wrongful trading'** was that it was exceptionally difficult to prove the necessary fraud. Therefore a further civil liability for 'wrongful trading' was introduced, which means that the **director will have to make such contribution to the company's assets as the court sees fit**.

Directors will be liable if the liquidator or administrator proves the following.

(a) The director(s) of the insolvent company **knew**, or **should have known**, that there was **no reasonable prospect** that the **company** could **have avoided insolvency**. This means that directors cannot claim they lacked knowledge if their lack of knowledge was a result of failing to comply with Companies Act requirements, for example preparation of accounts: *Re Produce Marketing Consortium 1989* (see below).

(b) The director(s) did not take **sufficient steps** to minimise the potential loss to the creditors.

Directors will be deemed to know that the company could not avoid insolvency if that would have been the conclusion of a **reasonably diligent person** with the **general knowledge, skill and experience** that might reasonably be expected of a person carrying out that particular director's duties. If the director has greater than usual skill then he will be judged with reference to his own capacity.

5.5 Other offences in relation to winding up

We saw in Chapter 12 that it is a criminal offence for directors to make a **false declaration of solvency** during a liquidation – further offences include the following.

5.5.1 Acting as a director whilst disqualified

S 15 **Company Directors Disqualification Act 1986** (HMSO, 1986) makes a person who **acts as a director whilst disqualified** personally liable for the company's debts. Directors of insolvent companies may be disqualified under the Act if the court deems they are unfit to be involved in the management of a company.

5.5.2 Phoenix companies

Phoenix companies are created by directors of insolvent companies as a **method of continuing their business**. Very often they have similar names as (or similar enough to suggest an association with) the insolvent company. S 216 Insolvency Act 1986 (HMSO, 1986) makes it a **criminal offence** where a director **creates such a company within five years of the original company being liquidated**. The person is liable for a fine or imprisonment. S 217 makes a person who creates such a company personally liable for its debts.

5.5.3 Fraud and deception

S 206 Insolvency Act 1986 makes it a criminal offence to **conceal** or **fraudulently remove company assets** or **debt** – including falsifying records. It is also an offence to **dispose of property** that was **acquired on credit** that has **not been paid** for.

5.5.4 Defrauding creditors

Once a winding up commences, s 207 Insolvency Act 1986 makes it an offence to make a **gift** of, or **transfer company property**, unless it can be proved there was no intent to defraud creditors.

5.5.5 Misconduct during a liquidation

A company officer may be liable for a number of offences due to their misconduct. These include:

- Not identifying company property to the liquidator.
- Not delivering requested books and papers to the liquidator.
- Not informing the liquidator if identified debts do not turn out to be debts.

5.5.6 Falsification of company books

The destruction, mutilation, alteration or falsification of company books is an offence under s 209 Insolvency Act 1986.

5.5.7 Omissions

It is an offence under s 210 Insolvency Act 1986 to omit material information when making statements concerning a company's affairs.

5.6 Examples: Offences in relation to winding up

The standard expected of a listed company director would be **higher** than for the director of a small owner-managed private company.

> *Halls v David and Another 1989*
>
> *The facts:* The directors sought to obtain relief from liability for wrongful trading by the application of what is now s 1157 Companies Act 2006. This stated that in proceedings for negligence, default, breach of duty or breach of trust against a director, if it appears that he has acted honestly and reasonably the court may relieve him wholly or partly from liability on such terms as it sees fit.
>
> *Decision:* S 1157 Companies Act 2006 is not available to excuse a director from liability under s 214.

> *Re Produce Marketing Consortium Ltd 1989*
>
> *The facts:* Two months after the case above, the same liquidator sought an order against the same directors this time, that they should contribute to the company assets (which were in the hands of the liquidator) since they had been found liable for wrongful trading.
>
> *Decision:* The directors were jointly and severally liable for the sum of £75,000 plus interest, along with the costs of the case. The judge stated that the fact that wrongful trading was not based on fraud was not a reason for giving a nominal or low figure of contribution. The figure should, however, be assessed in the light of all the circumstances of the case.

This case was significant for creditors, since the assets available for distribution in a winding up will (potentially) be much increased by a **large directors' contribution**. It serves as a warning to directors to take professional advice sooner rather than later. The prospect of making a personal contribution may prove much more expensive than winding-up at the appropriate stage.

5.7 Companies Act 2006 offences

The Companies Act 2006 (TSO, 2006) includes provision for a **large number of offences** in relation to the **management** and **operation** of a company.

5.7.1 Company records

Company records and **registers**, such as the register of members and record of resolutions **must be kept adequately for future reference**. Officers in default are liable to a fine (s 1135 Companies Act 2006). **Falsification** of **information, hiding falsification,** or **failing to prevent falsification** are also offences and the wrongdoer is liable to a fine (s 1138 Companies Act 2006).

5.7.2 Accounting records

Where a company fails to **keep adequate accounting records**, every officer who defaults is subject to a fine (s 387 Companies Act 2006). However, they have a **defence** if they **acted honestly** and the **circumstances** surrounding the company's business makes the default **excusable**.

5.7.3 Trading disclosures

Companies are required to disclose **certain information** (such as its name) in **specific locations**. If these disclosures are not made then defaulting officers are criminally liable for a fine and may also be liable for losses under the civil law.

5.7.4 Filing accounts

If a company fails to **file its accounts within the time limit following its year end** then any defaulting officer is liable to a fine (s 451 Companies Act 2006). However they will have a **defence** if they took **reasonable steps** to **ensure the requirements** were **complied with**.

5.7.5 False information

Under s 463 Companies Act 2006, officers are liable for making **false disclosures** in relation to the **directors' report**, **directors' remuneration report** and **summary financial statements** based on those reports. An officer is also liable under s 501 Companies Act 2006 for **providing false** or **misleading information to an auditor**. Punishment is either imprisonment or a fine.

5.8 The Fraud Act 2006

The **Fraud Act 2006** (TSO, 2006), to which directors and secretaries are subject, created a **single offence of fraud**, which a person can commit in three different ways by:

- **False representation**: dishonestly making a false representation of fact or law, intending thereby to make a gain for himself or another, or to cause another party loss, or to expose that party to the risk of making loss.

- **Failure to disclose information when there is a legal duty to do so**: dishonestly failing to disclose to another person information which he is under a legal duty to disclose, thereby intending to make a gain for himself or another, or to cause another party loss or expose that party to the risk of making loss.

- **Abuse of position**: occupying a position in which he is expected to safeguard, or not to act against, the financial interest of another person, and dishonestly abusing that position, thereby intending to make a gain for himself or another, or to cause another party loss or expose that party to the risk of suffering loss.

5.9 The Criminal Finances Act 2017

The **Criminal Finances Act 2017** (TSO 2017) potentially makes 'relevant bodies' criminally liable if 'associated persons' are involved in tax evasion.

A **relevant body** is defined by the Act as a company or partnership whether formed in the UK or elsewhere.

An **associated person** is anyone acting in the capacity of an employee, an agent, or any other person who performs services on behalf of the relevant body.

5.9.1 The offence

Under the Act, an **offence will be committed** by a relevant body if the following three stages occur:

- There is criminal tax evasion by a taxpayer or business under existing tax evasion law.

- An associated person of the relevant body, facilitated the tax evasion under existing aiding and abetting law.

- The relevant body failed to prevent the associated person from committing the aiding and abetting offence.

5.9.2 Defence

Under the Act, a relevant body has a defence if it can demonstrate that it **had reasonable prevention procedures in place**, or in the circumstances it was unreasonable or unrealistic to have such procedures in place.

It applies even if the business was not involved in the act or had no knowledge of it. The maximum penalty under the Act is a conviction and unlimited fine.

> Janice is employed as an accountant and tax advisor by Jones & Co LLP to provide all aspects of tax advice to clients. One of the firm's clients, Lucas Ltd, contacted Janice for help to minimise its tax bill for the current tax year. To keep the client happy, Janice suggested that they provide her with copies of fake purchase invoices so that she can include them in their accounts to reduce their profit for the year and therefore reduce their tax bill.
>
> Lucas Ltd has committed a tax evasion offence by providing fake purchase invoices in an attempt to reduce its tax bill. Janice has aided and abetted Lucas Ltd's tax evasion by suggesting how it can evade tax and by using the fake invoices to reduce the business' profit.
>
> Therefore the first two stages of an offence under the Criminal Finances Act 2017 have been committed. Jones & Co LLP will be liable under the Act unless it can demonstrate that it had reasonable prevention procedures in place, or in the circumstances it was unreasonable or unrealistic to have such procedures in place.

PART E CRIMINAL LAW

Chapter roundup

- Crime is **conduct prohibited by the law**. Financial crime can be international in nature, and there is a need for international cooperation to prevent it.

- Insider dealing is the statutory offence of **dealing** in securities while in **possession** of **inside information** as an insider, the securities being price affected by the information.

- The law on insider dealing has had some **limitations**, and the **market abuse offences** were brought in to reduce security-related crime.

- Money laundering is the attempts to **make money from criminal activity appear legitimate** by disguising its original source.

- In the UK, there are various offences relating to **money laundering**, including **tipping off** a money launderer (or suspected money launderer) and **failing to report** reasonable suspicions.

- **Bribery** is a serious offence which often relates to the **offering** and **receiving** of **gifts** or **hospitality**.

- **Criminal offences** in relation to **winding up** include: making a declaration of solvency without reasonable grounds; fraudulent trading; wrongful trading.

Quick quiz

1. Insider dealing is a criminal offence

   True ☐

   False ☐

2. Fill in the blanks

   Inside information is '…………………………………..' relating to a ………………….. of **securities** that are price-affected and not to securities generally.

3. Define money laundering.

4. Which of the following is not a UK offence relating to money laundering?

   A   Concealing the proceeds of criminal activity
   B   Tipping off
   C   Dealing in price affected securities
   D   Failing to report suspicion of money laundering

5. What is placement?

Answers to quick quiz

1. True. Insider dealing is a criminal offence.
2. Inside information is 'price sensitive information' relating to a particular issuer of securities that are price-affected and not to securities generally.
3. Money laundering is the term given to attempts to make the proceeds of crime appear respectable.

    It covers any activity by which the apparent source and ownership of money representing the proceeds of income are changed so that the money appears to have been obtained legitimately.
4. C. This could be insider dealing, if the person dealing was an insider and was using inside information.
5. Placement is the disposal of the initial proceeds of the illegal activity.

End of chapter question

Financial Conduct Authority

Explain the role of the Financial Conduct Authority as a regulator of company markets in the UK, paying particular attention to its role with regard to money laundering. **(5 marks)**

PART E CRIMINAL LAW

Answers to end of chapter questions

ANSWERS TO END OF CHAPTER QUESTIONS

1 Companies

(a) **A public limited company**

A public limited company is a company (an entity so registered under the Companies Act) that states in its constitution that it is a public company and has complied with the registration procedures for such a company.

Special registration procedures

As well as stating in the constitution submitted to the Companies Registrar that the company is public, a company registering as a public limited company must obtain a special trading certificate to allow it to trade.

Distinguished from a private company

A company which does not meet the criteria to be a public company is by default a private company. The key difference between them is that public companies are entitled to offer their shares to the public. Public companies may therefore (although they do not have to) be listed on stock exchanges, whereas private companies may not.

(b) **Parent and subsidiary company**

A parent company is a company which **controls** another company (the subsidiary) by virtue of one of:

- Holding a majority of voting rights in the other company
- Being a member of the other company able to appoint/remove directors
- Holding the right to exercise a dominant influence over the other company
- Controlling the voting rights in the other company
- Being a parent company of a company that fulfils one of the above

The parent company and the subsidiary company form a simple **group of companies**. Groups of companies can be much larger that two companies, as a company may control a large number of other companies (each of which is therefore a subsidiary) and subsidiary companies may also be parent companies. As can be seen in the last bullet point above, when a subsidiary company is also a parent company, its parent company is also a parent company of the subsidiary's subsidiary. This is illustrated in the following diagram.

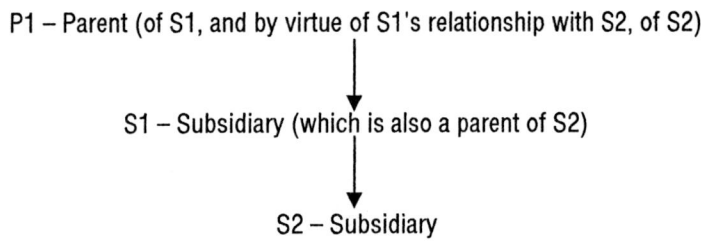

P1 – Parent (of S1, and by virtue of S1's relationship with S2, of S2)

S1 – Subsidiary (which is also a parent of S2)

S2 – Subsidiary

(c) **A multinational company**

A multinational company is one which produces and markets its products in more than one country. Such companies may also be listed on several different national stock exchanges, although it is not the multiple listing which renders a company multinational, but its actual operations.

The vast majority of companies in the world simply operate in one country, even if their products may be exported, but some huge multinational companies such as Microsoft or Coca Cola operate in many different countries and are genuinely global.

2 Incorporation and promoters

(a) (i) **Promoter**

A company is usually formed by a **promoter**, who is 'one who undertakes to form a company with reference to a given project and to set it going and who takes the necessary steps to accomplish that purpose'. It is a promoter who enters into pre-incorporation contracts.

Pre-incorporation expenses

A promoter cannot enter into a contract to be paid for expenses incurred before incorporation, such as drafting legal documents, because the company does not possess legal capacity prior to being incorporated. However, he can generally arrange that the first directors, of whom he may be one, should reimburse him or pay the bills.

(ii) **Pre-incorporation contract**

A **pre-incorporation contract** is a contract made in a company's name before it is formed. Companies are not bound by such contracts as they do not exist when the contracts are made.

Company cannot ratify

It follows that a company can never ratify a pre-incorporation contract made on its behalf. Since it did not exist when the pre-incorporation contract was made, it cannot be made a party to it.

Need for novation

Once the company is incorporated there must be **novation** for a pre-incorporation contract to be enforced. This means that a new contract is made with the same subject matter, or the terms of the contract modified to the extent that it constitutes a new offer.

(b) **Liability of promoter**

Although a company is not liable on a pre-incorporation contract the promoter may nevertheless incur personal liability in statute.

S 51(1)

S 51(1) of the Companies Act contains the statutory provisions relating to pre-incorporation contracts. It states that where a person contracts in the name of, or as agent for, a company before its incorporation, that person will be personally liable unless there is agreement to the contrary.

3 Articles

Content of articles

A company's articles of association form the basis of its constitution along with its resolutions and agreements. It lays down rules governing its **internal management** and the rights of its shareholders and directors.

The principal areas covered will be the issue and transfer of shares, members' rights and the conduct of general meetings, the appointment, dismissal, powers, responsibilities and liabilities of company directors, dividends, class meetings, communication with members and documents and records.

Where a company does submit its own articles on incorporation, these must be **signed** by the **subscribers** to the memorandum of association. Companies which do not submit articles on registration will be allocated default, or model, articles relevant to the type of company registered.

Legal effect of articles

S 33 states that the constitution of a company (and therefore its articles) **bind the company and its members** to the same extent as if they had been signed and sealed by each member and each member had covenanted to observe all their provisions. Thus the articles are treated as a binding contract between the company and its members and as a binding contract between the shareholders.

Thus the company's articles were enforceable by the company against one of its shareholders in *Hickman v Kent or Romney Marsh Sheepbreeders Association 1915*. The rule applies only where the shareholders' rights affected are their rights as members and not in any personal capacity or capacity as director: *Eley v Positive Government Security Life Assurance Co 1876*.

The case of *Rayfield v Hands 1958* illustrates the existence of a contract between company members under s 33. In this case the articles required that the directors should purchase the shares of any member wishing to transfer his shares and also that the directors should also be shareholders. When the directors claimed that their liability was not as members and that the article was not enforceable by members, it was held that the article created an enforceable contract between the claimant members and directors as members of the company.

The articles do **not constitute a contract with any third party** by virtue of s 33: *Eley v Positive Government Security Life Assurance Co 1876*. However, where a contract between a company and a third party fails to address an issue which is covered in the company's articles, the relevant provisions may be taken to supply a missing contract term: *Re New British Iron Co, ex p Beckwith 1898*.

If legislation enables a company to do something provided its articles contain appropriate authority, the company, in the absence of such authority, will need to **alter its articles** first of all before doing the thing permitted. The alteration must be *bona fide* for the benefit of the company as a whole, meaning the individual hypothetical member. Alterations cannot be made if their effect is to place the articles in conflict with the general law or statute. The courts will look with suspicion upon changes that give some members the power to expel others (*Dafen Tinplate Co Ltd v Llanelly Steel Co [1907] Ltd*), unless the benefit to the company is clear (for example expulsion of a member who is competing with the company: *Sidebottom v Kershaw Leese & Co Ltd 1920*). The fact that a contract with a third party may be broken by a change in the articles does not invalidate that change, however damages may be payable: *Southern Foundries v Shirlaw 1942*.

In some cases, provisions of a statute may prohibit a company from doing something notwithstanding anything to the contrary in its articles of association.

A company may alter any of its articles (usually) by the passing of a **special resolution** to that effect. However s 22 permits companies to 'entrench' provisions into their articles. This means specific provisions may only be removed or amended if certain conditions (which are more restrictive than a special resolution) are met.

4 Shares

(a) **Share capital**

A share is 'the **interest of a shareholder in the company measured by a sum of money**, for the purpose of a liability in the first place, and of interest in the second, but also consisting of a series of mutual covenants entered into by all the shareholders *inter se*'.

A share must be **paid for** and it gives a proportionate entitlement to **dividends**, **votes** and any **return of capital**. It also constitutes a form of bargain **between the shareholders**, underlying such principles as majority control and minority protection.

A share is a form of **personal property** carrying rights and obligations, which is **transferable** in accordance with the company's articles on transferability of shares. Shares in a public company are freely transferable provided the appropriate procedures are followed.

The **nominal value** of the share usually fixes the amount of the shareholder's liability, ie how much he can be required to contribute to the company's assets. The shareholder's right to share in the company is the right to receive a **dividend** in the company's profits and not a share of the company's **capital assets**.

(b) **Types of share capital**

(i) **Issued share capital**

This is the nominal value of all shares which have been **allotted to members and issued as share certificates**. Where part of its share capital has not been issued, this part is called the unissued share capital. A public company must have at least £50,000 issued share capital.

The issued share capital is the measure of the substance of a company.

(ii) **Paid up share capital**

This is the proportion of the nominal value of the issued capital actually **paid**. An allottee of shares must pay the **nominal value** of those shares plus any **premium due** on them.

Once the amount due has been paid, the shares are **'fully paid'**. However, it is possible for part of the payment (or all of the payment in the case of private companies only and very rarely) to be **deferred** to a future date (either fixed or on demand from the directors for example) or to be payable in **instalments**. In such cases the shares are referred to as **'partly paid'**. In the event of the shares being transferred, the unpaid capital passes with the shares as a debt payable by the holder at the time when payment becomes due.

In the case of public companies, at the time of allotment the company must receive payment for at least **one quarter of the nominal value of the shares and the whole of any premium**. Thus partly paid shares of a public company (except those issued under an employees' share scheme) must always be at least one quarter paid up.

5 Debentures and charges

(a) **Debentures**

There is no statutory definition of 'debenture' (though s 738 Companies Act 2006 states that a debenture includes debenture stock, bonds and any other securities of a company, whether or not constituting a charge on the assets of the company).

In essence, a **debenture** is a document which states the terms on which a company has borrowed money (creating or acknowledging the debt).

A debenture is often **secured** (by also creating a fixed or floating charge over some or all of the company's assets) but may be unsecured, in which case it is likely to be called an unsecured loan note to distinguish it from a secured debenture.

A debenture usually takes the form of a printed legal document, setting out the **terms** of the loan and providing for the payment of **interest** to the debenture holder (regardless of profits). It might be a single debenture or one of a series ranking ***pari passu*** (for example, where the directors or members provide different loan amounts at different times but all loans are intended to rank equally). It might be one which governs the issue of debenture stock subscribed to by a large number of lenders (typically the public at large).

(b) **Fixed charges**

A **fixed charge** attaches to a specific asset as soon as the charge is created. If the company fails to honour its commitment to pay interest or repay the amount borrowed or goes into liquidation, the asset will be passed to the chargeholder, or sold to realise the debt, and the proceeds of the sale will go to the fixed chargeholder in preference to preferential creditors and floating charges. The company cannot dispose of the asset without the consent of the chargeholder.

The fact that a document is called a fixed charge will not be conclusive where in fact the company is still permitted to deal with the charge without reference to the chargee: *R in Right of British Columbia v Federal Business Development Bank 1988*.

Examples of fixed charges are legal mortgages of shares or land, or charges over other property.

(c) **Floating charges**

A **floating charge** is:

(i) A charge on a **class of assets** of a company, present and future

(ii) Which class is in the ordinary course of the company's business **changing** from time to time, and

(iii) Until the holders enforce the charge the company may **carry on business** and **deal** with the asset charged: *Re Yorkshire Woolcombers Association Ltd 1903*.

A floating charge can apply to fixed assets and current assets. It does not attach to any assets until crystallisation (when it becomes a fixed charge).

6 Issuing shares

(a) **Issuing shares at a premium**

A company may issue shares for a price **in excess of the nominal value** of those shares. The excess is called the **'share premium'** and must be credited to a share premium account.

It is not necessary for the articles of association to include a **power** to issue shares at a premium since it is **implied**. Where the shares are issued for a non-cash consideration in excess of the shares' nominal value, the excess should still be credited to the share premium account, since the statutory rule applies to issues of shares 'at a premium whether for cash or otherwise'.

The general rule is that reduction of the share premium account is subject to the same restrictions as reduction of share capital.

(i) **No part** of the account can be distributed as **dividend**.

(ii) The account can be used to pay up fully paid shares under **a bonus issue** since this operation simply converts one form of fixed capital into another.

(iii) It can also be used to pay **issue expenses** and **commission** in respect of a **new share issue**.

The share premium account is included in the **'undistributable reserves'** when determining whether a **dividend** can lawfully be declared by a public company (which can only make a distribution if its net assets are not less than the aggregate of its called up share capital and undistributable reserves).

(b) **Issuing shares at a discount**

Every share has a nominal value and cannot be allotted at a discount to that value. A company must obtain in money or money's worth consideration of a value at least equal to the nominal value of the shares allotted plus the whole of any premium. If shares are allotted at a discount, the allottee (and subsequent ones) is liable to pay the full nominal value together with interest at the appropriate rate.

The issue of shares at a price which is less than the market value (but equal to or more than the nominal value) of existing shares does not contravene the provision.

In the case of **private companies only**, shares may be allotted for inadequate consideration by the acceptance of **goods or services** at an over-value. A blatant and unjustified overvaluation will not, however, be upheld. **Non-cash consideration must be independently valued in the case of public companies.**

7 Boards

(a) **Non-executive director**

A non-executive director is a fully appointed director of the company who does not have executive powers ie does not have a functional role in the company's management. Non-executive directors' primary duty is to attend meetings of the board, at which they are expected to play an objective, questioning role.

(b) **Executive director**

An executive director is a **director who performs a specific role in a company** under a service contract which requires a regular, possibly daily involvement in management.

Such directors are often employees of the company, and if they have **specific management duties**, they are often given a relevant title, for example, finance director or sales director.

The contrasting type of director, often found in listed, public companies where they are a requirement of the Corporate Governance Code, are non-executive directors, who simply serve on the board of directors.

(c) **Single board**

A single, sometimes known as unitary, board is the typical board structure in the UK and the US and many other countries. It is **where the company is managed by a single board of directors**.

Such a board may simply comprise executive directors, but may also include non-executive directors, particularly in listed, public companies, where a combination of executive and non-executive directors is encouraged by the Corporate Governance Code.

The single board has collective responsibility to manage the company and has power delegated to it as a collective body.

(d) **Supervisory board**

The supervisory board is the superior board in a system used in several countries, where there is a **dual-board system** comprising a **management board** and a **supervisory board**.

The supervisory board consists of members elected by the shareholders and the employees and it has an advisory role in relation to the business. It also carries out certain duties, such as electing members of the management board and receiving reports from the management board on company business.

8 Hydrangea

(a) **Calling of the meeting**

All the business can be handled by an AGM so no other general meeting is required.

Notice of the meeting

Notice of the AGM must be sent to every **member** of the company who is entitled to attend and vote at the meeting. It should also be sent to the directors and auditors. The notice should:

(1) Give adequate information concerning the **date, time and place** of the meeting.

(2) Specify it is an **AGM**.

(3) Describe the proposed **special resolution** as such.

(4) Give sufficient **details** of the **proposed business** at the meeting to enable recipients of the notice to understand what it is proposed to be done at the meeting.

Length of notice

The length of notice required for AGMs is 21 clear days notice.

Approving the accounts and re-electing directors

These resolutions are deemed ordinary business and should be passed by an ordinary resolution of the company, which is carried by a simple majority (over 50%) of votes cast.

Changing the company's name

Authority to change the name of a company requires a special resolution of the company, which means a 75% majority of votes cast is needed to pass it.

(b) **Voting rights of members**

The **rights** of members **to vote** and the **number of votes** to which they are entitled will be **determined by** the company's **articles**.

Show of hands

Voting is normally done by a **show of hands** by each member present in person. Each has **one vote**.

The chairman's declaration of the result on a show of hands (in the absence of it being fraudulent or manifestly wrong) will be conclusive. **Voting** by **show of hands** will **not be effective**, however, where a poll is properly demanded.

Polls

There is a statutory right to a poll wherever a special resolution is proposed. Voting on a poll may be demanded by at least **five members** or by **members representing at least one tenth of the voting rights** or by members holding **at least one tenth of the paid-up capital** conferring voting rights. (A company's articles cannot make these criteria more onerous from the shareholders' point of view.)

Where voting is on a poll, every member present may cast the **full number** of votes to which they are entitled. This is normally one per share held.

Voting rights of proxies

Every member entitled to **attend** and **vote** at a meeting may instead appoint at least one proxy to attend and vote for him. The proxy need not be a member.

Notice of the meeting must contain a statement which explains each member's **right to appoint** a non-member proxy. **Proxies may vote on a poll** since they have the same right to demand a poll as the member whom they represent. Most companies issue **two-way proxy cards** on which the member instructs his proxy to vote either for or against each resolution.

9 Statutory duties

The Companies Act 2006 includes seven statutory duties that directors must meet.

(a) **Duty to act within powers (s 171)**

This duty requires directors not to exceed the powers given to them by the company. In particular they must only exercise powers for the purpose for which they were conferred.

(b) **Duty to promote the success of the company (s 172)**

The principle of 'enlightened shareholder value' requires directors to act in a way which is most likely to promote the success of the company for the benefit of the members as a whole.

(c) **Duty to exercise independent judgement (s 173)**

Directors must exercise independent judgement. They must not delegate their powers or be swayed by the influence of others.

(d) **Duty to exercise reasonable skill, care and diligence (s 174)**

Directors have a duty to exercise the same standard of care, skill and diligence that would reasonably be expected of a reasonably diligent person with:

(i) The general knowledge, skill and experience which may be reasonably expected of a person in their position and

(ii) The general knowledge, skill and experience they actually have.

(e) **Duty to avoid conflicts of interest (s 175)**

The Act suggests a number of circumstances where a director's personal interests may conflict with the company's interests. Directors have a duty to avoid such circumstances.

(f) **Duty not to accept benefits from third parties (s 176)**

This duty prevents directors from accepting benefits from parties outside the company (usually bribes). It supports the duty under s 175 by preventing a potential conflict of interest.

(g) **Duty to declare an interest in proposed transaction or arrangement (s 177)**

Directors must declare the nature and extent of any proposed arrangement or transaction they may be involved in with the company either personally or through a third party. Disclosure may be given by written or general notice or a board meeting, but must be made to the directors, as disclosure to the members is not sufficient to discharge the duty.

Note only an explanation of five of the duties was required in the question.

10 Frank

Ultra vires acts

The approach taken by the Companies Act 2006 is to give security to commercial transactions for third parties, while preserving the rights of shareholders to restrain directors from entering an *ultra vires action*. S 39 provides that 'the validity of an act done by a company shall not be called into question on the ground of lack of capacity by reason of anything in the company's constitution'. S 40 provides that 'in favour of a person dealing with a company in good faith, the power of the directors to bind the company, or authorise others to do so, shall be deemed to be free of any limitation under the company's constitution'.

Consequently, the contract between Good plc and the supplier of alcoholic drinks is valid and enforceable and neither Good plc nor the other party can plead *ultra vires* to escape their obligations.

Frank's duties as director

While sections 39 and 40 deal with the company's transactions with third parties, however, the members may take action against Frank and the other director for permitting *ultra vires* acts. Their action will be based on the fact that the constitution specifically restricted the particular act and under section 171, the directors must abide by the company's constitution.

The directors owe a duty to the company to ensure that the company's assets are not used for *ultra vires* purposes. Where this is breached, the act can only be ratified by special resolution and separate special resolution will be needed to relieve the directors from liability for this breach. An action to make Frank liable to account for losses is not relevant since the contract proved to be profitable.

Internally, the *ultra vires* rule continues to operate between the company and its members. Shareholders have the right to restrain an ultra vires act. However, this is of no use where the act has already occurred.

The shareholders of Good plc might consider **altering the constitution** to broaden its objects and business operation by specific additions or alterations or by adopting the commonly used 'general commercial company' provision. It should bear in mind that retaining an object clause which is more detailed may be preferable with regard to securing investment in the company. The clause can be altered by the shareholders in general meeting passing a special resolution.

As managing director **Frank can exercise all the directors' powers** (Art 84) but he is also subject to limitations on those powers contained in the company's constitution. He is in breach of his authority in this case, but the contract cannot be challenged on this ground any more than on the *ultra vires* ground.

Ultimately, the shareholders of a company have the power to remove a director by passing an ordinary resolution to that effect (s 168). Henry would need to command a simple majority or have sufficient support from other shareholders to achieve this.

Insider dealing

Section 52 of the Criminal Justice Act 1993 provides that it shall be a **criminal offence to deal in securities while in possession of inside information as an insider**, the securities being price-affected by the information. It is necessary to show that the person with inside information either dealt in price-affected securities or encouraged another to deal in them, or disclosed the information.

'Dealing in securities' is widely defined and there is not doubt that Frank's purchase of shares would be covered by these provisions. 'Inside information' is defined as 'price-sensitive information' relating to a particular issuer of securities that are price-effected. The information must be specific or precise and, if made public, be likely to have significant effect on price. Again it appears that Frank, an insider by virtue of his position as a director, has inside information and has made use of that information in his purchase of shares.

The Act does contain some special and general defences. The latter are that the individual did not expect there to be a profit or avoidance of loss, or that he had reasonable grounds to believe that the information has been disclosed widely or that he would have done what he did even if he had not had the information.

None of these defences appear to apply in Frank's favour which means that he is liable to be convicted for the offence of insider dealing, the maximum penalties for which are seven years' imprisonment and/or an unlimited fine. Insider dealing has constituted a ground for disqualification for acting as a director under the CDDA 1986 (*R v Goodman 1993*).

At civil law, action could be taken against Frank for breach of the fiduciary duties owed by him as a director. A claim would be made for him to account to the company for the profits made on the purchase of shares.

11 Parsloe Ltd

The auditors had no contract with Parsloe Ltd and so they can only be sued in the tort of negligence, not in contract.

Parsloe Ltd relied upon the accounts laid before the AGM, but to sue for its economic loss it must establish that there was a 'special relationship': a professional relationship (the accountants gave the advice in their professional capacity) in which one party relies on the expertise of the other who knew or ought to have known that the other party would rely upon this advice: *Hedley Byrne v Heller & Partners [1964]*. Such a special relationship means that a fiduciary relationship exists (a relationship of trust and competence).

The case of *Caparo Industries v Dickman and others [1991]* however has set the modern standard (indeed the facts of this question are very similar to those in that case). This shows that it is important to look at the relationship between the parties. Firstly, how closely connected or 'proximate' were they? The defendant and claimant must be proximate so that the loss was not too remote. Secondly, was the defendant's loss foreseeable?

The then House of Lords in the *Caparo case* decided that the auditors' relationship with individual shareholders was not enough to give rise to a duty of care to shareholders as potential purchasers. It would have done so only if, at the time of signing their report, the auditors were aware of the acquiring company's interest. In this case, as in the *Caparo* case, they were not aware of it since it had not at that time been finally decided on.

Parsloe Ltd has no claim in negligence against the auditors of Matchingham plc as a duty of care cannot be established.

12 Liquidation

When a company cannot meet its **financial liabilities** it is likely to enter a process of liquidation. This process sees the company's **assets** realised and arrangements made to settle its **liabilities** where possible. Liquidation can be compulsory or voluntary.

Compulsory liquidation

Under this method, the company is forced into liquidation by one or more of its creditors.

Under s 122 of the Insolvency Act 1986 creditors may apply to the court for the compulsory liquidation of a customer for seven reasons. The two most important reasons are:

- The company **cannot** pay its debts.
- It is **just and equitable** to wind up the company (members may also apply).

Voluntary liquidation

Voluntary liquidation is a decision taken by the members to wind up the company. There are two methods that can be used.

- **Members' voluntary winding up** – where the company is solvent but the members decide to close the business down.
- **Creditors' voluntary winding up** – where the company is insolvent and the members decide to wind the company up in conjunction with the creditors.

Differences between compulsory and voluntary liquidation

Timing

A compulsory winding up commences (once granted by the court) on the day the court is presented with the petition. Voluntary liquidation commences on the day the resolution to wind up the company is passed.

Liquidator

The official receiver administers a compulsory winding up, the members and creditors chose and appoint a liquidator under the voluntary process. Unlike the official receiver, this liquidator is not an officer of the court.

Legal action

Unlike compulsory liquidation, under the voluntary process the company receives no automatic stay of legal proceedings. However the liquidator can apply to the court for any order that it would grant under compulsory liquidation.

Employment

Employees are not automatically dismissed under voluntary liquidation. In circumstances of compulsory or 'insolvent' liquidation, employment contracts are effectively repudiated as the company can no longer pay its staff.

13 Financial Conduct Authority

Financial Conduct Authority (FCA)

The Financial Conduct Authority is one of the regulators of the financial services industry and company markets and share exchanges in the UK. In this answer, we shall concentrate on its role with regard to companies. It is not a government agency, but has links to the government. It is a private limited company of which the UK government's treasury department is the guarantor. It is financed by the financial services industry.

Companies

Specifically in relation to companies, the FCA approves companies for listing in the UK, supervises companies and has powers of enforcement with relation to companies. It aims to secure an appropriate degree of protection for consumers in the market and to reduce the scope for financial crime (for example, market abuse and money laundering, both of which we consider below in more detail below).

The FCA is authorised to carry out investigations of companies when the following matters are suspected:
- Market abuse
- Misleading statements and practices
- Insider dealing
- Breaches of the Listing Rules of the Stock Exchange
- Money laundering

Money laundering

Money laundering is the term given to attempts to make the proceeds of crime appear respectable. It covers any activity by which the apparent source and ownership of money representing the proceeds of income are changed so that the money appears to have been obtained legitimately.

As discussed above, the FCA also has powers to conduct investigations into such activity. Money laundering is a criminal offence, so the FCA will work jointly with the National Crime Agency (NCA) and the police in respect of this crime.

Exam question bank

EXAM QUESTION BANK

Separate legal personality (November 2015)

Discuss the concept of separate legal personality in company law and the circumstances in which it can be lost. **(20 marks)**

Partnerships and companies (November 2016)

Compare and contrast the characteristics of a business organisation established as a general (unlimited) partnership and a business organisation incorporated as a company with model articles (unamended).

(20 marks)

Registering a company (November 2015)

Identify the key documents required to register a company under the Companies Act 2006 and analyse the legal effects of each of the documents. **(20 marks)**

Company name, pre-incorporation contracts and accounts (May 2017)

Jack Slater and Graham Dickson are builders who would like to form a private company limited by shares called Redbrick Limited (Redbrick). Jack is aware of another company within the local area called Redybrick Limited which operates a similar business to the construction business that will be undertaken by Redbrick Limited.

Required

(a) Discuss any legal risks that Jack and Graham are taking in incorporating a company with the name Redbrick Limited and consider any alternative course of action they could take to avoid these risks whilst still using this name. **(8 marks)**

(b) Just before incorporation, Jack signed a contract 'for and on behalf of Redbrick Limited' to secure storage premises for the new company. Discuss where liability lies in relation to this contract.
(5 marks)

(c) Following incorporation, explain to Jack and Graham what Redbrick's obligations will be in relation to the production and filing of accounts and whether Redbrick will need to appoint an auditor.
(7 marks)

(Total = 20 marks)

Incorporation: Rules and procedures (November 2014)

Sprayfinishing Solutions is a successful business providing industrial spray-painting services. The business has been operating as a partnership for the last five years. The two partners, Jed Baker and Tim Gregson, both work full time in the business and employ a team of 25 painters and 5 administrative staff. Over the last 12 months, Sprayfinishing Solutions has secured a number of large contracts and Jed and Tim have decided that the expanding business should become a limited liability company trading as Sprayfinishing Solutions Limited (SSL). The turnover of the business is in the region of £1.5 million and its balance sheet total is approximately £750,000. Current projections suggest that both measures will increase by approximately 20% over the next 12 months.

Jed and Tim have decided that the company will be incorporated with Model Articles (unamended) and ordinary shares of £1 each. They will each own one share and both be appointed as directors of the company.

Required

(a) Advise Jed and Tim as to the procedures that should be followed to incorporate SSL and what checks should be made before doing so. **(10 marks)**

(b) Advise Jed and Tim what SSL's obligations will be in relation to the production and filing of accounts and whether SSL will need to appoint an auditor. **(7 marks)**

(c) Jed and Tim explain that there have been issues in the past where Jed has spent large sums of money on machinery or supplies without consulting Tim. They have agreed that they want to keep a tight rein on finances and that in future they must both agree on any purchases in excess of £20,000. Advise Jed and Tim as to how an individual director's expenditure can be restricted. **(3 marks)**

(Total = 20 marks)

Issue and transfer of shares (May 2017)

KidsTime Limited (KidsTime) is a company which operates a chain of children's day nurseries. It has four directors, who all own shares in the company, and a further seven shareholders. KidsTime was incorporated in January 2010 and has Model Articles (unamended).

The directors now want to issue new ordinary shares in the company to themselves, but not to any of the other shareholders in the company. One of the directors, Helena Fiennes, also wants to sell some of her shares to her son David, who is not currently a shareholder in KidsTime.

Required

(a) Discuss the procedure that the directors of KidsTime must follow to issue new ordinary shares to themselves.

Note to candidates: You need not consider any fiduciary duties relevant to this transaction. **(9 marks)**

(b) Discuss the procedure that must be followed in order to transfer some of Helena's shares to David. **(6 marks)**

(c) How would your answer to b) differ if KidsTime's articles contained the following clause:

Any shares which a member wishes to transfer must first be offered to the existing members of the company in proportion to their existing shareholding, who have 21 days in which to accept or reject the offer. Any shares not accepted may be freely transferred. **(5 marks)**

(Total = 20 marks)

Allotment and types of shares (May 2015)

Keysure Limited (Keysure) is a local alarm and security company specialising in the security of commercial premises. Keysure was incorporated in 2010 with Model Articles (unamended) and ordinary shares of £1 each. Keysure is currently in need of a capital injection and one of the directors has asked his brother Tony, whether he would be interested in purchasing £20,000 of Keysure shares.

Required

(a) Advise Tony as to the benefits for him, if he were to become a shareholder of Keysure, in Keysure having a separate legal personality and the circumstances in which such benefits may be lost. **(9 marks)**

(b) Discuss the procedural steps Keysure must take in order to allot the shares to Tony, including any documentation and filing required. **(8 marks)**

(c) Tony holds preference shares in another company. Discuss the difference between ordinary and preference shares. **(3 marks)**

(Total = 20 marks)

Shareholder v debenture holder rights (May 2015)

Sartorial Limited (Sartorial) manufactures and distributes children's clothing to wholesalers and retailers. The company is very successful but would like to expand into online retail and requires a financial investment to do so. They have approached an investor, Kate Simms, who seems very keen. The directors of Sartorial have suggested that Kate either buys £25,000 worth of shares in the company, or loans the company £25,000 at an interest rate and with security over assets to be agreed.

Required

Discuss how Kate's rights would differ if she became a shareholder of the company compared to if she became a debenture holder. **(20 marks)**

Charges and guarantees (November 2015)

Ecowood Floors Limited (Ecowood) supplies and fits wooden floors sourced from sustainably managed forests. The directors and majority shareholders of Ecowood are two brothers, Michael and Thomas Daniels. Michael is very wealthy; Thomas is married to Isobel with two small children and much less wealthy than Michael. Ecowood would like to expand into supplying floors to commercial properties, predominantly boutique hotels and designer shops. Ecowood needs some additional finance to achieve this expansion and has approached City Bank plc (City Bank) who have agreed to lend Ecowood £80,000. City Bank has requested personal guarantees from the directors of Ecowood, as well as either a fixed or floating charge over Ecowood's assets.

Required

(a) Explain to the directors of Ecowood the implications of them granting personal guarantees in relation to City Bank's proposed loan to Ecowood. **(6 marks)**

(b) Advise Ecowood on the legal effect of granting either a fixed charge or a floating charge over Ecowood's assets and any procedures which must be complied with in relation to either such charge. **(10 marks)**

(c) Assume now that it has been decided that Michael, rather than City Bank, will lend the money to Ecowood. What procedures would Ecowood need to follow to put the loan in place? **(4 marks)**

(Total = 20 marks)

Maintenance of share capital (May 2015)

Discuss the rules in the Companies Act 2006 relating to the maintenance of share capital. **(20 marks)**

Director appointment and share purchase (November 2014)

Protech Limited (Protech) is a manufacturer of computer hardware incorporated in 2001 with Model Articles (unamended). Five years ago, a private equity firm, Globe Limited (Globe), invested £100,000 in Protech. It purchased 10,000 shares at £10 per share, which gave it a 20% shareholding and a position on the board of directors. Protech's shares are currently valued at £20 per share and Globe wants to realise its investment by selling its shares in Protech.

David Elms, a wealthy local entrepreneur, has expressed an interest in acquiring Globe's shareholding in Protech and becoming a director of Protech in place of Globe's representative on the board. In addition, he would like to be awarded a service contract for a period of three years.

Protech are considering, as an alternative, whether they could use the company's profits to buy back Globe's shareholding.

Required

(a) Discuss what Protech would need to do to effect the purchase of Globe's shares by David. **(6 marks)**

(b) Discuss what the procedure would be to appoint David to the board of directors and award him a three year service contract. **(6 marks)**

(c) Discuss what legal and procedural requirements Protech would be required to satisfy if its board of directors decided that Protech will buy back Globe's shares. **(8 marks)**

(Total = 20 marks)

Transactions with directors (May 2015)

Thomas Potts has been a shareholder in Similian Limited (Similian), an industrial chain manufacturer, for a number of years. He owns eight per cent of the shares in Similian but is not a director. Thomas has recently discovered that some of the directors of Similian, specifically Charles, Zainab and Stephanie, have engaged in various transactions with Similian. Thomas is very concerned about the activity of these directors and wants to bring their actions to the attention of the other shareholders in Similian. The transactions which are of concern to Thomas are:

(a) Last month, a company set up by Charles, of which he is the sole shareholder and director, was awarded a contract that Charles had previously been attempting to secure for Similian.

(b) In the last year, Zainab has received a number of loans from Similian totalling £30,000.

(c) Six months ago, Stephanie bought industrial vehicles and computer equipment from Similian for £150,000. The property was valued in Similian's company books at £200,000.

Required

Discuss what action, if any, Similian can take in respect of the transactions set out above and whether Thomas can requisition a meeting of Similian's shareholders to discuss these transactions. **(20 marks)**

Director appointment (November 2015)

Amy, Charles, Omar and Sarah are the directors of Dream Landscaping Limited (Dream Landscaping). Amy and Charles would like to bring an additional director onto the board of the company, to advise on Dream Landscaping's growth strategy and generally to improve financial performance. Omar and Sarah are opposed to the proposal.

Dream Landscaping has Model Articles (unamended). Omar and Sarah each hold 23% of the company's issued share capital and Amy and Charles hold 12% each. Omar is the chairman of the company.

Required

Advise Amy and Charles whether, and if so how, they can appoint a new director against the wishes of Omar and Sarah. **(20 marks)**

Allotment of shares and transactions (November 2014)

Sensations Limited (Sensations) manufactures and distributes luxury sweets and chocolates to high-end wholesalers and retailers. The company has gone from strength to strength since its formation two years ago and its net asset value is in the region of £200,000. It was incorporated with Model Articles (unamended). It has three shareholders, who are also directors, each of whom own 500 £1 ordinary shares.

The directors now wish to increase the level of investment in the company by allotting shares to Belinda Rosenberg, who has agreed to invest £100,000 cash in return for 1,000 £1 ordinary shares. They plan to spend approximately half of Belinda's investment on purchasing new delivery vans. One of the directors,

Charles Evans, has told the board that his wife, Jemima, is selling three vans she uses in her mobile hairdressing business and the board has decided to purchase the vans from Jemima. The vans are together valued at £80,000.

Required

(a) Discuss why Belinda is paying £100,000 for 1,000 shares when the shares have a nominal value of £1 each. **(3 marks)**

(b) Discuss the procedural steps Sensations must take in order to allot the shares to Belinda, including any documentation and filing required. **(9 marks)**

(c) Discuss any legal issues that should be considered and any procedures that should be followed in relation to the sale of the vehicles by Jemima to Sensations. **(8 marks)**

(Total = 20 marks)

Director duties, appointment and allotment of shares (May 2016)

Hassan Akram and Leo Baker are the only directors and shareholders of Extreme Clean Limited, a company which provides industrial cleaning to the hotel and restaurant industries. The company was incorporated five years ago with Model Articles (unamended). Hassan and Leo want to expand the business and have asked Leo's cousin, Georgina Higgins, to join the company as a director and shareholder, as she has extensive marketing experience and can assist with the expansion plans. Hassan and Leo each own 5,000 £1 ordinary shares. The shares are now worth £3 each and Georgina has agreed to invest £6,000 in the company in return for 2,000 shares.

Required

(a) Describe the duties of a company director for the benefit of the soon-to-be-appointed Georgina.
(8 marks)

(b) Advise the board of directors as to the ways in which Georgina can be appointed as a director, detailing the necessary procedures. **(5 marks)**

(c) Discuss the procedural steps the company must take in order to allot the shares to Georgina. **(7 marks)**

(Total = 20 marks)

Acquisition of shares, company re-registration (May 2014)

Coastal Pharmaceuticals Limited ('the Company') has been trading successfully for five years, and has just won a new lucrative contract to expand operations overseas.

The Company was incorporated on 12 March 2007 and has an issued share capital of £100,000 (100,000 £1 shares). The Company has five shareholders, each of whom holds 20% of the share capital.

The board of directors have received an offer from a third party who would like to acquire the entire issued share capital of the Company. The board have relayed the details of the offer to the shareholders. Four of the shareholders are keen to sell, but one, Pedro, is reluctant as he believes that these are exciting times for the company and further success will follow from the overseas operations.

Required

(a) If four shareholders sell their shares in response to the offer from the third party, advise what right (if any) the third party has to acquire Pedro's shares. **(7 marks)**

(b) The board of the Company have decided that they would like to re-register the company as a public limited company. Advise whether it is possible for the company to re-register as a public limited company and the procedure to do so. **(7 marks)**

(c) Following re-registration as a public limited company, Coastal Pharmaceuticals PLC intends to appoint Nick Smith as company secretary. Nick is the company's financial controller and has worked for the company for the last 10 years. Discuss whether Nick can be appointed as company secretary. **(6 marks)**

(Total = 20 marks)

Minority shareholders (November 2014)

Brakes Catering Limited (Brakes) is a catering company which provides national and international event catering. Harry Jackson and his wife Julia founded the company over 15 years ago but no longer hold positions on the board or significant shareholdings. The current directors are Martin Toller, Umara Khan and Kieran Dyer, each of whom owns 30% of the shares in Brakes. The remaining 10% is owned by a number of small shareholders, including Harry and Julia who own 5% and 2% respectively. Over the last 12 months, Harry and Julia have become increasingly frustrated with how the company is being run and do not believe that Martin, Umara and Kieran are acting in the best interests of the company and its shareholders.

Required

Discuss and analyse the statutory rules which would provide assistance to Harry and Julia as minority shareholders in this company. **(20 marks)**

Dividends and financial information (May 2014)

Xavier and Roberto each own 25% of the share capital of Leyland Limited. The remainder of the shares are owned by Paula (40%) and John (10%) who are the only directors of the company. The company has been trading for three years and has made a reasonable profit over the last twelve months.

The relationship between Xavier, Roberto, Paula and John has always been good. However Xavier and Roberto feel that they only have informal discussions with the other two about how the company is doing and feel that John and Paula are of the opinion that they can run the company without ever taking Xavier or Roberto's views or opinions on matters.

Required

(a) Discuss the rules relating to the ability of a private limited company to declare a dividend including the implications for the directors of the company if the rules are breached. **(12 marks)**

(b) Xavier and Roberto have not received any financial information about the company for 24 months. Discuss the obligations of the directors to produce financial information about the company and to provide information to Roberto and Xavier. **(8 marks)**

(Total = 20 marks)

Debentures, auditors and voting (May 2014)

Forresters Limited is a newly incorporated company. The company has adopted the Model Articles for private companies limited by shares without amendment. The board of directors require some advice as to the administrative requirements in respect of the company.

In addition the company has borrowed £150,000 from London Bank PLC to help with start-up costs and for working capital. The bank requires the loan to be secured by an all monies debenture containing both fixed and floating charges.

Required

(a) Discuss any registration requirements in respect of the debenture. **(5 marks)**

(b) Discuss the procedure for the company to appoint auditors. **(4 marks)**

(c) Discuss the role of auditors in a private company limited by shares. **(5 marks)**

(d) Explain the procedure to demand a poll at a shareholders' meeting, and analyse the effect on voting where a poll is demanded. **(6 marks)**

(Total = 20 marks)

Company accounts (November 2013)

Sarah is a shareholder in Oasis Limited. Sarah has held her shares for ten years. Since the appointment of a new financial director two years ago Sarah has received very limited financial information.

Required

Advise Sarah on the obligations of Oasis Limited in relation to the preparation of accounts including the procedures that must be followed to approve the accounts and any sanctions for breach. You need not consider the exemptions available to small and medium sized companies. **(20 marks)**

Company accounts and auditor liability (May 2015)

(a) Gerard Rimes is a shareholder in Vinematters Limited (Vinematters), a fine wine importing company. He is concerned by the limited financial information about the company which he receives. All he recalls receiving in the last twelve months is a summary financial statement.

Required

Advise Gerard on the obligations of Vinematters in relation to the preparation of accounts and the procedures required to approve these accounts. Vinematters is not a small or medium sized company.

(14 marks)

(b) Gerard is also a minority shareholder in Wineworld plc (Wineworld) and is considering purchasing a controlling interest on the basis of encouraging results and potential further growth shown in Wineworld's latest annual accounts. Gerard waits for the accounts to be approved at Wineworld's AGM and then purchases the shares. Four months later Wineworld is declared insolvent and it is discovered that the accounts approved at the AGM were inaccurate and contained misleading statements.

Required

Advise Gerard as to whether he has a claim against the auditors of Wineworld. **(6 marks)**

(Total = 20 marks)

Auditors (May 2016)

Omar Rashid is the newly appointed company secretary of Shopmart Limited, a company which operates a large chain of supermarkets. It has been brought to his attention that the company's current auditors have become ineligible and new auditors need to be appointed.

Required

Advise Omar on the requirements for eligibility as auditor, the ways in which auditors can be appointed and the duties and rights of the new auditors.

Your answer does not need to consider exemptions available to small and medium sized companies.

(20 marks)

Compulsory liquidation (November 2014)

Discuss the circumstances in which compulsory liquidation of a company is likely to occur. Consider the procedure to effect the liquidation and the outcomes of such liquidation. (20 marks)

Administration (May 2016)

Discuss in what circumstances an administrator may be appointed and explain the role of an administrator.

(20 marks)

Insider dealing (May 2016)

Henry Bradfield is the chief executive officer of Yensert plc, an oil exploration company listed on the London Stock Exchange. Henry was working from home and discussing on the telephone the fact that the company had just discovered a new drilling area which could be extremely profitable for the company. The family's nanny, Isabel Drake, overheard the conversation. Isabel is also a business and economics graduate student working towards her masters at the local university. The next day, without Henry's knowledge, she bought £3,000 worth of Yensert plc shares with the money set aside to pay next term's fees, hoping that their value would increase and that she would make a profit once the information became public.

Required

Advise as to the potential consequences under the Criminal Justice Act 1993 arising from the events set out above for:

(a) Isabel Drake (14 marks)
(b) Henry Bradfield (6 marks)

(Total = 20 marks)

Exam answer bank

Separate legal personality (November 2015)

The concept of the separate legal personality of a company following its incorporation is illustrated in cases such as *Salomon v A. Salomon & Co Ltd [1897]* AC 22 and gives rise to limited liability. Limited liability means that a shareholder in a company has limited liability for the debts of that company – liability is limited to the amount unpaid, if any, on members' shares. So, for example, if an individual shareholder has paid in full for his or her shares, and the company subsequently goes into insolvent liquidation, that shareholder has no liability for the company's unpaid debts and cannot be required to contribute to the assets of the company to pay off those debts. The concept of separate legal personality was confirmed in *Lee v Lee's Air Farming Ltd [1961]* AC 12 and more recently in *MacDonald v Costello [2011]* EWCA Civ 930.

There are circumstances in which the separate legal identity of the company can be lost, often referred to as situations where the veil of incorporation is lifted by the courts. This could result in the benefits of limited liability being lost.

Lifting the veil by statute to enforce the law:

There are provisions in the Companies Act 2006 which result in the benefits of limited liability being lost. For example, in circumstances where a public company does business without a trading certificate, the directors are liable to indemnify a third party for any loss or damage suffered as a result (s 767 Companies Act 2006). There are also Insolvency Act 1986 provisions that have the effect of removing limited liability for directors of a company in liquidation, where those directors are found liable for fraudulent or wrongful trading (ss 213–214 Insolvency Act 1986). Liability can result in directors being required to contribute to the assets of the company.

Lifting the veil to prevent evasion of obligations:

The courts may ignore the distinction between a company and its members and managers if the members use that distinction to evade their pre-existing legal obligations. Examples include to prevent the transfer of assets from one company to another in order to avoid a liability, as in *Re H and Others [1996]* 2 All ER 391 CA and to conceal the nationality of a company and avoid taxation, as in *Unit Construction Co Ltd v Bullock [1960]* AC 455.

Lifting the veil in group situations:

The principle of the veil of incorporation extends to the parent company/subsidiary relationship. Although parent companies and their pre-existing subsidiaries are part of a group under company law, they retain their separate legal personalities. In *Adam v Cape Industries plc [1990]* Ch 433, three reasons were put forward for identifying companies as one and lifting the veil of incorporation:

- The subsidiary is acting as an agent for the parent company;
- The group is to be treated as a single economic entity because of statutory provision;
- The corporate structure is being used as a facade to conceal the truth.

Partnerships and companies (November 2016)

The separate legal personality of a company gives rise to a number of characteristics which distinguish it from a general (unlimited) partnership governed by the Partnership Act 1890. Here, comparing a company incorporated with model articles, and such a partnership:

- Entity – A company is a legal entity separate from its members whilst a partnership has no existence outside of its partners.

- Liability – Members' liability can be limited but partners' liability is usually unlimited.

- Size – A company may have any number of members and a minimum of one, whereas partnerships must have a minimum of two partners.

- Succession – There is perpetual succession of a company – a change in ownership does not affect its existence. The default position in a partnership (unless amended by agreement) is that a partnership is dissolved when any of the partners leaves it.
- Owners' interests – Members own transferable shares but partners cannot assign their interests in a partnership.
- Assets – The assets in a company are owned by the company. The assets in a partnership are owned jointly by the partners.
- Management – A company must have at least one director (two for a public company) and the members elect directors to manage the company. All partners have a right to participate in management.
- Constitution – A company must have a written constitution (memorandum and articles) whereas a partnership may have a written constitution (partnership agreement) but is not compelled to do so.
- Accounts – A company must usually deliver accounts to the Registrar but partners do not have to send their accounts to the Registrar.
- Security – A company may offer a floating charge over its assets but a partnership may not usually give a floating charge on assets.
- Taxation – A company pays tax on its profit – directors are taxed on their income through the PAYE system and shareholders are taxed on their dividend income 10 months after the tax year. Partners extract 'drawings' on a weekly or monthly basis. No tax is deducted at that stage as income tax is payable on their share of the final profit for the year.

Registering a company (November 2015)

A company is formed and registered under the Companies Act 2006 when it is issued with a certificate of incorporation by the Registrar, after submission to the Registrar of a number of documents and a fee.

Memorandum of Association

This is a simple document signed by the subscribers. The memorandum states that the subscribers wish to form a company and they agree to become members of it. Before the Companies Act 2006, the memorandum was an extremely important document containing information concerning the relationship between the company and the outside world – for example its aims and purpose (its objects). The position changed with the Companies Act 2006 and most of the information contained in the old memorandum is now found in the articles of association. The essence of the memorandum has been retained, although it is now a very simple historical document which states that the subscribers (the initial shareholders):

- Wish to form a company under the Companies Act 2006; and
- Agree to become members of the company and take at least one share each if the company is to have share capital.

Articles of Association

The articles contain detailed rules and regulations setting out how the company is to be managed and administered. The Companies Act states that the registered articles should be contained in a single document which is divided into consecutively numbered paragraphs. Articles should contains rules on a number of areas including:

- Appointment and dismissal of directors;
- Powers, responsibilities and liabilities of directors;
- Board meetings;
- General meetings;
- Members' rights;
- Dividends;

- Decision making by directors and shareholders;
- Issue and transfer of shares;
- Documents and records;
- Company secretary.

Rather than a company having to draft their own articles and to allow companies to be set up quickly and easily, the Companies Act 2006 allows the provision of Model (or standard) articles that apply to companies by default unless excluded or amended.

Statement of proposed officers

This statement gives the particulars of the proposed directors and company secretary (if applicable). The persons named as directors must consent to act in this capacity. When the company is incorporated they are deemed to be appointed.

Statement of compliance

This is a statement that the requirements of the Companies Act 2006 in respect of registration have been complied with.

Statement of capital and initial shareholdings

A statement of capital and initial shareholdings must be delivered by all companies with share capital.

Form IN01

This document is submitted with those listed above and is the application for registration. It contains:

- The company's proposed name;
- The location of its registered office;
- The liability of its members;
- Whether the company is private or public;
- The intended address of the registered office.

Company name, pre-incorporation contracts and accounts (May 2017)

(a) It may be possible to incorporate Redbrick Limited, provided that there is no company with this name already on the register at Companies House.

However, the risk is that Redybrick might bring a passing off action against Redbrick, alleging that the similarity between the companies' names is causing confusion in the minds of the public, particularly as the two companies operate a similar business in the same geographical area. An injunction could be granted preventing Redbrick from using this name.

Alternatively, a complaint could be made to Companies House, alleging that the names are too similar, which may result in Redbrick being directed to change its name (s 67(1) Companies Act 2006). In addition, Redybrick may appeal to the Company Names Tribunal, alleging that Redbrick's name is too similar to its own and asking that a decision be made by the Company Names Adjudicator to require Redbrick to change its name.

To avoid these risks, Jack and Graham could decide to incorporate the company with a different name. Another option would be to conduct their business using a name different to that of their registered name Redbrick; ie, use a business or trade name. If they decide to do this, they must state the company's registered name on all documents used by the company, such as letters, invoices and receipts and it must be displayed at the company's business premises. Use of a different business name may not be enough to prevent a passing off action or an appeal to the Adjudicator by Redybrick Limited.

(b) The contract will constitute a pre-incorporation contract, as Jack has entered into the contract prior to the date of the certificate of incorporation, thus prior to the company's legal existence.

The company will not be bound by such a contract. Jack will be personally liable under s 51 Companies Act 2006. This is subject to any agreement to the contrary, but the words 'signed for and on behalf of Redbrick Limited' would not amount to such an agreement (see *Phonogram v Lane [1982]*).

If all parties agree, following incorporation, there could be a novation of the contract with Jack replaced as a party by Redbrick.

(c) For each accounting reference period, the directors of Redbrick must prepare accounts for its members and file them with the Registrar of Companies. They must include a balance sheet and a profit and loss account, to give a true and fair view of the company's assets, liabilities, financial position and profit or loss for the accounting reference period up to the accounting reference date (s 396 Companies Act 2006). The board of directors must approve the annual accounts and they must be signed by a director on behalf of the board.

A company is permitted to file abbreviated accounts with the Registrar of Companies if it is classed as 'small' by satisfying two of the following conditions:

- Annual turnover must be not more than £6.5 million
- The balance sheet total must be not more that £3.26 million
- The average number of employees must be not more than 50

Filing must be within nine months of the end of the accounting period.

A small company will also be exempt from the requirement to appoint an auditor and produce an audit report.

We do not have the requisite information to determine whether Redbrick is a 'small' company for these purposes.

Incorporation: Rules and procedures (November 2014)

(a) To incorporate Sprayfinishing Solutions Limited (SSL), Form IN01 must be completed and submitted to Companies House. This form contains details of the company's name, the situation of its registered office, the type of company it is to be incorporated as, its initial share capital, its first directors, its initial subscribers and a statement of the company's compliance with the provisions of the Companies Act 2006.

A copy of the company's memorandum should also be sent to Companies House. If SSL wanted to use a bespoke set of articles or to modify the provisions of the Model Articles, these would also need to be sent to Companies House, but as SSL want Model Articles (unamended), this is not necessary.

The appropriate fee should accompany the documents.

The Registrar of Companies will issue a Certificate of Incorporation provided the documents are in order. The number which appears on the Certificate of Incorporation is SSL's unique company number and the date on the certificate is the date that SSL legally comes into existence.

Before incorporation, the register of names at Companies House should be checked to make sure that the name, Sprayfinishing Solutions Limited, is not the same as that of an existing company or that it is not too similar to that of an existing company. If the former is the case, SSL will not be registered (s 66 Companies Act 2006). If the latter is the case, although it will be possible to register SSL, the existing company with the similar name may complain to the Registrar of Companies who may direct SSL to change its name.

(b) For each accounting reference period, the directors of SSL must prepare accounts for its members and file them with the Registrar of Companies. Where they are prepared in Companies Act format, they must include a balance sheet and a profit and loss account, to give a true and fair view of the company's assets, liabilities, financial position and profit or loss for the accounting reference period up to the accounting reference date (s 396 Companies Act 2006). The board of directors must approve the annual accounts and they must be signed by a director on behalf of the board.

A company is permitted to file abbreviated accounts with the Registrar of Companies if it is classed as 'small' by satisfying two of the following conditions:

- Annual turnover must be not more than £6.5million
- The balance sheet total must be not more that £3.26million
- The average number of employees must be not more than 50

SSL satisfies all three conditions and can therefore choose either to file a copy of the full accounts prepared for its members or to file an abbreviated version. Filing must be within nine months of the end of the accounting period.

As a small company, SSL will also be exempt from the requirement to appoint auditors and produce an audit report.

(c) Directors' expenditure can be restricted in the company's articles. This would require SSL to incorporate with a modified version of the Model Articles incorporating an appropriate special article or to amend the articles after incorporation by special resolution (s 21 Companies Act 2006). Alternatively, the directors could pass a resolution at a board meeting to the same effect which would be noted in the company's board minutes.

Issue and transfer of shares (May 2017)

(a) S 550 Companies Act 2006 allows directors to allot shares without authority from the company's shareholders (where there is only one class of share in issue and no relevant restriction in the company's articles of association). This section applies to a company incorporated on or after 1 October 2009, which is the case here. The Model Articles for private companies limited by shares do not contain restrictions on a director's authority to allot; therefore, the directors of KidsTime may allot themselves new shares without authority from the members.

However, the statutory rights of pre-emption found in s 561 Companies Act 2006 require these new shares to be offered first to KidsTime's existing shareholders in the same proportion as they currently own shares in the company. The Model Articles do not disapply the statutory rights of pre-emption; therefore, these rights will either have to be waived by the existing members or disapplied in relation to this transaction by the members passing a special resolution in general meeting s 569 Companies Act 2006. The meeting needs to be held on 14 days' notice (s 307 Companies Act 2006).

Form SH01 recording the allotment of the new shares must be sent to the Registrar of Companies, together with a copy of the special resolution disapplying the statutory pre-emption rights. New share certificates must be issued within two months (s 769 Companies Act 2006).

(b) The company currently has Model Articles which do not contain any restrictions on the transfer of shares except for Model Article 26, which gives the directors discretion to refuse to register a transfer of shares.

To begin the transfer process, Helena must execute a stock transfer form in respect of the shares she wishes to sell to David and send this, together with the relevant share certificates, to David, who must pay stamp duty of 0.5% on the stock transfer form. The stamped form can then be sent to the company together with the share certificates. The transfer must be put to the board of KidsTime for its formal approval. The board then has two months to decide whether to approve the transfer. If the board does not take a decision refusing to register the transfer within the two-month period, the board then loses the right to do so. If the transfer is approved, David must be sent a new share certificate within two months of the date upon which the stock transfer form was lodged with the company's 776 Companies Act 2006.

(c) This clause gives existing shareholders rights of pre-emption on the transfer of any shares in the company, similar to the statutory rights of pre-emption found in s 561 Companies Act 1986, which apply on the allotment of shares. The above process will therefore change because Helena must offer her shares to existing members of the company, who have a period of 21 days in which to decide whether to buy their proportion of the offer, before Helena can transfer her shares to David. If Helena attempted to transfer her shares to David without offering those shares first to the other members of the company, then action would be taken against Helena for breaching the articles of association. Such action could be brought either by KidsTime or by other members.

Allotment and types of shares (May 2015)

(a) A company is both an association of members and a person separate from its members. This means that a company is treated in law as having the capacity to enter into legal relationships, has perpetual succession and survives the death of its members. The leading case on this is *Salomon v A. Salomon & Co Ltd* [1897] AC 22 which shows that the concept of separate legal personality gives rise to limited liability. A company acquires separate legal personality on incorporation by registering and complying with the requirements of the Companies Act 2006. Once registered a company is defined as a 'body corporate' s 16(2). For Tony this means that as a shareholder of Keysure he would only be liable for the amount unpaid (if any) on any shares he purchases. He would not be liable for the debts of the company if it should subsequently go into any form of insolvency.

There have been a number of cases where the separate legal identity of the company has been ignored which could mean that the benefit of limited liability for Tony would be lost. This is referred to as lifting or piercing the veil of incorporation. For example, *Jones v Lipman* [1962] 1 WLR 832, where the company had been used by the shareholders as a means of avoiding personal legal obligations deliberately. Also in *Gilford Motor Co Ltd v Horne* [1933] Ch 935, Horne attempted to evade a covenant not to compete with the claimant by getting his wife to set up a company which carried on business in competition with the claimant. It was held that both the company and Horne were restrained from enticing away the claimant's customers.

There are also a number of statutory provisions which allow the corporate veil to be pierced. The Insolvency Act 1986 imposes personal liability on directors who are found guilty of wrongful trading (s 214) or fraudulent trading (s 213). Directors in these circumstances will be ordered to contribute to the assets of the company.

(b) S 550 Companies Act 2006 applies as Keysure is a private limited company with only one class of shares. This means that the directors have the authority to allot shares to Tony without seeking authorisation from the company's shareholders.

However, s 561 pre-emption rights will apply as the shares are being allotted for cash consideration. The impact of this provision is that when the directors issue the new shares they must first be offered to existing shareholders pro rata to their existing shareholding. This would mean that the shares Keysure is planning to issue must first be offered to the existing shareholders. This does not appear to be what the shareholders want, they want Tony to become a member of the company.

Pre-emption rights can be excluded in a company's articles (s 567), however this is not the case here as Keysure has Model Articles. Pre-emption rights can also be disapplied by special resolution (s 570). A special resolution could be passed by a 75% majority of shareholders at a general meeting or by way of written resolution.

A return of allotment of shares must be sent within one month to the Registrar of Companies on Form SH01 along with any special resolution disapplying the statutory pre-emption rights.

(c) Ordinary shares are the most common type of share in a company. They give their holders a proportionate share in any dividends and a right to the remaining divisible profits (and in liquidation, the assets) after prior interests eg creditors and prior charged capital, have been satisfied. They also give their holders the right to vote at company meetings. Preference shares is a term often used to embrace shares with a number of different rights (different to ordinary shares). The common characteristic of preference shares is that they will rank ahead of ordinary shares as to dividend payments but often do not give their holders the right to vote.

Shareholder v debenture holder rights (May 2015)

As a shareholder, Kate would be a member of the company. As a debenture holder she would be a creditor but not a member of the company.

A company's relationship with its shareholders is governed by its articles which operate as a contract between them and between the shareholders and each other and also governed by the Companies Act.

The relationship between a company and its debenture holders is regulated by the terms of the trust deed or other formal document and different provisions of the Companies Act. We have not been given any detailed terms of the debenture other than it is for £25,000 and the interest rate and security over assets are to be agreed.

There are a number of practical differences between a shareholder and a debenture holder:

- Voting – As a member of the company, a shareholder has the right to attend and vote at meetings. A debenture holder has no such automatic right, although he may have votes if the articles and deed allow although this is not very common.

- Income – A shareholder, even if he holds preference shares on which fixed dividends are due on specific days, can only receive dividends out of distributable profits. In addition, he cannot force the company to pay dividends *Bond v Barrow Haematite Steel Co* [1902] 1 Ch 353. By contrast, interest at the agreed rate must be paid on debentures even if that interest has to be paid out of capital.

- Rights on securities – The Companies Act confers pre-emption rights on shareholders, entitling them to first call on any new shares which are to be issued. Debenture holders have no right of objection to further loans and debentures being taken out, unless the trust deed sets out restrictions. However, there is no statutory restriction on debenture holders having debentures redeemed or purchased by the company. By contrast, there are detailed rules regulating redemption or purchase of a company's own shares.

- Rights if aggrieved – Shareholders have the right to complain to the court if the company is breaching the articles or acting in a manner unfairly prejudicial to the shareholders' interests. Shareholders can, by simple majority, remove directors from the board. We do not know how many shares Kate will have and whether other shareholders would vote in the same way as her. Debenture holders may have rights under the trust deed if the company breaches the agreement. These include the right to appoint a receiver or the right to enforce charges and sell the property under the charge to realise their debts. Their consent may also be required before the company deals with certain of its assets when the debenture holders have secured their loan by means of a fixed charge over those assets.

- Rights on liquidation – In liquidation debenture holders must be repaid in full before anything is distributed to shareholders.

Charges and guarantees (November 2015)

(a) As Ecowood is a limited company, the liability of the directors in relation to the loan from City Bank is, in theory, limited. However, if the directors give personal guarantees in respect of the loan, they are required to pay if the company defaults on the loan. This means that the directors' personal assets (houses, cars, savings etc) would be at risk.

If the guarantee is given by both directors for the full amount on a joint and several basis City Bank will be able to choose which of the directors to go against to recover the amount in default under the loan. Given the assets of the two directors are quite different, it seems likely that City Bank would pursue Michael, as he is 'asset rich'. Michael would however be able to claim against his brother to recover his 'share' of the amount he is required to pay to the bank. The guarantee could however be structured such that each of the directors are liable for a defined proportion of the loan eg £40,000 each.

(b) If Ecowood grants a charge over the company's assets in favour of City Bank it gives City Bank a prior claim over other creditors to repayment of its £80,000 loan out of the company's assets.

A fixed charge attaches to specific assets as soon as the charge is created. The fixed charge is likely to attach to assets which Ecowood will retain for a long period; for example, it may attach to Ecowood's premises. If Ecowood disposes of the charged assets, it will repay the loan out of the proceeds of sale so that the charge is discharged.

A floating charge is a charge on a class of assets which, in the ordinary course of business, is changing from time to time. The floating charge may attach to Ecowood's stock as the exact stock and stock levels will fluctuate over the period of the loan. Until crystallisation of a floating charge occurs, Ecowood can carry on business and deal with the assets which are charged. When it crystallises, it is converted into a fixed charge on the assets owned by the company at the time of crystallisation.

To be valid and enforceable, a charge must be registered within 21 days of creation by the Registrar of Companies. Ecowood would be responsible for registering the charge but City Bank may also register it, as it is interested in the charge. The Registrar should be sent a copy of the instrument by which the charge is created and a statement of particulars. The Registrar issues a certificate which is evidence that the charge has been registered.

(c) The company will convene a board meeting and record the transaction in board minutes, recording that the company is authorised to take the loan and the reasons for it. The company will draw up a loan agreement setting out the dates and amounts of the loan, the proposed repayments, rate of interest etc. As this is a loan from a director, there is a need to consider an s 177 Companies Act 2006 declaration of interest. There is perhaps no need to expressly declare interest as the board should already be aware of the interest.

Maintenance of share capital (May 2015)

Capital maintenance is a fundamental principle of company law. What this means is that capital contributed to a limited liability company must not be returned to shareholders. Limited liability companies should not be allowed to make payments out of capital to the detriment of company creditors. The Companies Act contains many rules which dictate how a company is to manage and maintain its capital to balance members' enjoyment of limited liability and creditors' requirements that the company shall remain able to pay its debts.

The above principle requires that shares must be paid for, or agreed to be paid for, in full. S 580 prohibits the issue of shares at a discount to their nominal value and makes the allottee liable for the difference between the issue price and the nominal value (s 580(2)).

As far as dividends are concerned, the capital maintenance principle requires that a company may only pay dividends to its shareholders out of distributable profits (s 830(1)). Capital cannot be used to fund dividend payments.

Companies are prohibited from buying their own shares, as this would effectively be a return of capital to the selling shareholder. However, under s 690, buy-back is permitted in certain circumstances. The relevant shares must be fully paid and, in the case of an off-market purchase, shareholders' approval by ordinary resolution is required prior to the transaction (s 694). The general rule is that the purchase price must be paid out of distributable profits, however private companies may purchase shares out of capital provided special resolution approval has been given (s 709 and s 713). There must be nothing in the company's articles prohibiting the use of capital in this way and the directors must make a statement of solvency, supported by an auditor's report. S 710 requires that capital can only be used to buy back shares to the extent that distributable profits and the proceeds of any fresh issue of shares made to fund the purchase have been used but fall short. Under s 734, the company's accounts are required to reflect a buyback of shares using capital.

The Companies Act 2006 has removed the prohibition against a company giving financial assistance for the purchase of its own shares in the case of a private company. A public company is prohibited from giving financial assistance for the purchase of its own shares, which includes using its assets as security for a loan used to buy its shares s 678(1) and s 677(1)(b). Financial assistance is permitted where the assistance is given in good faith in the interests of the company, and the principal purpose of the assistance is not the acquisition of shares or, if the assistance is for that purpose, it forms an incidental part of some larger purpose of the company, s 678(2).

In some circumstances, a company may wish to reduce its share capital, for example to write off losses or to return excess capital to shareholders. Such reductions of capital can only be effected if authorised by a special resolution and supported by a solvency statement (private limited company) or authorised by the court (public limited company). The option of using a statement of solvency is not available to a public company.

Director appointment and share purchase (November 2014)

(a) Shares are freely transferable subject to any restrictions contained in a company's articles (s 544 Companies Act 2006). Protech has Model Articles (unamended) which contain no restrictions on the right to transfer fully paid shares but directors may refuse to register the transfer under Model Article 26.

The transfer between Globe and David Elms must be put to the Protech board for its formal approval. Within two months, Protech must decide to either register the transfer and prepare a share certificate for David or give notice of their refusal to register the transfer. If Protech refuse to register the transfer, Globe would remain on the register of members of Protech holding the shares on trust for David whose beneficial interest would not be affected but he could not exercise all members' rights. It is unlikely that David would want to buy the shares if this were to be the case.

(b) A new director can be appointed by ordinary resolution of the shareholders in general meeting (Model Article 17(1)(a)) or by a decision of the directors in a board meeting (Model Article 17(1)(b)).

Any service contract for a director for longer than two years must be approved by an ordinary resolution (s 188 Companies Act 2006). David has indicated that he would like a service contract for a period of three years. The members of Protech must therefore convene a general meeting to approve the contract by ordinary resolution or pass an ordinary resolution by way of written resolution. The service contract (or particulars of it) must be available for inspection at Protech's registered office (s 228 Companies Act 2006).

(c) The directors of Protech should be aware that companies are prohibited from buying their own shares, as this would effectively be a return of capital to the selling shareholder (s 658 Companies Act 2006).

However, if a company's members approve the transaction, such purchases are permitted in some circumstances (s 690 Companies Act 2006):

- Out of distributable profits or the proceeds of an issue of new shares under the redemption of share rules;
- Out of capital (private company only).

It appears that Protech has distributable profits available.

The contract for the purchase of the shares must be approved in advance by an ordinary resolution of the members of Protech (s 694 Companies Act 2006). A copy of the proposed contract must be available for inspection by members at the registered office for 15 days before the general meeting or if a written resolution is used instead of a general meeting, the contract must be sent to all members. Members selling the shares cannot vote on the resolution, so Globe cannot vote.

Transactions with directors (May 2015)

Generally, must consider fiduciary duties. The Companies Act 2006 includes a statutory statement of the duties that a director owes to a company (ss 170-177). Although these duties take effect in place of the rules developed at common law, s 170(4) makes it clear that the statutory duties shall be interpreted in the same way as the corresponding common law rules. The case law that has developed regarding directors' duties is therefore still relevant in interpreting the provisions in the Companies Act 2006.

(a) The fiduciary duties owed by a director to the company involve a director acting in the best interests of the company and not for personal reasons benefiting him or herself. The rule extends to cover a personal profit arising as a result of a corporate opportunity coming to a director by reason of his or her office. If a director diverts a corporate opportunity to himself away from the company this is regarded as a breach of fiduciary duty, *Cook v Deeks* [1916] 1 AC 554. This approach is taken even where the company itself would not have been awarded the contract as in *Industrial Developments Consultants Ltd v Cooley* [1972] 1 WLR 443. Charles appears to have actively diverted a corporate opportunity away from Similian to a company in which he is the sole shareholder and director. He may be required to account for profits made as a result. The director's duties under the Companies Act 2006 directly relevant to the above situation are to avoid conflict of interest (s 175) and to declare at board meetings interests in existing and proposed transactions and arrangements with the company (s 177).

(b) The general rule set out in s 197 Companies Act 2006 is that loans to directors are prohibited, unless approved by an ordinary resolution of the members of the company. A memorandum must be made available to the members of the company setting out the nature of the transaction, the amount of the loan and the purpose for which it is required. This memorandum must be sent with a written resolution if the approval is to be given by written resolution or to be available before and at a general meeting where the resolution is to be proposed. Transactions in contravention of these provisions are voidable at the instance of the company and the director is liable to account for any gain made as a result of the transaction or indemnify the company for any loss. It appears that this will be the case for Zainab in relation to her loans from Similian. Zainab cannot rely on the exception under s 207 as it is possible that the individual loans were less that £10,000 but aggregated they are more than £10,000.

(c) The purchase of industrial vehicles and computer equipment from Similian by Stephanie should have been approved by the shareholders passing an ordinary resolution (simple majority of those present at a general meeting voting in favour), or the transaction should have been made conditional on this approval being obtained. The purchase is viewed as a substantial property transaction, provided the property is of the requisite value, and therefore requires approval under s 190 Companies Act 2006. Failure to obtain such approval makes the transaction voidable at the option of the company. The directors who approved the transaction, would also be liable to indemnify the company for any loss it has suffered and account to the company for any gain made as a result of the transaction (s 195). The requisite value is defined as exceeding £100,000 or 10% of the company's asset value. The property here was sold for £150,000 and would therefore fall within these provisions. Stephanie should also have declared her interest in the transaction as required by s 177.

Thomas has sufficient shares in Similian to requisition a general meeting, s 303. Thomas needs to deposit a signed requisition at Similian's registered office. The directors of Similian must call the meeting within 21 days of receiving the requisition and hold the meeting within 28 days of the notice calling it.

Director appointment (November 2015)

A new director can be appointed at a general meeting, where the members appoint by ordinary resolution (MA 17(1)(a)), or at a board meeting, where the board can appoint by board resolution (MA 17(1)(b)). There is no maximum number of directors under the Model Articles.

The most straightforward way of making the appointment would be at a board meeting by board resolution. The difficulty in this case is that two of the company's four directors are opposed to the new appointment. Decision making by directors must be by majority in number (MA 7(1)). However as Omar is the chairman and the chairman gets a casting vote (MA 13) it would not be possible to make the appointment by way of board resolution.

If Amy and Charles wish to try to persuade the company's other shareholders (30% of the company's shares are held by non-directors) to agree to the appointment of a new Finance Director they will have to requisition a general meeting following the procedure under s 303 Companies Act 2006.

Amy and Charles each hold 12% of the shares, so separately or together they have sufficient shares to validly requisition a general meeting under s 303 Companies Act 2006 (5% is needed).

Following their requisition, the board is obliged to call a general meeting within 21 days (s 304(1)(a) Companies Act 2006) of receiving the requisition and hold the meeting within 28 days (s 304(1)(b) Companies Act 2006) of the notice calling it. In the notice of the general meeting, the time, date and place of the meeting is stated in addition to the general nature of the business to be dealt with at the meeting (s 311 Companies Act 2006). On this basis, information that would appear in the register of directors if the new director were to be appointed would be circulated to members.

Amy and Charles need sufficient support from the other shareholders to pass the required ordinary resolution. They hold 24% of the shares between them, therefore they need shareholders holding more than 26% to vote with them to pass the resolution.

If the new director is appointed Form 288(a) recording the appointment must be completed and returned to Companies House. The company's register of directors must also be amended.

Allotment of shares and transactions (November 2014)

(a) The value per share of £1 is the nominal value of the share. It bears no relation to the market value of the share, which in this case is much higher at £100 per share (1,000 shares × £100 = £100,000). The difference between the nominal value of the share and its market value is known as the share premium. We have been told that Sensations has 'gone from strength to strength' since its incorporation.

(b) S 550 Companies Act 2006 applies as Sensations is a private limited company with only one class of shares. This means that the directors have the authority to allot shares to Belinda without seeking authorisation from the company's shareholders.

However s 561 Companies Act 2006 pre-emption rights will apply as the shares are being allotted for cash consideration. The impact of this provision is that when the directors issue the new shares they must be offered to existing shareholders pro rata to their existing shareholding. This would mean that the 1,000 shares Sensations is planning to issue must be offered in equal shares to the three existing shareholders each of whom currently own 500 shares. This does not appear to be what the shareholders want, they want Belinda to become a member of the company.

Pre-emption rights can be excluded in a company's articles (s 567 Companies Act 2006), however this is not the case as Sensations has Model Articles. Pre-emption rights can also be disapplied by special resolution (s 570 Companies Act 2006). This special resolution could be passed by way of a written resolution instead of convening a general meeting.

A return of allotment of shares must be sent within one month to the Registrar of Companies on Form SH01 along with any special resolution disapplying the statutory pre-emption rights.

(c) Here we have a situation whereby the company is purchasing an asset from Jemima Evans, the wife of director Charles Evans.

Under s 190 Companies Act 2006, when a director or a person connected with a director sells an asset to a company and that asset is deemed to be a 'substantial non-cash asset' the contract will need to be approved by the members by ordinary resolution.

Under s 191 Companies Act 2006, an asset worth between £5,000 and £100,000 (here asset is worth £80,000) will be 'substantial' if it exceeds 10% of the company's net asset value. Sensation's estimated net asset value is £200,000, therefore the asset being acquired from Jemima will be a substantial non-cash asset.

The transaction must be approved by ordinary resolution in a general meeting or by way of written resolution before the directors can enter into the contract. At the board meeting at which the contract is entered into, Charles Evans must declare his interest under s 177 Companies Act 2006 and pursuant to Model Article 14 must not vote or count in the quorum.

Director duties, appointment and allotment of shares (May 2016)

(a) The Companies Act 2006 ss 171–177 sets out the statutory duties that directors owe to their company (not the members):

- To act within their powers – in accordance with the company's constitution for the purposes the powers were conferred
- To promote the success of the company – with regard for stakeholder interests
- To exercise independent judgement – remain independent, not delegate and not be swayed by the influence of others
- To exercise reasonable skill, care and judgement – did the director act in a manner reasonably expected of a person performing the same role (objective test); did the director act in accordance with the skill, knowledge and experience they actually have (subjective test)
- To avoid conflicts of interests – where personal interests conflict with the company's interests
- Not to accept benefits from third parties – a benefit may create a conflict of interest.
- To declare an interest in proposed transactions – to be done before the company enters into the transaction.

Breach of these duties is a civil matter and can lead to damages, an injunction, repayment of profits made by a director, or restoration of property.

(b) Under the Model Articles (unamended) there are two possible methods by which Georgina can be appointed as a director:

- Model Article 17(1)(b) – the appointment can be made by the board. A simple majority of directors on a show of hands is required. This is the most straightforward method.

- Model Article 17(1)(a) – Georgina can be appointed by the shareholders passing an ordinary resolution. The ordinary resolution can also be effected by way of written resolution circulated to the members to avoid the need to call a general meeting.

After the relevant resolution has been passed the board must ensure that Form AP01 (particulars of a director's appointment) is sent to the Registrar of Companies within 14 days. Georgina's appointment should also be written up in the register of directors.

(c) As the company is a private company with only one class of shares, s 550 Companies Act will apply to the company. This statutory provision empowers directors to allot shares without obtaining express authority from the company's members.

As Georgina is offering cash consideration, s 561 Companies Act 2006 is relevant. It protects existing members from dilution of their shareholding as they are given a right of pre-emption (first refusal) in relation to new shares issued. However, the facts suggest that the other shareholders want Georgina to become a member as well as a director so s 561 is not helpful. It is possible for the other shareholders to disapply their rights of pre-emption in relation to this transaction by passing a special resolution (which can be done via written resolution to avoid the need to hold a general meeting).

Form SH01 recording the allotment of the new shares must be sent to the Registrar, together with the special resolution disapplying the statutory pre-emption rights.

Acquisition of shares, company re-registration (May 2014)

(a) There has been an attempt at a friendly takeover where the third party has made an approach to the board and the board have not rejected the offer outright but have relayed the offer to the shareholders, presumably as they believe it to be a good offer and in the interests of the shareholders.

In relation to the offer the terms must be the same in relation to all of the shares (as they are the same class of shares).

In this situation each shareholder has a 20% stake in the company, if four shareholders agree to accept the offer the third party will be able to acquire 80% of the issued share capital. This is not sufficient to be able to serve notice on the remaining shareholder requiring him to sell. In order to be able to do this the acquirer must be in a position to be able to acquire 90% of the issued shares.

(b) In order to re-register as a public company there are a number of requirements that must be fulfilled. A company is only able to re-register as a public company if its allotted share capital is a minimum of £50,000 of which a quarter must be paid up plus the whole of any premium. We know the company has an issued share capital of £100,000 but we do not know how much of it has been paid up; more information is required.

On the basis that the share capital requirement has been satisfied then the shareholders must pass a special resolution agreeing to the company becoming a public company. The company must then apply to the Registrar of Companies to be re-registered as a public company, along with the application form (RR01) together with, copies of the special resolution and the proposed new articles, details of the company's name and proposed secretary, balance sheet and auditors report confirming the company's net assets are not less than the called up share capital and distributable reserves (the balance sheet must not be more than seven months old) and the fee. Once these requirements have been satisfied the Registrar will issue a certificate of incorporation on re-registration.

(c) All PLCs must have a suitably qualified company secretary, s 273 Companies Act (2006) provides that the following are qualified:

- A person who has been employed as a secretary of a plc for three out of the last five years;
- A person who is a member of one of a list of qualifying bodies ACCA, CIMA, ICAEW etc;
- A qualified solicitor, barrister or advocate in the UK; or
- A person who by virtue of having held any other position or his being a member of a professional body appears to the directors to be capable of discharging the role.

From the information we have Nick is the financial controller. We will need to find out if he is a member of any of the relevant bodies otherwise the directors would need to be of the opinion that his experience and positions held to date make him a suitable candidate. In making their decision the directors should remember their duties.

Minority shareholders (November 2014)

Foss v Harbottle (1843) confirmed the rule that the majority shareholders control a company and consequently established a need for minority protection.

Since a company cannot protect itself, a member may bring an action to enforce the company's rights (a derivative action). The Companies Act 2006 introduced a statutory process for deciding whether or not a member has a right to bring a derivative action on behalf of the company (ss 260-264 Companies Act). This does not replace *Foss v Harbottle* but sets out additional rules (but it does abolish a 'fraud' requirement). Permission of the court is required to continue a derivative claim and any remedy awarded goes to the company (as the claim is brought in its name) – thus damages do not flow to the claimants directly. Further information is required from Harry and Julia as to how the company is being run to determine whether they could bring a derivative action but they need to be aware of the significant drawbacks in doing so.

Statutory protection for minority shareholders is also found in s 994 Companies Act 2006. A member may petition the court on the grounds that the affairs of the company are being conducted in a manner unfairly prejudicial to the interests of the members generally, or some part of the members. A petition may be made in respect of past, present or proposed future conduct. Examples include:

- Exclusion from management;
- Improper allotment of shares;
- Failure to call meetings;
- Making inaccurate statements to shareholders;
- Management using assets for personal benefit;
- Failure to pay dividends for prolonged period;
- Payment of excessive directors' bonuses or pension contributions; and
- Continued mismanagement causing financial damage.

Discussions with Harry and Julia are required to establish whether any of these grounds exist. If they make a successful application the court may make a variety of orders including regulating the company and authorising proceedings to be brought on its behalf. More commonly, courts tend to order that the shares of the minority are bought by the majority, or by the company, but this does not appear to be what Harry and Julia want.

In addition, a minority shareholder may use s 122(1)(g) Insolvency Act 1986 to petition that a company be wound up because it is 'just and equitable' to do so. Harry and Julia do not appear to want this outcome.

Dividends and financial information (May 2014)

(a) A dividend is a payment to the shareholders of a company representing a share of the profit that the company has made and a return on the shareholders' investments in the company.

Shareholders do not have an automatic right to a dividend; there is a process by which it is declared to be lawful.

A dividend may only be paid out of profits which are available for this purpose (defined in s 830 Co Act 2006 – basically with reference to the year-end accounts accumulated realised profits so far as not previously utilised by distribution less accumulated realised losses).

The process that must be followed is that the directors will consider what dividend if any ought to be declared and will make a recommendation of that amount. A general meeting will then be held where the question of declaring a dividend will be considered. To approve the dividend an ordinary resolution is required. The shareholders may in general meeting reject the recommendations of the directors with regard to the dividend or declare a dividend that is smaller than that recommended. They may not declare a dividend in excess of the amount recommended by the directors.

Once declared the dividend will be paid to the members.

Directors may during the course of an accounting period pay interim dividends to members, these do not need to be formally declared by ordinary resolution however the basic rule that they can only be paid out of distributable profits applies.

There are consequences for both shareholders and directors of unlawful dividends (ie one paid otherwise than out of distributable profits of the company). Directors will normally be personally liable. If directors honestly rely on properly prepared accounts which show a distributable profit, the directors will not be liable if it turns out that the assumptions or estimates used in preparing the accounts although reasonable at the time were in fact unsound.

Directors will be liable if:

- They declare a dividend which they know is paid out of capital;
- Without preparing accounts they declare a dividend which consequently turns out to be paid out of capital; or
- They make some mistake of law or interpretation of the constitution which leads them to recommend or declare an unlawful dividend, the directors may get some relief if they acted honestly and reasonably.

Shareholders will be liable if the member knew or had reasonable grounds to believe the dividend was unlawful.

A member may apply for an injunction to prevent a company paying an unlawful dividend. Members are not entitled to authorise the payment of an unlawful dividend or release the directors from liability for such. If a member knowingly receives an unlawful dividend it may not bring an action against the directors.

(b) The company has a duty to keep adequate accounting records that show the financial position of the company reasonably accurately s 386. The directors must produce a balance sheet that gives a true and fair view of the company's financial state at the end of the financial year and a profit and loss account that gives a true and fair view of the profit (or loss) for the financial year in question.

The directors must also prepare a directors' report reviewing the development of the company over the financial year and stating the amount (if any) of the dividend to be declared.

The Companies Act 2006 requires the accounts to be audited, the auditor must prepare a report to the shareholders confirming that the accounts give a true and fair view of the company's position and performance (to the standards laid out in the Companies Act 2006) and must confirm whether or not the directors' report is consistent with the accounts. Certain companies are exempt from the audit requirements, the conditions to be satisfied are: if in a financial year the company's turnover doesn't exceed £6.5 million and its balance sheet is not more than £3.26 million.

Once the accounts have been 'audited' the directors must approve them and they must be signed on behalf of the board.

Xavier and Roberto are entitled to receive copies of the accounts, the directors' report and the auditors' report (or summaries if Roberto and Xavier have agreed to accept shortened reports). The accounts and directors' and auditors' reports must also be sent to the Registrar of Companies within 9 months after the end of the relevant financial period.

The directors of Leyland Limited may be guilty of a criminal offence if they fail to send information as set out above to Roberto and Xavier.

Debentures, auditors and voting (May 2014)

(a) To be valid and enforceable all charges created by companies must be registered at Companies House within 21 days of their creation. The instrument creating the charge together with the requisite particulars of charge (form MG01) and the registration fee must be sent to the Registrar. If a charge is not validly registered it will be void against a liquidator, administrator and any creditor of the company. Every officer of a company in default of the registration requirements would also be liable to a fine (s 860(4)).

(b) Every company must appoint appropriately qualified auditors for each financial year. As Forresters is a newly incorporated company, the directors can appoint the first auditors to hold office until the first general meeting of the company at which their appointment can be considered by the shareholders.

To be appropriately qualified, auditors must be a member of a Recognised Supervisory Body. The following may not act as auditors:

- Any officer or employee of the company
- A partner or employee of such a person
- A partnership in which any of the above is a partner
- Any other person excluded by law

(c) Auditors are under a duty to review the balance sheet and profit and loss account of the company for the relevant financial year and prepare a report for the shareholders stating that the accounts give a true and fair view and have been properly prepared in accordance with the Companies Act (2006). The auditors' report must also consider and state whether or not the directors' report is consistent with the accounts.

In order to be able to prepare their report the auditors must review the accounts and carry out such investigations as are necessary to be able to form the required opinions and make the required statements. Auditors are entitled to have access to the books and accounts of the company at any time, a right to require information from the company's officers, employees and any other relevant persons. Auditors must receive copies of all written resolutions and can attend and speak at all general meetings of the company.

(d) Every holder of a voting share is entitled to attend a general meeting and vote on any resolutions considered. Voting under the Model Articles can take place by way of a show of hands or by demanding a poll. The difference in the outcome can be considerable. On a show of hands each shareholder is entitled to one vote. On a poll each shareholder is entitled to so many votes as the constitution provides (usually one vote per share).

A poll can be demanded at the meeting or in advance of the meeting. It can be demanded after the vote on a show of hands as long as the result has not yet been declared. A poll can be demanded by the chairman of the meeting, two or more shareholders having the right to vote at the meeting or one or more shareholders holding at least one tenth of the total voting rights.

Company accounts (November 2013)

Under the Companies Act 2006 a company has a duty to keep accounting records which are sufficiently adequate to explain the company's transactions and its financial position so that financial statements can be prepared s 386.

The directors are obliged to ensure that annual accounts for the company are prepared showing a true and fair view, the accounts must be laid before the members and then filed with the Registrar of Companies.

S 396 provides that the annual accounts must comprise of a balance sheet that gives a 'true and fair view' of the financial position of the company at the end of the financial year and a profit and loss account that gives a 'true and fair view' of the profit or loss for the financial year in question. The accounts must be prepared in accordance with the Companies Act format or the International Accounting Standards, if the latter a note to that effect must be included in the notes to the accounts.

In addition to the accounts, the directors must prepare a directors' report to accompany the accounts (s 415) containing details of all directors during the financial year, the principal activities of the company during the year and the amount of any dividend recommended by the directors. The directors must also produce a 'business review' which is an analysis of the company's performance and the risks that it may be facing (s 417). This review gives the shareholders an opportunity to assess how well the directors have fulfilled their duty to promote the success of the company contained in s 172.

Under s 475 the accounts must be audited by auditors appointed annually by the company (private companies are allowed to elect for automatic reappointment of its auditors) without the need for a shareholder resolution unless the articles provide for annual appointment or the shareholders pass a resolution to block the reappointment or an objection has been received by at least 5% of the shareholders who would be entitled to vote on a resolution appointing the auditors. The auditors must prepare a report on the accounts confirming the content complies with accounting standards, that the accounts give a true and fair view of the financial state of the company.

The accounts must be approved by the board and signed off, copies together with a copy of the auditor's report must be sent to all shareholders (s 423). The accounts must be submitted to the Registrar of Companies and copies to shareholders no later than 9 months after the end of the accounting period for the company.

The Company can send members a summary financial statement rather than full copies of the reports and accounts (s 426) however a member has the right to request a copy of the full accounts.

There are criminal penalties if the directors of Oasis Limited fail to send the accounts of the company to Sarah and the other shareholders. If the directors approve accounts that do not comply with the standard required by the Companies Act or the International Accounting Standards (as appropriate) they will be guilty of an offence.

Company accounts and auditor liability (May 2015)

(a) Under the Companies Act 2006 a company has a duty to keep accounting records which are sufficiently adequate to explain the company's transactions and its financial position so that financial statements can be prepared s 386.

The directors are obliged to ensure that annual accounts for the company are prepared showing a true and fair view, the accounts must be laid before the members and then filed with the Registrar of Companies. S 396 provides that the annual accounts must comprise of a balance sheet that gives a 'true and fair view' of the financial position of the company at the end of the financial year and a profit and loss account that gives a 'true and fair view' of the profit or loss for the financial year in question.

In addition to the accounts, the directors must prepare a directors' report to accompany the accounts (s 415) containing details of all directors during the financial year, the principal activities of the company during the year and the amount of any dividend recommended by the directors. The directors must also produce a 'business review' which is an analysis of the company's performance and the risks that it may be facing (s 417). This review gives the shareholders an opportunity to assess how well the directors have fulfilled their duty to promote the success of the company contained in s 172.

Under s 475 the accounts must be audited by auditors appointed annually by the company. The auditors must prepare a report on the accounts confirming the content complies with accounting standards and that the accounts give a true and fair view of the financial state of the company.

The accounts must be approved by the board and signed off. Copies together with a copy of the auditor's report must be sent to all shareholders (s 423). The accounts must be submitted to the Registrar of Companies and copies to shareholders no later than nine months after the end of the accounting period for the company.

The Company can send members a summary financial statement rather than full copies of the reports and accounts (s 426) however a member has the right to request a copy of the full accounts so Gerard can request a copy of the full accounts.

(b) Gerard had no contract with the auditors of Wineworld so he can only sue them in the tort of negligence, not in contract.

Gerard relied upon the accounts laid at the AGM but to sue for economic loss he needs to establish a fiduciary relationship *Hedley Byrne v Heller & Partners* [1964]. The House of Lords decided in *Caparo Industries v Dickman and others* [1991] that the auditors' relationship with individual shareholders was not enough to give rise to a duty of care to shareholders as potential purchasers. It would have done so only if, at the time of signing their report, the auditors were aware of the shareholder's interest.

The auditors were not aware of Gerard's interest since he had not finally decided to make the purchase so he has no claim against the auditors of Wineworld.

Auditors (May 2016)

No person may act as auditor if they become ineligible. They must resign with immediate effect and notify Shopmart Limited of their resignation, giving the reason (s 516 Companies Act 2006).

Membership of a Recognised Supervisory Body is the main prerequisite for eligibility as an auditor. An audit firm may be either a body corporate, a partnership or a sole practitioner. The auditor must hold an 'appropriate qualification'. A person holds an appropriate qualification if they:

- Have satisfied existing criteria for appointment as an auditor
- Hold a recognised qualification obtained in the UK
- Hold an approved overseas qualification.

The replacement auditors cannot take office until the previous auditor has ceased to hold office. Auditors can be appointed in different ways:

- By members – usually in general meeting by ordinary resolution. This may be done to fill a casual vacancy as has occurred with Shopmart Limited.

- By directors – usually in board meeting by majority. This may also be done to fill a casual vacancy. This would be the most straightforward option for Shopmart Ltd.

- By Secretary of State – only necessary if members fail to make an appointment – unlikely on the facts.

The statutory duty of auditors is to report to the members whether the accounts give a true and fair view and have been properly prepared in accordance with the Companies Act. In order to carry out the statutory duties, s 498 Companies Act 2006 requires the auditors to carry out such investigation as necessary to form an opinion as to whether:

- Proper accounting records have been kept and proper returns adequate for the audit have been received from branches.
- The accounts are in agreement with the accounting records.
- The information in the directors' remuneration report is consistent with the accounts.

The auditor's report must be read before any general meeting at which the accounts are considered and must be open to inspection by members. Auditors' remuneration must be disclosed in a note to the accounts. Auditors also have to make disclosure of other services rendered to the company and the remuneration received.

S 499 and 502 Companies Act 2006 set out the principal statutory rights for auditors to enable them to carry out their duties. These are:

- A right of access to records.
- A right to require from officers or employees information and explanations as necessary.
- A right to attend any general meeting and receive all notices and communications relating to such meetings.
- A right to speak at general meetings.
- A right to receive a copy of any written resolution proposed.

Compulsory liquidation (November 2014)

Compulsory liquidation of a company is likely to occur when the company is insolvent and involves applying to the court to wind it up. The most common reasons for compulsory liquidation are:

- The company is unable to pay its debts (s 122(1)(f) Insolvency Act 1986)
- It is just and equitable to wind up the company (s 122(1)(g) Insolvency Act 1986).

A creditor may apply to the court for compulsory winding up of a company on the basis that the company is unable to pay its debts. There are three permitted ways to show that a company is unable to pay its debts (s 123 Insolvency Act 1986):

- A creditor who is owed more than £750 serves the company with a written demand for payment and the company does not pay within 21 days;
- A creditor obtains judgment against the company for a debt and attempts to enforce judgment but no payment is obtained; or
- A creditor satisfies the court that the company is unable to pay its debts by proving either that the company cannot pay its debts as they fall due (commercial insolvency test) or that the company's assets are less than its liabilities (balance sheet test).

A member who is dissatisfied with the directors or controlling shareholders in relation to the management of the company may petition the court for the company to be wound up on the just and equitable ground. For such petition to be successful, the member must not be unreasonably refusing to pursue some other remedy. Examples of circumstances when companies have been wound up on the just and equitable ground include when:

- The only or main object(s) of the company can no longer be achieved;
- The company was formed for an illegal or fraudulent purpose;

- There is complete deadlock in the management of the company's affairs; and
- The understandings between members or directors which were the basis of the company have been unfairly breached by lawful action.

When a petition to bring proceedings for compulsory liquidation is presented to the court, a copy is also delivered to the company in case it wishes to object. It is also advertised so that other creditors may intervene if they wish. The court appoints the Official Receiver who takes control of the company's property and acts as liquidator (s 136 Insolvency Act 1986), with a view to realising value in the company's assets for the benefit of creditors. The Official Receiver may hold a meeting of members and creditors to appoint their own nominee as replacement liquidator. If different persons are nominated, the creditors' nominee takes precedence. The liquidation is deemed to have commenced at the time when the petition was first presented.

Having realised the company's assets, the liquidator distributes them in a prescribed order as follows:

(a) Costs
(b) Preferential debts
(c) Debts secured by floating charges
(d) Debts owed to unsecured ordinary creditors
(e) Deferred debts
(f) Members

Creditors with fixed and floating charges may appoint a receiver to sell the charged asset. Any surplus is passed on to the liquidator and, in the event of a shortfall, those with the benefit of the charge become unsecured creditors for the balance.

Administration (May 2016)

Administration is a corporate rescue procedure and an administrator is appointed to try to rescue a company as a going concern. The purpose of administration is to insulate the company from its creditors while it seeks:

- To save itself as a going concern, or failing that;
- To achieve a better result for creditors than an immediate winding up would secure, or failing that;
- To realise property so as to make a distribution to creditors.

Administration orders and liquidations are mutually exclusive. Once an administration order has been passed by the court, it is no longer possible to petition the court for a winding up order against the company. Similarly, once an order for winding up has been made, an administration order cannot be granted (except when appointed by a floating chargeholder).

Administration can be initiated with or without a court order. There are three sets of people who can appoint an administrator without reference to the court:

- Floating chargeholders.
- Directors.
- The company.

In addition, various parties can apply for administration through the court:

- The company.
- Directors.
- One or more creditors of the company.
- The Justice and Chief Executive of the Magistrates' Court following non-payment of a fine imposed on the company.

The court will grant the administration order if it is satisfied that the company is, or is likely to be, unable to pay its debts, and the administration order is reasonably likely to achieve the purpose of administration. Individual members cannot apply to the court for an administration order.

The effects of an administrator appointment is that a moratorium over the company's debts commences ie no creditor can enforce their debt during the administration period without the court's permission and all outstanding petitions for winding-up of the company are dismissed.

The administrator is an agent of the company and the creditors as a whole. He owes fiduciary duties to them and has a number of legal duties relating to notification to the company and creditors etc. He also requires a statement of affairs to be submitted to him. This sets out the company's property, debts and liabilities, details of creditors and any security they hold. He must consider the statement of affairs and within eight weeks, set out his proposals for achieving the aims of the administration. The proposals must be sent to the Registrar and the creditors and be made available to all members of the company. While preparing the proposals the administrator manages the affairs of the company and managers can only act with the consent of the administrator.

The administrator must either propose a rescue plan or state that the company cannot be rescued. He must call a meeting of creditors within 10 weeks of his appointment to either accept or reject the proposals.

The administration period ends when the administration has been successful or 12 months has elapsed from appointment of the administrator. This time period can be extended by court order or consent from appropriate creditors. Alternatively, the administrator may apply to the court if the purpose of the administration cannot be achieved or the company should not have entered into administration.

Insider dealing (May 2016)

(a) Under s 57 Criminal Justice Act 1993, Isabel has information as an insider if she has inside information from an inside source and she knows both of these things.

Under s 56 Criminal Justice Act 1993, Isabel has inside information as it:

- Relates particularly to Yensert plc
- Is specific or precise – it relates to the discovery of a new drilling area
- Does not appear to have been made public – only just discovered
- Is price sensitive/likely to have a significant effect on price – it would result in an increase in Yensert's share price

Isabel has this information from an inside source as she obtained it from Henry who is a director and the CEO of Yensert plc (s 57 Criminal Justice Act 1993). As a nanny to the family and business and economics graduate she will have known that she had inside information from an inside source.

Isabel has dealt in price-affected securities, by acquiring Yensert plc's shares, on a regulated market, the London Stock Exchange (s 52 and s 55 Criminal Justice Act 1993).

The defences under s 53 Criminal Justice Act 1993 which could be relevant to this dealing offence are unlikely to apply:

- She did not expect there to be a profit – contrary to facts.
- She had reasonable grounds to believe the information had been disclosed widely – contrary to facts.
- She would have done what she did even if she did not have the information – £3,000 was intended for university fees.

She is likely to be guilty of dealing s 52 Criminal Justice Act 1993. The sanctions include up to seven years in prison and/or an unlimited fine.

(b) Henry is unlikely to be guilty of an offence. Certainly, he has neither 'dealt', nor 'encouraged' under s 52 Criminal Justice Act 1993. He might be liable under s 52 if he had 'disclosed' inside information as a result of his phone call. However, this seems unlikely. Henry would likely be able to argue, successfully, either that he disclosed the information in the proper performance of his office s 52(2)(b) or that he did not expect Isabel to deal in the company's securities s 53(3)(a).

Mock exam 1
questions and answers

MODULE C

PROFESSIONAL EXAMINATION 1

PAPER 8 – COMPANY LAW

TUESDAY 28th NOVEMBER 2017

Time allowed – 3 hours

Candidates must answer FIVE questions in total
Questions 1–3 are mandatory and must be attempted
Candidates can choose a further TWO questions to answer from the remaining questions

Candidates should always give reasons for their answers and, where appropriate, support them by reference to decided cases and statutes.

You are allowed an additional 15 minutes reading time before the exam begins, during which you should read the question paper and, if you wish, make notes on the question paper. You are **not** allowed to open the exam script booklet and start writing or use your calculator during the reading time.

CREATING WORLD CLASS ACCOUNTANTS

Candidates MUST attempt ALL of the following THREE questions which are COMPULSORY

Question 1

Paul Harrison, a retired chef, has agreed to invest in a local catering company called Keen Cuisine Limited (Keen Cuisine). He will purchase 15,000 of the £1 ordinary shares (the only class of shares) for £15,000. Keen Cuisine is going to use the investment to purchase new industrial ovens. Paul has been provided with a copy of the company's articles of association which are Model Articles (amended).

Required

(a) Discuss the nature and significance of a company's articles of association. **(7 marks)**

(b) Discuss why Keen Cuisine has amended the Model Articles to include the following "Special Article":

Special Article 3

In accordance with section 567(1) of the Companies Act 2006, the rights of pre-emption under sections 561 and 562 shall not apply to an allotment of shares made by the company. **(7 marks)**

(c) Discuss the procedural steps necessary for Keen Cuisine to allot the shares to Paul, including any documentation and filing requirements. **(6 marks)**

(Total 20 marks)

Question 2

Discuss the different types of resolution which members of a private company can pass and explain the procedure for passing each of these types of resolution. **(20 marks)**

Question 3

Pet Matters Limited (Pet Matters) is a small company which manufactures a range of foods for domestic pets. As a result of increased competition in the market, Pet Matters has been struggling for the last couple of years and appears to be in financial difficulty. A bank loan from Royal Standard Bank plc was recently secured on the company's premises, it has not paid its employees for the last three months and it has failed to make a number of substantial payments to Jessops Farm Supplies Limited (Jessops) which supplies some of the key ingredients for Pet Matters products.

Required

(a) Discuss what statutory test must be satisfied for Jessops to be successful in applying to the court for a compulsory winding up of Pet Matters. **(10 marks)**

(b) How likely is Jessops to get its money? Discuss the order of payments on liquidation. **(10 marks)**

(Total 20 marks)

Candidates must answer TWO questions from questions 4, 5, 6, 7 and 8

Question 4

HeavenlyCocoa plc (HeavenlyCocoa) is a large chocolate manufacturing company which wants to acquire Choc Deluxe plc (Choc Deluxe), a company which produces luxury organic chocolates. HeavenlyCocoa has approached the board of directors of Choc Deluxe with an offer of £2.39 per share, which is four pence above the price at which Choc Deluxe shares are trading. Despite the fact that the board of Choc Deluxe did not recommend the offer, HeavenlyCocoa went ahead and made the offer to Choc Deluxe shareholders. By the end of the period in which HeavenlyCocoa's offer could be accepted, 90% of the shareholders of Choc Deluxe had accepted the offer. However, Brian, a close friend of the directors, who owns 10% of Choc Deluxe's shares, did not accept the offer.

Required

(a) Discuss whether the transaction would be classified as a friendly takeover or a hostile takeover and the difference between the two. **(8 marks)**

(b) Will HeavenlyCocoa now be able to compel Brian to sell his shares to HeavenlyCocoa and, if so, on what terms? **(6 marks)**

(c) Will Brian be able to compel HeavenlyCocoa to purchase his shares and, if so, on what terms? **(6 marks)**

(Total 20 marks)

Question 5

Discuss how the Companies Act 2006 regulates dealings between directors and their companies, with particular reference to long-term service contracts, substantial property transactions and loans.

(20 marks)

Question 6

Future Films Limited (Future Films) is a film production company which wants to expand into the production of television programmes. It plans to create a separate company, to be called Future Television Limited (Future Television), to pursue this proposed expansion. Future Television will have Model Articles and Future Films will own 80 per cent of the shares in Future Television. The remaining 20 per cent will be owned by private investors.

Required

(a) Discuss what the nature of the relationship will be between Future Films and Future Television. What company law rules will govern this relationship? **(10 marks)**

(b) Advise the directors as to the advantages and disadvantages of establishing Future Television by buying a company 'off the shelf'. **(10 marks)**

(Total 20 marks)

Question 7

Morgan Cycles Limited (Morgan Cycles) is a racing bike manufacturer specialising in track bikes. The company has Model Articles. Sam Frank is the Chairman of the board and there are three other directors, Jenny Frank, Tom Evans and Mike Edwards. Sam is very ambitious and would like to expand Morgan Cycles' business operations. It currently manufactures professional bikes but has not really exploited the market for amateur bikes. Sam has been in discussion with Royal Standard Bank plc about a business development loan of £300,000 to be secured by a floating charge. Sam intends to use the finance to invest in Morgan Cycles' production of new bike lines and related advertising campaigns.

Required

(a) Advise the board of directors of Morgan Cycles of the procedure for entering into the loan agreement with Royal Standard Bank plc, including the granting of the floating charge as security.

(10 marks)

(b) Advise Sam as to what would happen, if at the board meeting to approve the loan, he and Jenny voted in favour but Tom and Mike voted against. **(4 marks)**

(c) Analyse what rights Royal Standard Bank plc will have as a floating charge holder in the event that Morgan Cycles enters into the loan but later defaults on the terms of the loan. **(6 marks)**

(Total 20 marks)

Question 8

Fair Law Solicitors is a medium-sized law firm. A year ago, the firm started acting for Kite Properties Ltd (KPL). KPL specialises in purchasing high value properties and selling them on at a profit. The directors of the company advised Fair Law that the company's funding comes from profits and bank loans and KPL's bank statements support this.

Six months ago, the directors told their client partner at Fair Law that they were having some difficulties with the company's bank account. They asked if the company could use Fair Law's client account as a temporary measure. By this stage, KPL was one of Fair Law's most lucrative clients, so the partner agreed. Over the following six months, the partner allowed KPL to make in excess of one hundred high value deposits and withdrawals on the client account. None of the transactions related to any legal matter in which KPL was involved.

The partner is aware that Fair Law's Head of Finance has recently become suspicious that KPL's activities may involve money laundering. Not wanting to jeopardise the relationship with KPL, the partner has alerted KPL and withdrawn access to the client account.

Required

Advise Fair Law as to what, if any, offences may have been committed by KPL, the partner or Fair Law.

(20 marks)

MODEL ANSWERS

MODULE C

PROFESSIONAL EXAMINATION 1

PAPER 8 – COMPANY LAW

TUESDAY 28th NOVEMBER 2017

> Valid alternative points, whether or not they are shown in the Model Answers, will be given credit where appropriate.
>
> The answers to this Mock Exam are as provided by the AIA and have not been amended in respect of subsequent changes to legislation, case law or accounting standards.

Question 1

This question covers a company's constitutional documents and allotment of shares. Parts 8.1 and 8.2 of the syllabus and RQF learning outcomes 1 and 2. AIA text chapters 3 and 4.

(a) The articles of association are a constitutional document of the company. The articles are a public document open to inspection at Companies House. They create a contract between the company and each of its members.

The articles contain detailed rules and regulations setting out how the company is managed and administered. The Companies Act 2006 (CA 06) states that a company's articles should be contained in a single document divided into consecutively numbered paragraphs. Articles should contain rules on a number of areas:

- Directors – appointment, powers, responsibilities, and decision-making etc.
- Shares – classes of shares, share certificates, share transfers, dividends etc.
- Shareholders – general meetings and voting at general meetings etc.
- Administrative arrangements – documents, records, communication, indemnity and insurance etc.

Companies can draft their own bespoke articles based on the above principles. Alternatively, the CA 06 provides standard articles – known as Model Articles – that apply by default, unless a company chooses to exclude or modify them. Different Model Articles are available for different types of companies. It is common, as for Keen Cuisine Limited, that a company adopts the appropriate Model Articles as the basis of their articles of association, and then makes a number of changes by amending the Model Articles and/or introducing Special Articles.

(b) S561 CA 06 states that when a company allots ordinary shares for cash consideration, the shares must first be offered to existing shareholders pro rata their existing shareholding. The purpose of this provision is so that shareholders have the option of retaining their current shareholding percentage on a further issue of shares ie to ensure their shareholding is not diluted. S562 CA 06 sets out how offers under s561 must be communicated to shareholders.

This can cause some difficulties when allotting shares to new shareholders. The company must either:

- Get a waiver from the existing shareholders
- Pass a special resolution to disapply the pre-emption rights in relation to a specific allotment (s569 CA 06)
- Include a provision in the articles disapplying pre-emption rights generally (s567 CA 06).

By including Special Article 3, Keen Cuisine has chosen to disapply pre-emption rights generally in its articles. This means that shareholders' percentage shareholding is not protected from dilution but allotting shares to new shareholders, such as Paul, is more straightforward.

(c) S550 CA 06 applies as Keen Cuisine is a private limited company with only one class of shares. This means that the directors have the authority to allot shares to Paul without seeking authorisation from the company's shareholders as there are no restrictions on issue in the articles which Keen Cuisine have adopted.

Ordinarily, s561 CA 06 pre-emption rights would have applied as the shares are being allotted for cash consideration. The impact of this provision is that when the directors issue new shares they must be offered to existing shareholders pro rata to their existing shareholding. However, this is not the case as Special Article 3 disapplies pre-emption rights, so the shares can be offered to Paul without first having to be offered to existing shareholders pro rata.

A return of allotment of shares must be sent within one month to the Registrar of Companies on Form SH01 and the company's register of members and register of allotments must be updated.

> **Additional areas where credit might be given, note this is not an exhaustive list:**
> - Discussion of issue of shares for non-cash consideration not being subject to statutory pre-emption.
> - Discussion of the meeting of directors that will be necessary to effect the allotment.

Question 2

This question covers the types of resolutions which members of a private company can pass and the procedure for passing the resolutions. Part 8.3 of the syllabus and RQF learning outcome 3. AIA text chapter 8.

Members of a private company can pass ordinary resolutions and special resolutions.

Ordinary resolutions are passed by a simple majority (more than 50%) of the votes cast by those entitled to vote. An ordinary resolution is the decision making tool for most business within a company (s282 CA 06). Examples of where an ordinary resolution would be required include a vote to:

- Remove a company director (s168 CA 06)
- Approve a directors' long term service contract (s188 CA 06)
- Approve the sale to or purchase from a director of a substantial asset (s190 CA 06) etc.

14 days' notice is required.

Special resolutions are passed by at least 75% of the votes cast by those entitled to vote. A special resolution is required for major changes in a company (s283 CA 06). Examples of where a special resolution would be required include a vote to:

- Change a company's name (s77 CA 06)
- Restrict the company's objects or alter the company's articles (s21 CA 06)
- Disapply pre-emption rights (s569 CA 06)
- Reduce the company's share capital (s641 CA 06)
- Purchase of the company's own shares from capital (s716 CA 06) etc.

14 days' notice is required.

CA 06 indicates where a special resolution is required. If CA 06 does not specify the type of resolution needed, stating only that "a resolution of the company is required", then no more than an ordinary resolution is legally needed. However, unless CA 06 prevents it from doing so, a company would be free to include provision in its articles insisting on a special resolution, if it prefers a greater number of members to be in favour before that particular matter is passed.

Apart from the size of the majority, the main differences between the types of resolution are:

- The text of a special resolution must be set out in full in the notice convening the meeting, and it must be described as a special resolution. This is not necessary for an ordinary resolution if it is routine business.
- A signed copy of every special resolution must be delivered to the Registrar for filing. Although some ordinary resolutions, particularly those relating to share capital have to be delivered for filing, many do not.

Both ordinary and special resolutions can be passed:

- On a show of hands at a general meeting – members representing the requisite majority of members who are entitled to vote, do so in person or by proxy (s282(3), 283(4) CA 06)
- On a poll at a general meeting – members representing the requisite majority of the total voting rights of members who are entitled to vote, do so in person or by proxy (s282(4), 283(5) CA 06)
- By way of written resolution (without the need for a physical meeting) – members representing the requisite majority of the total voting rights of all eligible members (s282(2), 283(2) CA 06).

MOCK EXAM 1 ANSWERS

Written resolutions may be proposed by directors (s291 CA 06) or by members holding 5% of the voting rights (s292 CA 06). They are subject to strict rules to ensure that all members are notified of the business to be transacted and how and when they may vote. The written resolution must be sent to all shareholders together with a statement informing them how to signify acceptance and the date (known as the "lapse date") by which the resolution will fail if it is not approved by the requisite majority. In the absence of anything to the contrary in a company's articles (there is nothing in the Model Articles) the lapse date will be 28 days from the circulation date (s297 CA 06). The directors should also ensure that, where necessary, required documentation (eg copies of service agreements for s188 CA 06) accompany the written resolutions and are made available at the company's registered office. Shareholders do not all have to sign the same resolution and any number of counterparts can be issued.

> **Additional areas where credit might be given, note this is not an exhaustive list:**
>
> - Reference to extraordinary resolutions which largely ceased to exist on the implementation of CA 06 other than in relation to existing requirements in a company's memorandum or articles or a contract such as a shareholders agreement.
>
> - Consideration of the difference in passing an ordinary/special resolution at a general meeting where the majority relates to those in attendance in person or by proxy as opposed to passing an ordinary/special resolution by written resolution where the majority relates to the total voting rights ie all members.

Question 3

This question covers compulsory liquidation. Part 8.6 of the syllabus and RQF outcome 4. AIA text chapter 12.

(a) A creditor, such as Jessops, may apply to the court for a compulsory winding up. There are seven statutory reasons which can be cited and are found in s122 Insolvency Act 1986. The most relevant reason for Jessops would be that the company is unable to pay its debts (s122(1)(f)).

If Jessops petitions on the basis that Pet Matters is unable to pay its debts, it is effectively petitioning on the grounds of the company's insolvency. There are three ways for Jessops to do that:

- Assuming that it is owed more than £750, Jessops serves Pet Matters with a written demand for payment and the company does not pay the debt or offer reasonable security within 21 days. There does not appear to be grounds here for Pet Matters to deny it owes the amount.

- Obtain judgment against Pet Matters for the debt and attempt and fail to enforce the payment because there are insufficient assets available.

- Satisfy the court that, taking into account the contingent and prospective liabilities of Pet Matters, it is unable to pay its debts. Jessops may show this in one of two ways:

    - The commercial insolvency test – by proof that Pet Matters cannot pay its debts as they fall due, or

    - The balance sheet test – by proof that the company's assets are less than its liabilities.

It seems likely that Jessops will succeed with their application for a compulsory winding up on the basis that Pet Matters is unable to pay its debts under the commercial insolvency test.

(b) In a compulsory liquidation, the liquidator distributes the assets that remain after any fixed chargeholder has satisfied its secured debt by appointing a receiver to sell the asset. This means that Royal Standard Bank plc will appoint a receiver to sell Pet Matters' premises to repay its loan. If there is any surplus, the bank will pass this on to the liquidator.

The assets that remain will be distributed as follows:

- Costs – these include the costs of selling the assets, the liquidator's fee and all incidental costs.
- Preferential debts – employees' wages, accrued holiday pay, contributions to an occupational pension fund and money borrowed to pay wages.
- Debts secured by floating charges – subject to the ring-fenced "prescribed part" (see below).
- Debts owed to unsecured ordinary creditors – a proportion of assets, known as the "prescribed part", is ring-fenced for unsecured creditors. This proportion (which is subject to a statutory maximum) is 50% of the first £10,000 of realisations of debts secured by floating charge and 20% of floating charge realisations thereafter (subject to a maximum of £600,000).
- Members – any surplus (unlikely in a compulsory liquidation as a company is solvent if it has a surplus) is distributed to members according to their rights under the articles or terms of issue of their shares.

In addition to the bank loan, there are outstanding preferential debts - wages and possibly related items such as holiday pay and pension contributions.

Jessops will fall in the category of being an unsecured ordinary creditor which means it will be low down the order of distribution and unlikely to be paid in full.

Additional areas where credit might be given, note this is not an exhaustive list:
- Discussion of a petition on the just and equitable ground, by a member aware of the company's difficulties and dissatisfied with the management by the directors or controlling shareholders.

Question 4

This question covers the topic of takeovers including the acquisition and sale of minority shareholdings. Part 8.5 of the syllabus and RQF outcome 4. AIA textbook chapter 4.

(a) A takeover of a company (the target) occurs when control (ownership) of the target is taken over by another company (the offeror or bidder) by buying shares from their current owners. Takeovers are usually classed as either friendly (recommended) or hostile.

Friendly takeover – this is a situation where a target company's management and board of directors agree to an acquisition by another company. In a friendly takeover, a public offer is made by the offeror, and the target board will publicly approve the terms, which may yet be subject to shareholder or regulatory approval. In most cases, if the board approves an offer from an offeror, on the basis that it is in the best interests of shareholders, the shareholders will vote to pass it as well. The key determinant in whether the buyout will occur is if the price per share being offered. The offeror will offer a premium to the current market price, but the size of this premium (given the company's growth prospects) will determine the overall support for the buyout within the target.

Hostile takeover – this is where the target does not approve of the acquisition and fights against it. The offeror approaches the target's board with the terms of an offer but the board rejects it as not being in the best interests of shareholders. Regardless of this, the offeror announces its intention to make an offer, then goes ahead and makes the offer to shareholders.

The facts here indicate that this will be a hostile takeover, perhaps because the four pence premium is not considered to be enough for the board to recommend the offer as in the best interests of shareholders.

(b) A key aspect of the rules on takeovers is that if a large majority of shareholders (90% or more by nominal value and voting rights) like the terms of the offer and agree to sell their shares before the offer lapses, the offeror can then choose to buy-out the minority shareholders (here the remaining shares in Choc Deluxe).

They do this by giving them a "squeeze-out" notice within a maximum of three months after the takeover offer has lapsed (s979 CA 06). Any shares in the target that were already owned by the offeror at the date of the takeover are excluded when calculating the 90% threshold.

The squeeze-out notice requires the minority shareholders to sell their shares to the offeror on the terms of the takeover offer and also requires the offeror to buy them (s981 CA 06). So if HeavenlyCocoa wants to acquire the remaining shares in Choc Deluxe it can.

(c) HeavenlyCocoa may choose to live with there being a minority of shareholders, who did not accept the offer, still holding shares in the company, and therefore choose not issue a squeeze-out notice for compulsory acquisition. Even if HeavenlyCocoa is happy to live with the minority shareholders, once it reaches the 90% threshold it must within one month give the minority shareholders notice of their right to sell under s983 CA 06.

And those minority shareholders (Brian, in our question) may compel HeavenlyCocoa to buy their shares under the "sell-out" provisions of s983 but only if:

- The offeror has acquired 90% of the shares in the target before the period within which the offer can be accepted, and
- The shareholder (Brian) writes to the acquirer requiring their shares to be purchased on the same terms as the original takeover offer or on such other terms as may be agreed (s985 CA 06).

Unlike for squeeze-out notices, any shares in the target already owned by the offeror at the date of the takeover are included when calculating the 90% threshold for sell-out.

Additional areas where credit might be given, note this is not an exhaustive list:

- Discussion of offeror revising the terms of its offer so that a hostile takeover could become recommended.

Question 5

This question covers the regulation of dealings between the company and its directors. Part 8.3 of the syllabus and RQF learning outcome 3. AIA text chapter 9.

Under s177 CA 06, directors are required to disclose to the other directors the nature and extent of any interest, direct or indirect, that they have in relation to a proposed transaction or arrangement with the company. Even if the director is not a party to the transaction, the duty may apply if they are aware, or ought reasonably to be aware, of the interest. For example, the interest of another person in a contract with the company may require disclosure under this duty if that other person's interest is a direct or indirect interest on the part of the director.

Directors are required to disclose such an interest before the company enters into the transaction. Disclosure can be made by written notice, general notice or verbally at a board meeting. Disclosure to members is not sufficient, it must be to other directors as well and the declaration must set out the nature and extent of their interest. If the declaration becomes void or inaccurate, a further declaration should be made.

Under s177(6) CA 06, no declaration of interest is required if the director's interest cannot reasonably be regarded as likely to give rise to a conflict of interest, or to the extent that the other directors either already are, or ought reasonably to be aware of it.

Under Model Article 14, if a director is interested in a transaction he may not count as participating in the decision-making process of the board for quorum or voting purposes. This provision may be excluded.

Long term service contracts

The terms of a service contract will normally be for the director and the company, acting through the board, to decide (Model Article 19). However, in certain circumstances, s188 CA 06 must first be complied with.

This provides that where the guaranteed term of a director's employment is, or may be, longer than two years, the company may not agree to such a provision unless it has been approved by an ordinary resolution of the members. This is so that a service contract provision which could result in an ex-director receiving a very substantial payment if he was dismissed, can be first scrutinised by the company's members.

Furthermore, the resolution itself must not be passed unless a memorandum setting out the proposed contract has been on display at the company's registered office for at least 15 days prior to the members' meeting or is attached to a written resolution sent to the eligible members.

Substantial property transactions

The authorisation of most contracts merely requires director consent. However, under s190 CA 06, when a director or a person connected with a director is either selling an asset to or acquiring an asset from the company, consideration needs to be given as to whether that asset is deemed to be "a substantial non-cash asset". Where it is, the contract will need to be approved by the members by ordinary resolution before the directors can successfully conclude matters. Approval from the members can either be sought before the contract is entered into or the contract can be made conditional upon such consent.

The rules to determine what is a substantial non-cash asset are set out in s191 CA 06:

- An asset worth less than £5,000 is never substantial
- An asset worth in excess of £100,000 is always substantial
- An asset worth between £5,000 and £100,000 will be substantial if it exceeds 10% of the company's asset value.

Loans

Usually, whether a company is to lend money or not will be a decision for its directors under their delegated powers (Model Article 3). However, where the proposed loan is to a director of the company, s197 CA 06 makes such lending subject to the prior consent of the company's members by ordinary resolution unless the loan is for:

- Expenditure on company business (s204 CA 06)
- The cost of the directors defending himself against legal proceedings in connection with the company (s205 CA 06)
- The cost of the directors defending himself against investigation by any regulatory authority regarding matters relating to the company (s206 CA 06)
- £10,000 or less (s207 CA 06).

In this context, a "loan" to a director would also include indirect "lending" by the company such as it agreeing to guarantee the director's own personal borrowing from another lender eg a bank.

Additional areas where credit might be given, note this is not an exhaustive list:

- Discussion of other dealings between the company and its directors eg quasi-loans (s198 CA 06), unapproved credit transactions (s197 CA 06) or non-contractual payments to directors for loss of office (s217 CA 06).
- Discussion of requirement to declare interest in existing transactions or arrangements (s182 CA 06).

Question 6

This question covers group companies and off the shelf companies. Part 8.1 of the syllabus and RQF learning outcome 1. AIA text chapters 1 and 2.

(a) Future Films will be the parent company and Future Television will be a subsidiary. The two companies will form a simple group of companies.

The parent company is a member of the subsidiary and here owns a majority of the voting rights in the subsidiary. As an 80 per cent shareholder, it has the right to exercise a dominant influence over the subsidiary by virtue of provisions contained in the subsidiary's Model Articles and the CA 06. It has the right to appoint or remove a majority of its board directors and therefore has a great degree of influence at board level. At general meetings, it can pass all ordinary and special resolutions on its own.

The importance of the parent and subsidiary company relationship is recognised in company law in a number of provisions, the main ones being:

- A subsidiary may not ordinarily be a member of its parent company (s136 CA 06)

- A parent company must generally prepare group accounts in which the financial situation of parent and subsidiary companies are consolidated as if they were one person (s399 CA 06)

- Since directors of a parent company may control its subsidiary, some rules designed to regulate the dealings of companies with directors also apply to its subsidiaries eg loans to directors (s197 CA 06).

(b) Buying a company off the shelf avoids the administrative burden of registering a company. The main advantages are that the following documents will not need to be filed with the Registrar by Future Films in respect of Future Television:

- Memorandum and Articles (not actually necessary in this instance as Model Articles)
- Application for registration
- Statement of proposed officers
- Statement of compliance
- Statement of capital and initial shareholdings
- Fee (although there is obviously a cost associated with purchasing a company off the shelf).

This is because the specialist has already registered the company. It will therefore be a quicker and possibly cheaper way of incorporating a company. There will also be no risk of potential liability arising from pre-incorporation contracts.

The disadvantages relate to the administrative changes that will be required to the company after it has been purchased to make it compatible with Future Television's needs:

- The nominee directors will need to resign and the real directors be appointed

- The company is likely to have Model Articles which the directors may want to amend – not in this instance though, they are happy with Model Articles

- The directors may want to change the name of the company – yes, this is the case, the company is to be called Future Television Limited

- The subscriber shares will need to be transferred and the transfer recorded in the register of members

- The correct number of shares need to be allotted to Future Films and the agreed private investors.

Additional areas where credit might be given, note this is not an exhaustive list:

- Mention of how 'veil piercing' applies (or no longer applies) to corporate groups.

Question 7

This question covers borrowing and charges. Part 8.2 and 8.3 of the syllabus and QCF learning outcomes 2 and 3. AIA text chapters 5 and 9.

(a) The CA 06 states that unless there are any restrictions in a company's articles, it has unlimited capacity (s31 CA 06). Morgan Cycles has Model Articles, which do not contain any restrictions on its capacity, therefore would include the power to borrow for purposes incidental to its business or trade and to create charges over its assets.

Under Model Article 3, directors are responsible for the management of the company's business, for which purpose they may exercise all the powers of the company. Therefore, the decision to borrow from Royal Standard Bank plc and grant a floating charge as security is one that can be taken by the directors in a board meeting.

A board meeting should be convened on reasonable notice and details of the loan, its terms and the floating charge should be tabled and discussed and the directors should then vote on the matter. Voting is on a show of hands and a majority in favour will pass the resolution. If it is resolved to enter into the loan and the floating charge, two directors or one director and the company secretary should be authorised to execute the relevant documents.

Once executed the floating charge should be registered with the Registrar of Companies within 21 days to be valid and enforceable. Application for the charge to be registered can be made by the company or by any other person interested in the charge (s859A CA 06). To apply to register a charge, a statement of particulars relating to the charge must be delivered to the Registrar. A certificate is issued which is conclusive evidence that the charge has been duly registered.

(b) If Sam and Jenny vote in favour of the resolution and Tom and Mike vote against, as voting at a board meeting is on a show of hands, there will be deadlock.

The company has Model Articles so this situation will be resolved by Model Article 13, which states that if the numbers of votes for and against a proposal are equal, the Chairman has a casting vote. Sam will therefore have a casting vote and will vote in favour and the resolution will be passed.

(c) It would be usual for the floating charge granted by Morgan Cycles to Royal Standard Bank plc to contain charges over all or substantially all of the company's property and the right to appoint an administrator if Morgan Cycles defaults on the loan.

The appointment of an administrator by a floating charge holder is an out-of-court process. If there are no prior floating charges then Royal Standard Bank plc will file at court a notice of appointment, a statement that the administrator consents to act and that the purpose of the administration is likely to be achieved and a statutory declaration that the administrator is qualified to act. If there is a prior floating chargeholder, Royal Standard Bank plc will have to give the charge holder two days prior written notice before appointing an administrator.

Additional areas where credit might be given, note this is not an exhaustive list:

- Credit for discussing procedure for entering into loan by way of general meeting but board meeting is most appropriate.

Question 8

This question covers money laundering. Part 8.3 and 8.5 of the syllabus and RQF learning outcome 4. AIA text chapter 13.

The offence which must be considered is money laundering. Money laundering is generally defined as the process by which the proceeds of crime, and the true ownership of those proceeds, are changed so that the proceeds appear to come from a legitimate source.

Law and regulations relevant to money laundering are found in the Proceeds of Crime Act 2002 and the Money Laundering Regulations 2007.

There are three acknowledged phases to money laundering:

- Placement – the initial disposal of the proceeds of the illegal activity into an apparently legitimate business activity or property. This would be putting the proceeds of some illegal activity, although it is not certain from the facts that there is such activity, into KPL which appears to be a legitimate property business.

- Layering – this is the transfer of monies from one business to another or one place to another to conceal the original source. This would be the transfer of funds from KPL to Fair Law's client account and the subsequent deposits and withdrawals.

- Integration – once it has been layered, the money appears to be legitimate funds.

There are three categories of criminal offence under the Proceeds of Crime Act:

- Laundering – this is the acquisition, possession or use of the proceeds of crime or assisting another to retain the proceeds of crime by concealing, disguising, converting, transferring or removing the criminal property.

- Failure to report – this is in respect of an individual relevant person failing to disclose knowledge or suspicion of money laundering.

- Tipping off – this is disclosing information to any person which may prejudice an investigation.

More information is needed in relation to the original source of KPL's funds to determine whether the offence of money laundering has been committed by KPL, although the activity does have many of the hallmarks of money laundering. If this is the case, it seems likely that the partner will have committed the offence of failing to report and tipping off.

The penalties are a maximum sentence of 15 years' imprisonment and/or a fine for knowingly assisting in the laundering of criminal funds, and for failure to report or tipping off, five years' imprisonment and/or a fine.

The Money Laundering Regulations apply to a wide range of organisations including accountants and auditors and solicitors. As each organisation is different, systems have to be designed appropriate to each organisation to ensure there are:

- Internal reporting procedures
- Due diligence in relation to clients
- Record-keeping
- Employee training.

The facts suggest that Fair Law may have failed to implement these measures.

This is a criminal offence punishable with a maximum sentence of two years' imprisonment and/or a fine, irrespective of whether money laundering has taken place (further investigations are needed to determine whether the initial proceeds are as a result of illegal activity). Civil penalties may also be imposed.

Additional areas where credit might be given, note this is not an exhaustive list:
- None

Mock exam 2
questions and answers

MODULE C

PROFESSIONAL EXAMINATION 1

PAPER 8 – COMPANY LAW

TUESDAY 22nd MAY 2018

Time allowed – 3 hours

**Candidates must answer FIVE questions in total
Questions 1–3 are mandatory and must be attempted
Candidates can choose a further TWO questions to answer from the remaining questions**

Candidates should always give reasons for their answers and, where appropriate, support them by reference to decided cases and statutes.

You are allowed an additional 15 minutes reading time before the exam begins, during which you should read the question paper and, if you wish, make notes on the question paper. You are **not** allowed to open the exam script booklet and start writing or use your calculator during the reading time.

Candidates MUST attempt ALL of the following THREE questions which are COMPULSORY

Question 1

Pitch Perfect Limited (PPL) manufactures and installs artificial turf in schools and sporting venues. The company needs a cash injection in order to develop the next generation product. PPL has approached City Bank plc (City Bank), who is happy to lend PPL £300,000. City Bank has requested either a fixed or floating charge over PPL's assets and personal guarantees from the directors.

Required

(a) Advise PPL on the legal effect of granting a fixed or floating charge over the company's assets and any procedures which must be complied with in relation to the charge. **(10 marks)**

(b) Advise the directors of PPL about the implications of them granting personal guarantees in relation to the loan. **(4 marks)**

(c) Assume now that three years ago, PPL borrowed £70,000 from a wealthy individual. The loan was secured by way of a floating charge on PPL's assets and was also correctly registered within the prescribed time limits. If PPL now grants a fixed charge over the company's assets to City Bank, advise which charge would prevail. **(6 marks)**

(Total 20 marks)

Question 2

Analyse how the rights of a shareholder in a company differ from the rights of a debenture holder in a company, including any differences that arise where the company is being wound up. **(20 marks)**

Question 3

Webdesign Solutions is a successful business which has been providing web design services to a broad range of clients for the last three years. The business has been operating as a partnership. The three partners, Ashley Burton, Charlie Dawson and Ethan French, all work full time in the business and employ a team of five web designers and one administrative member of staff.

Over the last twelve months, Webdesign Solutions has secured a number of large, lucrative contracts and Ashley, Charlie and Ethan have decided that the expanding business should become a limited liability company called Webdesign Solutions Limited (WSL). The turnover of the business is in the region of £700,000 and its balance sheet total is approximately £250,000. Current projections suggest that both turnover and balance sheet total will increase by approximately twenty five per cent over the next twelve months.

Ashley, Charlie and Ethan have decided that the company will be incorporated with Model Articles (unamended) and ordinary shares of £1 each. They will each own one share and be appointed as a director of the company.

Required

(a) Advise Ashley, Charlie and Ethan as to the procedures that should be followed to incorporate SSL and what checks should be made before doing so. **(10 marks)**

(b) Advise Ashley, Charlie and Ethan what WSL's obligations will be in relation to the production and filing of accounts and whether WSL will need to appoint an auditor. **(10 marks)**

(Total 20 marks)

Candidates must answer TWO questions from questions 4, 5, 6, 7 and 8

Question 4

Divine Destinations Limited (DDL) is a luxury travel company which has a number of stores and a significant online presence. The company has performed extremely well since its first store opened five years ago and has a net asset value of around £500,000. It is now looking for investment to increase the number of stores in order to establish a nationwide network.

DDL was incorporated with Model Articles (unamended). It has four shareholders, who are also directors, each of whom owns 100,000 £1 ordinary shares.

Required

(a)   Discuss whether the directors of DDL can issue 100,000 £1 shares to a new investor who is not currently a shareholder of DDL. **(7 marks)**

(b)   What difference would it make if the new investor was only prepared to pay £50,000 for the 100,000 shares it wished to buy in DDL? **(6 marks)**

(c)   Assume now that DDL wishes to purchase some fixtures and fittings valued at £25,000. Advise DDL what additional steps would need to be taken if those fixtures and fittings are being purchased from one of the directors' spouses? **(7 marks)**

(Total 20 marks)

Question 5

Discuss the options available to a company wanting to effect a share buy-back, including the relevant legal and procedural requirements. **(20 marks)**

Question 6

Graham Price, Felix Shaw and Lucy Drake are directors and shareholders in an advertising company called Visualise Limited (Visualise). The company has been in existence for over twenty years. Six years ago, Visualise adopted new articles of association in line with the Companies Act 2006 Model Articles (unamended).

Recently, Graham has expressed a desire to retire. He would like to vacate his position on the board of directors and sell his shares. Lucy's husband, Andrew, is keen to buy Graham's shares and to take his position on the board of directors. Graham is happy with the price that Andrew is offering and Felix and Lucy are happy for Andrew to join the board.

Required

(a)   Discuss the procedural steps necessary for Graham to transfer his shares to Andrew. **(8 marks)**

(b)   Advise the board of directors as to the procedures for Andrew to replace Graham on the board. **(8 marks)**

(c)   What additional procedures are necessary if Visualise wants to offer Andrew a three year service contract? **(4 marks)**

(Total 20 marks)

Question 7

Anthony Bird and Clare Davidson want to set up a company selling party accessories online. They plan to call the company Party Pieces Limited (PPL). Anthony, who is very keen to get the new business established, has already entered into a number of contracts with suppliers on behalf of the company prior to its incorporation.

Required

(a) Discuss the advantages of establishing the business as a private limited company. **(12 marks)**

(b) Advise Anthony and Clare as to who is liable for the contracts that have already been entered into with suppliers on behalf of the proposed company. **(8 marks)**

(Total 20 marks)

Question 8

Oil Investigation Limited (OIL) is a medium-sized oil exploration company. The Chief Executive Officer, Vinod Khan, is a strong advocate of ethical exploration and of the high standards the company maintains in all areas of regulation and governance.

Daniel Prescott is an employee of OIL in the department responsible for identifying and promoting new areas of exploration. A new area has recently been identified and an environmental impact report has been commissioned. A month ago, Daniel paid Will Jamieson, the author of the environmental impact report, to state that the impact on the local environment of extracting oil from this area would be significantly less than it would actually be.

Daniel's actions have been exposed in the local newspaper and OIL has been criticised for failing to prevent his behaviour.

Required

Advise OIL as to what, if any, offences it may be alleged that OIL has committed, what defence may be available to OIL and how that defence would operate. **(20 marks)**

MODEL ANSWERS

MODULE C

PROFESSIONAL EXAMINATION 1

PAPER 8 – COMPANY LAW

TUESDAY 22nd MAY 2018

Valid alternative points, whether or not they are shown in the Model Answers, will be given credit where appropriate.

The answers to this Mock Exam are as provided by the AIA and have not been amended in respect of subsequent changes to legislation, case law or accounting standards.

# MOCK EXAM 2 ANSWERS

Question 1

This question covers charges over the assets of a company and personal guarantees. Part 8.2 of the syllabus and RQF learning outcomes 2 and 3. AIA text chapter 5.

(a) If PPL grants a charge over the company's assets in favour of City Bank it gives City Bank a prior claim over other creditors to repayment of its £300,000 loan out of the company's assets.

A fixed charge attaches to specific assets as soon as the charge is created. The fixed charge is likely to attach to assets which PPL will retain for a long period, for example, it may attach to PPL's premises. If PPL disposes of the charged assets, it will repay the loan out of the proceeds of sale so that the charge is discharged.

A floating charge is a charge on a class of assets which, in the ordinary course of business, is changing from time to time. The floating charge may attach to PPL's stock as the exact stock and stock levels will fluctuate over the period of the loan. Until crystallisation of a floating charge occurs, PPL can carry on business and deal with the assets which are charged. When it crystallises, it is converted into a fixed charge on the assets owned by the company at the time of crystallisation.

To be valid and enforceable, a charge must be registered within 21 days of creation by the Registrar of Companies. PPL would be responsible for registering the charge but City Bank may also register it, as it is interested in the charge. The Registrar should be sent the instrument by which the charge is created and the details of the charge. The Registrar issues a certificate which is evidence that the charge has been registered.

(b) As PPL is a limited company, the liability of the directors or shareholders in relation to the loan from City Bank is, in theory, limited. However, if the directors give personal guarantees in respect of the loan, they are required to pay if PPL defaults on the loan. This means that the directors' personal assets (house, cars, savings etc.) would be at risk. If several directors give a personal guarantee (or give a single guarantee jointly and severally), City Bank does not have to take action against all of them but can claim the whole amount from one guarantor and is most likely to be motivated by the liquidity of a director's assets.

(c) Different charges over the same property can be given to different creditors but it is then necessary to determine the priority of the charges.

A floating charge created before a fixed charge will only take priority over the fixed charge if, when the fixed charge was created, the fixed chargee had notice of a clause in the floating charge preventing a later prior charge. If no such clause existed or City Bank had no notice of any such clause because PPL did not disclose it, the fixed charge would have priority as it attaches to the asset when the charge is created and the floating charge only attaches on crystallisation.

> **Additional areas where credit might be given, note this is not an exhaustive list:**
> - Discussion of how directors who have given personal guarantees and had a claim brought against them may pursue co-directors.
> - Discussion of the situation if the later charges had been a floating charge – the earlier charge would have priority as two floating charges take priority according to the time of creation.

Question 2

This question covers rights of debenture holders and shareholders, including on winding up. Parts 8.2 and 8.6 of the syllabus and RQF learning outcomes 2 and 4. AIA text chapters 4, 6 and 12.

Although both debenture holders and shareholders own transferable securities in the company, there are many important differences between the rights of debenture holders and shareholders. Shareholders are members of the company and own part of the company. Debenture holders are not members of the company, they are simply creditors.

A company's relationship with a shareholder is governed by the company's articles which represent a contractual document between the company and its shareholders, and the Companies Act 2006 (the Companies Act). A company's relationship with a debenture holder is governed by the terms of the debenture document and different provisions of the Companies Act.

In relation to the cost of investment, shares may not be issued at a discount to nominal value but debentures may be issued at a discount to nominal value.

Statutory pre-emption rights offer some protection to shareholders in the event of a proposed new issue of shares. Although there is no statutory protection available to debenture holders, the debenture document will almost certainly contain a negative pledge preventing the company from granting any other charges over the assets secured by the debenture.

Shareholders have a right to attend and vote at general meetings, whereas debenture holders are not automatically afforded such rights, although the terms of the articles and debenture may confer such rights.

If shareholders are aggrieved by the company's behaviour, the shareholders can go to court to seek redress for ultra vires transactions, unfairly prejudicial conduct or to pursue a derivative claim. If the terms of the debenture document are breached, the most likely remedies would be the right to appoint a receiver or the right to enforce security and sell any property subject to a charge to recover debts. Shareholders can also remove a director by ordinary resolution under s168, no such right exists in relation to debenture holders.

Shareholders, even if they hold preference shares on which fixed dividends are due on specific dates, have no legal right to force a company to pay dividends (in any event, dividends can only be paid if a company has sufficient distributable profits). Conversely, the interest owing to debenture holders must be paid, regardless of whether or not the company has sufficient profits.

There are statutory restrictions on redeeming shares but there are no restrictions on redeeming debentures.

If the company goes into liquidation, debenture holders will be repaid in priority to shareholders who are the last people to be paid in a winding-up.

In a compulsory liquidation (and often in a voluntary one) the liquidator distributes the assets that remain after any fixed charge debenture holder has satisfied its secured debt following appointment of a receiver. The priority is then debenture holders where the debenture is secured by floating charge and then debenture holders where the debenture is unsecured. A proportion of assets (known as the "prescribed part") is "ring-fenced" for unsecured creditors. This proportion (which is subject to a statutory maximum) is calculated as 50 per cent of the first £10,000 or realisations of debts secured by floating charge and 20 per cent of the floating charge realisations thereafter (subject to a prescribed maximum on £600,000).

Additional areas where credit might be given, note this is not an exhaustive list:

- In relation to tax, dividends on shares are paid out of a company's post-tax distributable profits. In relation to debentures, interest is deducted from a company's profits before tax is calculated.

Question 3

This question covers incorporation of a private limited company and the company's accounting obligations. Parts 8.1 and 8.4 of the syllabus and RQF learning outcomes 1 and 3. AIA text chapter 2 and chapter 11.

(a) To incorporate Webdesign Solutions Limited (WSL), Form IN01 must be completed and submitted to Companies House. This form contains details of the company's name, the situation of its registered office, the type of company it is to be incorporated as, its initial share capital, its first directors, its initial subscribers and a statement of the company's compliance with the provisions of the Companies Act 2006 (the Companies Act).

A copy of the company's memorandum should also be sent to Companies House. If WSL wanted to use a bespoke set of articles or to modify the provisions of the Model Articles, these would also need to be sent to Companies House, but as WSL wants Model Articles (unamended), this is not necessary.

The appropriate fee should accompany the documents.

The Registrar of Companies will issue a Certificate of Incorporation provided the documents are in order. The number which appears on the Certificate of Incorporation is WSL's unique company number and the date on the certificate is the date that WSL legally comes into existence.

Before incorporation, the register of names at Companies House should be checked to make sure that the name, Webdesign Solutions Limited, is not the same as that of an existing company or that it is not too similar to that of an existing company. If the former is the case, WSL will not be registered (s66). If the latter is the case, although it will be possible to register WSL, the existing company with the similar name may complain to the Registrar of Companies who may direct WSL to change its name.

(b) For each accounting reference period, the directors of WSL must prepare accounts for its members and file them with the Registrar of Companies. Where they are prepared in Companies Act format, they must include a balance sheet and a profit and loss account, to give a true and fair view of the company's assets, liabilities, financial position and profit or loss for the accounting reference period up to the accounting reference date (s396). The board of directors must approve the annual accounts and they must be signed by a director on behalf of the board.

A company is permitted to file abbreviated accounts with the Registrar of Companies if it is classed as "small" by satisfying two or more of the following conditions:

- Annual turnover must be not more than £6.5million
- The balance sheet total must be not more that £3.26million
- The average number of employees must be not more than 50

WSL satisfies all three conditions and can therefore choose either to file a copy of the full accounts prepared for its members or to file an abbreviated version. Filing must be within nine months of the end of the accounting period.

As a small company, WSL will also be exempt from the requirement to appoint auditors and produce an audit report.

Additional areas where credit might be given, note this is not an exhaustive list:

- Discussion of "micro-entities" and whether WSL would qualify – no. Annual turnover must be not more than £632,000, balance sheet total not more than £316,000 and average number of employees not more than 10.

Question 4

This question covers issue of shares and substantial property transactions. Parts 8.2 and 8.3 of the syllabus and RQF learning outcomes 2 and 3. AIA text chapter 4.

(a) S550 Companies Act 2006 (Companies Act) applies as DDL is a private limited company with only one class of shares. This means that the directors have the authority to allot shares to the new investor without seeking authorisation from the company's shareholders.

However s561 pre-emption rights will apply as the shares are being allotted for cash consideration. The impact of this provision is that when the directors issue the new shares they must be offered to existing shareholders pro rata to their existing shareholding. This would mean that the 100,000 shares DDL is planning to issue must be offered in equal shares to the four existing shareholders each of whom currently own twenty five per cent of the shares each. This does not appear to be what the shareholders want, they want the new investor to become a member of the company so the additional funds are available.

Pre-emption rights can be excluded in a company's articles (s567), however this is not the case as DDL has Model Articles. Pre-emption rights can also be disapplied by special resolution (s570). This special resolution could be passed by way of a written resolution instead of convening a general meeting.

(b) The consideration here is the issue of shares at a discount. S580 prohibits the issue of shares at a discount to their nominal value. The nominal value here is £1 and the proposal is that 100,000 shares are issued for £50,000 – a discount of 50 pence or 50 per cent. If the new investor only wants to invest £50,000, then the maximum number of shares issued would be 50,000, which would mean that the new investor would hold a smaller percentage than the existing shareholders. If he/she wanted to be an equal shareholder ie hold 100,000 shares, the minimum payable would be £100,000. More would be payable if the valuation of DDL's shares exceeded £1 per share.

(c) Here we have a situation whereby the company is purchasing assets from Helen Brent, the wife of a director.

Under s190, when a director or a person connected with a director sells an asset to a company and that asset is deemed to be a "substantial non-cash asset" the contract will need to be approved by the members by ordinary resolution.

Under s191, an asset worth between £5,000 and £100,000 (here asset is worth £25,000) will be "substantial" if it exceeds ten per cent of the company's net asset value. DDL's estimated net asset value is £500,000, therefore the asset being acquired from Helen will not be a substantial non-cash asset – five per cent.

If the assets had been substantial, the transaction would have to be approved by ordinary resolution in a general meeting or by way of written resolution before the directors could enter into the contract. At the board meeting at which the contract is entered into, the director would have to declare his interest under s177 and pursuant to Model Article 14 could not vote or count in the quorum.

Additional areas where credit might be given, note this is not an exhaustive list:

- Discuss the possibility of transferring shares at less than nominal value but understand that this does not bring investment into the company – funds go to transferor.
- Acceptable to issue shares at a premium.

Question 5

This question covers maintenance of capital and the circumstances in which a company can buy its own shares. Part 8.2 of the syllabus and RQF learning outcome 2. AIA text chapter 6.

Under s658 Companies Act 2006 (the Companies Act) a company cannot acquire its own shares. However, this prohibition is subject to exceptions in s659, which includes a company's buy back of its own shares by way of specified procedures. The Companies Act sections 690-736 sets out the law relating to a company buy back of shares.

Legal and procedural requirements relation to a public company buy back of shares

The essential rule for public companies is that no purchase or redemption is to be financed out of a company's capital. A buy back can only be financed out of profits properly available for distribution to a company's members or from the funds arising from an issue of shares. The purchase can either be effected by way of a market or off-market purchase. A market purchase must be authorised by ordinary resolution and is a purchase by a public company under the normal market arrangements of a recognised investment exchange. An off-market purchase is any other purchase. The procedural requirements for an off-market purchase are detailed below.

Legal and procedural requirements relating to private company buy-back of shares

Private companies can only effect a buy back by way of an off market transaction. The contract for the purchase of shares must be approved by ordinary resolution (s694(2)). A copy of the contract must be made available for inspection at the company's registered office for fifteen days prior to the general meeting to approve. The contract must also be made available at the meeting itself. The members who are selling their shares back to the company should not vote on the resolution approving the purchase.

Private companies have an additional financing option available to them that is not available to public companies. Under s709, private companies are permitted to use the company's capital to finance the purchase of their own shares, although the controls are rigorous. Furthermore, the company must first use all of its available profits and the proceeds of any fresh issue of shares to fund the buy back before being able to make a payment out of capital under s710. In addition, the company must not have any relevant restrictions in its articles.

There are a number of procedural requirements that a private company must satisfy in order to effect a payment out of capital, including:

- The directors must make a statutory declaration to the effect that the company is solvent and will remain so for the following year, and this declaration must be supported by report of the auditors;
- The company must pass a special resolution authorising the procedure (again the members selling their shares back to the company should not vote);
- A shareholder who did not vote for the resolution or a creditor (for any amount) may within five weeks apply to the court to cancel the resolution which may not be implemented until the five weeks have elapsed;
- A notice must be placed in the Gazette and an appropriate national newspaper or every creditor must be informed under s719.

> **Additional areas where credit might be given, note this is not an exhaustive list:**
> - If the company goes into insolvent liquidation within a year of making a payment out of capital the person who received the payment and the directors who authorised it may have to make it good to the company.
> - Less onerous rules apply where the payment out of capital relates to the purchase of own shares for the purpose of or pursuant to an employees' share scheme.
> - Mention might also be made of the exception for small buy backs out of capital by private companies that do not exceed £15,000.

Question 6

This question covers transfer of shares, appointment and retirement of directors and service contracts. Parts 8.2 and 8.3 of the syllabus and RQF learning outcomes 2 and 3. AIA text chapter 4 and chapter 9.

(a) Shares are generally freely transferable in accordance with and subject to restrictions contained in the company's articles, s544 Companies Act 2006 (the Companies Act). The Model Articles (unamended) contain no restrictions on the right to transfer fully paid shares but directors may refuse to register the transfer (Model Article 26). The transfer is put to the board for its formal approval, which must be given within two months of its presentation to the company. No evidence on the facts that the directors will refuse to register.

The member selling his shares, Graham, must execute a stock transfer form in respect of the shares he wishes to sell and send this, together with the relevant share certificates, to the new shareholder, Andrew, who must pay stamp duty of ½% on his stock transfer form. The stamped form can then be sent to the company together with the share certificate. Andrew must be sent a new share certificate within two months of the date upon which his stock transfer form was lodged with the company. The new shareholder will also be entered on the register of members and register of transfers (optional).

(b) Graham should serve a letter of resignation on Visualise with the appropriate notice period. This should be in accordance with any service contract he is party to. Form TM01 should be filed at Companies House and the register of directors and directors' interests should be written up accordingly.

Under the Model Articles (unamended) there are two possible methods by which Andrew can be appointed as a board director:

- Model Article 17(1)(b) - the directors can vote at a board meeting. A simple majority on a show of hands is required. This is the most straightforward method.

- Model Article 17(1)(a) – Andrew can be appointed by the shareholders passing an ordinary resolution. The ordinary resolution can also be effected by way of written resolution circulated to the members to avoid the need to call a general meeting.

After the relevant resolution has been passed the board must ensure that form AP01 (particulars of a directors appointment) is sent to the Registrar of Companies within 14 days. Andrew's appointment should also be written up in the register of directors and register of directors' interests.

(c) Any service contract for longer than two years must be approved by an ordinary resolution. If Visualise wants to offer Andrew a service contract for a period of three years the members of Visualise must convene a general meeting to approve the contract by ordinary resolution or pass an ordinary resolution by way of written resolution.

Additional areas where credit might be given, note this is not an exhaustive list:

- Discuss display obligations relating to long term service contracts.

MOCK EXAM 2 ANSWERS

Question 7

This question covers incorporation of a company and pre-incorporation contracts. Part 8.1 of the syllabus and RQF outcome 1. AIA text chapters 1 and 2.

(a) The main advantages of establishing the business as a private limited company are:

- **Separate legal entity** – a legal identity separate from its members.
- **Owners' liability is limited** – members' liability is limited to their unpaid contribution on their share capital.
- **Perpetual succession** – a change in ownership does not affect its existence.
- **Credibility and prestige** – a private limited company can suggest the business has permanence and is committed to effective and responsible management. It gives both suppliers and customers a sense of confidence and many companies, particularly larger businesses, will not deal with an entity that's not a limited company.
- **Possible tax benefits** – corporation tax rates are lower than income tax rates and companies generally have a more benign set of rules around allowable expenses and reliefs. There is also a range of allowances and tax-deductible costs that can be offset against a company's profits.
- **Options when raising new capital** – there is a greater range of possibilities for companies compared to sole traders or partnerships. Companies can issue new shares to existing shareholders or new investors and can also create floating charges.
- **Exit from the business** – this can be achieved very easily with a company by the sale of shares in the company.

(b) The contracts with suppliers will be pre-incorporation contracts. These are contracts purported to be made by a company (Party Pieces Limited) or its agent (Anthony) at a time before the company has been formed. A company can never ratify contracts made on its behalf before it was incorporated. It did not exist when the pre-incorporation contracts were made so one of the conditions for ratification fails.

Party Pieces Limited may enter into new contracts with these suppliers on the same terms after it has been incorporated. This is known as novation. However, there must be sufficient evidence that the company has made a new contract. Mere recognition of the pre-incorporation contracts by performing them or accepting benefits under them is not the same as making a new contract.

S51 Companies Act 2006 (the Companies Act) covers liability in relation to pre-incorporation contracts and makes whoever has signed the contract before the company is legally incorporated personally liable. This is the case regardless of how the contract was signed. Anthony is therefore personally liable in relation to the contracts. Anthony could have avoided liability either by leaving the contracts in draft (so not binding) until the company is formed, or by clearly agreeing with the suppliers that he was not to be personally liable under the contracts.

Consider from a commercial perspective whether Clare is happy with the terms of the contracts, and if so, likely that the company will effect a novation. Only if Clare were dissatisfied with the terms of the contracts would she leave Anthony liable.

Additional areas where credit might be given, note this is not an exhaustive list:

- Discussion of level of regulation of companies and whether an advantage to have legislation etc. that governs with appropriate flexibility for medium, small and micro companies or whether more advantageous to operate as a sole trader/partnership in a less regulated environment.

Question 8

This question covers bribery. Parts 8.3 and 8.5 of the syllabus and RQF learning outcome 4. AIA text chapter 13.

The offence which must be considered is corporate failure to prevent bribery. It is committed by an organisation that fails to prevent a bribery offence being committed by a person who performs services for it in any capacity – such as agent, employee or subsidiary.

The Bribery Act 2010 (Bribery Act) is the legislation that governs this area of law and under the Bribery Act an organisation includes a company such as OIL.

OIL would have a defence to this offence if it could prove that it had in place "adequate procedures" designed to prevent persons associated with it from committing bribery. Daniel Prescott, as an employee, would be considered to be associated.

These "adequate procedures" are not defined in the Bribery Act but the Secretary of State's non-prescriptive published guidance on adequate procedures is based around six principles:

- **Proportionate procedures** – OIL must have in place procedures which are aimed at preventing bribery. The scale and complexity of the procedures should be proportional to the size of the organisation. More information is needed on the size of OIL.

- **Top-level commitment** – OIL's senior management should be committed to preventing bribery and should foster a culture that sees bribery as unacceptable.

- **Risk assessment** – OIL should assess the nature and extent of their exposure to bribery from both inside and outside the organisation. Some industries are seen as, by their nature, more susceptible to bribery and therefore risk assessments in these areas should be seen as even more stringent – query whether the oil exploration is such an industry.

- **Due diligence** – OIL should perform due diligence procedures including in respect of employees such as Daniel Prescott and others who perform services for the organisation or on its behalf, in order to mitigate the risk of bribery.

- **Communication** – anti-bribery policies and procedures should be embedded in the fabric of the organisation and communicated both internally and externally. This is likely to include relevant training if proportionate to the risk.

- **Monitoring and review** – the anti-bribery policies and procedures should be regularly monitored and reviewed. Amendments and improvements must be made as appropriate.

Whether OIL had adequate procedures is a matter for the courts who will look at the particular circumstances an organisation is faced with. However, the onus is on OIL to prove that its procedures are adequate.

Additional areas where credit might be given, note this is not an exhaustive list:

- The maximum penalty that can be imposed if OIL is found guilty is an unlimited fine. However, if found guilty, it is likely that OIL's business will also suffer loss of reputation and compensation will be payable for civil claims against the directors for failing to maintain adequate procedures.

Case index

Case index

Case	Page
A company 1983, Re	211
Adams v Cape Industries plc 1990	16
Aerators Ltd v Tollit 1902	48, 49
Aldermanbury Trust 1993, Re	157
Allen v Gold Reefs of West Africa Ltd 1900	41
Ashbury Railway Carriage & Iron Co Ltd v Riche 1875	43
Bamford v Bamford 1969	158, 163
Barings plc 1998, Re	157
Bond v Barrow Haematite Steel Co 1902	59, 78
Borland's Trustee v Steel Bros & Co Ltd 1901	57
Brown v British Abrasive Wheel Co 1919	41
Burland v Earle 1902	170
Burnham Marketing Services Ltd 1993, Re	157
Bushell v Faith 1970	40, 153
Centrebind Ltd 1966, Re	209
Cimex Ltd 1994, Re	80
City Equitable Fire and Insurance Co Ltd 1925, Re	165
Clemens v Clemens Bros Ltd 1976	179
Continental Assurance Co of London plc 1996, Re	156
Cook v Deeks 1916	170, 179
D' Jan of London Ltd 1993, Re	166
Dafen Tinplate Co Ltd v Llanelly Steel Co (1907) Ltd 1920	42
Daniels v Daniels 1978	179
Dorchester Finance Co Ltd v Stebbing 1977	166
Dunlop Pneumatic Tyre Co Ltd v Dunlop Motor Co Ltd 1907	48
Ebrahimi v Westbourne Galleries Ltd 1973	15, 185, 211
Eley v Positive Government Security Life Assurance Co 1876	45
Ewing v Buttercup Margarine Co Ltd 1917	48
F G Films Ltd 1953, Re	15
Firedart Ltd, Official Receiver v Fairall 1994, Re	156
Foss v Harbottle 1843	178
Freeman & Lockyer v Buckhurst Park Properties (Mangal) Ltd 1964	160
GE Tunbridge Ltd 1995, Re	80
German Date Coffee Co 1882, Re	211
Gilford Motor Co Ltd v Home 1933	14
Grayan Building Services Ltd 1995, Re	157
Greenhalgh v Arderne Cinemas Ltd 1946	61
Greenhalgh v Arderne Cinemas Ltd 1950	40
Greymoat Ltd 1997, Re	156
Griffiths 1997, Re	157
GSAR Realisations Ltd 1993, Re	157
H and Others 1996, Re	15
Halls v David and Another 1989	243
Hickman v Kent or Romney Marsh Sheepbreeders Association 1915	45
Hogg v Cramphorn 1966	163
House of Fraser plc v ACGE Investments Ltd 1987	61
Howard Smith Ltd v Ampol Petroleum Ltd 1974	163

CASE INDEX

Industrial Development Consultants Ltd v Cooley 1972 ... 167

John Smith's Tadcaster Brewery Co Ltd 1953, Re ... 61
Jubilee Cotton Mills Ltd v Lewes 1924 ... 27

Lee Behrens & Co 1932, Re ... 170
Lee v Lee's Air Farming Ltd 1960 ... 12
London & General Bank (No 2) 1895 ... 10

MacDonald v Costello 2011 ... 13
Maidment v Attwood and Others 2012 ... 182
Monolithic Building Co Ltd 1915, Re ... 81
Multinational Gas & Petrochemical Co v Multinational Gas and Petrochemical Services Ltd 1983 ... 16

New British Iron Co, ex parte Beckwith 1898, Re ...
Nicholas v Soundcraft Electronics Ltd 1993 ...

O'Neill v Phillips ... 182
Ooregum Gold Mining Co of India v Roper, 1892 ... 97
Overend Gurney & Co v Gibb 1872 ... 166

Panorama Developments (Guildford) Ltd v Fidelis Furnishing Fabrics Ltd 1971 ... 172
Patent File Co 1870 ... 74
Pavlides v Jensen 1956 ... 166
Pender v Lushington 1877 ... 45
Percival v Wright 1902 ... 162
Peso Silver Mines v Cropper 1966 ... 167
Produce Marketing Consortium Ltd 1989, Re ... 241, 243

R in Right of British Columbia v Federal Business Development Bank 1988 ... 79
R v Goodman 1993 ... 156
Rayfield v Hands 1958 ... 45
Re A Company 1983 ... 181, 185
Re A Company 1986 ... 181
Re Astec (BSR) plc 1998 ... 182
Re Bird Precision Bellows 1986 ... 180
Re Cumana 1986 ... 181
Re DR Chemicals Ltd 1989 ... 181
Re Elgindata Ltd 1991 ... 181
Re Five Minute Car Wash Service Ltd 1966 ... 181
Re German Date Coffee Co 1882 ... 184
Re London School of Electronics 1985 ... 181
Re McGuinness and Another 1988 ... 181
Re R A Noble & Sons (Clothing) Ltd 1983 ... 180
Re Ringtower Holdings plc 1989 ... 182
Re Yenidje Tobacco Co Ltd 1916 ... 185
Regal (Hastings) Ltd v Gulliver 1942 ... 167, 170

Salomon v Salomon & Co Ltd 1897 ... 12
Sevenoaks Stationers (Retail) Ltd 1991, Re ... 157
Sharp v Dawes 1876 ... 139
Shuttleworth v Cox Bros & Co (Maidenhead) Ltd 1927 ... 41, 46
Sidebottom v Kershaw, Leese & Co Ltd 1920 ... 41
Siebe Gorman & Co Ltd v Barclays Bank Ltd 1979 ... 80
Smith v Fawcett 1942 ... 158, 162
Southern Foundries (1926) Ltd v Shirlaw 1940 ... 40, 153

Twycross v Grant 1877 .... 24, 182

Unit Construction Co Ltd v Bullock 1960 15

White v Bristol Aeroplane Co Ltd 1953 61
Williams and Another v Natural Life Health Foods Ltd 1998 171
Wragg 1897, Re 98

Yenidje Tobacco Co Ltd 1916, Re 211
Yorkshire Woolcombers Association Ltd 1903, Re 79

CASE INDEX

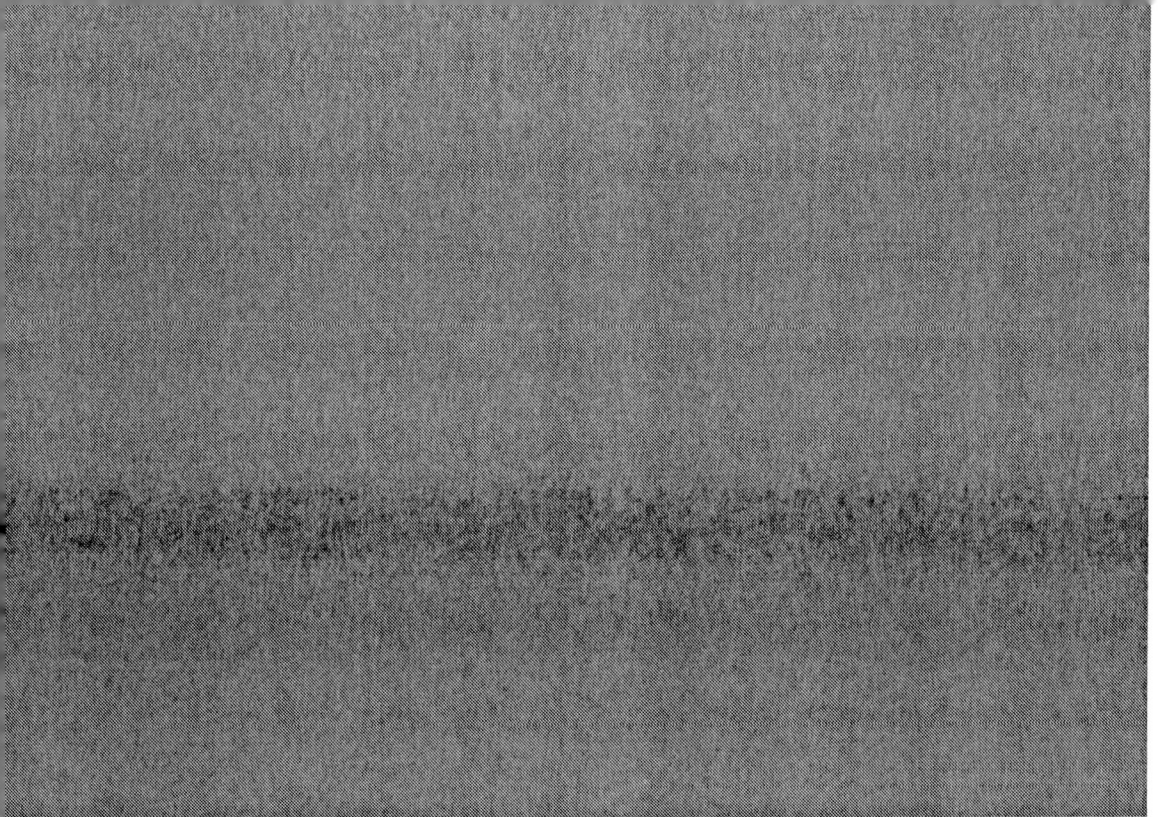

Index

Note. **Key Terms** and their page references are given in **bold**.

Accounting records, 190
Accounting reference date, 30
Accounting reference period, 9
Administration, 218
Administrator, 217, 220
Administrator's power, 221
Administrator's proposals, 220
Agent of the company, 220
Allotment of shares, 63, 99
Allotted share capital, 58
Alteration of the articles, 39, 158
Alternate directors, 148
Annual accounts, 190
Annual general meeting (AGM), 114
Apparent authority, 159
Appointment of directors, 150
Articles, 27, 57
Articles of association, 39
Associated person, 244
Auditor, 132
Auditor remuneration, 194
Authorised share capital, 57

Balance sheet test, 210
Becoming a member, 56
Board meetings, 149
Board of directors, 149
Bonus issue, 66
Bribery Act 2010, 238
Bribery, 238
Business name, 49

Called up share capital, 58
Capital maintenance, 90
Capital redemption reserve, 102
Centrebinding, 209
Certificate of incorporation, 27
Chairman, 138
Change of name, 47
Charge, 79
Chartered corporations, 6
Chief executive officer, 149
Class of shares, 57
Class rights, 59
Commencement of business, 29
Commercial insolvency test, 210
Committees, 149
Community interest companies (CICs), 6
Companies Act, 27
Company, 4, 6, **182**

Company auditor, 193
Company Directors Disqualification Act 1986, 154
Company investigations, 121, 123
Company limited by guarantee, 8
Company secretary, 171, 173
Company unable to pay its debts, 210
Company's letterheads and other forms, 30
Compensation, 151
Composition of the single board, 116
Compulsory liquidation, 84, 210
Confirmation statement, 33
Conflict of interest, 170
Contributories, 213
Corporate governance, 112
Corporate governance statement, 115, 195
Corporate personality, 4
Corporations, 6
Corporations sole, 6
Court order where there is unfair prejudice, 182
Creditors' meeting, 221
Creditors' voluntary liquidation, 208
Criminal Finances Act 2017, 244
Criminal Justice Act 1993, 232
Crystallisation, 80
Crystallisation, 80, 82

De facto directors, 148
De jure directors, 148
Debenture, 75
Debenture trust deed, 76
Debentures
　advantages, 77
　disadvantages, 77
Declaration of solvency, 208, 241
Derivative claims, 184
Differences between private and public companies, 8
Director, 112, 148, 218
Directors' disqualification under model articles, 154
Directors' personal liability, 170
Directors' powers, 159
Disapplication of pre-emption rights, 66
Discount, 97
Discrimination against minority, 179
Disqualification of directors, 153, 155
Disqualification undertaking, 154
Distinction between sole traders and partnerships, 4
Distributable profit, 101
Distributing dividends, 100

INDEX

Diversion of contracts, 179
Dividend, 57, **100**, 102
Duties of auditors, 194
Duties of promoters, 24
Duty of directors, 161, 164

Enhanced due diligence, 237
Enterprise Act 2002, 217
Equity (share), 59
Equity share capital, 59
European companies, 12
Exclusion of pre-emption rights, 65
Executive director, 148

Fiduciary duty, 24, **161**, 164
Fiduciary position, 161
Financial assistance, 96
Financial crime, 232
Financial statements, 114
Fixed charge, 79
Floating charge, 79, 80, 81, 212
Floating chargeholders, 218
Fraud on the company, 178
Fraudulent trading, 14, 156, 241

General meeting, 163
Group accounts, 10

Holding and subsidiary companies, 10
Holding out, 159

Ignoring separate personality, 13
Ineligible for appointment, 193
Initial accounts, 103
Inside information, 233
Insider dealing, 232
Insolvency Act 1986, 14, 15
Inspection of directors' service agreements, 152
Interim accounts, 103
Issue of shares, 64
Issued share capital, 58
Issuing shares at a premium and at a discount, 95, 97

Joint money laundering steering group, 238
Just and equitable ground, 210
Just and equitable winding up, 184

Knowledge gap, 113

Lack of independence, 193
Legal personality, 4, 12
Legal regulation of corporate governance, 120
Liability for trading without trading certificate, 13
Liability limited by guarantee, 6
Liability limited by shares, 6
Lifting the veil, 13
Limited by guarantee, 6, 47
Limited companies, 6
Limited liability, 5
Limited liability of members, 4
Limited liability, 5, 6
Liquidation, 155, **206**
Liquidator, 207, 209, 214
Loan capital, 58, 74
London Gazette, 30, 213
Loss of capital by public company, 132

Maintenance of capital, 90
Majority control, 178
Management board, 116
Managing director, 149
Medium companies regime, 11
Meetings, 130
Member, 56, 214
Members' voluntary liquidation, 208
Memorandum of association, 8, 160
Micro-entities regime, 11
Micro-entity, 192
Minority protection, 178, 179
Minutes, 141
Money Laundering Regulations 2017, 236
Money laundering, 234
Moratorium, 220
Multinational company, 11

Name, 7
Nominal value, 57
Non-cash consideration, 98
Non-executive director, 149, 165
Notice, 134
Number of directors, 149

Off the shelf companies, 28
Offences in relation to winding up, 241
Official receiver, 212
Order for compulsory liquidation, 212
Ordinary resolutions, 132
Ordinary shares, 59
Owner-managed businesses, 112

Paid up share capital, 58
Par, 97
Parent company, 10
Partly paid shares, 97
Passing of property to controlling shareholders, 179
Passing-off action, 48
Phoenix company, 14
Poll, **140**
Powers of directors, 158
Pre-emption rights, **65**
Pre-emption rule, 8
Preference dividend, 59
Preference shares, 58, **59**, 60
Preferential debts, 81, 214
Pre-incorporation contract, **25**, 26
Premium, 99
Principal, 159
Priorities on liquidation, 214
Priority dividend entitlement, 59
Priority of charges, 81
Private company, **7**, 8, 9, 30, 98
Profits available for distribution, **101**
Promoter, 24, 25
Proxy, **139**
Public company, **7**, 30, 47, 98
Public, 7

Quasi-partnership company, 180
Quasi-partnership, 15
Quorum, **138**

Ratification, 164
Redeemable shares, **93**
Reduction of share capital, 90, 158
Register of charges, 83
Register of debentureholders, 33, 76
Register of directors, 32
Register of members, 32
Register of people with significant control, 32
Registered companies, 6
Registered number, 27
Registers, 30
Registrar, 4
Registrar of companies, 7, 27, 150
Registration procedures, 26
Relevant accounts, 103
Relevant body, 244
Removal of directors, 152
Removal of the auditor from office, 197
Remuneration of directors, 150
Requisitioning a resolution, 136

Re-registration procedures, 28
Resignation of auditors, 196
Return of capital, 60
Rights issue, **65**
Rights of auditors, 195, 198
Rights of secured debentureholders, 84
Rights of unsecured debentureholders, 84
Romalpa clause, 81
Rotation of directors, 152

Secretary of State, 47
Separate legal personality, 12
Service contract, **33**
Shadow directors, 148
Share capital, 57
Share premium, **99**
Share, **57**
Shareholders, 57, 112
Shareholders' agreements, 46
Show of hands, **140**
Simplified due diligence, 237
Single alternative inspection location (SAIL), 31
Single board
   advantages, 117
   criticisms, 117
Single member private companies, 142
Small Business, Enterprise and Employment Act 2015, 26, 148
Small companies regime, 11
Sole traders, 4
Solvency statement, **90**
Special notice, **135**
Special resolutions, 132, 158
Stakeholders, 112
Stamp duty, 66
Stamp Duty Reserve Tax, 67
Statement, 27
Statement of affairs, 213
Statutory books and records, 30, 31
Statutory corporations, 6
Statutory rights of minorities, 186
Stock exchange requirements, 120
Stock exchange, 9
Subdivide shares, 61
Subscriber shares, 56
Substratum, 211
Supervisory board, 116
   advantages, 117
   criticisms, 117

Termination of auditors' appointment, 196
The registrar of companies, 31
The rule in *Foss v Harbottle*, 178

Trading certificate, 30
True and fair view, 194
Two-tier system, 116
Types of capital, 57
Types of company, 6
Types of debenture, 75

Ultra vires, 43
Underwriting fees, 97
Undistributable reserves, 102
Unfair prejudice, 62
Unfairly prejudicial conduct, 180
Unitary board of directors, 116
Unlimited liability company, 6
Unrestricted objects, 43

Vacation of office, 152
Variation of class rights, 60
Veil of incorporation, 13
　lifting the veil, 13
Voluntary codes of corporate governance, 114
Voluntary liquidation, 207
Voting, 140
Voting rights, 10

Winding up, 206
Written resolutions, 133
Wrongful trading, 156, 241

NOTES